YAMUNA RIVER PROJECT

NEW DELHI URBAN ECOLOGY

Iñaki Alday and Pankaj Vir Gupta

With essays by
Keshav Chandra, Rana Dasgupta,
Peter Debaere, John Echeverri-Gent,
Daniel Ehnbom, and Pradip Saha

Edition coordinated by
Joseph Brookover Jr

AN ESSENTIAL FUTURE

The Yamuna River Project (YRP) aims to help the city of New Delhi and its citizen stakeholders reimagine and transform the sacred, yet polluted Yamuna River as it flows through India's capital. The Yamuna River Project confronts the dilemmas of Delhi's urban reality, with a precise, analytical, multi-disciplinary, research-based methodology. This approach facilitates a dynamic collaboration between the intellectual speculations generated within a University and their application for a range of knowledge partners governing a city, including municipal authorities, political leaders, citizens' advocates and non-government organizations.

As one of the most rapidly urbanizing mega-cities in the developing world, New Delhi confronts serious challenges, revealing inadequacies in planning, urban design, and social equity. These limitations are emerging at a time of economic uncertainty and ecological fragility. As a result, the citizens of the world's largest democracy live amidst unprecedented environmental degradation. Existing governance structures have been hard pressed to keep up with the pace of the complex, rapidly evolving dynamics of climate change. Toxic air and septic waters are simply collateral damage in this circumstance. Overburdened public health systems are fraying as more citizens are exposed to the adverse consequences of these environmental ills in daily life. These millions continue to suffer, often silently, as they inhabit, without recourse, these imperfect urbanites.

Governance

Political leadership, limited by the relatively brief tenure of elected office, and challenged by the pace of change, often resorts to political grandstanding. In New Delhi, policy-making often seems at an impasse, unable to conceptualize a systematic, long-term urban vision for the humanity that constitutes a city. Governments, confronting the limitations of five-year long electoral cycles, often default to short-term solutions, perpetuating an illusory construct of urban progress. Increasingly, the call for "smart cities", automated and propelled by artificial intelligence, is seen as a panacea. Over the past decade, it has become increasingly evident that no single entity—elected or appointed to 'lead' the city—has the experience to 'resolve' rapid urban degradation. In fact, it has become evident that the existing structure of urban governance may be part of the problem. That is, governance structures that are designed to operate with a historically limited mandate, are now being asked to address novel problems that demand both agility, and cross-disciplinary functionality. A plethora of municipal agencies, often working at cross-purposes, without accountability, fail to address the synthetic nature of the city. Thus, agencies tasked with water-supply and sewage treatment have little to do with entities that manage solid waste management; development authorities entrusted with planning housing and work-space, consistently fail to estimate the growth of the city, condemning millions of people to forage for a foothold in squatter settlements lacking even the most basic amenities; public transportation administrators fail to synchronize existing and new multi-modal transport systems.

Within this fragile equilibrium, active engagement with best-practice models for identifying, synergizing, and upgrading urban systems, governance and ecology, has never been more critical.

The River

The Yamuna River is a living ecological entity with her own seasonal cycle of flow, complex hydraulic dynamics, and shifting floodplain territory. For centuries, the river has existed as a significant geographic presence within the northern Indian landscape. In myth and in religion, in prose and poetry, in song and in lore, the Yamuna has been immortalized as a primordial Goddess. For centuries, the river constituted not just the defining axis, but also the ecological and agricultural lifeline of the many settlements preceding present day Delhi. It is impossible to imagine the city of Varanasi without the illuminating presence of lamps adorning the Ganga; or to disengage the Holkar capital of Maheshwar, famous for its weavers and looms, from its anchor on the banks of the Narmada, where the rising humidity provides an atmospheric condition perfect for blending cotton fiber with silk, creating the famed Maheshwari silk. Delhi and the Yamuna were once so conjoined. Even today, the sandstone walls of Mughal era monuments abutting the floodplain reveal watermarks of the Yamuna. But all this is in the past. Long gone are the days when the citizens of Delhi swam, fished, and strolled freely on the banks of the Yamuna.

In this age, characterized by geologists as the Anthropocene—when patterns of human settlement are significant influencing forces on environment and climate—urban populations in mega-cities have far exceeded the carrying capacity of their designed infrastructure. In New Delhi, the Yamuna has been reduced to a poorly managed sewage drain, absent both from the urban landscape and from the public imagination. The fight for citizens' survival inflicts even deeper damage to an already fragile ecological circumstance. Urban development justified in the name of civic prosperity is often misleadingly defined in opposition to environmental security. In the hardscrabble urbanity of the present India megacity, there is little room for the ecologically sacred.

The Diagnosis

Originating in the Himalayas, and emerging from the Yamunotri glacier, the Yamuna River negotiates dams and barrages, irrigating thousands of acres of agricultural land, before it flows into New Delhi. North of Delhi, the volume of fresh water in the Yamuna is able to dilute organic matter and fertilizers, absorbing pollution from pesticides and agricultural runoff, while maintaining a level of dissolved oxygen capable of supporting aquatic life, birds, and vegetation. However, the river receives an unholy welcome upon her arrival in Delhi.

At the Wazirabad barrage, all of the Yamuna's water is dammed and diverted, partially quenching the capital city's insatiable thirst. Just after this Barrage, the Najafgarh Drain—formerly the perennial Sahibi River—provides the only flow to the Yamuna, bringing with it, sixty percent of the river's total pollution load. Comprising of untreated sewerage, solid waste, industrial and chemical effluent, and urban detritus, the flow of the Najafgarh drain depletes the water of all oxygen content, rendering it incapable of supporting any form of life.

The quality of the water is not in fact the problem. Billions of dollars have been invested in large water-based infrastructure projects, without achieving any substantial success in cleaning the river. Polluted water is the consequence and an indicator of 150 years of urban evolution, an empirical measure of the last fifty years of rapid, largely unplanned growth, and, in summary, of severe social and environmental inequality in the city. As Rana Dasgupta points out in his essay, British rule changed the historic relation between Delhi's population and the water, transforming both a sacred and a secular interface, into a commodity of uncertain origin. From inhabiting the many 'ghats' that lined the river, and offering an unobstructed experience of civic and religious life amidst the Yamuna river, Delhi's population grew detached from the river, receiving a poorly regulated, often contaminated, and, at best, intermittent supply of precious water, through an intricate maze of pipes and meters. A water mafia sprung into action, quickly monetizing an opportunity to drill illegal wells, pump unregulated water, and supply tankers to a parched populace.

Delhi's citizens are now completely detached from their river, only part of a larger detachment from the formerly shared consciousness of public space, and, in fact, from the concept of a 'commons'. This detachment is the underlying cause of Delhi's environmental dilemma. The Yamuna river, perceived as an incarnate Goddess, is incapable of supporting physical life.

The legal protections offered to the Yamuna (and to the Ganges river), entrusted with the rights of living entities, fail to deter the agencies that poison them. This contradiction reflects the dilemmas of a complex society, confronting a critical moment of exponential population growth, social inequality and convoluted municipal governance. The perennial flows of raw sewage from the capital city into in the Yamuna, are simply a reflection of the inequity of a city without planning, with a severe lack of infrastructure. Thus, the floodplain of the Yamuna reveals urban slums of unprecedented density, without any provision for the safe supply of drinking water, nor for sewerage treatment, without education and health facilities. This disenfranchised population, encroaching upon the floodplain, scraping a meager livelihood from the margins, suffers again from an unrelenting cycle of monsoon floods.

The restoration of a healthy equilibrium between the river and the city is also a matter of survival. India faces the consequences of climate change on enormous scale, with monsoon floods killing thousands of people every year, and causing significant damage to urban infrastructure, ruining lives and livelihoods. The consequences of a one hundred-year flood event–likely to occur more frequently with increasing global warming–will be devastating. Urban sprawl, fueled by the lack of planning, has reduced the available forest cover; ecological and agricultural area per inhabitant in the National Capital Territory of New Delhi has shrunk dramatically in the past few decades. The reduction of forested area, diminished local food production and poor soil permeability, has created a social and ecological crisis of extreme urgency. The effects of climate change are seen not only in more recurrent floods, but also in droughts and heat island effects with substantial impact on the most vulnerable populations.

Many Municipal agencies, as well as social and environmental organizations continue working in Delhi to reverse this situation. The Delhi Jal Board (Delhi Water Authority), confronting a mammoth task of creating infrastructure for water and sewerage treatment, has, for the first time, started to integrate urban design and planning strategies in its development manifest. The Delhi Government has taken a critical first step in consolidating a few of the agencies that deal with water, flood control, irrigation, and environment, under a single-point leadership structure. The Ministry of Water Resources may now be considering the empowerment of a Yamuna River Development Authority, streamlining the complexity of governance of water and rivers.

The Methodology

The Yamuna River Project has sought to engage this dilemma with a multi-faceted approach. Applying broad based, intellectually diverse, research experience, the Yamuna River Project has forged a credible partnership with existing governance structures, and established a paradigm for influencing significant remediation policies. Developing a transparent, collaborative and open-source methodology, the project functions as a critical front for the confluence of academic leadership, with cultural, environmental, and political systems of governance.

The project methodology questions and investigates the causes and origins of Delhi's environmental situation from many perspectives–historic, social, technological and cultural. A critical element of this approach is the commitment to the development of a vision, a conceptual framework, to explore potential avenues for transformation. This vision reimagines the urban environment, evaluating and testing ecologies that facilitate sustainable urban growth and accountable governance. Finally, the Yamuna River Project proposes speculations: holistic interventions that define systematic urban strategies, and generate new typologies that respond to the specificity of Delhi. The thesis of this approach postulates that 'water is the consequence', reflecting the ethos of the present urbanity.

The breadth of this methodology is only possible in the context of an independent research university, acting as a multidisciplinary think tank. As pointed by George Steiner (Universitas, 2013), the pivot of the university is its intellectual and civic freedom, and this capacity to engage in independent excellence, remains unfettered by the utility of the knowledge so produced. The university has an almost infinite capacity to add and combine disciplines and areas of expertise, therefore developing innovative interdisciplinary connections. Institutions like the University of Virginia are thus multicultural by nature, nimble enough to deploy academic resources across diverse cultural environments.

On the other hand, contradicting or complementing Steiner's vision, today's leading universities feel the urgency of engaging with the most critical issues of our time, extending their reach and collaborating beyond the campus. The implication on these urgencies requires dealing with the complex issues and the difficulties of management and implementation. To that end, multidisciplinary teams become key, ranging from abstract and very specific areas of knowledge to disciplines that engage naturally with politics, social dynamics, design, or planning.

The intellectual apparatus for the Yamuna River Project encompasses multiple and interrelated points of view: ecology and culture, history and infrastructure, economics and design, are some of the many combinations explored. The vision for the planning, and creation of dynamic public spaces emerges as a conclusion drawn from detailed investigations of the physicality of the city fabric, and the armatures of governance, culture, religion, ecology, public health or infrastructure. Conceptualized as systems, the layers of complexity of the city and its ecological territory, are intertwined as a "design methodology."

The Vision

The dilemmas of New Delhi—or for that matter, any Indian or global megacity—a critical level of air and water pollution, scarcity of affordable housing, acute shortage of community space, are not radically different from the dysfunction of some European river cities only a few decades ago. Although Delhi and the Yamuna represent an acute urban crisis, this is only one of the many similar crises on the planet, in which a lack of planning, rapid growth and climate change redounds as a lack of basic infrastructures and cultural attachment. The resulting social inequality is dramatically visible in the ecology of an environment that once was the reason for the city to exist—its rivers—and in the pollution of the most precious substance for life—its waters.

The remedy for New Delhi's defiled Yamuna, and her once sacred waters, will need to holistically address the causes of pollution, and redress the inequality within the city. The Yamuna River Project seeks to foster this change. We recognize a basic fact of the Anthropocene era—the cities that we design and make now, are the cities that we shall inhabit in the future and with which the planet itself shall have to live. It is present day human intent and intervention that shall ensure the sustainability and survival of the future city—a city predicated on our ability to secure ecology from our own advances. We therefore equate social prosperity with ecological stewardship. The Yamuna and all its tributaries, the flows and the floodplains, are the base for reformulating Delhi's commons. They are to become the public space and ecological spines of the new socio-ecological structure of the city.

As co-founders of the Yamuna River Project, we have marshaled the resources of the University of Virginia and forged an innovative collaboration with the Delhi Jal Board, generating meaningful solutions for the crises afflicting the Yamuna River. Developing a transparent, collaborative, and open-source methodology, the Yamuna River Project functions as a critical front for the confluence of academic leadership, and cultural, environmental, and political systems.

We are optimistic that many restorative opportunities are latent in the neglected space of interaction between River and City. What if the Yamuna River floodplain may be reimagined as an urban nucleus, communicating a value system that situates the capital city within its original riparian ecology? In this sense, the Yamuna River Project is entrusted with the task of redefining a sanctuary within a megacity. As Dan Ehnbohm's essay so eloquently suggests, the new reality of the Yamuna River would, once again, be tethered to an awareness of the sacred, celebrated in image and in song. In a world where we have vanquished nature, the river city relationship would be an inseparable ethical identity. The citizens of the city would make a commitment to secure and nourish the river—making her sacred again—and New Delhi would forge another identity, a commitment to a new ecology.

SKETCH of the ENVIRONS of DELHI

Miles

F.S. White...Surveyor.

References
1. The Palace
2. Suleemgurh
3. Jumma Musjid, Lat 28°39'
4. Cantonments & Cashmeer gate
5. Kabul gate
6. Lahor gate
7. Ferash khanuh kreekee
8. Ajmeer gate
9. Toorkmangate
10. Dilhee gate
11. Deriah Gunj gate & Cantonment
12. Rajghat gate & Cantonments

Var" 5° East

PALUM

Chiragh Delhi

Moonalee

Tughluqabad

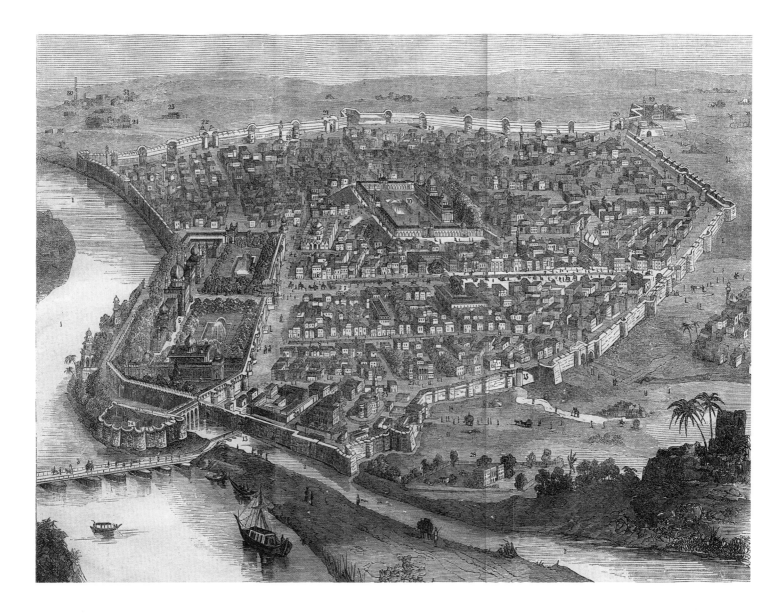

The City of Delhi Before the Siege (above):

The Illustrated London News, January 16, 1858. Original image sourced from DELHI, 1857 provided by Prof. Emerita Frances Pritchett, Columbia University in Sept 2013

Sketch of the Environs of Delhi (left):

Drawn by F.S. White, National Archives of India, 1807.

Delhi is a city of cities: Qila Rai Pithora, Mehrauli, Siri, Tughlaqabad, Firozabad, Shergarh, and Shahjahanabad were the original seven. The city preserves remnants of these empires scattered along the western bank of the Yamuna River. Delhi's earliest history traces back over 3,500 years to mythic origins, as recounted in the Hindu Epic, Mahabharata. Archaeologists believe that the ancient city known as Indraprastha might have developed along the western bank of the Yamuna, between Feroz Shah Kotla and Humayun's Tomb. Subsequent empires constructed their citadels on hills to the west of the Yamuna, but continued to rely on the river for access to trade.

Early urban settlements concentrated in the south around the eleventh century site known as Lal Kot or Qila Rai Pithora. The military advantage of rich alluvial soils lead to continued growth along the river, including the Mughal citadel of Purana Qila in 1533 and later, Shahjahanabad in 1639. The walled city of Shahjahanabad, now known as Old Delhi, depended on the river as a means of defense and trade. Delhi's urban fabric would begin to shift away from the Yamuna with the occupation of the British East India Company in 1803 but the preserved ruins from the city's past carry lessons on how new generations can relate to this legendary land.

TOMAR
1060 - 1180

1. Surajkund - 731
2. Lal Kot - 1060

CHAUHAN
1180 - 1192

1. Qila-i-Rai Pithora - 1182

KHALJI
1290 - 1320

1. Alai Dorwaza - 1311

TUGHLAQ
1320 - 1451

1. Baradari at Sadhna Enclave - 14th ce.
2. Hazrat Nizamuddin Ki Baoli - 1321
3. Tughlaqabad Fort - 1321
4. Agrasen Ki Baoli, 1324
5. Hauz Khas, 1350
6. Feroz Shah Kotla, 1354

GHURID
1192 - 1206

*no major monuments were
built during this era*

SLAVE
1206 - 1290

1. Qutb Minar - 1193

LODI
1451 - 1526

1. Lodi Garden, 1517
2. Tomb at Sadhna Enclave, 15th ce.
3. Bijri Khan, 15th ce.
4. Bara Lao Ka Gumbad and Baradari, 15th ce.
5. Gol Gumbad, 15th ce.
6. Maqbara Paik, 15th ce.

MUGHAL
1526 - 1803

1. Purana Qila, 1533
2. Humayun's Tomb, 1572
3. Mohd Quli Khan's Tomb, 16thce
4. Dara Shikoh, 1639
5. Jama Masjid, 1644
6. Red Fort, 1648
7. Turkman's Gate, 1658
8. Kaushal Minar, 17th ce.
9. Jantar Mantar, 1724
10. Qudsia Bagh, 1748
11. Safdarjung's Tomb, 1753

Historic Delhi's Geography

Delhi's urbanity was closely integrated with its natural environment. The first forts were built along the southern ridge. Shahjahanabad, the capital of Mughal India, was bounded by the Yamuna River and surrounded by the forested ridge. Expansive alluvial plains were ideal for agriculture, tombs, and urban villages. A network of rivers and streams connected these landscapes and was an integral part of civic life. Topographical features informed the location of major roads and allowed for a massive floodplain to the east which managed the influx of seasonal monsoon waters. Settlement avoided the floodplains, instead expanding across the open plains to the west.

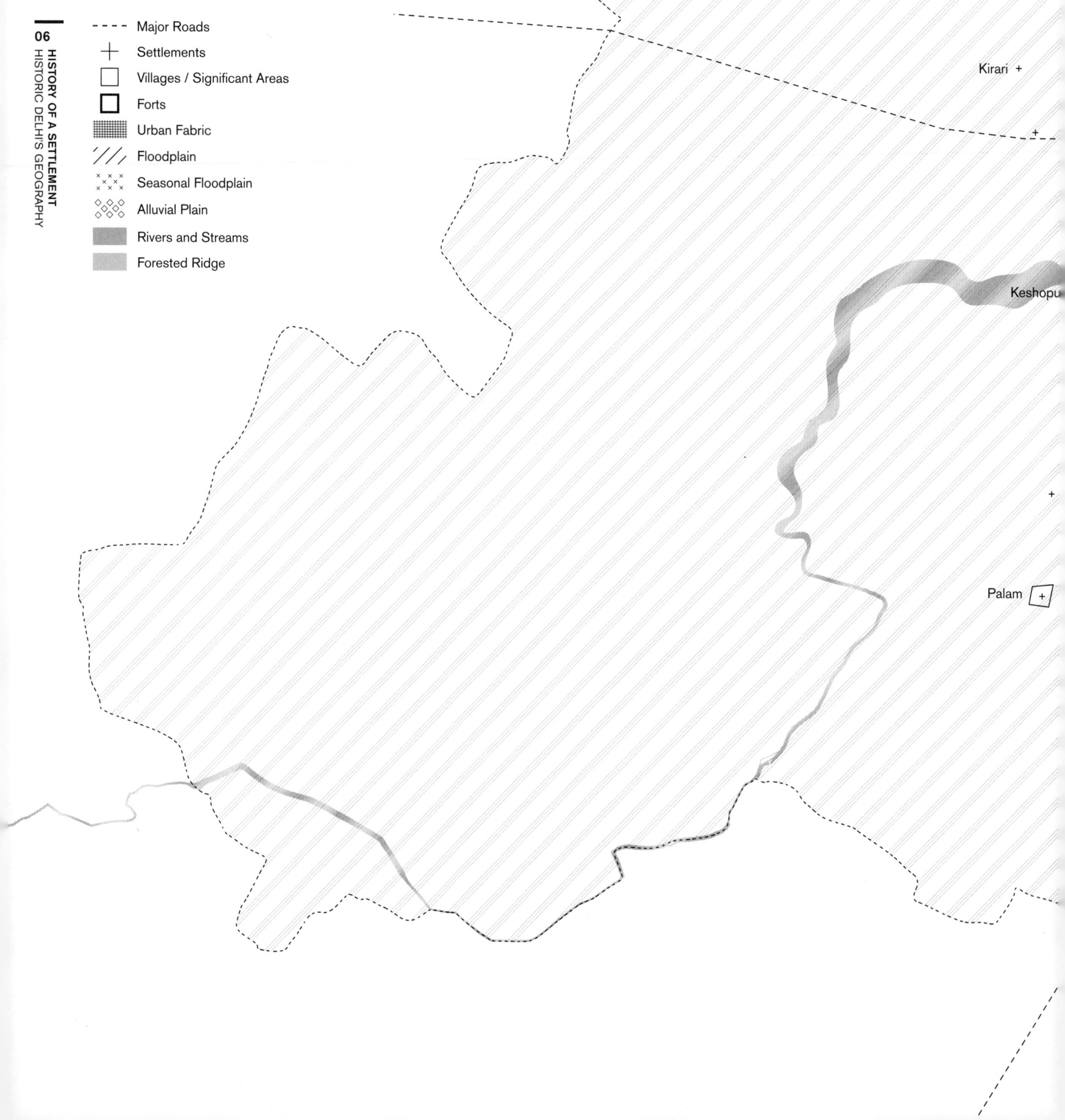

- - - - Major Roads

+ Settlements

☐ Villages / Significant Areas

☐ Forts

▦ Urban Fabric

/// Floodplain

××× Seasonal Floodplain

◇◇◇ Alluvial Plain

▨ Rivers and Streams

▨ Forested Ridge

Kirari +

Keshopu

Palam +

HISTORICALLY, DELHI'S URBAN STRUCTURE WAS CLOSELY INTEGRATED WITH ITS NATURAL ENVIRONMENT.

Khera Khurd
Burari
Jahangirpura
Shahbad
Samaypur
Mukundpur
Jharoda
Haiderpur
Shalimar Bagh
Wazirabad
Naharpur
Pitampura
Rajpura
Chandrawal
Wazirpur
Madipur
Rampura
Subzi Mandi
Shahjahanabad
Kailash Nagar
Basai
Pahari
Paharganj
Tihar
Raju Bazaar
Feroz Shah Kotla
Jantar Mantar
Talkatora
Nangal
Purana Qila
Patparganj
Humayun's Tomb
Safdarjung's Tomb
Nizamuddin
Moti Bagh
Mehram Nagar
Okhla
Sarai Jullena
Hauz Khas
Ber Sarai
Shahpur Jat
Jasola
Chirag Dilli
Madanpur
Qila Lal Kot
Lado Sarai
Madangir
Mehrauli
Khanpur
Deoli
Tughlaqabad
Badarpur

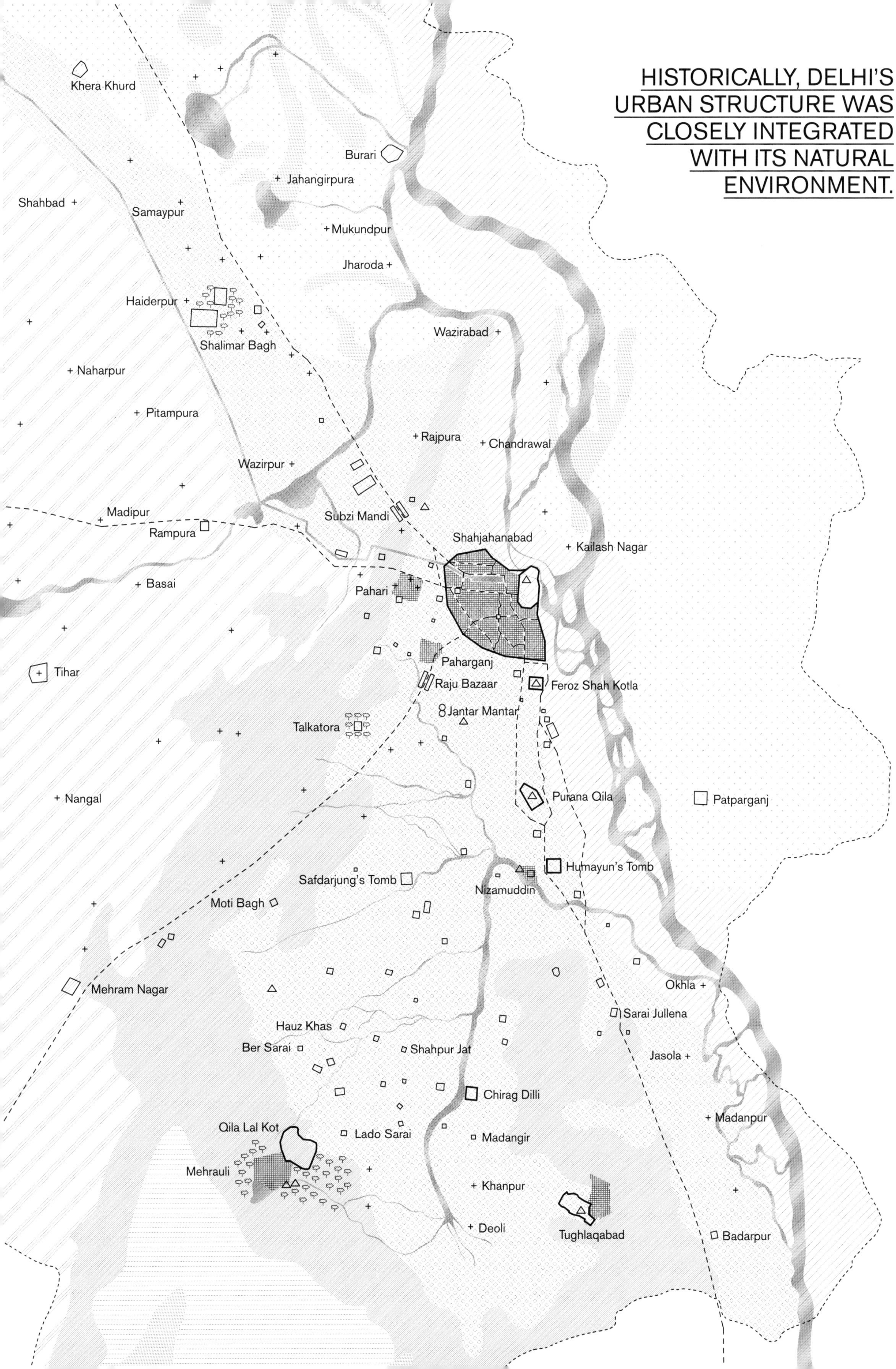

The Red Fort Complex, Lahori Gate

Mughal Delhi

The seventeenth century city of Shahjahanabad retains a prominent place within Delhi's ever-expanding urban fabric. The Mughal Emperor, Shah Jahan, decided in 1638 to construct a new capital somewhere between Lahore and the then capital city of Agra since Agra had outgrown its constricting walls. Architects and astrologists selected a new site for the capital on high ground along the western bank of the Yamuna, north of Agra, in present day Delhi. Here they constructed the imperial palace, The Red Fort, to sit directly on the Yamuna's bank, further surrounded by massive stone walls that fortified the city's perimeter. This location along the Yamuna offered important strategic advantages and the river directly enabled urban life through a constant source of water for drinking and irrigation which was further supplemented by canals.

The Red Fort's typology echoes an earlier Indian urban form of fortified palaces revived by the Mughals. Palaces along rivers also created a new riverfront garden typology. The classical organizing principle of palaces during the Mughal period would typically place garden pavilions at the center of a quadrilateral layout. Within the Red Fort's riverfront garden, three imperial pavilions sit along the wall closest to the river. This location offers breezes and an appearance of grandeur when viewed from the river.

Although the course of the Yamuna River has since naturally shifted further east, Mughal influence typified by the Red Fort Complex and surrounding city of Shahjahanabad stand testament to an urban form once shaped by a symbiotic relationship to the river.

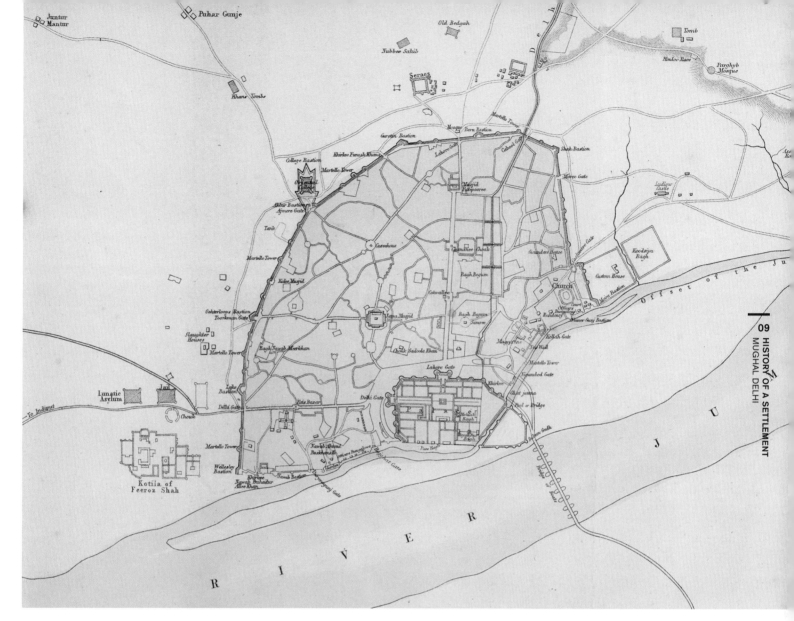

Plan of Delhi and its Environs - 1857 (above):

Edward Weller. The Weekly Dispatch. Duke Street, Bloomsbury. 1857. Original image sourced from DELHI, 1857 provided by Prof. Emerita Frances Pritchett, Columbia University in Sept 2013.

View of Delhi from the River Showing the King's Palace (left):

Robert Montgomery Martin. 'The Indian Empire', vol 3. c.1860.

Delhi from the Ridge Camp 1857

A view from the Illustrirte Zeitung, 14 Nov. 1857. Scan sourced from DELHI, 1857 (1858) provided by Prof. Emerita Frances Pritchett, Columbia University in July 2007

YAMUNA AS GODDESS AND ICON

Daniel Enhborn
Associate Professor, Art History
University of Virginia

The Yamuna River is one of the most sacred rivers of India and for millennia has been considered to be a goddess, the daughter of Surya, the sun god, and the twin sister of Yama, the god of death. She is frequently invoked in the Rig Veda (composed c. 1700-1100 BCE), but she is seen in the visual arts only from the early 5th century of the Common Era, when she and her companion river goddess Ganga begin to be depicted flanking the entrances of temples, a practice that has continued (Figure 1).

She inhabits both literal and metaphysical space in India—one of the most sacred places in the religious geography of the subcontinent is the Triveni Sangam in Allahabad (ancient Prayaga), the place where she joins the Ganga and the now mythical Sarasvati rivers. This is the site of the great Kumbha Mela every twelve years, the largest assemblage of humans on the planet, when millions of pilgrims come to bathe in the holy waters. It is this intertwining of the literal and the metaphysical that gives the sacred rivers of India their resonance with those who revere them. They are real rivers that transcend their physical existence to transport the pilgrim to a metaphysical geography where gods and goddesses can take human form and can be apprehended, if only partially, by their devotees.

Yamuna is dark in color. Her vehicle is a tortoise, an animal associated with creation in Vedic literature, and now endangered by pollution. The river is directly linked to Krishna, one of the most popular deities in India today, and as Kalindi she becomes his wife. The Yamuna is connected to the god from his infancy, when his father carries him away from the dangers of Mathura, his birthplace, to be raised by foster parents across the river. He sports in the river with the women of his village, and still today the holy places associated with his youth draw pilgrims to the banks of the Yamuna where, as in all the sacred waters of India, ritual bathing gives redemption from sin. In the twenty second chapter of Book Ten of the Bhagavata Purana, the standard Sanskrit account of the life of Krishna, it is told that cowherd women who wished to marry Krishna worshiped the goddess Katyayani on her banks (BPX.22.1-8), though in the earliest known representation of the theme in painting the goddess's image is replaced by that of Krishna himself (Figure 2). In the picture, the Yamuna flows along the bottom of the scene as the women worship on her bank, her waters filled with lotuses and geese. In this way she becomes a common if subtle presence in Indian painting, particularly in narrative illustrations of the Krishna story. The river is a constant presence in representations of the youthful Krishna, such as when he plays the flute as Gopala, the protector of cows (Figure 3). This importance is pan-Indian—Yamuna as both goddess and river appears throughout the subcontinent in places far distant from her geographical location.

If the Yamuna is essential to Hinduism, she plays a major role in Islamic India too. She flows past the eastern side of the great Red Fort of Delhi, built by Shah Jahan from 1639 to 1648. Once close to the fort (Figure 4), the river is now at some distance from the structure, but she was an integral part of the urban fabric of Shahjahanabad, today called Old Delhi. The Yamuna remains a central feature of the urban setting of Agra, where the Red Fort of Agra, the Taj Mahal, and a few other sites bear witness to the many gardens, tombs, and palaces that once graced the banks of the river.

In closing, within the narratives of the Yamuna is a story that may serve as a metaphor and perhaps an inspiration for controlling the pollution that has turned the river into what it is today. In

Figure 1:

*"The River Goddess
Yamuna and Attendants"*

*India, Rajasthan, circa 800
Sculpture Red sandstone Los
Angeles County Museum of
Art From the Nasli and Alice
Heeramaneck Collection,
Museum Associates
Purchase (M.79.9.10.2a)*

Figure 2:

"Leaf from a Bhagavata
Purana series"

*The Cowherd Women of
Vraja Observing the Vow
of Katyayani. India, The
Delhi-Agra region, perhaps
Mathura, ca. 1520 – 1530.
Opaque color on paper The
Fralin Museum of Art The
University of Virginia Museum
purchase with Curriculum
Support Fund 1994.11.*

Book Ten of the Bhagavata Purana there is a story of fatal pollution in the Yamuna and of its cause, the serpent Kaliya (BPX.15.47-52 and 16.1-67). The once pure river waters become poisoned from the venom of the serpent king, and as his foster mother swoons and his foster father must be restrained from following him, Krishna leaps into the water to grapple with the snake. After disappearing for a long time under the water, the god reappears, triumphant, and dances on the battered hoods of the defeated serpent. As his family and companions express joy, the wives of Kaliya plead with Krishna to spare their husband's life. The compassionate god agrees, sending them back to their original home on an island in the sea, and the waters of the Yamuna are once again pure, cleansed of pollution. Divine intervention may be an unlikely solution in modern times, but perhaps with proper management of input to the river the day when her waters are pure can come again.

Bibliography

Sinha, Amita, and D. Fairchild Ruggles, "The Yamuna Riverfront, India: A Comparative Study of Islamic and Hindu Traditions in Cultural Landscapes", Landscape Journal 23:2 (2004), pp. 141-152.

von Stietencron, Heinrich. Ganga und Yamuna: Zur Symbolischen Bedeutung der Flussgöttinnen an Indischen Tempeln (Wiesbaden, 1972).

Viennot, Odette. Les Divinités Fluviales Ganga et Yamuna: Aux Portes des Sanctuaires de l'Inde; Essai D'évolution D'un Thème Décoratif (Paris, 1964).

15

YAMUNA AS GODDESS AND ICON
DANIEL ENHBORN

Figure 3:

"Venugopala"

The work of Ustad Hasan (active ca. 1750-1770). India, Rajasthan, Bikaner. Dated V.S 1823/ A.D. 1766. Opaque color and gold on paper. Private Collection. Ex-Maharaja of Bikaner Collection.

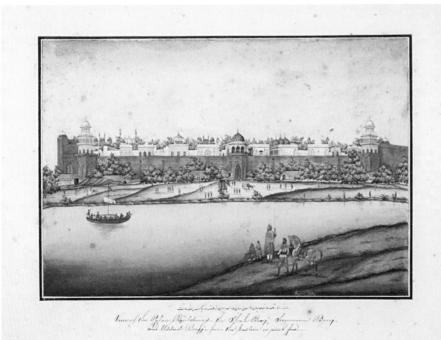

Figure 4:

"Leaf from a portfolio by Ghulam Ali Khan" (fl. 1817-55)

The Red Fort of Delhi from the Yamuna River. Inscribed "View of the Palace Buildings of the Shah Boorj, Summer Boorj, and Ussud Boorj from the Eastern or river face." India, Company Style, Delhi, c. 1852-54. Watercolor on paper. Sold at Bonham's London, 23 Apr 2013, Lot 352. Present location unknown. Photograph courtesy Bonham's, London.

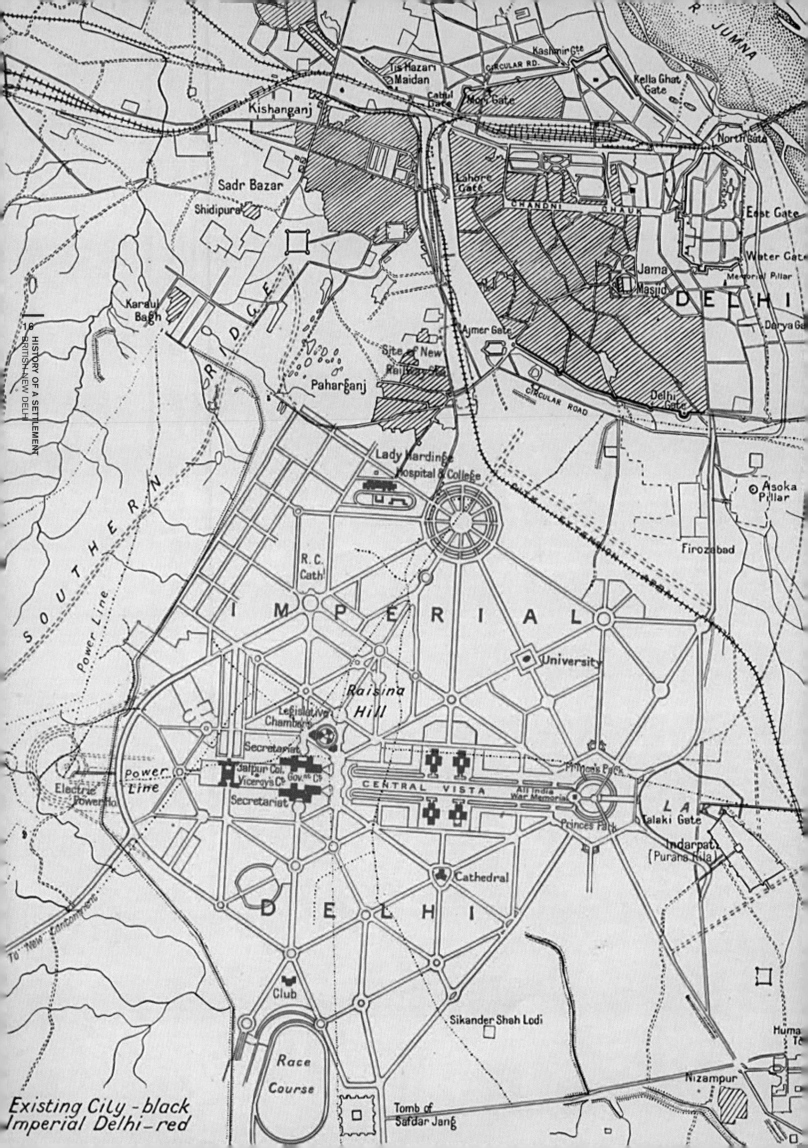

Existing City – black
Imperial Delhi – red

**Lutyens' Projected
"Imperial Delhi" (far left):**

*Encyclopedia Britannica,
11th ed., 1910-12*

Lutyens' Delhi (left):

*An aerial view of the completed city
of New Delhi with the war memorial
at the end of Kingsway. Photo
courtesy of Centre for South Asian
Studies, University of Cambridge
accessed on July 6th, 2017
at: http://nerdyindian.blogspot.
com/2014_11_01_archive.html*

Lutyens Delhi:

*"India Gate in the 1940s"
"Rashtrapati Bhavan Looking East"*

British New Delhi

In 1803, Shahjahanabad came under British control. Forced assimilation took a more aggressive tone after the Mutiny of 1857 when the British intensified the process of establishing their rule architecturally and militarily. In 1874 they annexed villages outside the walls in preparation for a new kind of urban growth. Infrastructure improvements expanded quickly, especially after 1900, culminating in the British declaration of Delhi as the Empire's capital in 1911. Lutyens' design for New Delhi in 1911 developed on a plain to the southwest of Old Delhi, drawing the city away from the river. Its monumental and geometric design was influenced by western precedents in Paris, Rome, and Washington D.C. in contrast to the dense and organic fabric of Shahjahanabad. Wells, graves, and villages were cleared in favor of avenues and monuments. Bureaucrats filled this new zone while clerks, workers, and traders were pushed to the south and west. India's independence in 1947 brought thousands of refugees and accelerated population growth. Delhi's 1962 Master Plan helped bring some order to the uncontrolled growth by dividing the city into "self-sufficient neighborhoods" but Delhi's dramatic population growth has left the Yamuna polluted, inaccessible, and forgotten.

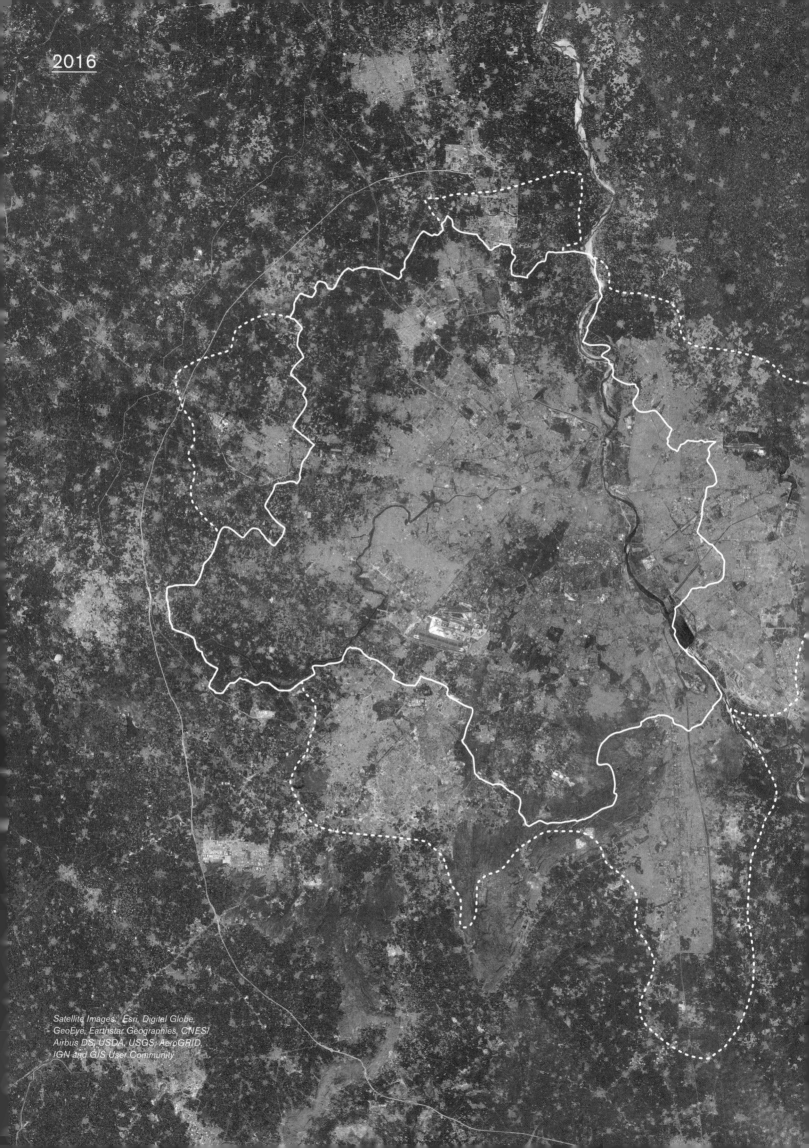

2016

DELHI'S MODERN EVOLUTION

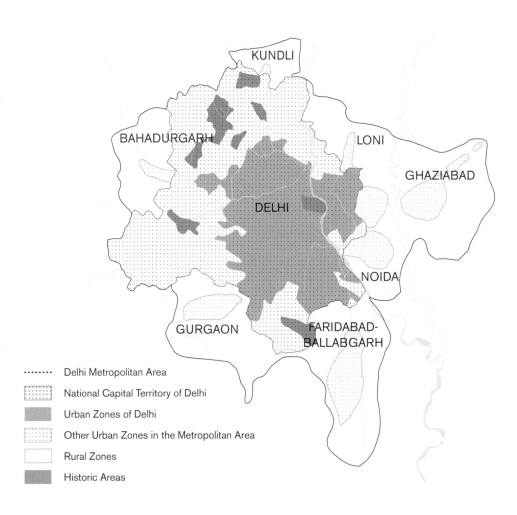

KUNDLI

BAHADURGARH

LONI

GHAZIABAD

DELHI

NOIDA

GURGAON

FARIDABAD-
BALLABGARH

········· Delhi Metropolitan Area

National Capital Territory of Delhi

Urban Zones of Delhi

Other Urban Zones in the Metropolitan Area

Rural Zones

Historic Areas

Then the city that had been planned so carefully over the centuries was overtaken by events. Independence and Partition brought enormous waves of refugees from East and West Pakistan; migration continued to swell Delhi long after the violence was over. Rapid industrialization and economic modernization has led to an explosion of wealth and employment opportunities for all classes in the capital causing people to flock to the city for economic opportunity. Birth rates remain high and rural migrants come not just from the corners of the small National Capital Territory but from surrounding states, especially Uttar Pradesh, Bihar, Haryana, Madhya Pradesh and Punjab.

Delhi's urban fabric has necessarily expanded to accommodate rising an ever growing population. Delhi has been undeniably successful in melting away its rural population and replacing it with city-dwellers through the annexation of dense villages and the development of agricultural fields into planned colonies and urban villages. Delhi has gone from 82.4% urban to 97.5% urban in just 50 years. There is no end in site for this relentless urbanization.

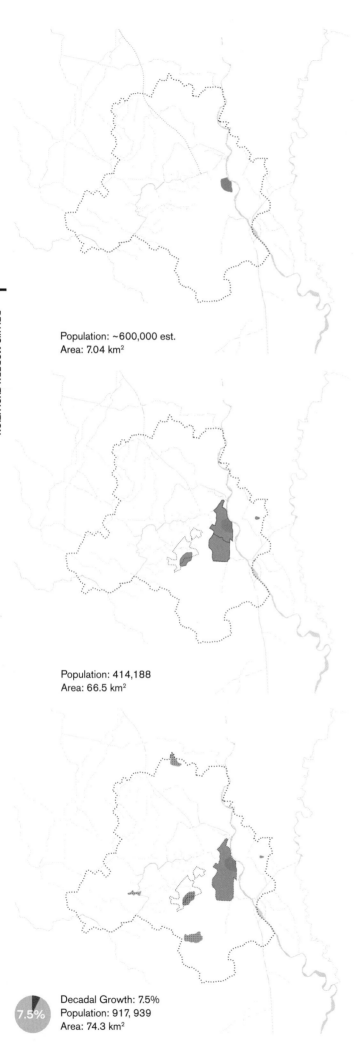

1648

1526: Delhi falls under Mughal rule
1628: Mughal Emperor, Shah Jahan, restores the 14th century Western Yamuna Canal
1639: Shah Jahan, initiates the construction of a new capital along the banks of the Yamuna River known as Shahjahanabad
1648: The Red Fort reaches completion.
Mid 18th Century: Delhi raided by Marathas

- - - - - National Capital Territory of Delhi

- - - - - - Western Yamuna Canal

  Yamuna River

  1648

Population: ~600,000 est.
Area: 7.04 km^2

1911

1803: Delhi occupied by the British
1857: Indian Mutiny
1870: The British begin restorations of the Western Yamuna Canal and construct the Tajewala Barrage. This diverted the river through the Western and Eastern Yamuna Canals
1911: Sir Edwin Lutyens commissioned by British to design a new capital in Delhi
1912: The British move into New Delhi
1931: Lutyens' construction in New Delhi is completed

- - - - - National Capital Territory of Delhi

- - - - - - - District Boundaries

  Yamuna River

  1911

Population: 414,188
Area: 66.5 km^2

1941

1947: Delhi achieves independence from the British, India and Pakistan partitioned
1947-1964: Jawaharlal Nehru serves as Delhi's prime minister

470,000 refugees from Punjab and Sindh move to Delhi
320,000 Muslims migrate from Delhi to Pakistan

- - - - - National Capital Territory of Delhi

- - - - - - - District Boundaries

  Yamuna River

  1941

  5,000 people per sq/km

Decadal Growth: 7.5%
Population: 917, 939
Area: 74.3 km^2

7.5%

1961

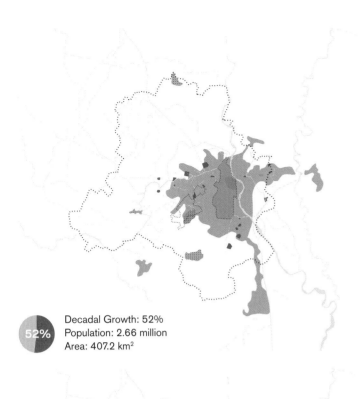

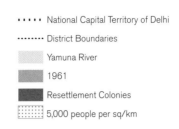

1956: Under the States
Reorganization Act, Delhi's Union
Territory is formed
1962: Master Plan for Delhi
formalized, to be implemented in 1981

- - - - - National Capital Territory of Delhi

· · · · · · · · District Boundaries

Yamuna River

1961

Resettlement Colonies

5,000 people per sq/km

Decadal Growth: 52%
Population: 2.66 million
Area: 407.2 km²

52%

1981

NORTHWEST
NORTH
NORTHEAST
WEST
CENTRAL
SOUTHWEST
EAST
NEW DELHI
SOUTH

1991: Delhi's National Capital Territory
established
1998: Delhi Jal Board Constituted
1999: The Hathnikund Barrage is
completed, replacing the 19th century
Tajewala Barrage
2010: Delhi hosts the Commonwealth
Games

———— National Capital Territory of Delhi

· · · · · · · · 1995 District Boundaries

Yamuna River

1981

Existing Resettlement Colonies
New Resettlement Colonies

0 - 500 people per sq/km
500 - 4,000 people per sq/km
4,000 - 10,000 people per sq/km

Decadal Growth: 53%
Population: 6.21 million
Area: 965.1 km²

53%

2011

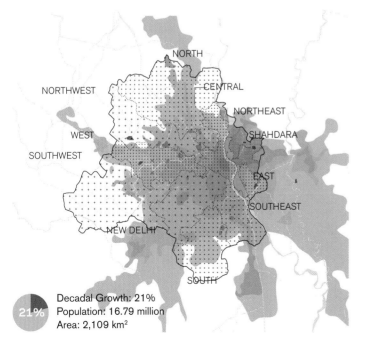

NORTH
CENTRAL
NORTHWEST
NORTHEAST
WEST
SHAHDARA
SOUTHWEST
EAST
SOUTHEAST
NEW DELHI
SOUTH

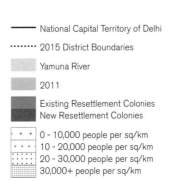

2015: Delhi redistricted
2016: The Delhi Jal Board begins to
draft Delhi Water Conservation Act
which will set up the Bureau of Water
Efficiency

———— National Capital Territory of Delhi

· · · · · · · · 2015 District Boundaries

Yamuna River

2011

Existing Resettlement Colonies
New Resettlement Colonies

0 - 10,000 people per sq/km
10 - 20,000 people per sq/km
20 - 30,000 people per sq/km
30,000+ people per sq/km

Decadal Growth: 21%
Population: 16.79 million
Area: 2,109 km²

21%

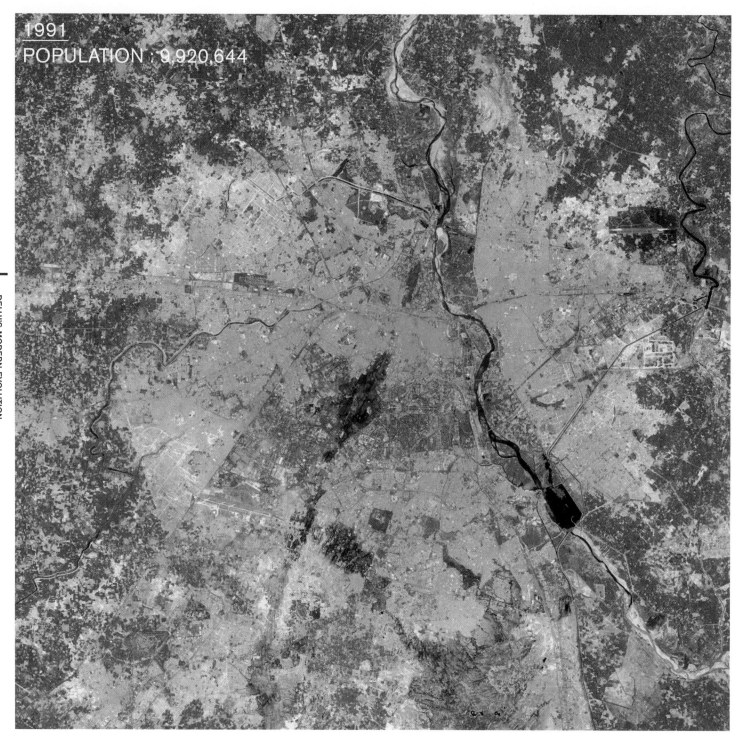

Delhi's Exponential Expansion

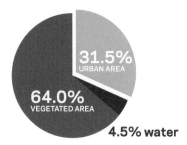

31.5%
URBAN AREA

64.0%
VEGETATED AREA

4.5% water

Year	Population
1991	9,421,000
2001	13,850,000
2011	16,787,000
2021	20,483,000
2031	23,442,000

Utilizing remote sensing and LANDSAT satellite observations of land cover, data is obtained in order to determine how human populations within the New Delhi region have expanded and how land use has changed over the last decades. This information is critical for future urban planning and hydrological modeling efforts of the Yamuna River System. Over the past decades, Delhi and its surrounding territory have undergone immense vegetation loss in conjunction with exponential growth in agricultural and urban areas. This growth increases pollution levels and presents an issue of wastewater runoff

during the monsoon season which is harmful to the entire Yamuna region. These images reveal a dangerous future for Delhi with certain districts seeing over 20% loss in vegetation cover. They also show little results from environmental efforts to increase vegetation. If this trend continues, and Delhi is to urbanize further without environmental considerations, the pollution and runoff into the Yamuna is only likely to worsen. The dramatic changes of land cover over the past 25 years illustrates just how vital it is that exponential expansion be addressed holistically by designers, government authorities, and society as a whole.

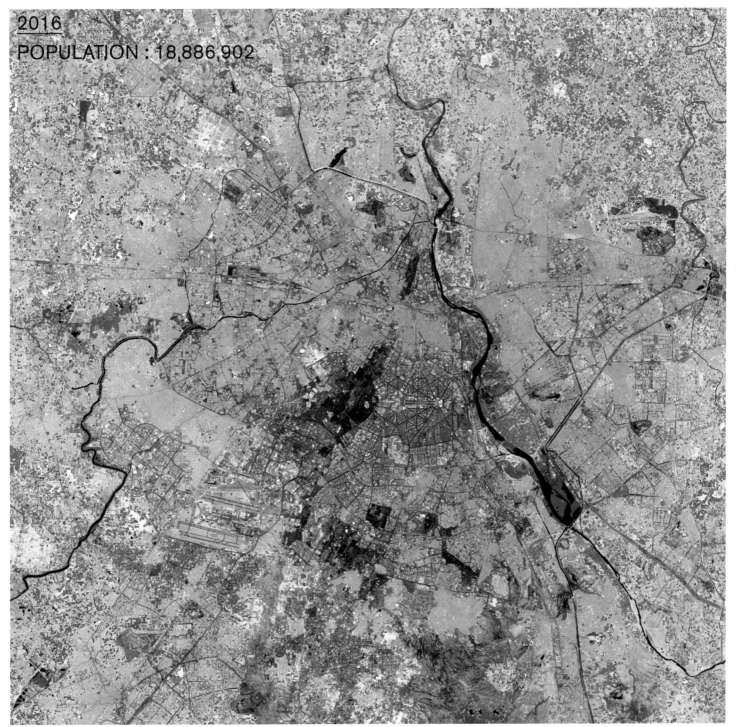

2016

POPULATION : 18,886,902

Research Director: M. Reidenbach, Associate Professor of Environmental Sciences

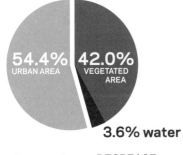

54.4% URBAN AREA

42.0% VEGETATED AREA

3.6% water

35% DECREASE IN FORESTED AREA

35% DECREASE IN AGRICULTURAL AREA

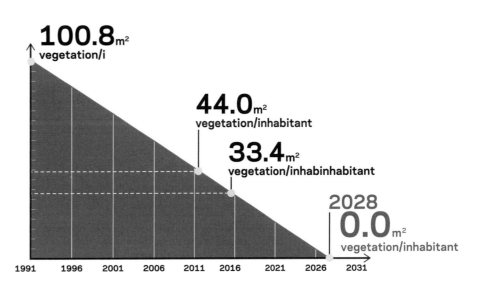

100.8m² vegetation/i

44.0m² vegetation/inhabitant

33.4m² vegetation/inhabinhabitant

2028
0.0m² vegetation/inhabitant

1991   1996   2001   2006   2011   2016   2021   2026   2031

Modern Delhi's Geography

Modern Delhi demonstrates a complete disregard
for the relationship between urbanity and the natural
environment which characterized the historic city.
Original settlements may remain but the city has turned
its back on the Yamuna River. The expansive floodplain
has been eliminated due to urban development and
streams have been turned into a system of "managed"
drains. What results from ignoring the role of nature in
supporting a sustainable urbanity are not surprising.
Delhi constantly suffers a severe lack of clean drinking
water, some of the worst air pollution in the world,
and is beset by other issues of growth, inadequate
sewage treatment, and lack of a clean food supply.

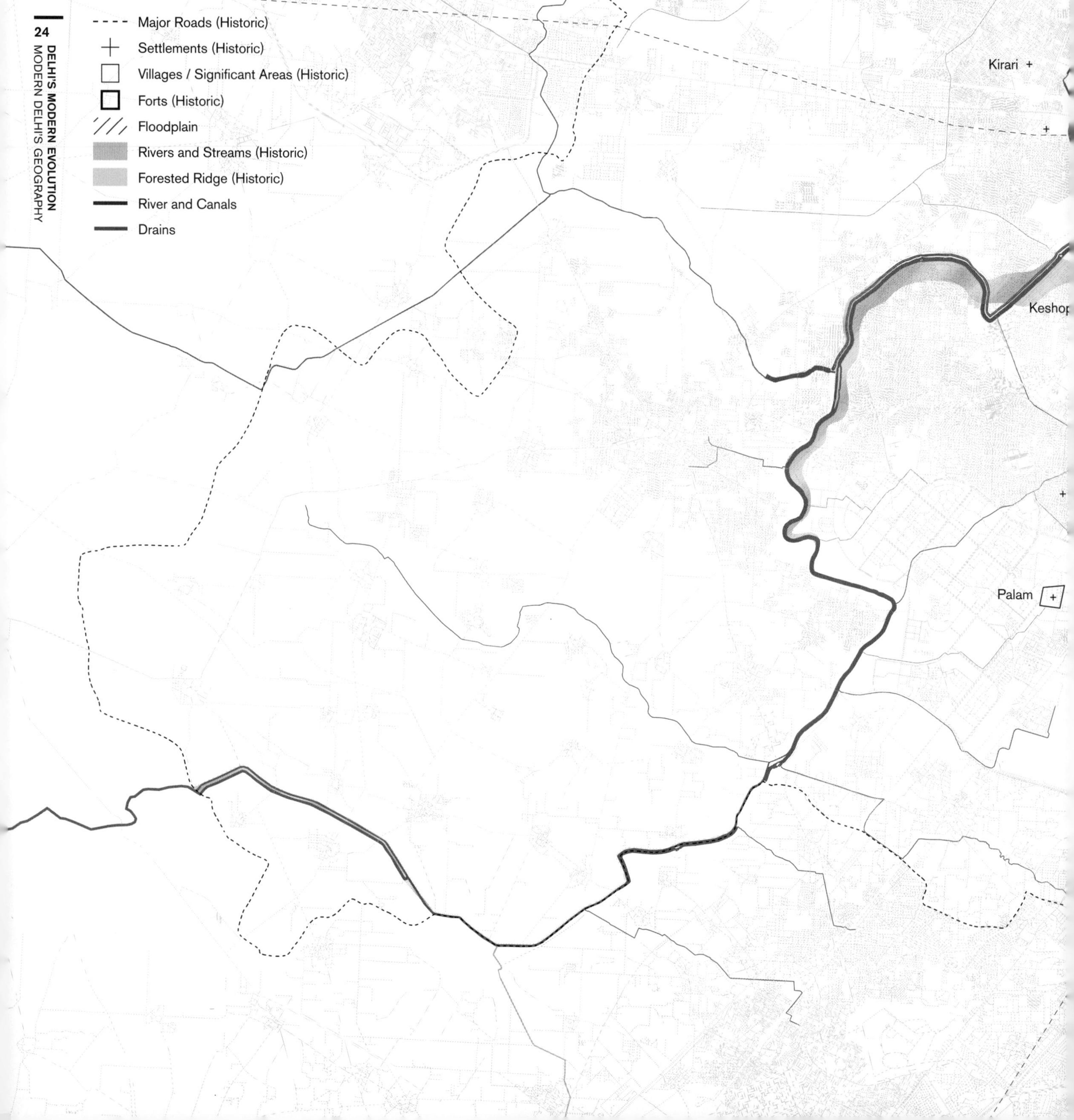

- - - - Major Roads (Historic)

╶╂╴ Settlements (Historic)

☐ Villages / Significant Areas (Historic)

▢ Forts (Historic)

/// Floodplain

▨ Rivers and Streams (Historic)

▨ Forested Ridge (Historic)

▬ River and Canals

▬ Drains

Kirari +

Keshop

Palam ▢+

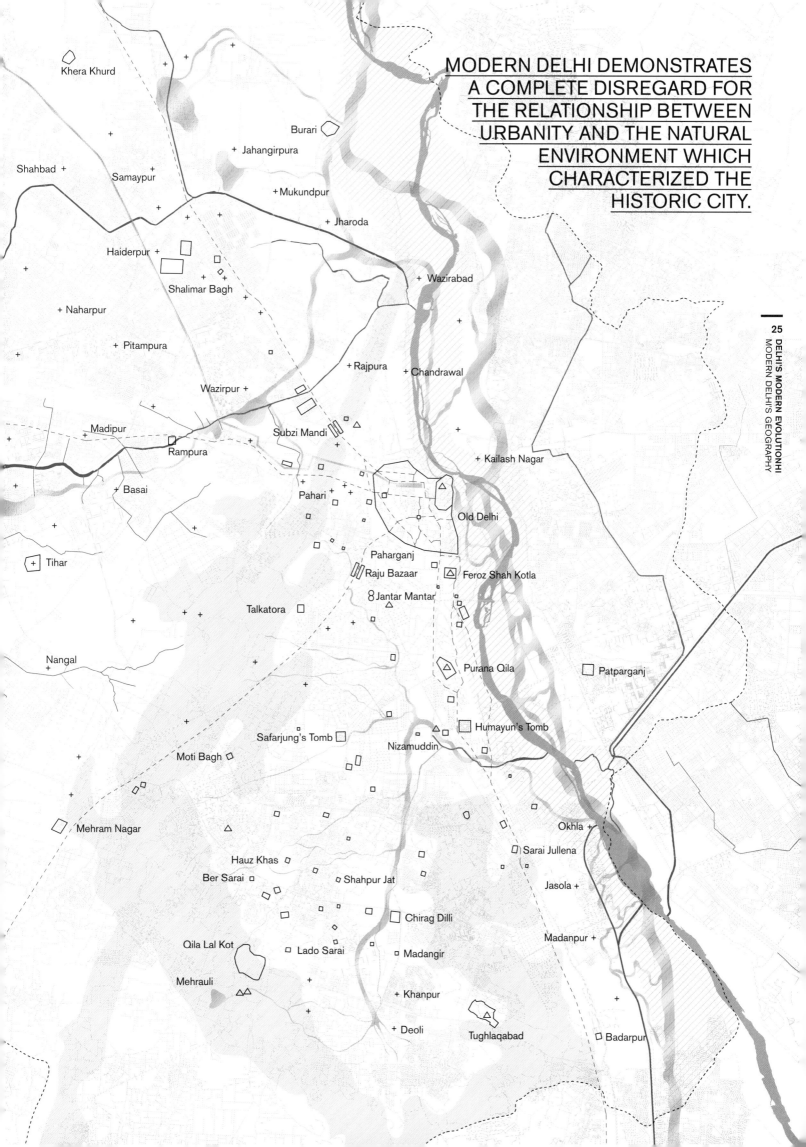

MODERN DELHI DEMONSTRATES
A COMPLETE DISREGARD FOR
THE RELATIONSHIP BETWEEN
URBANITY AND THE NATURAL
ENVIRONMENT WHICH
CHARACTERIZED THE
HISTORIC CITY.

Khera Khurd

Burari

Jahangirpura

Shahbad

Samaypur

Mukundpur

Jharoda

Haiderpur

Wazirabad

Shalimar Bagh

Naharpur

Pitampura

Rajpura

Chandrawal

Wazirpur

Kailash Nagar

Madipur

Subzi Mandi

Rampura

Basai

Pahari

Old Delhi

Tihar

Paharganj

Raju Bazaar

Feroz Shah Kotla

Jantar Mantar

Talkatora

Purana Qila

Patparganj

Nangal

Safarjung's Tomb

Humayun's Tomb

Moti Bagh

Nizamuddin

Mehram Nagar

Okhla

Hauz Khas

Sarai Jullena

Ber Sarai

Shahpur Jat

Jasola

Chirag Dilli

Qila Lal Kot

Lado Sarai

Madangir

Madanpur

Mehrauli

Khanpur

Deoli

Tughlaqabad

Badarpur

Master Plan for Delhi 2021:

*Land Use Plan 2021, Delhi
Master Plan, January 19, 2007.
Accessed September 13, 2017.
http://delhi-masterplan.com/zonal-
plans-mpd-2021/land-use-plan/*

Delhi 2021 Master Plan

The city currently operates under outdated planning prescriptions; its last master plan was approved in 1990. A master plan was completed in 2001 for "Delhi 2021" yet never approved, and planning is currently underway for "Delhi 2031" under the leadership of the Delhi Development Authority (DDA).

The Delhi 2021 master plan attempted to address Delhi's complexities through a zoning plan for areas that were already developed. No strategic vision was presented that holistically addressed how the city would accommodate the World Bank's estimate of ten million additional inhabitants by 2050, continued decimation of vegetated and agricultural land brought on by urban sprawl (as revealed though Matt Reidenbach's LANDSAT research), how the city would manage increased disaster risk brought on by climate change, or how Delhi's ecology could be revitalized and integrated into urban life.

However, there were a few disparate ideas in the Delhi 2021 master plan document which, if unified in a single proposal, could produce an inspired vision to "make Delhi a global metropolis and world-class city, where all people have productive work, a better quality of life and live in a sustainable environment." This new vision would redevelop Delhi's existing urban fabric, imagining the drains and waterfront as overlapping blue and green networks which form urban corridors for public recreation and water bioremediation, support an intermodal transport network which links work centers and residential areas, and structures the city's future growth alongside ecological considerations.

"MASTER PLANS" HAVE FAILED TO PROVIDE A STRATEGIC VISION WHICH ADDRESSES DELHI'S URBAN COMPLEXITIES, ENDANGERED ECOLOGIES, AND EXPONENTIAL URBAN GROWTH.

Master Plan for Delhi, 1962

Master Plan for Delhi, 2001

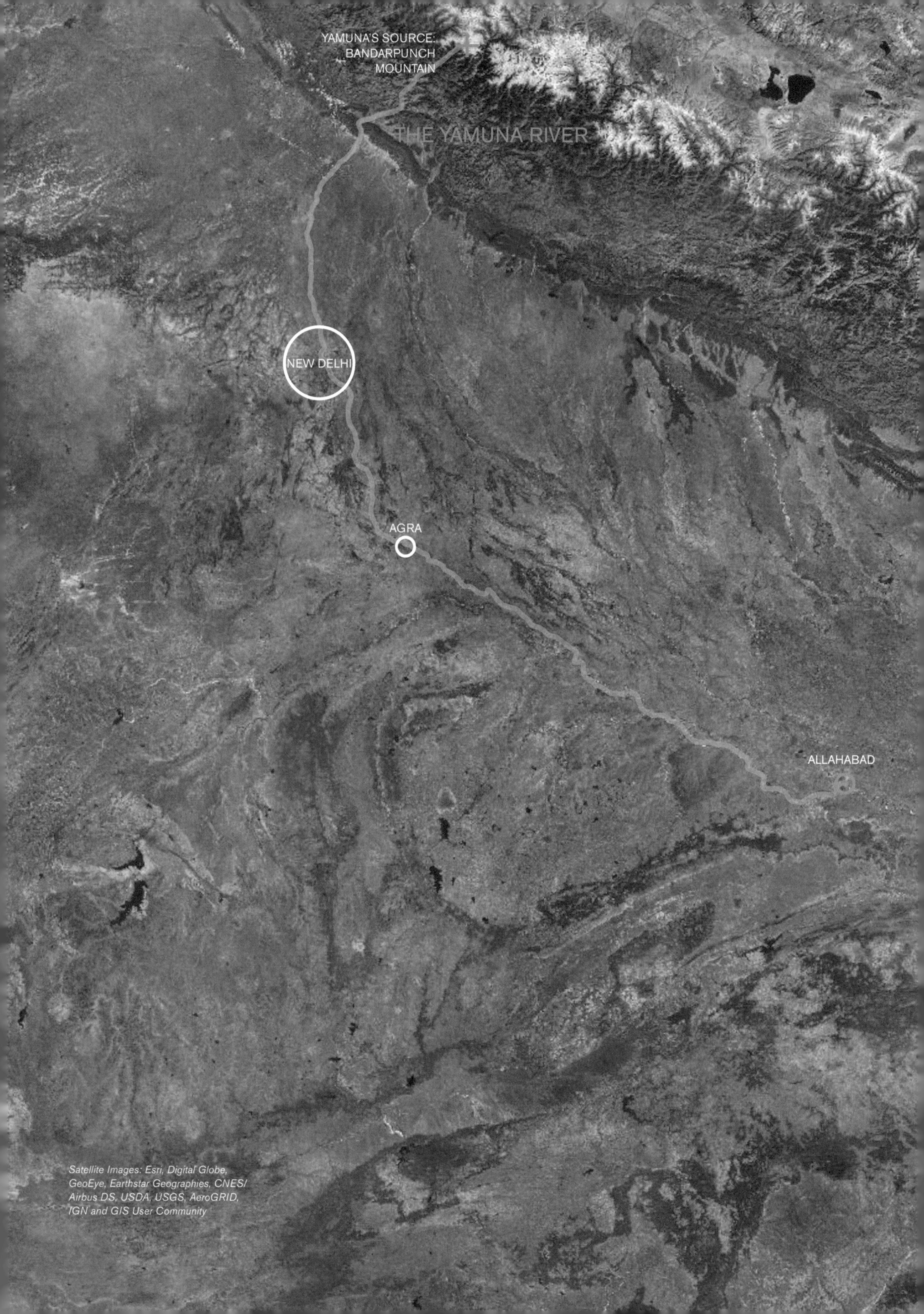
YAMUNA'S SOURCE:
BANDARPUNCH
MOUNTAIN
THE YAMUNA RIVER
NEW DELHI
AGRA
ALLAHABAD

Satellite Images: Esri, Digital Globe, GeoEye, Earthstar Geographies, CNES/Airbus DS, USDA, USGS, AeroGRID, IGN and GIS User Community

DELHI'S WATERS

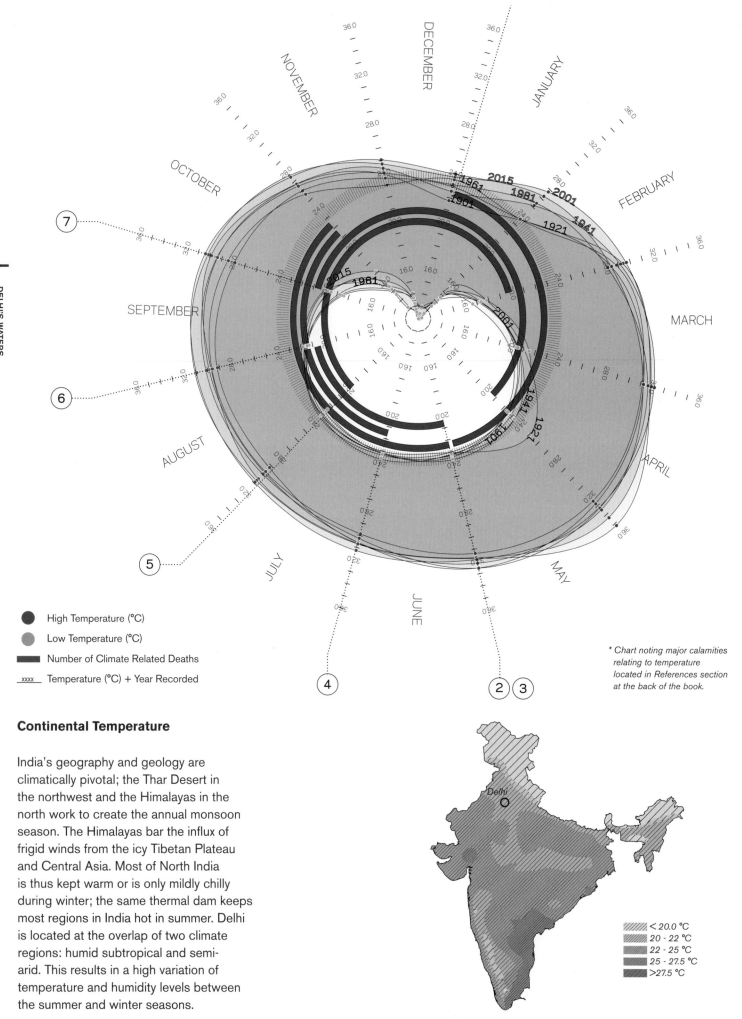

High Temperature (°C)

Low Temperature (°C)

Number of Climate Related Deaths

xxxx Temperature (°C) + Year Recorded

* Chart noting major calamities
relating to temperature
located in References section
at the back of the book.

Continental Temperature

India's geography and geology are
climatically pivotal; the Thar Desert in
the northwest and the Himalayas in the
north work to create the annual monsoon
season. The Himalayas bar the influx of
frigid winds from the icy Tibetan Plateau
and Central Asia. Most of North India
is thus kept warm or is only mildly chilly
during winter; the same thermal dam keeps
most regions in India hot in summer. Delhi
is located at the overlap of two climate
regions: humid subtropical and semi-
arid. This results in a high variation of
temperature and humidity levels between
the summer and winter seasons.

Delhi

< 20.0 °C
20 - 22 °C
22 - 25 °C
25 - 27.5 °C
>27.5 °C

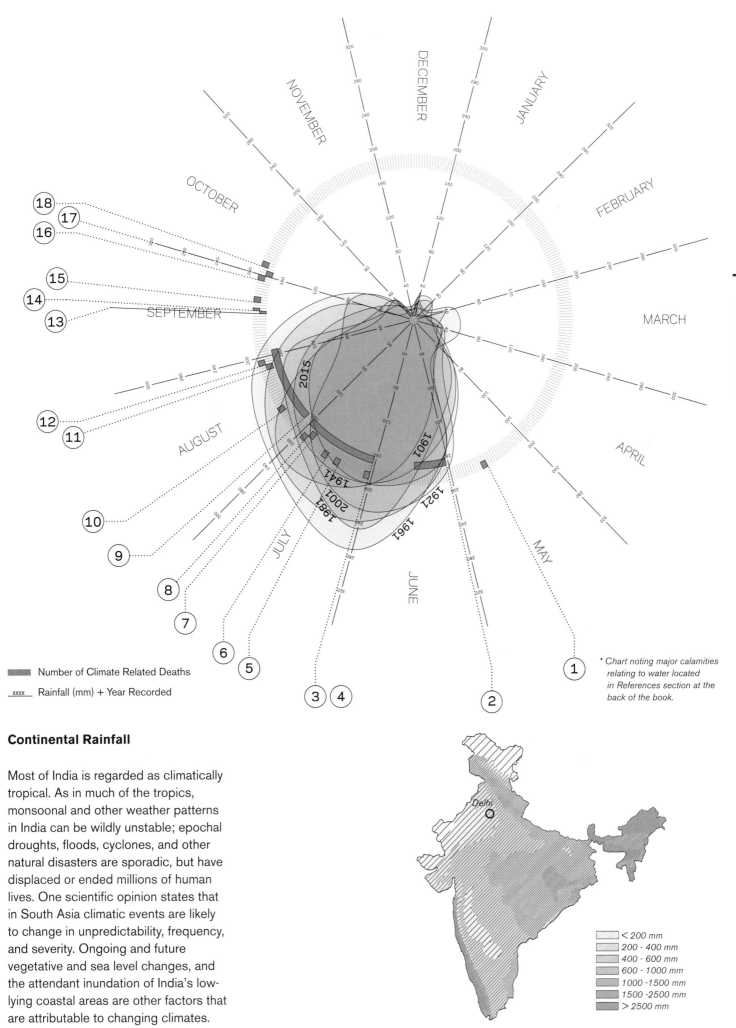

NOVEMBER
DECEMBER
JANUARY
OCTOBER
FEBRUARY
SEPTEMBER
MARCH
AUGUST
APRIL
JULY
MAY
JUNE

2015
1901
1941
1981
2001
1921
1961

Number of Climate Related Deaths

xxxx Rainfall (mm) + Year Recorded

* Chart noting major calamities
relating to water located
in References section at the
back of the book.

Continental Rainfall

Most of India is regarded as climatically
tropical. As in much of the tropics,
monsoonal and other weather patterns
in India can be wildly unstable; epochal
droughts, floods, cyclones, and other
natural disasters are sporadic, but have
displaced or ended millions of human
lives. One scientific opinion states that
in South Asia climatic events are likely
to change in unpredictability, frequency,
and severity. Ongoing and future
vegetative and sea level changes, and
the attendant inundation of India's low-
lying coastal areas are other factors that
are attributable to changing climates.

Delhi

< 200 mm
200 - 400 mm
400 - 600 mm
600 - 1000 mm
1000 -1500 mm
1500 -2500 mm
> 2500 mm

2016 Monsoon Onset (Southwest Monsoon)

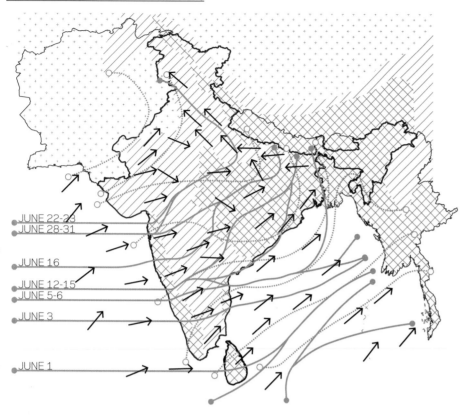

JUNE 22-23
JUNE 28-31

JUNE 16

JUNE 12-15
JUNE 5-6

JUNE 3

JUNE 1

2016 Monsoon Retreat (Northeast Monsoon)

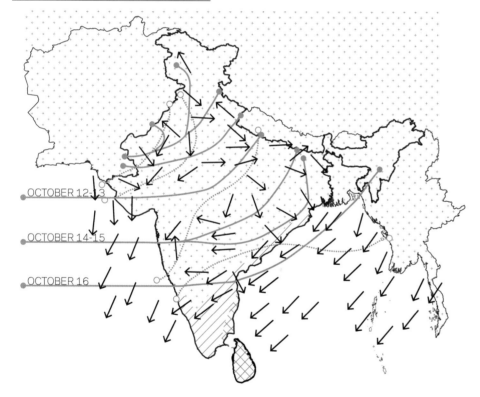

OCTOBER 12-13

OCTOBER 14-15

OCTOBER 16

○·············○ Normal Monsoon Progression

○————○ Actual Monsoon Progression

Very Light Rainfall

Moderate Rainfall

Heavy Rainfall

Monsoon

The monsoon provides over 80% of India's annual rainfall and generally occurs during a four month period between June and October. The country depends on monsoon waters to irrigate its massive agricultural economy, to bring cooler temperatures across the continent, to refill groundwater levels, and to provide adequate river flows. The Yamuna sees 80% of its flow during monsoon months and it is critical that the Yamuna is allowed to broaden into its full monsoonal floodplain to properly recharge groundwater, flush out silt and still water algae, and refresh good levels of bacteria in the soil to correct the imbalances of pollution.

However, the amount of water that flows through the Yamuna in Delhi is less than 30% of its original flow, and may be as low as 3% during the dry non-monsoon months due to infrastructures that divert water. A 2013 study concluded that anything less than 50-60% flow throughout the year causes serious damage to the entire river system, even beyond Delhi. At present levels of flow, the river cannot fully recharge groundwater and bacteria in aquifers can not break down nitrates when the soil is not thoroughly wet. This diminished flow is insufficient to dilute untreated sewage emptying into the Yamuna and silt buildup will make occasional floods even more catastrophic. Nor can this polluted river support biodiversity that is native to this area. Further downstream, a river that flows with less depth and velocity impoverishes the interface between the delta and the sea, an ecosystem upon which many livelihoods depend.

MONSOON WATERS PLAY A CRITICAL ROLE IN THE ECOLOGY OF THE YAMUNA RIVER BASIN AND DIRECTLY IMPACT DRINKING WATER SUPPLIES AND IRRIGATION RESOURCES ACROSS NORTHERN INDIA.

Average Temperature

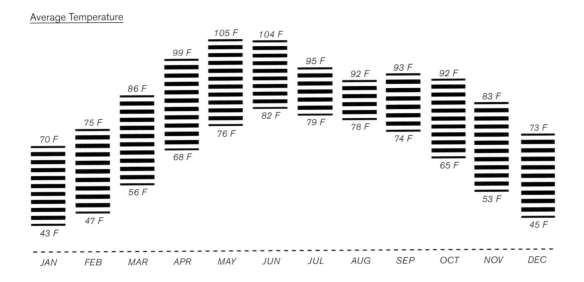

| JAN | FEB | MAR | APR | MAY | JUN | JUL | AUG | SEP | OCT | NOV | DEC |

70 F / 43 F — 75 F / 47 F — 86 F / 56 F — 99 F / 68 F — 105 F / 76 F — 104 F / 82 F — 95 F / 79 F — 92 F / 78 F — 93 F / 74 F — 92 F / 65 F — 83 F / 53 F — 73 F / 45 F

Humidity and Pressure

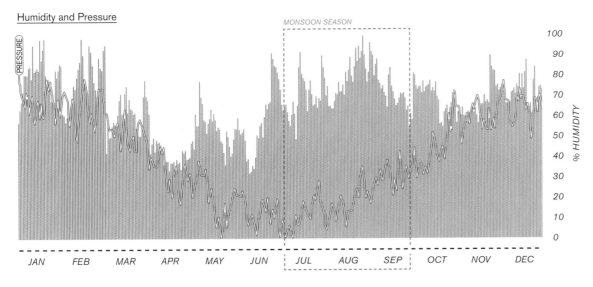

MONSOON SEASON

PRESSURE

% HUMIDITY
100
90
80
70
60
50
40
30
20
10
0

| JAN | FEB | MAR | APR | MAY | JUN | JUL | AUG | SEP | OCT | NOV | DEC |

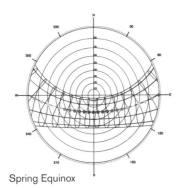

Spring Equinox

After the spring Equinox on March 21, the Sun advances north of the equator and is over the Indian subcontinent.

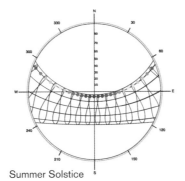

Summer Solstice

By mid-May, heat over the Indian subcontinent forms a low pressure area over Northwest India.

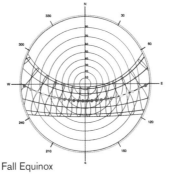

Fall Equinox

The low pressure pulls moisture rich air that rises and precipitates, marking the onset of the Southwest monsoon.

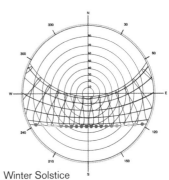

Winter Solstice

Indian landmass starts to cool from the monsoon rains and an increasing pressure causes the monsoon's retreat.

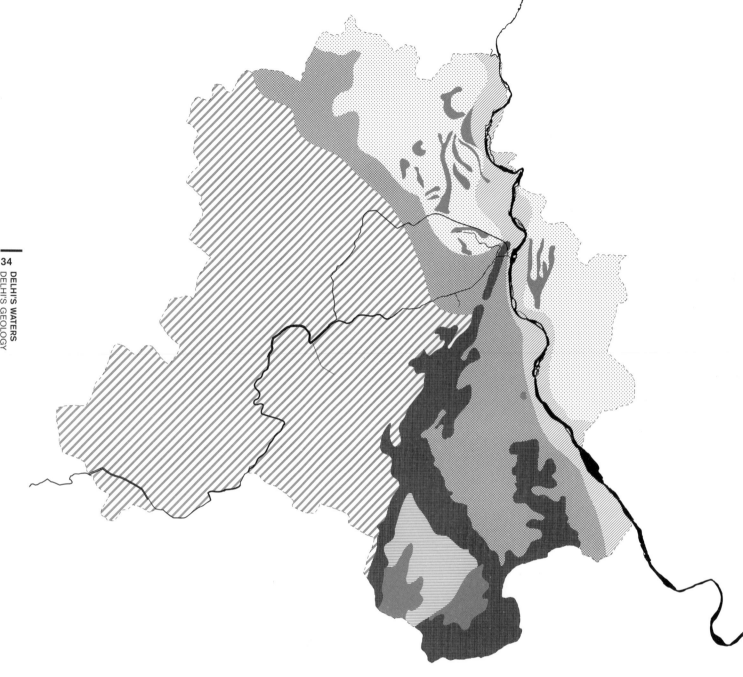

Delhi's Geology

Active Floodplain

Old Khadar Floodplain

Old Bhangar Alluvial Plain

Ridge

Elevated Sandy Surface

Plateau / Ravines

Old Sagar Alluvial Plain

Indian is composed of three distinct geologic features: the triangular plateau to the south which extends into the Indian Ocean, the Himalayan mountain range which rings the country to the west, north, and east, and the expansive Indus-Ganga Plain that runs through much of northern and eastern India. Climatic conditions, particularly seasonal monsoons, are interrelated with India's geologic features. High and low pressure systems draw humid air from the Indian Ocean over the Indian plains until the weather system is diverted by the Himalayas. The resulting monsoon rains feed rivers and contribute to the fertility of the Indus-Ganga Plain whose characteristics shaped settlement patterns and supported India's agricultural economy. Alluvial soils

found in the Indus-Ganga Plain, through which the Yamuna and Ganga Rivers flow, support extensive agricultural cultivation, which still continues today. Eventually this gave rise to large urban populations such as New Delhi.

India's geologic features continue to impact it cities. In 2011 The World Bank and United Nations co-published the 'Natural Hazards and UnNatural Disasters-the Economics of Effective Prevention' report stating around 200 million city dwellers in India will be exposed to life-altering storms and earthquakes by 2050. Potential threats are exacerbated when we consider that many Indian cities are outgrowing the capacity of their roads, water supplies, and sewage disposal systems.

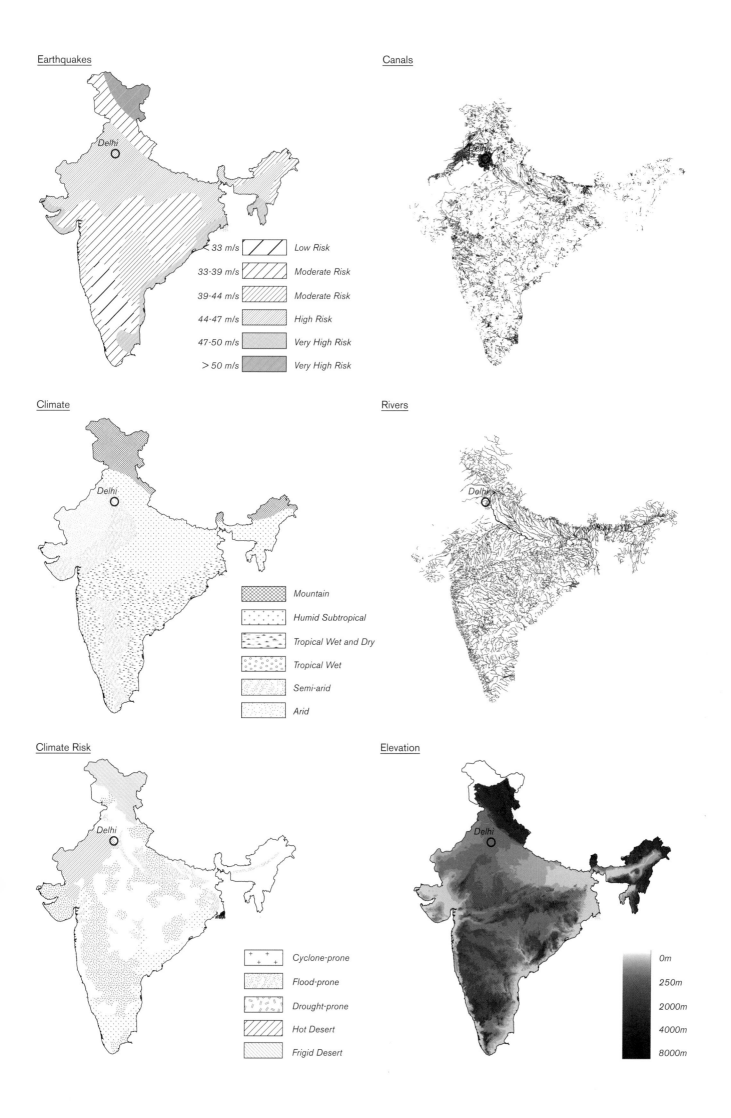

Earthquakes

< 33 m/s	Low Risk
33-39 m/s	Moderate Risk
39-44 m/s	Moderate Risk
44-47 m/s	High Risk
47-50 m/s	Very High Risk
> 50 m/s	Very High Risk

Canals

Climate

	Mountain
	Humid Subtropical
	Tropical Wet and Dry
	Tropical Wet
	Semi-arid
	Arid

Rivers

Climate Risk

	Cyclone-prone
	Flood-prone
	Drought-prone
	Hot Desert
	Frigid Desert

Elevation

	0m
	250m
	2000m
	4000m
	8000m

Delhi

Hindu Rao •
Baoli

● Red Fort
Baoli

■ Feroz Shah Kotla
Baoli

Ugrasen •
Baoli

Purana Qila ◈
Baoli

Nizamuddin Dargah •
Baoli

• Loharheri
Baoli

Wazirpur •
Baoli

■ Hauz Khas
Bundh

Rajon Baoli
Gandhak Baoli

Hauz-i-Shamsi ■
Bunch

▱ Tughlaqabad Fort
Baoli

1807 River and Streams

● Bundh or Baoli

Historic Bundhs and Baolis

From the 13th to the 15th centuries, Delhi's rulers oversaw a series of public engineering works that protected their city from torrential rains, stored water for use during the dry season, and distributed water during the uneven course of India's monsoon cycle. These waterworks supported a population of several hundred thousand people and many animals in forts and villages. Now their ruins in modern Delhi stand as testament to a network that functioned in harmony with human settlement and the environment.

Along a 35-kilometer section of Delhi's ridge, tanks called bundhs were constructed every three kilometers. Some called "wet bundhs" retained water year-round, while others held water only in the dry months. These bundhs ensured that monsoon water was available throughout the year for irrigation and household purposes while also filling defensive moats. Two major bundhs that still hold water, with positive benefits for the water table, are those at Hauz Khas and Hauz-i-Shamsi. Baolis, also known as stepwells, act as underground tanks, composed of a circular water-well and a descending stairway leading down through various levels. They may be either extremely utilitarian in appearance or embellished with beautiful patterns, monumental stonework, and even sculptures. Designed for ease of use and maintenance, with steps leading to the bottom, they may be used at any time of year, even when the water table is extremely low.

Ugrasen Baoli, New Delhi

Rajon Baoli, New Delhi

Gandhak Baoli, New Delhi

DELHI'S HISTORIC BUNDHS AND BAOLIS STAND AS TESTAMENT TO A NETWORK OF PUBLIC SPACES THAT FUNCTIONED IN HARMONY WITH THE SEASONS, LANDSCAPE, AND THE YAMUNA RIVER ITSELF.

1. The Yamunotri Glacier of the Bandarpunch Peaks in the Lower Himalayas acts as the source for the Yamuna River.1   30°48'16.68"N 79° 7'26.15"E

The Yamuna forms the western boundary of the Ganga-Yamuna Doab Region - the largest alluvial fertile plain in the world.   29°30'20.25"N 77° 7'8.04"E

The Yamuna winds through the Shivalik Hills of the Lower Himalayas, serving as a catchment for its many tributaries.   30°47'14.05"N 78° 8'11.39"E

After nearly 330km the Yamuna enters New Delhi. Here the river is dead: no longer a source of life, it has been turned into a sewer.   28°38'38.60"N 77°15'11.26"E

GOBIND SINGH RESERVOIR

HIMALAYAN MOUNTAINS

YUMUNOTRI GLACIER

HIMALAYAN MOUNTAINS

GANGOTRI

DAKPATHAR BARRAGE

ASSAN BARRAGE

PH 14
PH 15
PH 16
PH 17

HARIDWAR BARRAGE

UPPER GANGA CANAL

BHAKRA NANGAL DAM

HIMACHAL PRADESH
HARYANA

**97% OF WATER
FLOW IS DIVERTED
AT HATHNIKUND**

HATHNIKUND BARRAGE

PH 18
PH 19

WESTERN YAMUNA CANAL

EASTERN YAMUNA CANAL

PH 20

PUNJAB
HARYANA

PH 1
PH 2
PH 3
PH 4

TAJEWALA BARRAGE

DRY RIVER BED

YAMUNA RIVER

PATHRALA BARRAGE
YAMUNANAGAR
HAMIDA BARRAGE

PH 10

BEHAT

PH 11

CHECK DAM

GANGA RIVER

PH 6

PH 12

SAHARANPUR

PH 7

KARNAL

PH 8

MUNAK HEAD

MUNAK ESCAPE*

JIND

PANIPAT

HARYANA
UTTAR PRADESH

SHAMLI

KHUBRU HEAD

DRY RIVER BED

KANDHAL

ROHTAK

SONIPAT

HINDON RIVER

KAKROI HEAD

DRAIN NO. 8

BARAUT

PH 9

HARYANA
DELHI

* During the monsoon season
or when the Western Yamuna
Canal is undergoing maintenance,
the Munak Escape can release
water into the dry Yamuna
River bed allowing Wazirabad
WTP to draw from the Yamuna
River. Sonia Vihar WTP can
also draw from the Yamuna
River if water supplies from the
Ganga Canal are interrupted.

BAWANA
15 MGD

WAZIRABAD*
135 MGD

SONIA
VIHAR*
141 MGD

HAIDERPUR
226 MGD

*WAZIRABAD
BARRAGE*

MURADNAGAR

BHAGIRATHI
107 MGD

UTTAR PRADESH
DELHI

SUPPLEMENTARY DRAIN

CHANDRAWL
94 MGD

NAJAFGARH DRAIN

NANGLOI
40 MGD

DRAIN

DRAIN

PRIMARILY SEWAGE

DRAIN

DWARKA
43 MGD

OKHLA BARRAGE

OKHLA
20 MGD

DELHI
HARYANA

DHANSA REGULATOR

HARYANA
UTTAR PRADESH

GOKUL BARRAGE

ALLAHABAD

CHAMBEL RIVER

BETWA RIVER

KEN RIVER

	Major Barrage		→	Flow Direction
	Head Regulator			Raw Water Pump
	Canal / River			Water Treatment Plant (WTP)
	Water Pipe		●	Urban Center
	Political Boundary		○	Water Source

Yamuna River Canal System

About 92% of Yamuna River water is utilized for irrigation and 8% is used as drinking water for people and livestock. After passing through many cities, agricultural fields, and industrial lands, Delhi receives 55% of its drinking water from the canal system. The two largest canals of the Yamuna System are the Western Yamuna Canal and the Eastern Yamuna Canal, both of which originate at the Hathnikund Barrage in the state of Haryana, 250km north of Delhi. They respectively irrigate 486,000 hectares and 191,000 hectares annually. The Western Yamuna Canal was commissioned in 1335 and five centuries later the British added the Eastern Yamuna Canal, rebuilt the Western Yamuna Canal, and added the barrage at Hathnikund. Rebuilt in 2002, this barrage now diverts a majority of the river, leaving only residual flows of 3% to continue down the Yamuna River to Delhi.

The Western Yamuna Canal's main canal, branches, tributaries, and minors total 1,220km of waterways. They distribute water widely throughout Haryana, but Delhi asserts its right to some of this flow. In 1994 the NCT of Delhi and Haryana agreed to settle disagreements over water rights, but disputes remain. As Haryana's increasingly utilizes flood irrigation and shifts toward more water-intensive crops, farmers who face changing market forces are apt to tap into water that flows past their villages meant for Delhi. In 2016, farmers blocked the canals for several days and disrupted supply to seven water treatment plants in Delhi.

Hathnikund Barrage - Western and Eastern Yamuna Canals Begin

Eastern Yamuna Canal Enters Delhi

FROM THE HATHNIKUND BARRAGE IN THE HIMALAYAN FOOTHILLS TO WAZIRABAD BARRAGE IN DELHI, A DISTANCE OF OVER 250KM, THERE IS NO WATER FLOW IN THE YAMUNA RIVER DURING THE DRY SEASON.

Satellite Images: Esri, Digital Globe, GeoEye, Earthstar Geographies, CNES/Airbus DS, USDA, USGS, AeroGRID, IGN and GIS User Community

Panipat Refinery at the Western Yamuna Canal

Dadupur Power Station on the Western Yamuna Canal

Eastern Yamuna Canal South of Rataul

WESTERN YAMUNA CANAL
400 MGD

EASTERN YAMUNA CANAL
120 MGD

Bawana
15 MGD

Sonia Vihar
141 MGD

Haiderpur
226 MGD

Wazirabad
135 MGD

GANGA CANAL
250 MGD

Chandrawl
94 MGD

Bhagirathi
107 MGD

Nangloi
40 MGD

Dwarka
43 MGD

Okhla
26 MGD

- - - Zone of Vulnerability

——— Canals

○ Water Source

● Water Treatment Plant

One located at the edges of the city, many of Delhi's water treatment plants have since been engulfed by urban expansion, limiting the plants' ability to increase capacity. Additionally, these vital infrastructures are gated off from the surrounding neighborhoods, rendering the plants as islands in places of extreme density completely disconnected from daily urban life.

Nangloi WTP

Wazirabad WTP

Water Treatment Plants

The Yamuna River is a vital resource for New Delhi. The city has two primary sources of drinking water: surface water from the Yamuna and Ganga Canals and ground water which is recharged by the Yamuna. Of the water that reaches Wazirabad Barrage from the Yamuna River, 100% is redirected during the dry season and channeled from the river by a network of pipes into the city. Robbing the floodplain of its traditional flows, the groundwater level has dramatically decreased during the last decades. After traveling to the city, canal water is filtered using activated charcoal at nine water treatment plants. Every day 822 million gallons of drinking water is distributed through 9000 km of pipes, 550 pumping stations, and stored in 61 underground reservoirs. Approximately 40% of this water is lost during distribution.

This network of piped water still does not cover significant areas of the city because informal urban expansion exceeds the capacity of the city to plan even the most basic of urban infrastructures. So, a significant portion of the population must turn to illegal water networks. This water is pumped from wells, often in areas with polluted groundwater, and its extraction exacerbates the groundwater level crisis. Water, as in many parts of the world, is a major source of inequality, and despite governmental policies to assuage cost, often the least privileged segments of the population pay the highest prices for scarce and polluted water.

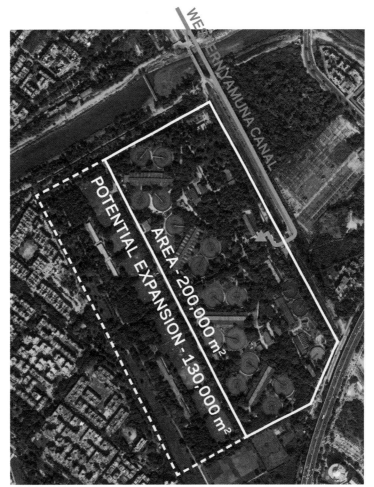

POTENTIAL EXPANSION - 130,000 m²

AREA - 200,000 m²

WESTERN YAMUNA CANAL

Haiderpur WTP

Water Treatment Capacity

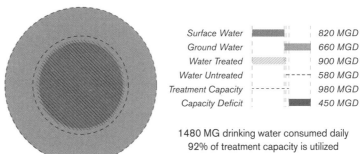

Surface Water	820 MGD
Ground Water	660 MGD
Water Treated	900 MGD
Water Untreated	580 MGD
Treatment Capacity	980 MGD
Capacity Deficit	450 MGD

1480 MG drinking water consumed daily
92% of treatment capacity is utilized
Only 10% of ground water is treated daily

Sonia Vihar WTP

Bhagirathi WTP

Okhla WTP

Water Treatment Capacity

92.0%
WTP CAPACITY UTILIZED

Drinking Water Sources

Surface Water	820 MGD
Western Yamuna Canal	*400 MGD*
Eastern Yamuna Canal	*120 MGD*
Ganga Canal	*250 MGD*
Ground Water	660 MGD
Ranney Wells	*580 MGD*
Tube Wells	*80 MGD*

Water Treatment Process

Though overwhelmed by demand and lacking sufficient capacity to supply clean water to the entire city, Delhi's water treatment plans, run by the Delhi Jal Board, stand as pillars of hope in the struggle to deliver clean water to all of Delhi's citizens. Founded in 1998, The Delhi Jal Board (DJB) is responsible for "the production and distribution of drinking water and also for collection, treatment, and disposal of domestic sewage in the Capital." Everyday, DJB supplies potable drinking water to the city through pipes or water tankers, packaged water to areas disconnected from water infrastructure, treats and disposes of waste, supplies biogas, sludge manure, and treated wastewater, and continuously tests water samples for organic and chemical pollutants. DJB is

able to provide 890-905 million gallons of drinking water per day to the city, even during the dry summer months, with about 83% of households connected to piped water supply. Thirteen labs located in strategic locations around the city, operate 24/7 conducting multiple checks along all stages of the water treatment process—from raw sewage to consumer taps. Future expansion of the water network will cover planned and unplanned urban developments and connect over 800 unauthorized colonies to treated water. There is no margin of error in the water treatment process. Electrical grid interruptions, plant malfunctions, a spike in pollutant levels, civil unrest, and monsoon floods threaten Delhi's water supply with catastrophic consequences.

The Yamuna River at Wazirabad WTP   *Collection Inlet*

Pump House 1

Sludge Thickener

Typical Water Treatment Plant

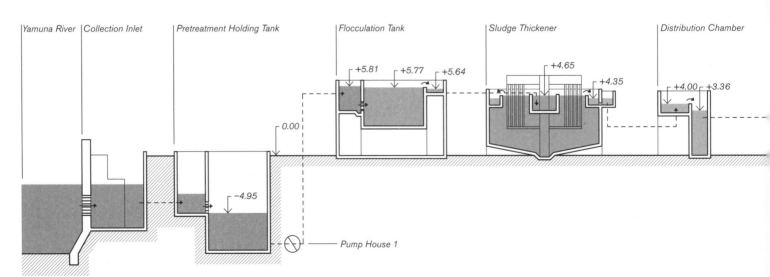

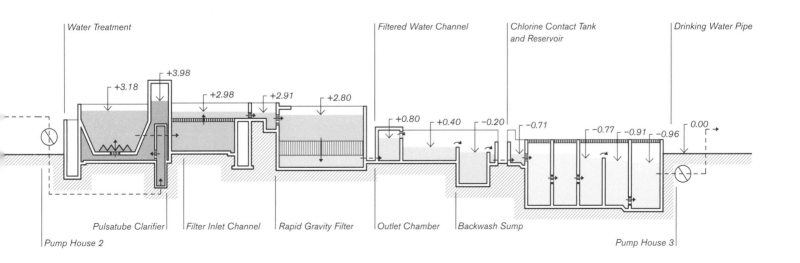

Water Treatment

Filtered Water Channel

Chlorine Contact Tank
and Reservoir

Drinking Water Pipe

+3.98

+3.18

+2.98

+2.91

+2.80

+0.80

+0.40

−0.20

−0.71

−0.77

−0.91

−0.96

0.00

Pulsatube Clarifier

Filter Inlet Channel

Rapid Gravity Filter

Outlet Chamber

Backwash Sump

Pump House 2

Pump House 3

Water Treatment Building

EXISTING WATER TREATMENT PLANTS ARE
EFFICIENTLY RUN AND IF MORE RAW WATER
IS ASSURED BY THE SURROUNDING STATES,
DELHI COULD INCREASE ITS WATER TREATMENT
CAPACITY TO MEET THE NEEDS OF THE ENTIRE
CITY. OFTEN ENGULFED BY URBAN FABRIC, THESE
PLANTS COULD SERVE AS PUBLIC PARKS THAT
EDUCATE CITIZENS ON THE IMPORTANCE, AND
VULNERABILITY, OF THEIR SHARED WATER
RESOURCES.

Pump House 3

Drinking Water Pipe

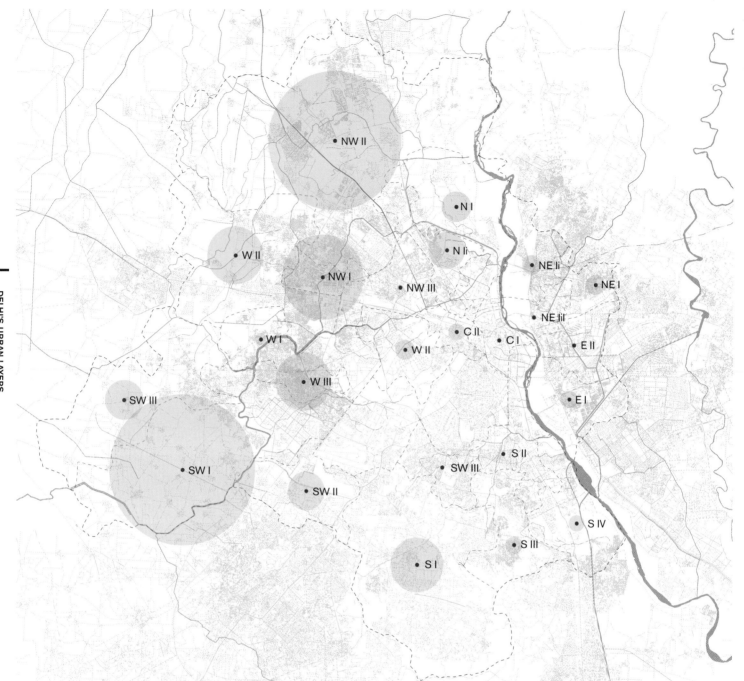

Zone	# Tankers	Weekly Visits
East I	17	684
East II	6	177
West I	11	499
West II	19	813
West III	77	4700
North I	26	1238
North II	32	1506
Northwest I	62	3418
Northwest II	99	5613
Northwest III	5	190
Central I	2	140
Central II	10	665
Northeast I	18	784
Northeast II	20	774
Northeast III	7	153
South I	38	2227
South II	2	42
South III	18	693
South IV	27	677
Southwest I	114	6089
Southwest II	65	3182
Southwest III	2	99
Departmental Flex	250	

Water Command Areas	
Haiderpur	*226 MGD*
Sonia Vihar	*141 MGD*
Wazirabad	*135 MGD*
Bhagirathi	*107 MGD*
Chandrawl	*94 MGD*
Dwarka	*43 MGD*
Nangloi	*40 MGD*
Okhla	*20 MGD*
Bawana	*15 MGD*
Cmn. Wealth Games	*1 MGD*

The Jal Board has established nine water command areas responsible for water quality control for the city of New Delhi. The quality control process begins at field stations north of the city and continues through the entire treatment process at the plants allowing the Jal Board to continuously determine the extent of treatment required.

District	MGD Available	Extraction	Net Draft
Central	1.88	1.65	88%
East	6.05	7.88	130%
New Delhi	2.98	5.09	171%
North	7.36	2.55	35%
Northeast	8.93	11.53	129%
Northwest	89.71	122.28	136%
South	34.33	83.43	243%
Southwest	96.88	207.71	214%
West	33.45	37.32	112%
Delhi NCR	281.57	479.44	170%

Drinking Water Delivery

The Delhi Jal Board (DJB) is charged with distributing potable water to Delhi's citizens. The DJB estimates that 17% of the population does not have piped connections, and as many as 700,000 cannot rely on their piped water due to other customers stealing water. The northern and western edges of the city continue to grow at rates which exceed the government's planning abilities and lack this infrastructure the most. In theory, the DJB must meet the difference between piped supply and total demand by delivering water to customers in water tankers. To meet this need, the DJB deploys 1000 water tankers to fixed locations and on an emergency basis when there has been a break in service. But this number is dwarfed by the estimated 2000 private tankers that illegally extract water from borewells and sell it at punishing prices to households, informal settlements, hotels, hospitals, and factories.

According to one estimate, the DJB is able to provide just more than 82% of the city's per capita water needs. In 2016 the DJB announced a plan to provide piped connections to every house in every informal settlement in Delhi. But until this plan is realized, and existing problems of leakage and uneven distribution that leave millions of households underserved are resolved, the black market—reeling in as much as $64 million annually—remains the most efficient delivery system of water for many in Delhi.

Piped Drinking Water Infrastructure

Delhi Jal Board Water Tankers

ACCESS TO CLEAN WATER IS ONE OF THE GREATEST CHALLENGES FACING NEW DELHI.

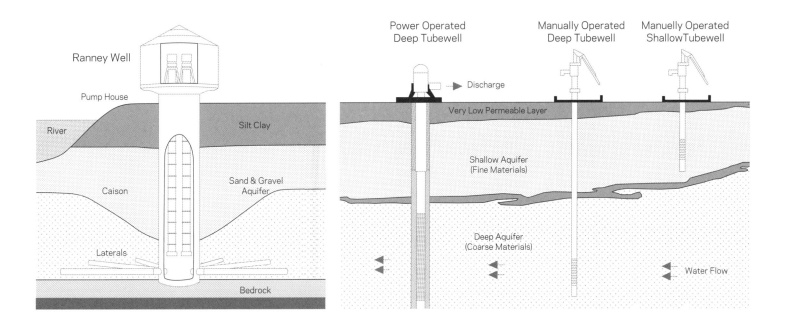

THE ECONOMICS OF WATER: A PROGRAMMATIC OUTLOOK

Peter Debaere
Associate Professor, Darden School of Business
University of Virginia

Fresh water is a precious resource that is without substitute. It is also essential for life. Any living being needs water and so does every ecosystem or society. Whatever we do uses water, and in many instances lots of water. In recent years, the water challenges the world faces in India, the United States and many other places have gotten more attention. How we address the water challenges has also been evolving. There is growing willingness to study water from an economic perspective, see Griffin (2015). The study of water and water scarcity has traditionally been linked to engineering. This came with a focus on water supply and water infrastructure such as canals, dams, etc. With increased competition for scarce water among agriculture, cities and the environment, whether water is distributed efficiently, and how flexibly the water allocation can adjust to unexpected climate events have become key questions. One could argue that the updated UN development goals for 2030 (Figure 1) ask for a larger role of social sciences in thinking about water. In this short essay, I highlight three programmatic issues that define an integrated, economic approach to water, rather than enumerate all the water challenges of specific countries or locations. Water should be studied as part of an evolving (global) economy.

Figure 1

Post 2015 UN Water Development Goals Source: UN

Post-2015 UN Water Development Goals.
1. Achieve universal and equitable access to safe and affordable drinking water for all.
2. Achieve access to adequate and equitable sanitation and hygiene for all, end open defecations, paying special attention to the needs of women and girls and those in vulnerable situations.
3. Improve water quality by reducing pollution, eliminating dumping and minimizing release of hazardous chemicals and materials, halving the proportion of untreated wastewater and at least doubling recycling and safe reuse globally.
4. Substantially increase water-use efficiency across all sectors and ensure sustainable withdrawals and supply of freshwater to address water scarcity, and substantially reduce the number of people suffering from water scarcity.
5. Integrate water resources management at all levels, including through trans-boundary cooperation as appropriate.
6. Protect and restore water-related ecosystems, including mountains, forests, wetlands, rivers, aquifers and lakes.

I. Produce the right products in the right spot

Many places experience water stress, but the world is not running out of its renewable resource: fresh water. The key is to match available water with consumers when and where it is needed, which hinges on producing the right products in the right spot. The latter is all the more important because of huge variation in how much water is needed to produce various products and in how water resources are distributed worldwide.

Hoekstra and Mekonnen (2012) have documented that direct, residential water use through drinking, bathing, doing laundry etc. is dwarfed by the vast amounts of water it takes to produce the goods that we consume (Figure 2). On average U.S. citizens' direct water use is about 100 gallons a day, but it takes 39 gallons to get a single glass of wine to the table, and a couple thousand for a pound of beef. There are thus huge differences in how much water is absorbed by our consumption. Note that agricultural products tend to have a heavy water footprint: Agriculture is responsible for ¾ of global water consumption.

Water is also very unevenly distributed. Some places have a hundred times more (renewable) water available per person than others (Exhibit 3). Within larger countries a similarly uneven distribution is often observed. India is endowed with 1500m3 of renewable water per person, which is a multiple of what Middle Eastern countries have. However, this number obscures the significant climate differences among very dry versus wet areas, as well as the often very uneven precipitation that is concentrated in monsoon months.

With much variation in regional water availability as well as in products' water intensity, it is of utmost importance to produce products in places that are best fit for their production, which is exactly what the economic principle of comparative advantage suggests. Countries or regions that are relatively abundant in water should specialize in water intensive products and crops. They should produce more than they need and export to water-scare regions. Relatively water scarce regions, in turn, should produce products that need less water and exchange these as well.

Producing goods that do not match the relative availability of water in an area creates water stress. Hence, economic policies should support regions' comparative advantage, see Debaere (2014). It is hard to defend the generous subsidies in very arid Saudi Arabia which made it an exporter of water-intensive wheat in the 1990s and contributed to the depletion of its aquifers. Should California be the preferred spot to grow low-value but water intensive alfalfa? We need to investigate the division of labor of cities and their hinterlands carefully since the majority of larger cities globally lie in routinely water-stressed basins.

Product	Virtual Water Content
glass of wine	109 liters (29 gallons)
tomatoe	50 liters (13 gallons)
pizza	1259 liters (332 gallons)
1 kilo of pork	5998 liters (1583 gallons)
1 kilo of beef	14515 liters (4079 gallons)

Figure 2

Examples of the Virtual Water Content of Products Source: Water Footprint Network

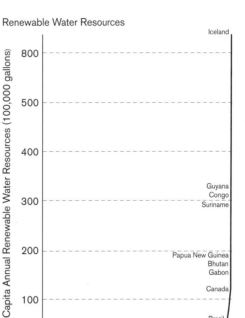

Figure 3

Uneven Distribution of Water (renewable water per capita) Source: FAO data, own graph

Allowing water-abundant regions to specialize and produce water-intensive products presupposes easy shipping to and from less water-abundant regions. Upgrading transportation infrastructure in many emerging economies that reduce transportation costs (also in terms of time) may hence improve more adequate local water use. The same is true for the legal and tax burdens to interstate commerce, and the high international tariffs. India's unbound and applied tariff in agriculture, for example, is respectively 113 and 33 %, or respectively 10 and 3 times that of the European Union. All of these hurdles are not conducive to efficient water use and can potentially give way to water stress.

II. Increase Water Productivity

To limit local water stress, it is essential to decouple economic (and population) growth from water use. More should be done with less water, which requires rising water productivity. Routinely, economic development and population growth are seen as drivers of water use. Careful analysis shows a more intricate relationship. Long-term water use in the United States, for example, has stabilized and decreased since the mid-1970s in spite of a more than doubled U.S. GDP and 60% increase in population (Figure 4). The literature on the Environmental Kuznets curve suggests a hump-shade relationship between per capita income and natural resource consumption and/or pollution.

Sectoral change and technological change (broadly defined) play major roles in decoupling water use and growth. Economies undergo structural changes. Agricultural economies are gradually more geared towards manufacturing and services, because of human and physical capital accumulation, and many factors unrelated to water. Such changes impact water use directly because manufacturing and services' water productivity is an order of magnitude larger than agriculture's. Value added (GDP) in manufacturing and services per unit of water can be a hundred times higher

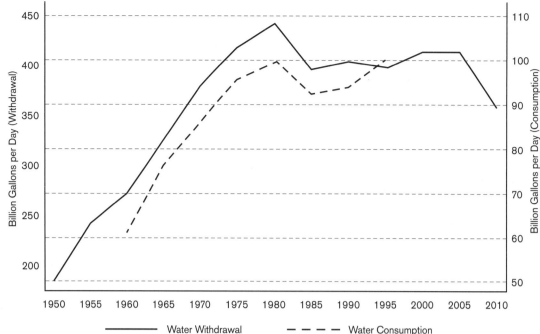

Figure 4

*U.S. Water Withdrawal
(consumption)
since 1950
Source: Debaere
and Kurzendoerfer
(2017, forthcoming)*

than in agriculture. Hence, furthering education and development, or for that matter, any policy that facilitates a transition out of agriculture into manufacturing and services, may help overall water use.

More efficient technology, better design and regulation constitute a second way to improve water productivity. Drip irrigation for agriculture (instead of flood irrigation) should help, and so should recirculating cooling systems (rather than once-through) in thermal electricity generation, industrial and residential water recycling, and smart ways of laying out cities. Policies that enhance water productivity are water-friendly policies. Ultimately, however, both water productivity and comparative advantage are linked to proper water pricing: because of water scarcity, water prices will tend to be higher and water-scarce areas will export less water intensive products. Similarly, higher productivity sectors will (because of their higher ability to pay) attract more water. Water prices can also affect water use in other meaningful ways.

III. Charging the Right Water Price

When a good is freely available, there tends to be over-consumption and wasteful use. In spite of this, scarce water is often available at subsidized rates, and overuse and shortage ensue. In part, the ready and free availability of water derives from its very nature as an open access resource. Without any restrictions on water access, everyone uses as much as he or she sees fit without regard for the overall depletion of the resource: rivers stop reaching their mouth, and aquifer levels drop, which can be amplified by energy subsidies to reduce water pumping costs. This is the familiar tragedy of the commons, Hardin (1968). To avoid it, one needs to regulate and limit water access and not make it available for free.

While determining the exact price of water is not trivial, pricing water properly has many desirable effects. A positive price of water supports water conservation and limits overuse. A price of water creates an incentive to save water, and to invest in water saving technology such as drip irrigation, recycling, etc. Putting a price on water in cities also provides funds for water utilities to upgrade and maintain their water infrastructure, and to reduce revenue loss due to leaks or lack of billing: For Delhi, Global Water Intelligence (2015) reports 52 % non-revenue water. More importantly, pricing water invites public-private partnerships, as private companies with better access to capital than resource-strapped communities can potentially tap into a steady stream of payments and hence a return on investment. Finally, a price on water is an incentive for innovation in water-saving technology.

Putting a price on water is not popular, not without challenges, and is often misunderstood. Pricing water comes with responsibilities. Only when water services work effectively, when the quality of the water delivered is high, and when there is good governance (no corruption) can consumers be enticed to pay higher water prices. Increased pricing with persisting water supply interruptions and leaks will not be tolerated. Moreover, prices should increase gradually and predictably. And if private partners have water rate setting power, they will have to be transparent, vetted, and supervised by the community.

There are, however, powerful misunderstandings with regard to water that hamper water pricing. It is often argued that water is a human right and should hence be available for free. Most will agree that since water is essential for life, one wants universal access to safe and drinkable water for essential needs (drinking, hygiene). It is an open question whether water use beyond this is a human right: Is water to water the lawn, clean one's car, or growing crops a human right? Note also that there are ways of charging a price that respect people's socioeconomic status. One could provide water credits to the poor for basic necessities for example, or by a broader stroke, one could have water tariffs (block tariffs) increase with use.

What about the objection that water in poorer countries will hurt the poor? It is not at all obvious that this is true, see Olmstead (2003). The poor are often the ones that are not connected to the water net. More stable revenue for water utilities may encourage utilities to expand water supply to poorer neighborhoods. Moreover, because the poor often have no ready access to drinking water, they tend to pay a much higher direct or indirect price for water. The poor are often dependent on water trucked in from elsewhere and the racketeering that may come with it. Alternatively, children and women may spend valuable time hauling water that could be devoted to school, education or employment.

Conclusion

In a water-strapped world in which cities, agriculture and the environment compete for water, the question of how to allocate water efficiently and equitably takes central stage. Addressing water challenges is not always a question of improving supply. Better management of water resources may reach into areas such as transportation infrastructure or development policies that are not always thought of as the purview of water policy. Giving water an explicit price (or taking into account the relative scarcity of water) will have to be part of how we guarantee water use in the future.

1 To be clear, economics and engineering in many instances will compliment each other. As Briscoe (2011) pointed out while discussing the UN development goals, countries' needs are different, and we should avoid projecting the situation of advanced economies (with relatively established water infrastructures) onto emerging economies. In India or Bangladesh, for example, which do not have precipitation year-round, investment in capturing and storing water ("the hard approach") may still have a more important role to play than the economic ("soft") approach.

2 See Johannson et al (2002), Rogers et al (2002). A few principles should guide pricing. Water should be priced at marginal cost, i.e. at the cost to supply the last (most expensive) unit of water. There should also be full cost recovery: water tariffs should pay for construction, maintenance and upgrading of water infrastructures. While these principles are clear, how to exactly translate them into pricing is not trivial, Briscoe (1997).

Bibliography

Briscoe, J., 2011, Invited Opinion Interview: Two Decades at the Center of World Water Policy, Water Policy, 13, p. 147-160.

Briscoe, J., 1997, Managing Water as an Economic Good: Rules for Reformers, Water Supply, 15, 4, Yorkshire, p. 153-172.

Debaere, P. and A. Kurzendoerfer, 2017, Decomposing U.S. Water Withdrawal since 1950, JAERE, forthcoming.

Debaere, P., The Global Economics of Water: Is Water a Source of Comparative Advantage, American Economic Journal: Applied Economics, April, p. 32-48.

Global Water Intelligence, 2014, Global Water Market 2014, Oxford, UK.

Griffin, R., 2016, Water Resource Economics, MIT Press, Cambridge.

Hardin, G., 1968, The Tragedy of the Commons, Science, 162, p. 1243-1248.

Hoekstra, A., and M. Mekonnen, 2012, The Water Footprint of Humanity, Proceedings of the National Academy of Science, April, p. 3232-3237.

Olmstead, S., 2003, Water Supply and Poor Communities: What's Price Got to Do with it?, Environment: Science and Policy for Sustainable Development, 45:10, p. 22-35.

Johansson, R., Tsur, Y., Roe, L., Doukkali, R., and A. Dinar, 2002, Pricing Irrigation Water: A Review of Theory and Practice, Water Policy, 4, p. 173-199.

Rogers, P., de Silva, R., and Bhatia, R., 2002, Water is an Economic Good: How to Use Prices to Promote Equity, Efficiency, and Sustainability, Water Policy, 4, p. 1-17.

Whittington, D., W. Hanemann, C. Sadoff, and M. Jeuland, 2008, The Challenge of Improving Water Sanitation Services in Less Developed Countries, in: Whittington, D., W. Hanemann, C. Sadoff, and M. Jeuland, Foundations and Trends in Microeconomics, Vol. 4, p. 469-609.

**EXTREMELY
HAZARDOUS**
500-1500 mg/L
11-33 times acceptable levels

HAZARDOUS
45-500 mg/L
1-11 times acceptable levels

ACCEPTABLE
1-45 mg/L
acceptable standard levels

*Ground water nitrate levels
according to drinking water specifications*

Ground Water Pollution

In 2013 Delhi's Central Groundwater Board reported dangerous levels of nitrates in the groundwater at many of Delhi's 162 hydrograph monitoring stations. Levels were generally safe in the East and Northeast Districts, but throughout the rest of the city, some readings indicated levels ranging from twice as high to 30 times as high as those deemed safe by the World Health Organization. Groundwater in Delhi is regularly contaminated because of runoff from fertilized fields and landfills, cattle sheds and unlined drains, untreated sewage, and unhygienic conditions around boreholes. Altogether nearly 50% of groundwater samples were found unsuitable for drinking on account of nitrates, heavy metals, dissolved solids,

fluoride, and miscellaneous trace metals. Since 25% of the population does not receive piped municipal water (and those that do often receive inadequate supplies), boreholes are dug by the thousands. While the Delhi Jal Board lists around 4,000 official tubewells and 16 rammey wells, they estimate that 465,000 illegal borewells supply millions with their water. These illegal sources are neither tested nor treated. Furthermore, illegal tanker trucks extract water to sell on the black market, exposing people to harmful contaminants and depleting depletes the water table. Only two districts out of nine are extracting water within safe limits for adequate recharge. The other seven districts are over-exploiting the groundwater, at an average level of 170%.

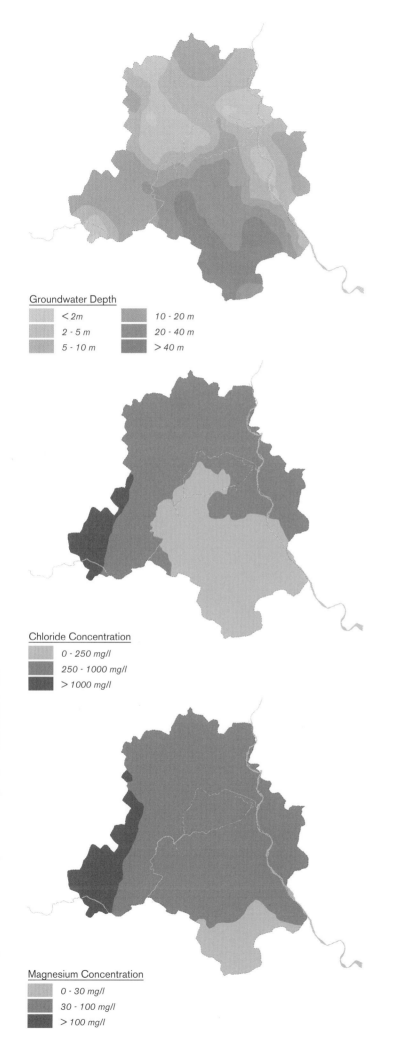

OVER THE PAST DECADE, 49%
OF DELHI'S WELLS SHOWED
A DROP IN GROUNDWATER
LEVELS. OVER 60% OF THESE
RECORDED A DROP OF
ALMOST 2M; SOME WELLS ARE
DECLINING AS MUCH AS 2M
ANNUALLY.

Groundwater Depth

- < 2m
- 2 - 5 m
- 5 - 10 m
- 10 - 20 m
- 20 - 40 m
- > 40 m

Chloride Concentration

- 0 - 250 mg/l
- 250 - 1000 mg/l
- > 1000 mg/l

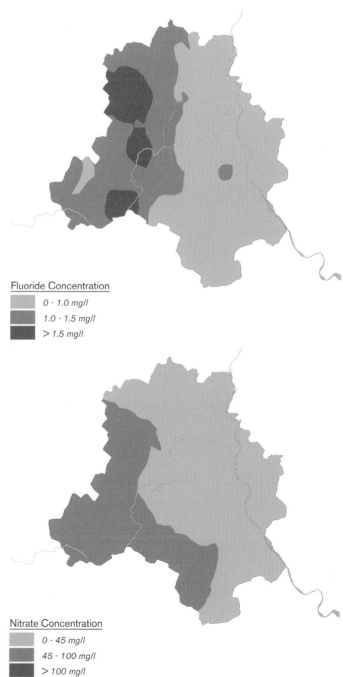

Fluoride Concentration

- 0 - 1.0 mg/l
- 1.0 - 1.5 mg/l
- > 1.5 mg/l

Magnesium Concentration

- 0 - 30 mg/l
- 30 - 100 mg/l
- > 100 mg/l

Nitrate Concentration

- 0 - 45 mg/l
- 45 - 100 mg/l
- > 100 mg/l

• Narela
10 MGD

Rohini •
15 MGD

Rithala
80 MGD

Coronation Pillar
40 MGD

Timarpur •
6 MGD

Yamuna Vihar
45 MGD

Bakkarwala •
67 MGD

Nilothi
60 MGD

Keshopur
72 MGD

Delhi
Gate Nalla
17.2 MGD

Sen Nursing
Home Nalla
2.2 MGD

Comm. Games
Village
1 MGD

Kondli
90 MGD

Chilla
9 MGD

Najafgarh •
5 MGD

Pappankalan
40 MGD

• Delhi
8 MGD

Okhla
170 MGD

Kapashera •
5 MGD

Vasantkunj •
5 MGD

Ghitorni •
5 MGD

Molarbandh
.67 MGD

• Mehrauli
5 MGD

—— Drains

● Sewage Treatment Plant

/// Sewered Area

SEWAGE TREATMENT PLANTS VS.
CITY GROWTH OF DELHI

ORIGINALLY, DELHI'S SEWAGE
TREATMENT PLANTS WERE LOCATED
AT THE PERIMETER OF THE CITY. WITH
THE RAPID GROWTH THAT THE CITY
HAS UNDERGONE OVER THE PAST
20 YEARS, THE SEWAGE TREATMENT
PLANTS NOW EXIST WITHIN THE CITY
LIMITS. 45% OF DELHI'S RESIDENTS
ARE NOT CONNECTED TO THE
SEWAGE SYSTEM.

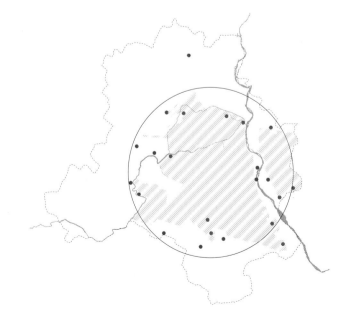

Drains and the Sewage System

Delhi's rapid growth presents many significant challenges for its urban sewage infrastructure. Unplanned growth has taken place without sewage pipes and waste water runs through the streets to open drains. More than 45% of Delhi's population is not connected to this basic infrastructure, and population growth is not slowing anytime soon. Major causes of water pollution in Delhi, besides domestic sewage, are industrial effluents, solid waste, excessive use of agricultural fertilizers, and agricultural slaughtering facilities. Twenty-two drains flow directly into the Yamuna and 60% of the pollution levels are caused by two main drains, the Najafgarh Drain and the Supplementary Drain. Sewage treatment plant (STPs) capacity is being increased to meet estimated treatment needs. However, the primary difficulty of capturing unregulated sewage and wastewater and directing it into the STPs remains.

Alternative strategies to conventionally engineered infrastructures are under discussion. Future tertiary treatment through wetlands would improve water quality after treatment and before it is released back into the main drains or infiltrates the soil to contaminate groundwater. In certain neighborhoods, decentralized systems of biodigesters and green filters could be the most effective strategies. Wetlands and green filters have the additional potential to create quality public space and ecological zones for indigenous vegetation and fauna.

NAJAFGARH DRAIN

AREA - 320,000 m²

Keshopur STP

Over 720 MDG Sewage Generated

63.0% TREATED

Sewage Treatment Capacity

75.0% UTILIZED

Satellite Images: Esri, Digital Globe, GeoEye, Earthstar Geographies, CNES/Airbus DS, USDA, USGS, AeroGRID, IGN and GIS User Community

Yamuna Vihar STP

Nilothi STP

Pappankalan STP

Narela
10 MGD

Bawana
15 MGD

Rohini
15 MGD

Rithala
80 MGD

Haiderpur
226 MGD

Coronation Pillar
40 MGD

Bakkarwala
.67 MGD

Nangloi
40 MGD

Nilothi
60 MGD

Keshopur
72 MGD

Najafgarh
5 MGD

Dwarka
43 MGD

Pappankalan
40 MGD

Delhi
8 MGD

Kapashera
5 MGD

Vasant Kunj
5 MGD

Mehrauli
5 MGD

Gh
5 M

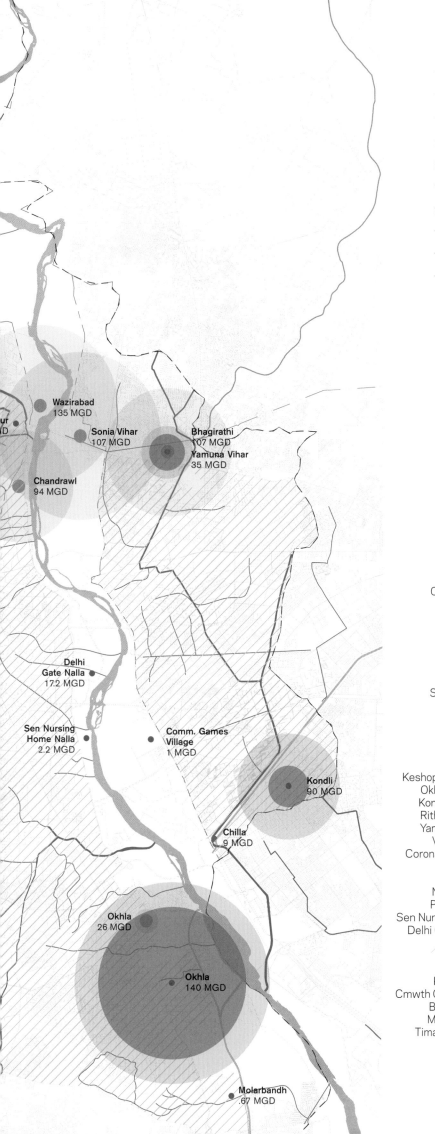

AN INSUFFICIENT–YET QUICKLY EXPANDING–TREATMENT CAPACITY AND LEAKY, OVERLAPPING SEWAGE AND WATER SYSTEMS COMPLICATE THE ABILITY OF DELHI TO PROVIDE ADEQUATE DRINKING WATER AND SEWAGE COLLECTION FOR ITS 25 MILLION PEOPLE.

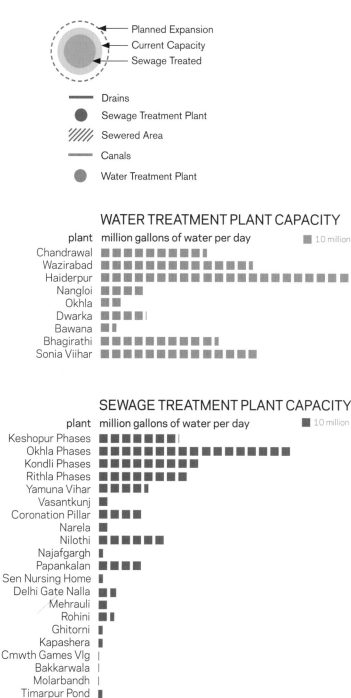

← Planned Expansion
← Current Capacity
← Sewage Treated

—— Drains
● Sewage Treatment Plant
////// Sewered Area
—— Canals
● Water Treatment Plant

WATER TREATMENT PLANT CAPACITY

plant	million gallons of water per day	■ 10 million
Chandrawal		
Wazirabad		
Haiderpur		
Nangloi		
Okhla		
Dwarka		
Bawana		
Bhagirathi		
Sonia Viihar		

SEWAGE TREATMENT PLANT CAPACITY

plant	million gallons of water per day	■ 10 million
Keshopur Phases		
Okhla Phases		
Kondli Phases		
Rithla Phases		
Yamuna Vihar		
Vasantkunj		
Coronation Pillar		
Narela		
Nilothi		
Najafgargh		
Papankalan		
Sen Nursing Home		
Delhi Gate Nalla		
Mehrauli		
Rohini		
Ghitorni		
Kapashera		
Cmwth Games Vlg		
Bakkarwala		
Molarbandh		
Timarpur Pond		
Chilla		

EXCRETA IN THE PUBLIC DOMAIN

Pradip Saha
Environmental Communicator, Artist, Journalist
New Delhi, India

The city used to be on the west side of the river. Over the years, the eastern side became built up, too. Now, there is a river in the middle of the city. Topographically, the river is situated at the lowest part of the city. In the minds of the citizens, as well as the city fathers, the river really is situated at the bottom. And hydrology determines that all of our sins show up in the river. We cannot hide it. The river has always remained as witness to bad urban development, throughout the history of civilization.

Urbanization at a breakneck speed is always presented as a glory, but it causes a disproportionate shift in the use of various natural resources. Water is no exception. Our cities, for some strange 'coincidence', always had a lake or two or a river close by. We depended on them. But over a period, we blocked natural water flows with concrete and our water bodies died. This was good news for the land developers. After all, we live on land, not in water! Slowly, as we urbanites forgot about our rivers and lakes, we lost respect, and eventually completely disengaged with our water bodies.

But we need water, and per capita water use in a city is much more than that in a village. Delhi, being a pampered city, needs more water per capita than other cities. We need water to drink, to cook, to bathe, to wash clothes and cars, to water plants, to extinguish fire, and to settle the dust during the worst air pollution days. Water travels a convoluted journey to Delhi. The city picks up all the water from the Yamuna as the river enters the city, cleans the water as much as possible, then distributes it to citizens. But the amount is too little for Delhi's great thirst. So it is augmented by water from Haryana, Uttar Pradesh, and from as far as Tehri Dam in Uttarakhand, all of which comes at a great cost of pipes and pumps to Delhi. Delhi then uses and misuses this supply, losing some, mixing the rest with our excreta, sends it through an array of sewage treatment plants with their great cost of pipes and pumps, and finally dumping it back to the Yamuna through some 20 drains.

Sewage treatment is a highly capital intensive system. It is also an electromechanical system that needs 24/7 electricity for pumping dense sewage and clariflocculator in the treatment plant. There is no comprehensive standard for the quality of treated water. Storm-water and sewage become mixed during the monsoon and overwhelm Delhi's sewage treatment plants, collapsing the system and resulting in waste water that is completely untreated. There is a large population that is not connected to the system, whose excreta goes straight into the river. In general, 80% of water used in a city becomes sewage, even water that is diverted from sources other than the Yamuna. As a result, the Yamuna is ill fated. Total water use in the city exceeds the small trickle of water that still flows down the Yamuna; the river receives more sewage from the city than the water it brings in.

There is a missing link too. A large part of the population that does not receive municipal water, yet can afford the investment, mines groundwater. Many households have a submersible pump. In addition, the water in private tankers sold to households is also pumped up from the ground. Clearly no one knows the amount of groundwater being extracted yet alone the amount of water poured into the river as sewage. This has serious implications, as the city fathers cannot know how much sewage is to be treated, and therefore our treatment capacity always runs at a deficit.

The result can be smelled in the river. Visually, it is just grey dirty water with fecal matter and other chemicals including traces of heavy metal bubbling away. The water has a very high biochemical oxygen demand (BOD) and hardly any dissolved oxygen. It is a dead water body. But it is our divine duty to bring the dead to life, if only for the amazing opportunities it creates. There are plans hatched to 'clean' the Yamuna, and they are costly. Large infrastructure projects are always welcome, though it is easy to overlook the difficulty of running those systems perfectly after the initial capital investment.

By now, a few thousand crore of Indian Rupees (a few hundreds of millions US$) has gone into cleaning the river. The exercise confirms that there is no positive correlation between money spent and dissolved oxygen in that river. The Yamuna remains a dead river. We have put a noose around the sacred goddess. There is a barrage upstream at Wazirabad in North Delhi that blocks the river, and the Wazirabad water treatment plant sucks all the water Yamuna brings to Delhi, cleans it and distributes it to some of the citizens. From Wazirabad to the next barrage at Okhla, the 22 kilometers of Yamuna does not have any fresh water during the dry season. This stretch of the river by the city has only a mix of semi-treated and untreated water pouring from the drains. No wonder it is a dead river: we have sucked all the breath from the water.

Let us assume that all sewage treatment plants treat sewage up to the desired quality as defined by Delhi's Central Pollution Control Board. Let us also assume that there are surprise inspections to check their operation. Still it is not enough since the reality is that when sewage treatment plants lack minimum riparian water quality standards they are generating only semi-treated water. Treated water is expected to have a BOD level of 10 mg per litre, and fecal coliform of less than 100 MPN per litre. Even if we pour only treated water of this quality into the river, it will not help because the same Pollution Control Board tells us that bathing water should have a BOD level of less than 3 mg per litre and fecal coliform of 1.8 MPN per litre. Yet after Wazirabad, the Yamuna has a BOD level of 26 mg per litre. On an auspicious day, one can happily take a dip in holy shit only.

All the sewage generated in the city is not connected to the system, and may never will be. The vast population in Delhi's slums are not connected with the centralized sanitation system and people who do not even have toilets are persecuted for open defecation. We forget that everybody's excreta reaches the river, even those connected to the sewage infrastructure made possible by state construction and subsidy. But it is the open defecators that get a bad name even though the city has left them to their own devices; by default, poor people use less water and generate less sewage.

Even then, sewage from connected establishments does not completely reach the treatment plants, and the sewage that does reach treatment plants is not treated completely. The city keeps on growing horizontally and vertically. More people are convinced they must move to the city. The sewage load keeps on increasing and the stipulated standard of treated water is inadequate if the treatment plants are to be a new water source for a revitalized Yamuna river. The expense for this kind of centralized system with 24/7 electric supplies is clearly beyond our means.

The utter disregard for nature and powerless people are similar and have come out of a certain mindset. The culture and education system do not provide any engagement with our immediate natural systems and teach us only to exploit nature. When we suddenly wake up and think of doing something for the river, all we can conjure up is 'Riverfront Development'. Invariably, these kinds of plans immediately exclude a sizable population who are managing their livelihoods out of the river. Urban infrastructure development and beautification plans are allowed to encroach upon the river and its floodplain, but poor people residing there suddenly become eyesores. Additionally, most river and floodplain developments treat the river as engineered canals. We forget a river's ecological and socio-economic aspect. Can we change that?

It is fashionable to talk about water. But we do not talk about excreta. It's high time that we talk about sanitation in a scientific and appropriate manner. The excreta coin has water on the other side, and we can never achieve our goal towards clean water unless we manage our excreta. Yamuna, the river by the city called Delhi, is only about excreta. In the absence of any public engagement, we are going to see only capital-intensive systems propagated by vested interests chasing an impossible dream. Citizens of Delhi should immediately claim ownership of their dirty Yamuna. Only then can the river be clean.

DELHI'S SOCIOECONOMICS

30,000 and Above

20,000-30,000

10,000-20,000

Less than 10,000

India and Delhi are densely populated with a high percentage of the population living with multiple families per household. Still a young population, India is well situated for decades of continued economic growth and rising living standards.

Many of India's households have seen an improved standard of living in the past decade with the middle and upper classes growing in number while the number of lower class households have decreased. However, as a percentage of the whole, the middle class has barely increased, representing potential roadblocks to further economic improvement.

Number of Households by Class

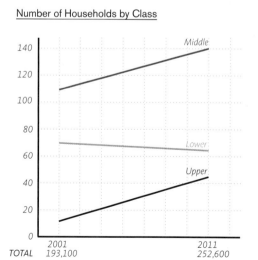

Percentage of Households by Class

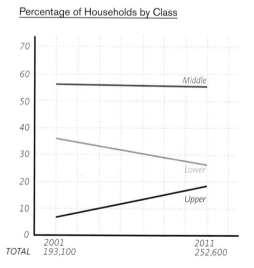

Population Density and Demographics

As with many developing cities, Delhi attracts a high number of migrants hoping to take advantage of opportunities for education and employment, and send money home to their rural villages. As India's capital, Delhi offers many bureaucratic and service industry jobs. The share of jobs in hotels, restaurants, transportation, insurance, banking, trade, and telecom continue to grow, as do average income levels. Recently the average Delhi income reached Rs 3 lakh (US$4700), the highest in the nation and three times the average Indian income. However, this high level of income puts a premium on real estate and drives up the cost of living.

77% of Delhi's urban fabric has been constructed in the last 40 years, a faster rate than that of other world cities like London or Tokyo whose urban areas were 90% in place by the 1970s. Although Delhi strives to be a modern planned city, the rate of growth has made it nearly impossible to keep up with the demand for adequate infrastructure, housing, and healthy living conditions. On the outer edges of the city the Delhi Development Authority (DDA) cannot build housing fast enough for people in the lower and middle-income levels. Informal settlements, which constitute about 75% of Delhi's housing stock, are relegated to these edges of development as well, raising the density levels of outer suburbs and further stressing inadequate infrastructural systems and social services.

Data sourced from the 2002 and 2011 Indian Census
http://censusindia.gov.in/

Urban Household Income Distribution (INR) - 2005

Lower Class	0
1st percentile	1,200
5th percentile	11,500
10th percentile	17,000
25th percentile	28,873
Middle Class	45,000
50th percentile	51,200
75th percentile	94,800
90th percentile	152,000
Upper Class	180,000
W.Bank Mid Class	*200,000*
95th percentile	210,000
99th percentile	396,000
Mean	75,266

Mean Household Income per Education Level (INR) - 2005

None	21,734
1-4 Standard	25,984
5-9 Standard	35,718
10-12 Standard	53,982
Some College	69,230
College Graduate	114,004
W.Bank Mid Class	*200,000*
Mean	47,804

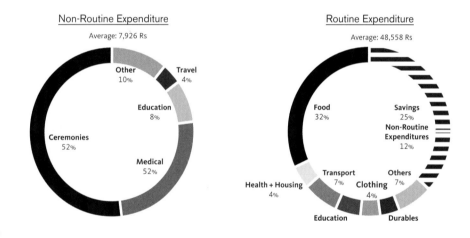

Non-Routine Expenditure
Average: 7,926 Rs

- Other 10%
- Travel 4%
- Education 8%
- Ceremonies 52%
- Medical 52%

Routine Expenditure
Average: 48,558 Rs

- Food 32%
- Savings 25%
- Non-Routine Expenditures 12%
- Others 7%
- Clothing 4%
- Durables
- Education
- Transport 7%
- Health + Housing 4%

Household Size

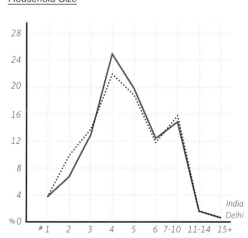

India
Delhi

Age Distribution

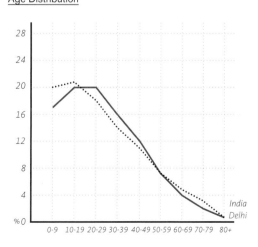

India
Delhi

Household Expenditures + Income

Food is by far the greatest household expenditure in India with medical care acting as another major expense. Amazingly, the average household savings rate is 25% across the nation perhaps representing the uncertainty of future income security or a mindset of planning for long term investments and important celebrations.

Around 50% of Indian households are considered to be middle class or higher with education levels significantly contributing to income. However, even if one is considered upper class in India, they often exist below a level of income considered average world 'middle class' by the World Bank.

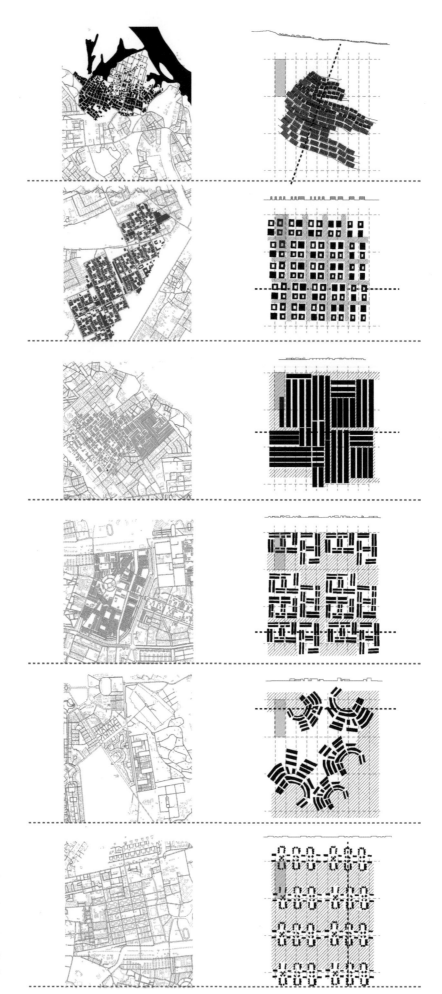

Housing Spacial Patterns

Various urban patterns are visible along the Yamuna River corridor in Delhi. An analysis of the relationship between these urban patterns and their construction quality reveals that areas suffering from poor housing quality and a lack of open space are often located near the Yamuna River and its historic floodplain. These conditions are especially clear in the neighborhoods of East Delhi where expansive development has occurred only recently.

Urban Fabric   *Spacial Pattern*

Housing

Less than one quarter of Delhi's population lives in "planned colonies," where infrastructure is adequate and ownership rights are fully established. The rest inhabit colonies with varying degrees of legality and services. Some areas are officially labeled "Slum Designated Areas." One of these, at an estimated two million people, is in the medieval walled city, an area designed for 60,000. The government generally makes their peace with this overcrowded and unsanitary area, preferring to address informal settlements that spring up due to newer arrivals.

However, a large portion of Delhi's population lives in squatter settlements on public lands, parks, or road berms. These areas lack formal infrastructure systems and are afforded no legal recognition—they are often subjected to forced removal and resettlement. Similarly, unauthorized colonies begin with no legal tenure as groups of people take over public or private lands for their communities. The colonies also lack proper infrastructure or services but are largely permanent in terms of their building materials and commercial activity. For reasons of political expediency these areas are often granted some legal status and basic government services. The government claims urban villages on the outskirts of the city as areas ripe for commercial development. Turned over to real estate developers, construction is not held to high planning standards and growth tends to be rapid and unchecked.

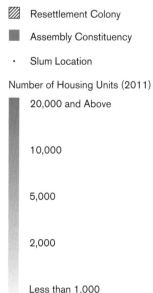

Resettlement Colony

Assembly Constituency

· Slum Location

Number of Housing Units (2011)

20,000 and Above

10,000

5,000

2,000

Less than 1,000

Rural
5.8%

JJ CLUSTER
14.8%

URBAN VILLAGE
6.4%

UNAUTHORIZED
AND REGULARIZED
COLONIES
18%

WALLED CITY
19.1%

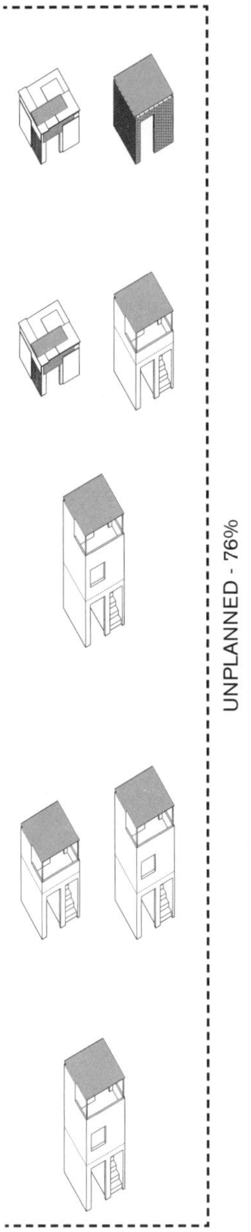

UNPLANNED - 76%

VILLA

BUILDERS FLAT

APARTMENT

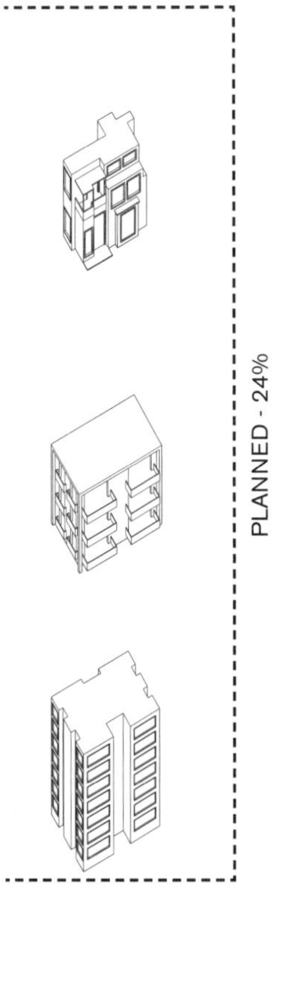

PLANNED - 24%

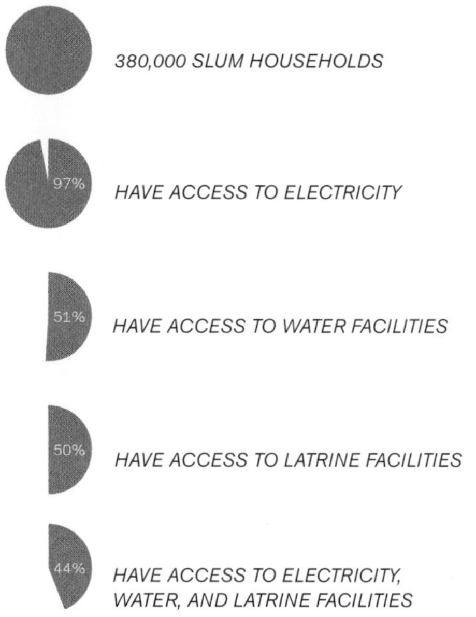

380,000 SLUM HOUSEHOLDS

97% *HAVE ACCESS TO ELECTRICITY*

51% *HAVE ACCESS TO WATER FACILITIES*

50% *HAVE ACCESS TO LATRINE FACILITIES*

44% *HAVE ACCESS TO ELECTRICITY,*
WATER, AND LATRINE FACILITIES

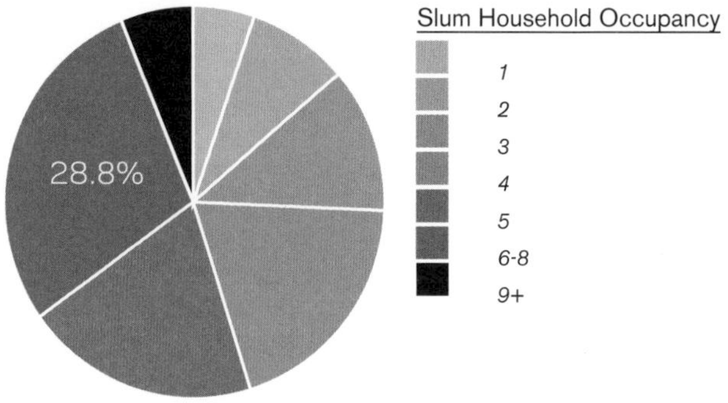

28.8%

Slum Household Occupancy
1
2
3
4
5
6-8
9+

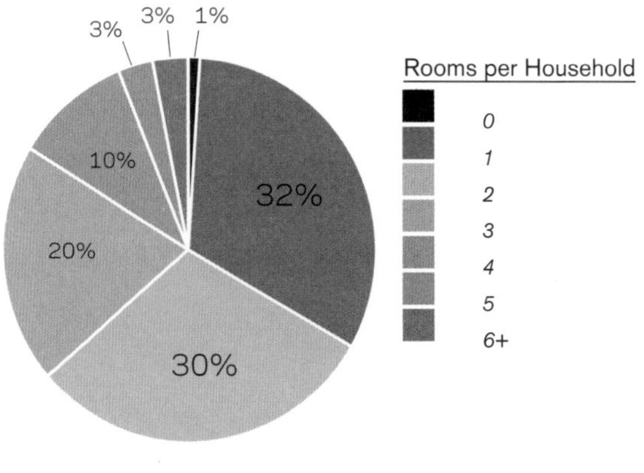

3% 3% 1%
10%
20%
32%
30%

Rooms per Household
0
1
2
3
4
5
6+

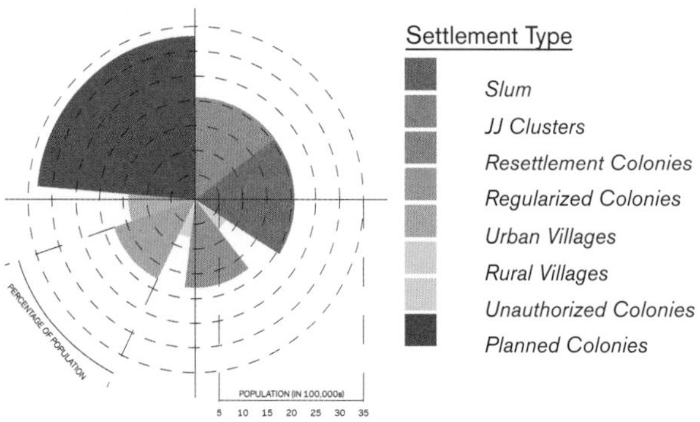

Settlement Type
Slum
JJ Clusters
Resettlement Colonies
Regularized Colonies
Urban Villages
Rural Villages
Unauthorized Colonies
Planned Colonies

PERCENTAGE OF POPULATION

POPULATION (IN 100,000s)
5 10 15 20 25 30 35

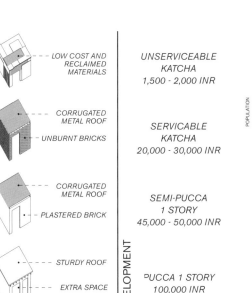

LOW COST AND
RECLAIMED
MATERIALS

UNSERVICEABLE
KATCHA
1,500 - 2,000 INR

CORRUGATED
METAL ROOF

UNBURNT BRICKS

SERVICABLE
KATCHA
20,000 - 30,000 INR

CORRUGATED
METAL ROOF

PLASTERED BRICK

SEMI-PUCCA
1 STORY
45,000 - 50,000 INR

STURDY ROOF

EXTRA SPACE

PUCCA 1 STORY
100,000 INR

.5 FLOOR LIVING
SPACE

SHOP

PUCCA 1.5 STORY
130,000 INR

1 FLOOR LIVING
SPACE

SHOP WITH
TOILET

PUCCA 2 STORY
150,000 INR

1.5 FLOOR
LIVING SPACE

SHOP WITH
TOILET

PUCCA 2.5 STORY
200,000 INR

INCREMENTAL DEVELOPMENT

RAINWATER
HARVESTING

TERRACES
OWNED PROPERTY
STREET ENTRANCE

VILLA
4+ BEDROOMS
1800+ SQM
UPPERCLASS

PRIVATE
BALCONY
RENTED
PROPERTY
1-2 UNITS
PER FLOOR
SMALL PLOT

BUILDERS FLAT
2-5 STORIES
1-2 BEDROOMS
PER UNIT
70-100 SQM
MIXED INCOME

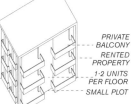

LARGE
PLOT
OUTDOOR
GREEN SPACE

APARTMENT
6-12 STORIES
2-4 BEDROOMS
PER UNIT
70-100 SQM
GATED COMMUNITIES

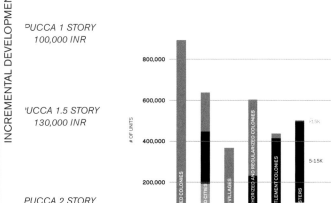

Distribution of Housing Types

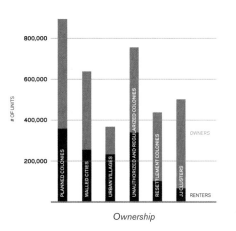

Income According to Housing Type

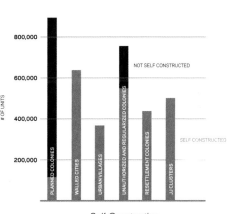

Ownership

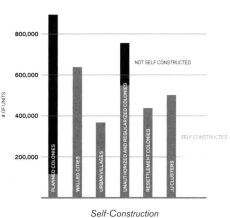

Self-Construction

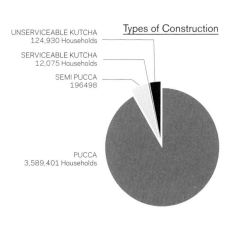

Types of Construction

UNSERVICEABLE KUTCHA
124,930 Households

SERVICEABLE KUTCHA
12,075 Households

SEMI PUCCA
196498

PUCCA
3,589,401 Households

Housing Stock

The 2011 Delhi Census states that 68% of people own their own homes and 32% pay rent. However, this statistic does not accurately capture the status of much of Delhi's population. There is a difference between those who own their homes and property outright, and those who are simply not paying rent on their dwelling because they have built illegally on private or publicly owned lands. Since well over half of the city lives in one kind of informal settlement or another, it is likely that this arrangement distorts the overall picture of homeownership.

Among the majority of households that do not reside in planned colonies, it is very common to build one's own home. These are generally basic structures of brick and cement. If made properly with a concrete roof, they can be built up two or more stories. While residents depend on the government to manage public works that require planning and large investments, most households are content to construct their own homes incrementally over time.

Agricultural Land

Agricultural Production (2011)

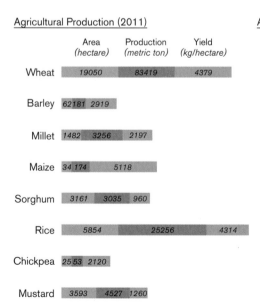

	Area (hectare)	Production (metric ton)	Yield (kg/hectare)
Wheat	19050	83419	4379
Barley	62181	2919	
Millet	1482	3256	2197
Maize	34.174	5118	
Sorghum	3161	3035	960
Rice	5854	25256	4314
Chickpea	25.53	2120	
Mustard	3593	4527	1260

Agricultural Area (2005 - 2011)

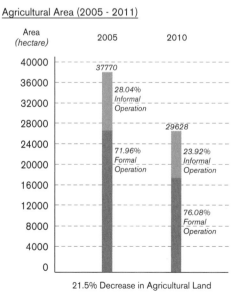

21.5% Decrease in Agricultural Land

Agricultural Land Area (2011)

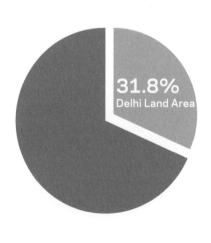

31.8% Delhi Land Area

~475 sqkm of Agriculture Land

Agriculture

Only a small percentage of Delhi's population is classified as rural. Yet in the area surrounding this territory, agricultural interests still take precedence—agriculture fields occupy more than 50% of the land in the Yamuna River Basin. The majority of farmland in this region is held by farmers who cultivate marginal-sized farms of 1 hectare or less. These farms are at the mercy of middlemen to set prices and distribute food efficiently which often leads to inflated consumer costs and substantial food waste. Delhi keeps a steady demand for milk, meat, and eggs; livestock counts have increased at a rate of 1.5% per annum from 1997 to 2007. The Yamuna Basin supports three distinct crop seasons which advantages farmers and attracts migrant workers from other states. This fertility allows agricultural land to be sown more than once per year, and therefore cropping intensity in the basin is more than 100%. To the west of Delhi, extensive canal infrastructure supports cropping intensities of up to 200%. Many farmers have occupied their farms for generations, but their methods present an urgent public health hazard. Excessive use of fertilizers pollute groundwater sources and the Yamuna River. Crop burning, used to clear land before the sowing season, creates extremely hazardous air quality conditions. And if that is not enough, food grown near the toxic Yamuna River is sold in markets around the city. Efforts to prevent these practices have largely failed to make an impact.

Agricultural Flood Plain

Illegal Groundwater Pumping

Agricultural Cycle

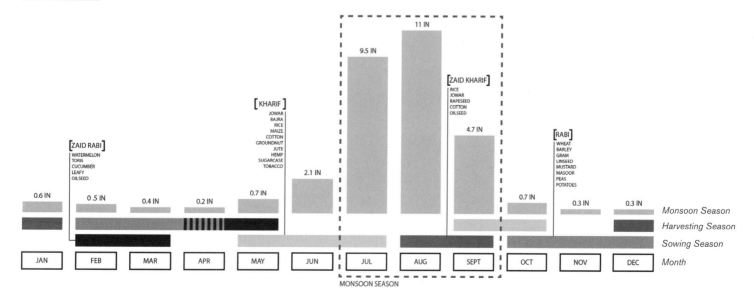

MONSOON SEASON

[ZAID RABI]
WATERMELON
TORIS
CUCUMBER
LEAFY
OILSEED

[KHARIF]
JOWAR
BAJRA
RICE
MAIZE
COTTON
GROUNDNUT
JUTE
HEMP
SUGARCASE
TOBACCO

[ZAID KHARIF]
RICE
JOWAR
RAPESEED
COTTON
OILSEED

[RABI]
WHEAT
BARLEY
GRAM
LINSEED
MUSTARD
MASOOR
PEAS
POTATOES

0.6 IN | 0.5 IN | 0.4 IN | 0.2 IN | 0.7 IN | 2.1 IN | 9.5 IN | 11 IN | 4.7 IN | 0.7 IN | 0.3 IN | 0.3 IN

JAN | FEB | MAR | APR | MAY | JUN | JUL | AUG | SEPT | OCT | NOV | DEC

Monsoon Season
Harvesting Season
Sowing Season
Month

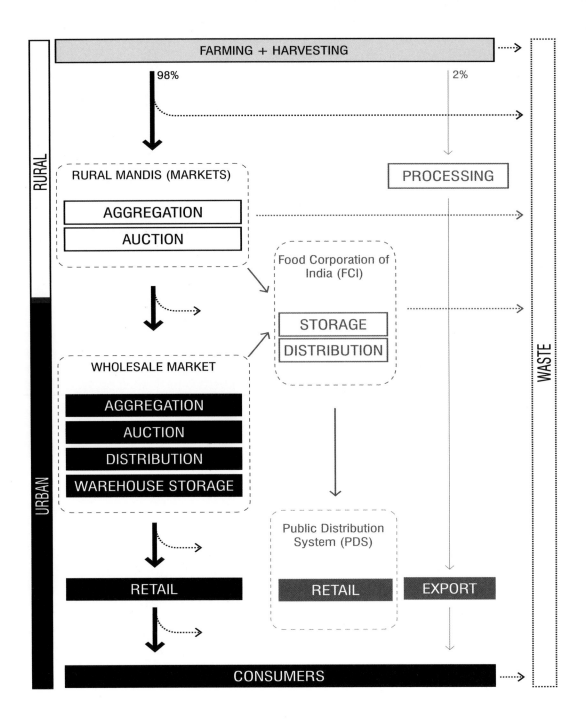

Food Distribution Network

Food distribution in India is hampered by inefficiency and corruption. While India holds the second-largest stockpile of surplus grain stores in the world, half of the nation's fruit and vegetables spoil before arriving to market. This is due to the lack of quality storage and infrequency of distribution from storehouses. Less than 4% of Indian foodstuffs are transported by cold chain and waste could be reduced by enlarging India's fleet of refrigerated trucks, but the diesel motors that cool the produce are highly polluting, and contribute to the nearly 600,000 premature pollution-related deaths in India each year.

A World Bank study claims that when states withdraw their allotted food supplies from federal warehouses, just 41.4% of it actually reaches the poor households it was intended to assist. Advocates say that more than 252 million poor Indians often go hungry as a result, many of them children. Additionally, throughout the distribution chain, officials take a cut to sell to traders and pocket the profit. These problems highlight the advantages of growing food in proximity to urban markets. As Delhi expands, consumers move closer to rural areas and further from traditional markets. Food produced in proximity to where people live and sold in urban markets may require little or no storage and removes middlemen from the distribution network. Solutions to these problems will require coordinated strategies from both private and government partners.

Wholesale Market - Extra Large Scale

Specialty Shop - Large Scale

Street Market - Medium Scale

Temporary Market - Small Scale

MARKETS

Over 15,000 tons of fruit and vegetables are brought each day to the 76 acre complex North of New Delhi. Poor access, congestion, small shops, drainage, no organized waste disposal, and poor infrastructure typify this place - it is at maximum capacity.

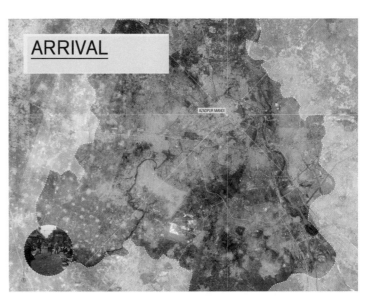

ARRIVAL

After traveling through multiple middle men and government markets, produce arrives at Azadpur Mandi, where it is sorted, traded, and sold. The market operates during all hours of the day, and is most active at night when trucks transport goods through the city.

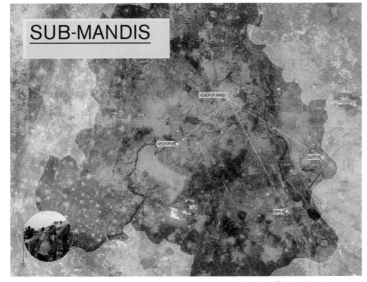

SUB-MANDIS

From Azadpur Mandi, produce travels through sub-mandis like Okhla, Keshopur, and Gazipur.

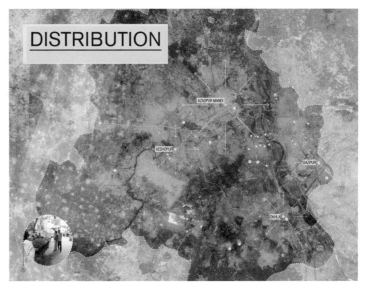

DISTRIBUTION

From sub-mandis, fruits and vegetables are distributed to smaller fruit and vegetable markets throughout the city. Produce can be traded as many as 4-5 times between markets and retailers before it reaches consumers, resulting in severe price inflation.

- ● Deemed Universities
- ● State Universities
- ⊙ Central Universities

Education Network

MANY PRIMARY
AND SECONDARY
SCHOOLS LACK BASIC
INFRASTRUCTURE
SUCH AS QUALITY
CLASSROOMS AND
TOILETS. ONLY 56% OF
THE 59,000 POSITIONS
IN DELHI ARE FILLED BY
PERMANENT TEACHERS.

Public Facilities - Education

Delhi is home to 26 public universities and nearly 6000 primary and secondary schools as of 2015. Enrollment numbers 4,430,000 students and free education is offered to children ages 6 to 14. Literacy rates stood at 89.89% in 2011, up from 70.85% in 2001, which surpasses the national average of 63%. Delhi ranks at the top of the country, along with pro-education states Kerala and Tamil Nadu, in achieving educational goals for girls. However, with an overall dropout rate of 22.9% in Standards I-X, exacerbated by a lack of basic necessities and erratic attendance rate among children from slum areas, it is almost impossible to tell how many students are falling through the cracks. The current ruling party has made education a key issue, doubling the budget allocated for schools and promising to renovate its 1000 government schools by adding classrooms and toilets where needed. Yet Delhi also faces a shortage of teachers—10,000 teachers needed to free existing teachers from administrative burdens and only 56% of the 59,000 positions in Delhi are filled by permanent teachers.

Educational Institution Enrollment (2016)

Elementary Education Grade I - VII
Total Schools - 5,751
Total Enrollment - 3,007,010 (.87 Girls to Boys Enrollment)
Total Teachers - 132,631 (Pupil-Teacher Ratio: 22)
(56% Public Schools | 44% Private Schools)

Secondary Education Grade VIII - XII
Total Schools - 2061
Total Enrollment - 1,208,151 (.87 Girls to Boys Enrollment)
Total Teachers - 47,316 (Pupil-Teacher Ratio: 26)

Population Receiving Education (2011)

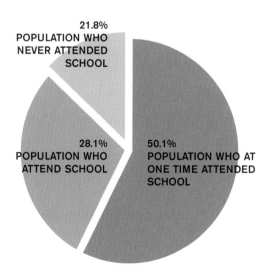

21.8%
POPULATION WHO NEVER ATTENDED SCHOOL

28.1%
POPULATION WHO ATTEND SCHOOL

50.1%
POPULATION WHO AT ONE TIME ATTENDED SCHOOL

Literacy Rates (Delhi)

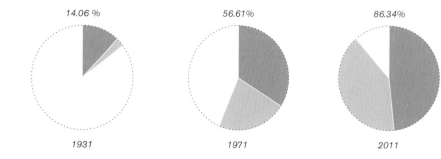

14.06 %   56.61%   86.34%

1931   1971   2011

Literacy Rates by District (2011)

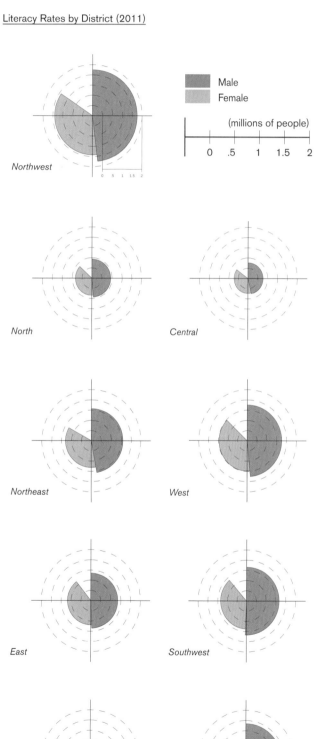

Male
Female

(millions of people)

0   .5   1   1.5   2

Northwest

North   Central

Northeast   West

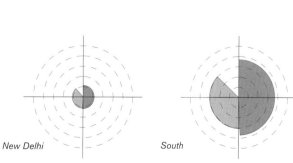

East   Southwest

New Delhi   South

● Major Stadiums

⊙ Minor Sports Facilities

● Museums

⊙ Monuments, Memorials, Temples, Mosques

Public Facilities - Culture

Delhi draws in people from the farthest corners of India giving it best claim to serving as the "melting pot" of India. Many people from around the world call Delhi home and numerous festivals represent both major and minor religions—some, like Delhi's own flower festival and procession of Phool Walon Ki Sair, transcend religious affiliation altogether. Delhi has twice hosted the Asian Games (1951 and 1982) and was the second Asian city to host the Commonwealth Games in 2010. It also hosted the 2010 Hockey World Cup and was a host city for the Cricket World Cup in 1987, 1996, and 2011. Jawaharlal Nehru Stadium, built in 1982 and renovated in 2010, is a world class stadium capable of hosting 60,000 spectators for sporting events and 100,000

for concerts. Red Fort, Humayun's Tomb and Qutb Minar are recognized as UNESCO World Heritage Sites. Jama Masjid is among the largest mosques in the world, and Akshardham Temple, on the banks of the Yamuna, is the world's largest temple. An additional 1200 heritage buildings and 175 monuments around the city have been designated with national heritage status. A plethora of embassies, foreign journalists, and educational institutions contribute to the intellectual and cosmopolitan nature of the city. Galleries, concerts, plays and restaurants cater to a creative crowd that looks far beyond the national bureaucracy for inspiration. A rejuvenated Yamuna River could become a cultural focus alongside the spiritual significance it has always embodied.

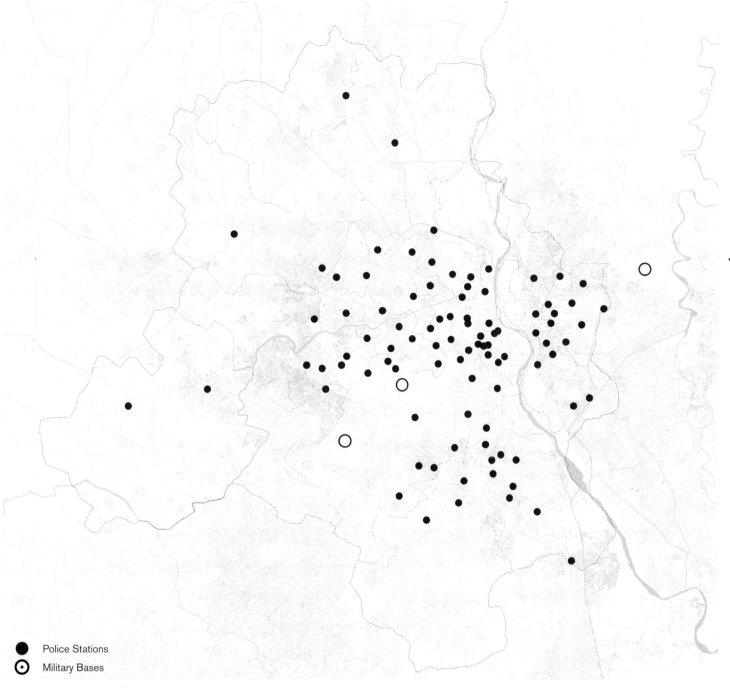

● Police Stations

◉ Military Bases

Reported Crimes in Delhi

209,519	2016
191,377	2015
155,654	2014
80,184	2013
54,287	2012
53,353	2011
51,292	2010
50,251	2009
49,350	2008
56,065	2007
57,963	2006

Public Facilities - Security

There is one policeman for every 253 people in Delhi, much higher than the national average of one policeman for every 761 people. Yet only 46% of these officers are assigned to public security, the rest primarily fill security details for ministry and bureaucrat VIPS or serve as orderlies to government officials. The number of cops assigned to VIP duty is one tenth of the total police force in the entire country. Studies indicate that police respond slowly to crime and discourage victims from filing reports. A public survey in 2016 concluded that more than half of the crimes in Delhi go unreported, and of those that are reported, less than half result in an official investigation with approximately 26% of those cases being solved. Recently, changes

were made to encourage crime reporting and since this announcement, the crime rate has shot up in every category: murder, rape, kidnapping, molestation, and robbery. The police assert that this is due to their effective campaign to register every case. Still, even the police commissioner agrees with critics that say "village attitudes" in areas surrounding Delhi worsen the situation for women and increase the rates of rape and molestation. These ideas filter into the population and often reinforce the presumptions of a police force that is largely composed of officers from surrounding states. Views on violence, caste, and acceptable behavior can become the norm for police personnel unless checked by careful training programs.

- ● Private Hospitals
- ⊙ Public Hospitals
- • Dispensary

Healthcare Network

ACCESS TO QUALITY
HEALTHCARE IS
EXTREMELY LIMITED
TO MANY IN DELHI.
THE GOVERNMENT
HAS RECENTLY
STATED A GOAL OF
CONSTRUCTING A
SYSTEM OF FREE
CLINICS THAT PROVIDE
ACCESS WITHIN 5KM
OF EVERY RESIDENT.

Public Facilities - Healthcare

In 2016, the Indian Institute of Tropical Meteorology reported that premature deaths due to air pollution had decreased life expectancy in Delhi by and average of 6.3 years. It was calculated that the cost of these deaths was INR 3,840,000 crore (USD 640 billion). This amount is ten times higher than the total annual expenditure, public and private, on healthcare in the nation. Such problems are widespread and systematic. Delhi is seeking to make healthcare more local and responsive to everyday needs. By February 2017 the Aam Aadmi government had opened 110 neighborhood clinics operating a battery of diagnostic and treatment programs. The majority of ailments can be quickly treated; more serious cases are transported to hospitals for specialist care. Each clinic is equipped to offer 212 diagnostic tests and dispense 110 essential drugs for free to the local population. Clinics are even starting to show up at night shelters for the homeless. In all, 1000 distributed clinics are planned. The government hopes to guarantee access to a neighborhood clinic within 5 km of every resident.

Average Expenditure per Hospitalization (2014)

Assam	INR 52,368 (USD 812.92)
Chandigarh	INR 37,243 (USD 578.13)
Delhi	INR 37,049 (USD 575.12)
Haryana	INR 35,217 (USD 546.68)
Andhra Pradesh	INR 33,671 (USD 522.68)
Uttar Pradesh	INR 33,402 (USD 518.50)
Punjab	INR 31,978 (USD 496.40)
Himachal Pradesh	INR 31,160 (USD 483.70)
Maharashtra	INR 31,028 (USD 481.65)
Bihar	INR 28,058 (USD 435.55)

Insurance Coverage (2014)

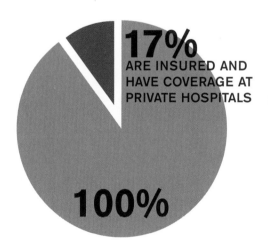

17%
ARE INSURED AND HAVE COVERAGE AT PRIVATE HOSPITALS

100%

BELOW POVERTY HAVE COVERAGE AT PUBLIC HOSPITALS

Number of Hospitals by District

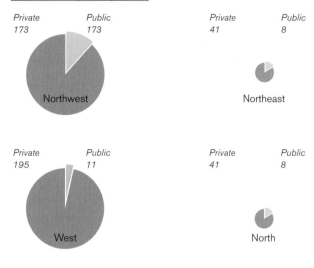

Private 173   Public 173
Northwest

Private 41   Public 8
Northeast

Private 195   Public 11
West

Private 41   Public 8
North

Private 82   Public 10
Southwest

Private 95   Public 10
East

Private 61   Public 20
New Delhi

Private 50   Public 19
Central

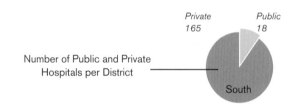

Private 165   Public 18

Number of Public and Private Hospitals per District

South

India Institute of Medical Sciences

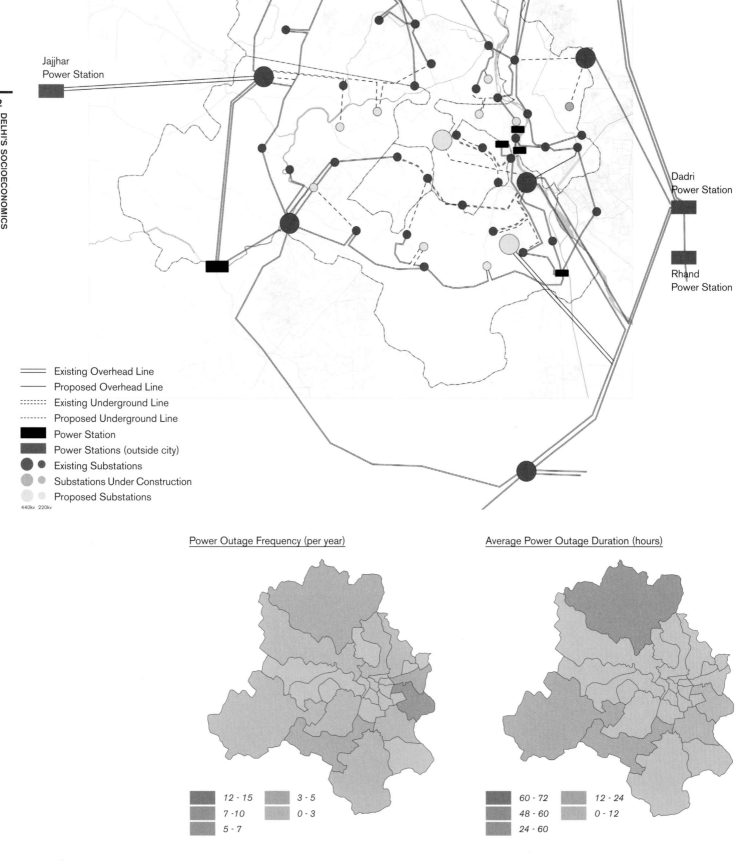

Bhwani
Power Station

Jajjhar
Power Station

Dadri
Power Station

Rhand
Power Station

Existing Overhead Line
Proposed Overhead Line
Existing Underground Line
Proposed Underground Line
Power Station
Power Stations (outside city)
Existing Substations
Substations Under Construction
Proposed Substations
440kv 220kv

Power Outage Frequency (per year)

Average Power Outage Duration (hours)

12 - 15   3 - 5
7 -10   0 - 3
5 - 7

60 - 72   12 - 24
48 - 60   0 - 12
24 - 60

Energy

Delhi's energy demand has doubled in the past decade, rising even more rapidly than its population. Household air conditioning use is driving this demand, accounting for 28% of monthly power consumption during hot months. Energy demand from air conditioners could increase ten times by 2030. The government subsidizes 50% of energy consumption up to 400 kwh for households, substantially above the population's average consumption of 181 kwh. It is easy to see how demand continues to top supply when cost is kept artificially low. To meet this growing demand, Delhi produces more energy from coal-powered plants every year due to cheap operating costs and their ability to provide reliable baseload power. Delhi's lack of performance in renewable energy stands out. A Greenpeace India report in 2013 showed that Delhi failed to meet even 1% of its target for renewables, despite ideal conditions for solar panels on urban rooftops.

Energy distribution companies argue that the government sets energy prices too low, even with the provided subsidies. As of March 2017, distribution companies had an outstanding bill of INR 4,911 crore (USD 818 million) owed to the Delhi government. This non-payment of bills prevents the government from completing power projects needed to meet the ever-increasing electricity demand. This situation also delays repair and maintenance which has led to major unplanned shutdowns.

Energy Consumed (kWh/Month)

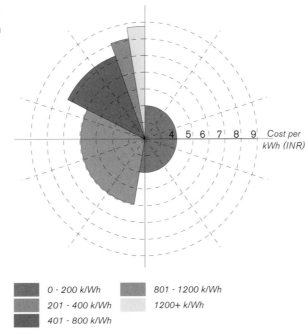

■	0 - 200 k/Wh	■	801 - 1200 k/Wh
■	201 - 400 k/Wh	■	1200+ k/Wh
■	401 - 800 k/Wh		

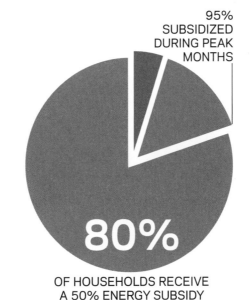

95% SUBSIDIZED DURING PEAK MONTHS

80%

OF HOUSEHOLDS RECEIVE A 50% ENERGY SUBSIDY UNDER 400 kWh/month

THE POWER GRID STRUGGLES TO KEEP UP WITH AN EXPANDING POPULATION WHICH INCREASINGLY RELIES ON AIR CONDITIONING TO ALLEVIATE HARSH CLIMATE CONDITIONS.

Energy Consumption, Demand, and Deficit

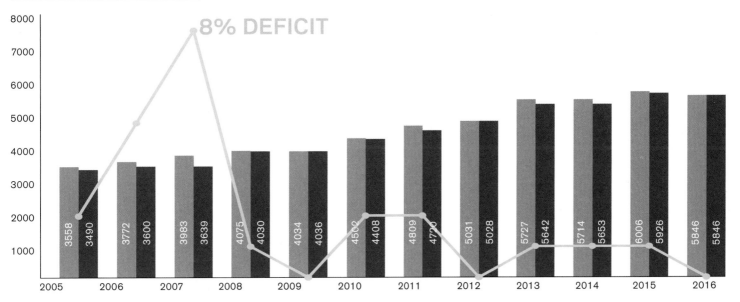

8% DEFICIT

	2005	2006	2007	2008	2009	2010	2011	2012	2013	2014	2015	2016
	3558 / 3490	3772 / 3600	3983 / 3639	4075 / 4030	4034 / 4036	4502 / 4408	4809 / 4720	5031 / 5028	5727 / 5642	5714 / 5653	6006 / 5926	5846 / 5846

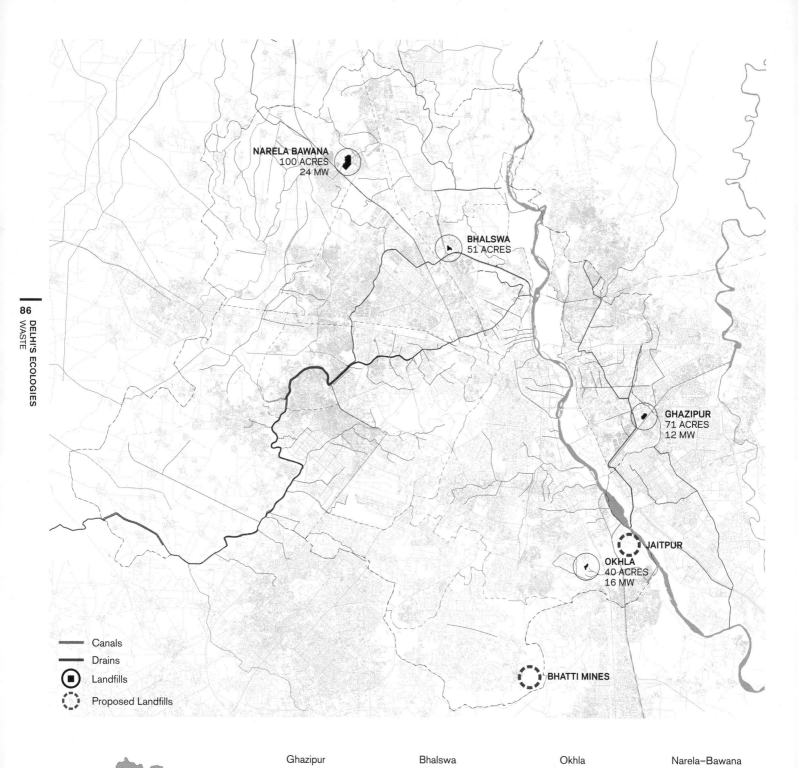

NARELA BAWANA
100 ACRES
24 MW

BHALSWA
51 ACRES

GHAZIPUR
71 ACRES
12 MW

JAITPUR

OKHLA
40 ACRES
16 MW

BHATTI MINES

Canals
Drains
Landfills
Proposed Landfills

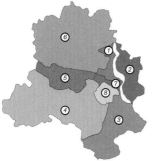

District	Tonnes / Day
① North Delhi	6,045 per sqkm
② East Delhi	15,908 per sqkm
③ South Delhi	4,866 per sqkm
④ Southwest Delhi	2,396 per sqkm
⑤ West Delhi	8,607 per sqkm
⑥ Northwest Delhi	3,631 per sqkm
⑦ Central Delhi	12,201 per sqkm
⑧ New Delhi	1,785 per sqkm

Ghazipur

280,000 sqm
71 Acres
45m Height

Waste to Energy
Plant:
Capacity - 1,300 MTD
Generates - 12 MW

Bhalswa

206,000 sqm
51 Acres
40m Height

Okhla

161,000 sqm
40 Acres
48.5m Height

Waste to Energy
Plant:
Capacity - 1,950 MTD
Generates - 16 MW

Narela–Bawana

404,000 sqm
100 Acres
15-20m Height

Waste to Energy
Plant:
Capacity - 4,000 MTD
Generates - 24 MW

Waste

Only 83% of solid waste is collected. 80% of this waste is either compostable or recyclable yet only 29% of collected waste is treated. Three of the four landfills are due for closure but locating land for new landfills understandably encounters opposition. Local residents strongly resist the introduction of such a horror into their communities. On an average day, 10,000 tons of garbage are dumped onto these waste mountains where decomposition leads to spontaneous methane fires that burn continuously. Their neighbors must deal with persistent stench, respiratory problems, and skin infections caused by smoke and gases. The uncollected waste ends up in informal landfills, empty lots, roadsides, the drain system, and eventually, the Yamuna River.

While millions of tons of garbage are disposed of legally each year, much disposal is unregulated. Factories, labs, hospitals, and power plants throw away about 600,000 tons of hazardous and industrial waste with no designated plan for its proper disposal. Solutions may lie in finding smaller sites to handle specialized processing. Segregation of waste into recyclable, biodegradable, and non-biodegradable, beginning at the household level, would have a significant impact by reducing the amount of waste entering these overburdened landfills. Sorting waste traditionally belongs to a particular class of people and many are reluctant to sort at source—one estimate finds that only 2% of Delhiites sort waste at source.

10,000 Tonnes of Waste Collected

650 Trucks Climb Landfills and Dump Waste

190 - 240 Tonnes Burned

Accounts for 9% of Air Pollution

1.4 Million Liters of Toxic Leachate Contaminates Groundwater

THERE ARE FOUR LANDFILLS IN DELHI, THREE OF WHICH ARE OVERDUE FOR CLOSURE—NONE OF THESE WERE DESIGNED TO EXCEED 15 METERS IN HEIGHT. THE OKHLA LANDFILL IS ALMOST 50 METERS TALL.

Waste Generated Daily

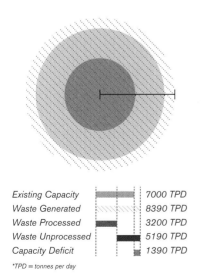

Existing Capacity		7000 TPD
Waste Generated		8390 TPD
Waste Processed		3200 TPD
Waste Unprocessed		5190 TPD
Capacity Deficit		1390 TPD

TPD = tonnes per day

Fires at Bhalswa Landfill

DELHI'S FORMAL WASTE MANAGEMENT SYSTEM IS OVERWHELMED. OF THE UNKNOWN PERCENTAGE OF WASTE PROCESSED DAILY, 80% CAN BE RECYCLED OR COMPOSTED. ONLY 5% ACTUALLY IS, FURTHER STRESSING THE SYSTEM.

recyclables
collected once per week or bi-weekly

types:
plastic (8% of recycled waste)
glass
paper / cardboard
metal
e-waste (32% of recycled waste)
compostables

only 5% of
recyclable and
compostable waste
is collected

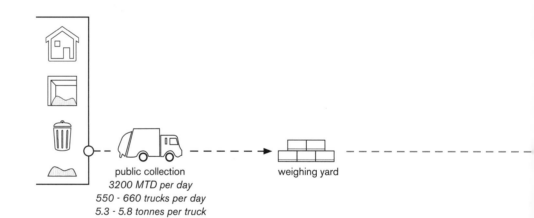

private recycling co.
*fee for collecting
covers 15% of
households*

weighing yard

hired waste pickers
waste is segregated

waste collectors
are paid for collecting

dalau by municipality
*waste is segregated
12-16 tonne capacity
serves 10-15,000 people*

dealers
*sell recyclables
rs 5 ($.08) per kg*

mixed waste
collected once per week

sources:
households
dalau (managed municipality dump site)
waste bins
open dump space (unmanaged)

3.2 kg generated per day per household
20% of waste needs to go to a landfill
30% of waste can be recycled
50% of waste can be composted

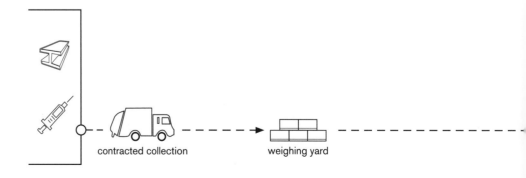

public collection
*3200 MTD per day
550 - 660 trucks per day
5.3 - 5.8 tonnes per truck*

weighing yard

special waste
managed on a contractual basis

sources:
institutions
imports

types:
construction materials (60% recycled)
hospitals
factories
imported waste

contracted collection

weighing yard

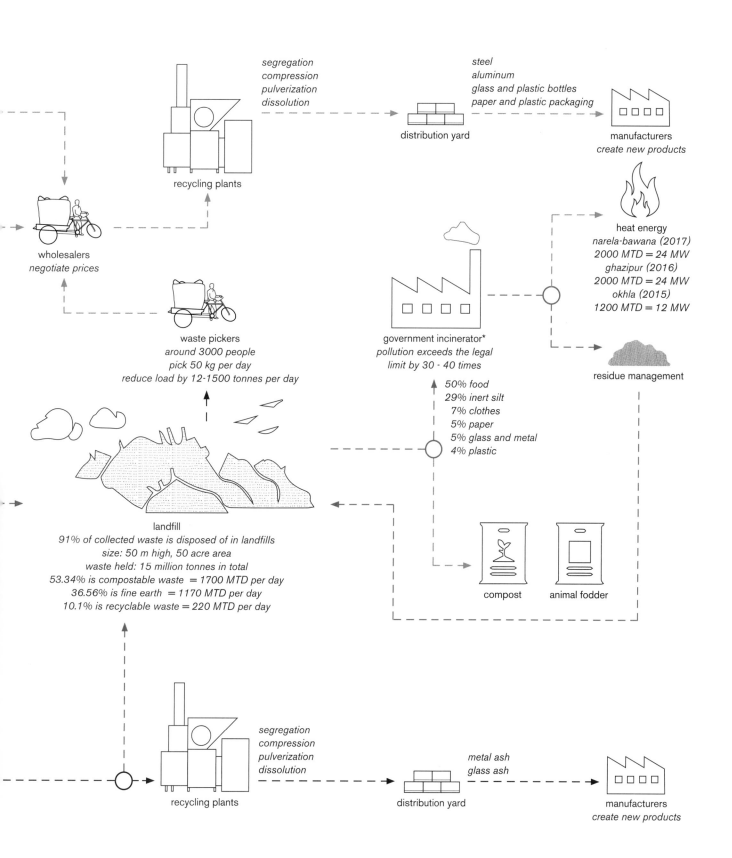

segregation
compression
pulverization
dissolution

steel
aluminum
glass and plastic bottles
paper and plastic packaging

distribution yard

manufacturers
create new products

recycling plants

heat energy
narela-bawana (2017)
2000 MTD = 24 MW
ghazipur (2016)
2000 MTD = 24 MW
okhla (2015)
1200 MTD = 12 MW

wholesalers
negotiate prices

government incinerator*
pollution exceeds the legal
limit by 30 - 40 times

residue management

waste pickers
around 3000 people
pick 50 kg per day
reduce load by 12-1500 tonnes per day

50% food
29% inert silt
7% clothes
5% paper
5% glass and metal
4% plastic

landfill
91% of collected waste is disposed of in landfills
size: 50 m high, 50 acre area
waste held: 15 million tonnes in total
53.34% is compostable waste = 1700 MTD per day
36.56% is fine earth = 1170 MTD per day
10.1% is recyclable waste = 220 MTD per day

compost   animal fodder

segregation
compression
pulverization
dissolution

metal ash
glass ash

recycling plants

distribution yard

manufacturers
create new products

THE CITY IS IN THE PROCESS OF ALLEVIATING PRESSURE ON OVERBURDENED LANDFILLS. SPECIALIZED RECYCLING CENTERS ARE IMPROVING ISSUES OF WASTE SEGREGATION AND NEW INCINERATOR PROJECTS WILL REDUCE THE VOLUME OF NEW AND EXISTING WASTE WHILE PROVIDING A NEW SOURCE OF ENERGY.

standard recyclables
collected once per week

types:
plastic containers, packages, trays, labels, caps
77% of collected plastic waste recycled (2010)

plastic bottles (remove caps and labels)
72% of collected plastic bottles recycled (2010)

glass bottles

aluminum and steel cans

weighing yard

government
recycling facility

used paper
collected once per week

types:
newspaper
cardboard boxes
miscellaneous

weighing yard

combustibles
collected twice per week

types:
food waste
cooking oil
clothes and fabric
twigs and leaves
leather and rubber
plastic products with unremovable stains
paper other than used paper

weighing yard

government incinerator

non-combustibles
collected twice per month

ceramics and glass
metal
small home appliances
spray cans, lighters, gas cartridge bottles
products containing mercury

weighing yard

incombustible waste
processing center

large sized waste
need apply for pickup by recycling-centers or
manufactures and pay associated fees for service
and processing

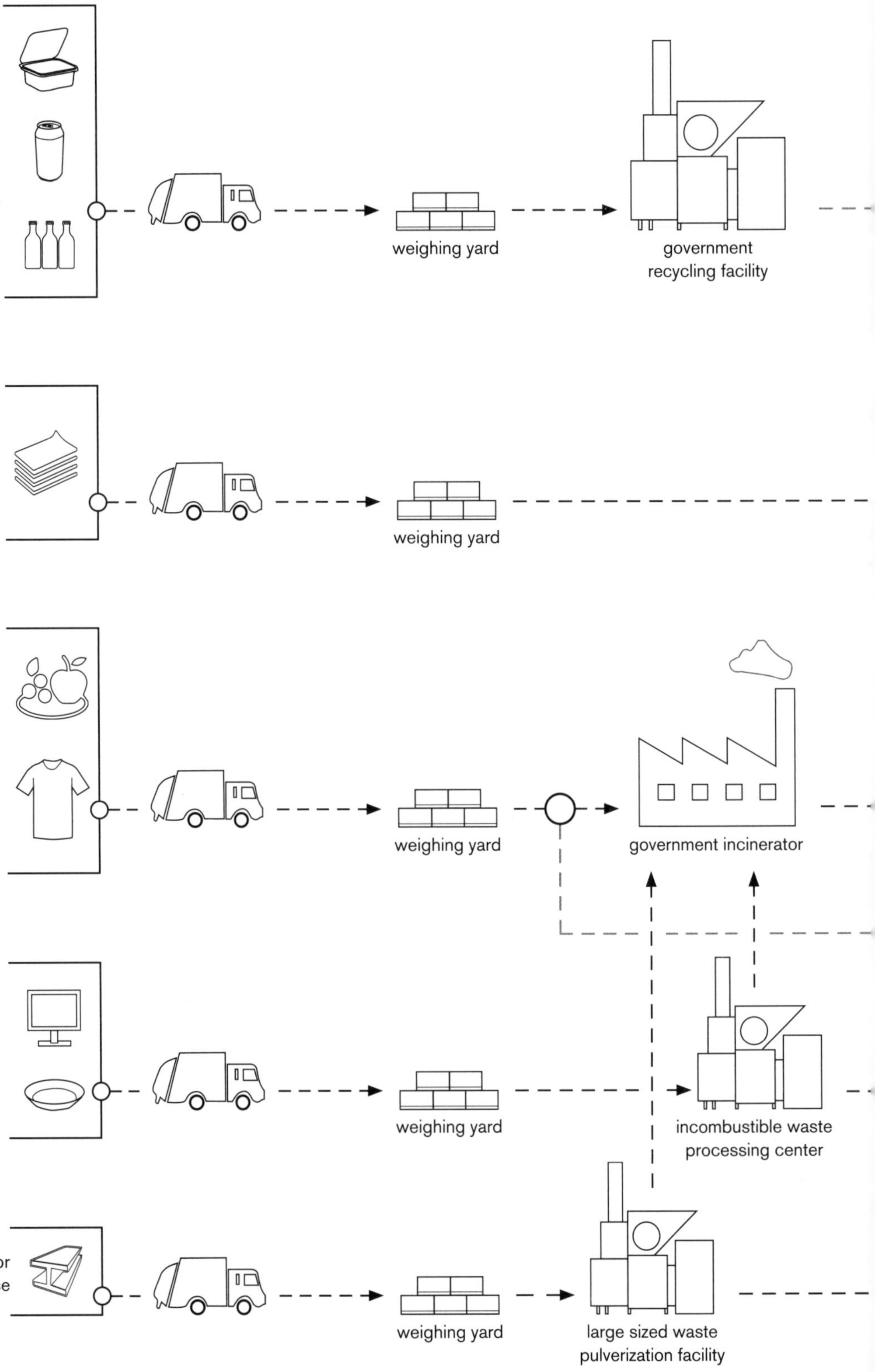

weighing yard

large sized waste
pulverization facility

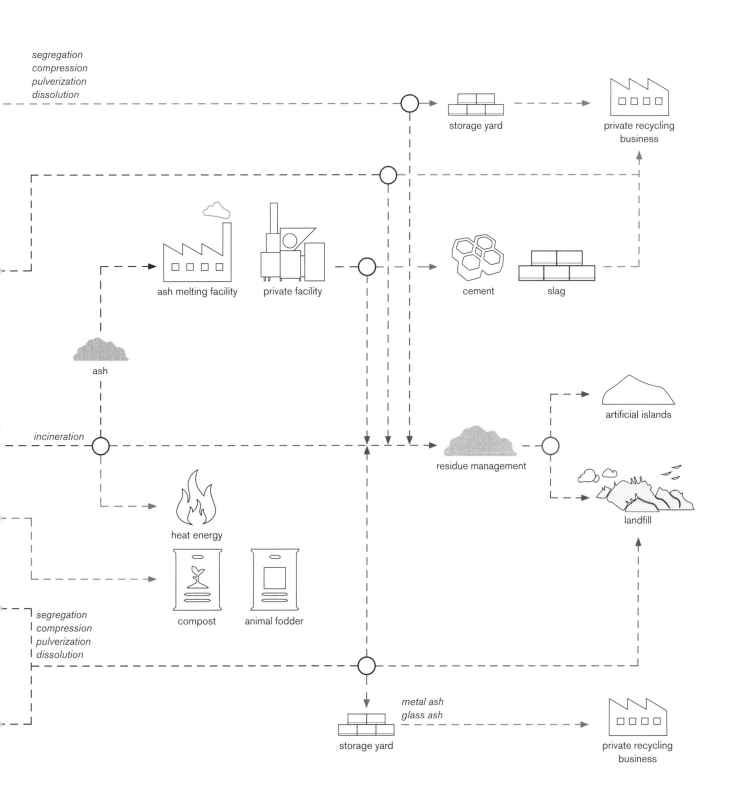

segregation
compression
pulverization
dissolution

storage yard

private recycling
business

ash melting facility   private facility

cement   slag

ash

incineration

residue management

artificial islands

landfill

heat energy

compost   animal fodder

segregation
compression
pulverization
dissolution

metal ash
glass ash

storage yard

private recycling
business

Air Pollution Levels

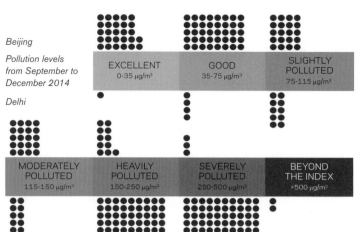

Beijing

Pollution levels from September to December 2014

Delhi

EXCELLENT 0-35 μg/m³	GOOD 35-75 μg/m³	SLIGHTLY POLLUTED 75-115 μg/m³

MODERATELY POLLUTED 115-150 μg/m³	HEAVILY POLLUTED 150-250 μg/m³	SEVERELY POLLUTED 250-500 μg/m³	BEYOND THE INDEX >500 μg/m³

Air Quality

Air quality readings taken in November 2016 officially made Delhi the most polluted major city in the world. While traditional offenders like Beijing, Mexico City, and Los Angeles score in the 50-100 range on the Air Quality Index, at one point, Delhi's was literally off the charts, registering at 999. Schools were closed, construction projects halted, and hospitals reported a sharp increase in patients with severe respiratory problems Even on a good day, Delhi's baseline pollution levels are unacceptable. The city receives emissions from heavily populated Punjab as well as smoke from crop burning on Haryana farms. Yet above all, Delhi's way of life pollutes the air. Much of the city's solid waste is burned, construction and infrastructure projects churn up dust. Over 7 million vehicles, many of which are emission heavy diesels, are on the road and their numbers increase every day. Beyond the limits of the NCT, coal-fired power plants, brick kilns, and other industries are heavy contributors to the high levels of PM2.5 pollutants. Such emissions are nearly impossible for Delhi to regulate since they are outside the administrative boundaries of the city. But this only underscores the importance of the government setting standards for the sectors it can influence, such as waste burning, transportation, and households and industries within its jurisdiction. Government agencies and municipal corporations need to coordinate efforts if any progress is to be seen.

PM2.5 Concentration Average Over Time

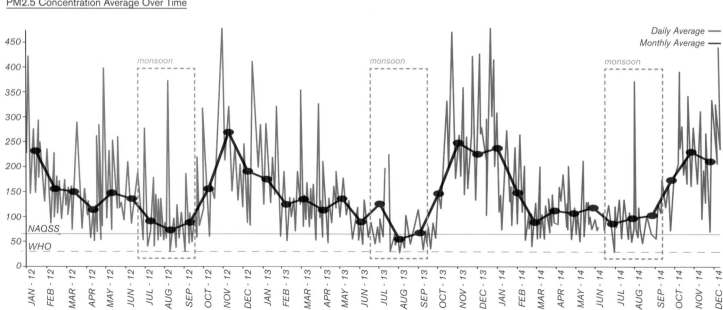

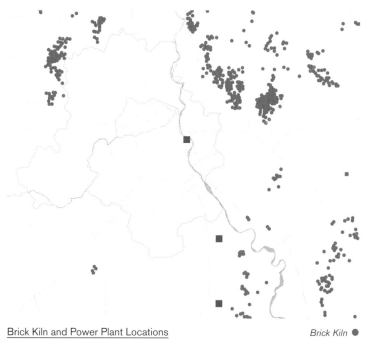

Brick Kiln and Power Plant Locations

Brick Kiln ●
Power Plant ■

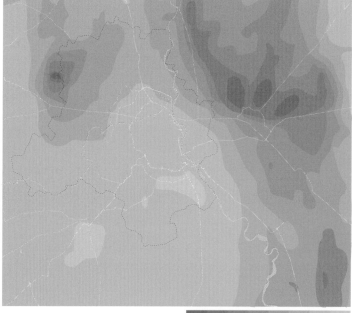

Brick Kiln Pollution

35% 30% 25% 20% 15% 10% 5% 0%

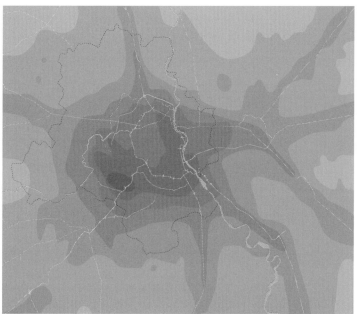

Vehicular Pollution

35% 30% 25% 20% 15% 10% 5% 0%

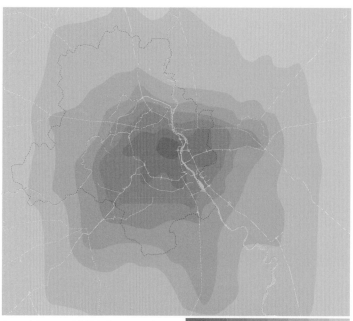

Annual Average PM2.5 Concentration

160 140 120 100 80 60 40 20

Pm2.5 Pollutants	Amount
Vehicle Exhaust	~25%
Biomass Burning (including seasonal open fires, cooking, and heating)	~20%
Industry	~15%
Soil and Road Dust	~15%
Diesel Generators	~10%
Open Waste Burning	~10%
Power Plants	~05%
Outside Urban Airshed	~20%

AIR QUALITY
READINGS TAKEN
IN NOVEMBER
2016 OFFICIALLY
MADE DELHI THE
MOST POLLUTED
MAJOR CITY IN
THE WORLD.

6.4
YEARS
LIFE EXPECTANCY
LOST DUE TO AIR
POLLUTION

Forested Land

IT IS CLEAR THAT CERTAIN AREAS OF DELHI HAVE A MORE FAVORED STATUS WHEN IT COMES TO ACCESSIBILITY OF GREEN SPACES–76% OF THE PLANNED OPEN SPACE IS SOUTH OF THE RIDGE, IN DISTRICTS OCCUPIED BY HIGH-INCOME GROUPS.

East Delhi Public Open Space

Green Space

Delhi lays dubious claim to the term "Green City". It hosts more green cover than any other metropolitan city in India with parks, extensive campus greens, plantings along drains, and two biodiversity parks constituting 15% of total urban land area. However, these statistics are misleading as poor quality and lack of accessibility renders much of these public spaces unusable. It is clear that certain areas of Delhi have favored status when it comes to accessibility of green spaces—76% of planned open space is south of the Ridge, in districts occupied by high-income groups. The stress of Delhi's rapid urbanization inevitably strains even the tiny pocket parks distributed throughout residential areas of the city. These spaces often become informal waste dumping grounds or are eyed by municipal agencies and real estate developers for construction projects that often do not benefit local communities. Injuries, assaults, and even deaths have occurred at neighborhood parks. Municipal officials lay the blame on lack of funding, a deficit of 1,400 gardeners, and a thin police presence after dark.

12.7%
GREATER DELHI URBAN AREA FORESTED

~190 hectares of Forested Land

Deer Park at Hauz Khas Reservoir

District	Forest Hectares	% of area
Central	5.14	20.56
New Delhi	17.25	49.29
South	82.14	32.86
East	3.28	5.13
Northeast	3.97	6.60
North	4.53	7.68
Northwest	17.04	3.87
Southwest	48.60	11.54
West	6.82	5.29

Public Green Space at Feroz Shah Kotla

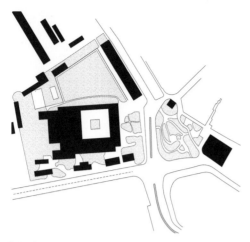

Elementary School

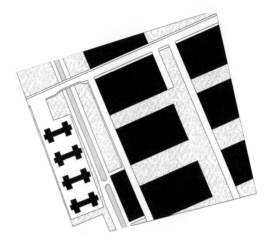

Planned Community

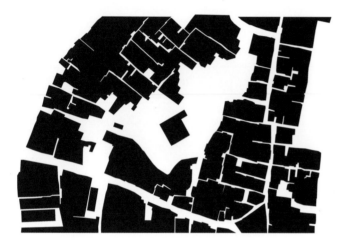

Unplanned Open Space

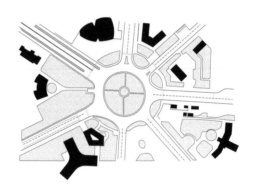

Roundabout

Drain Edge I

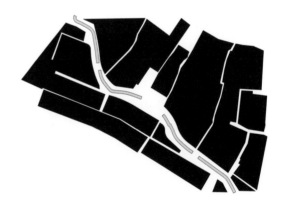

Drain Plaza

Drain Edge II

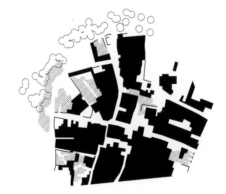

Informal Landfill

96
DELHI'S ECOLOGIES
OPEN SPACE

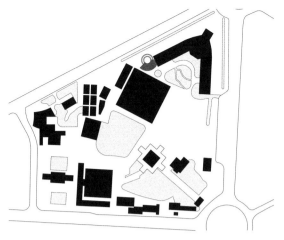

Institutional Grounds

High Density Pockets II

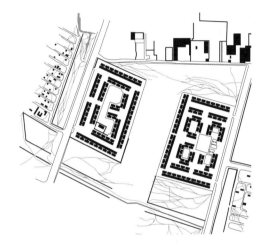

Planned Courtyard Housing

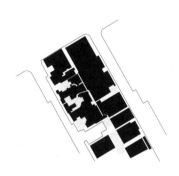

Alley Thoroughfares

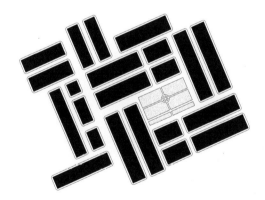

Planned Pocket Park

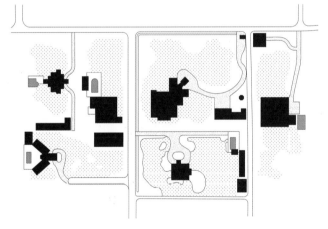

Low Density Villas

Open Space

Delhi's density is often the first layer of urban fabric one notices in satellite photos or from walking the streets. But as one looks closer another layer starts to appear. From neighborhood plazas to undeveloped urban lots and spaces along drain edges, there is a significant amount of unplanned open space existing within Delhi's urban fabric. These open spaces take on the character of surrounding neighborhoods, serving as places of commercial activity, leisure, and play. These open spaces present an opportunity for design interventions that support existing urban life while introducing new social and ecological functions.

High Density Pockets I

- - - - Future Highway
──── Primary Highway
──── Major Roads
///// Intermodal Node

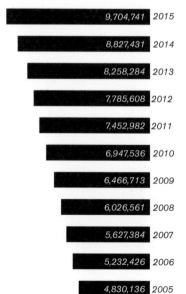

Number of Vehicles in Delhi

9,704,741	2015
8,827,431	2014
8,258,284	2013
7,785,608	2012
7,452,982	2011
6,947,536	2010
6,466,713	2009
6,026,561	2008
5,627,384	2007
5,232,426	2006
4,830,136	2005

Road Network

Delhi's road network accounts for 21% of total land area, far above the world urban average of 12-15%. The rate of increase in the network is about 0.33% per year over the last decade and the number of vehicles has grown at a rate of 7-8% per year. Outer arterial roads carry 80% of the city's daily traffic and are frequently congested, particularly during rush hour. The city has turned to constructing flyovers to help ease congestion, yet parking on the side of the road and other encroachments continually slow down traffic. In addition to the daily burden of too many cars on the roads, Delhi experiences extraordinary but regular challenges of waterlogged roads during monsoon rains, and heavy smog that limits visibility. A research institute says most roads lack safety norms necessary to protect pedestrians and cyclists, many of whom have no choice but to travel on these flyovers to access their neighborhoods.

Highway planning and construction is often swayed by political pressure instead of planning goals and is a common source of graft for municipal officials, developers, and contractors. In 2008, a toll road was built from Delhi to Gurgaon, a booming Haryana suburb. This project expanded access for commuters from Gurgaon and connected others to interstate highways. But poor planning and driving habits caused traffic to constantly clog at toll plazas. Mayhem, frustration, and occasionally violence resulted causing one plaza to be removed by court order.

National Rail Network

Metro Network + Stop

Bus Network

Intermodal Node

Daily Metro Ridership in Delhi

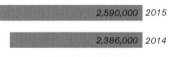

2,590,000	2015
2,386,000	2014
2,190,000	2013
1,926,000	2012
1,660,000	2011
1,259,000	2010
919,000	2009
722,000	2008
625,000	2007
484,000	2006
268,000	2005

Public Transportation Network

Since it opened in 2002, the Delhi Metro has been a shining success story for the city and the nation as a whole. There are only 8 metro systems in the country, with 324 km of track as of September 2016; Delhi operates 218 km of that track. It stands as the 12th longest metro system in the world, tenth in terms of ridership. Currently there are 6 lines and 164 stations serving Delhi and the satellite cities of Noida, Ghaziabad, Faridabad and Gurgaon. Phase III, expected to be completed by 2018, will add ring connectors to the radial lines. The extensions will add 167.27 km of track and make Delhi's network the fifth largest in the world. Another 100 km are planned for a Phase IV, which has a 2022 deadline. But the best metro system cannot work unless riders can efficiently access stations, a role buses can fill. Bus ridership has declined every year since 2012-2013, and a Bus Rapid Transit system piloted in 2008 was scrapped in 2016 due to poor implementation. Even though more riders use the bus than the metro, there is poor coordination between the two systems. Ridership may continue to decline unless all public transportations types are treated as a single network. In 1998 the Supreme Court ruled, in the interests of public health, that all buses, taxis and three-wheelers must convert their engines to compressed natural gas (CNG). Rapid improvements in the air quality followed. However, gains have been erased over the past two decades by the steady increase of private vehicles on the street.

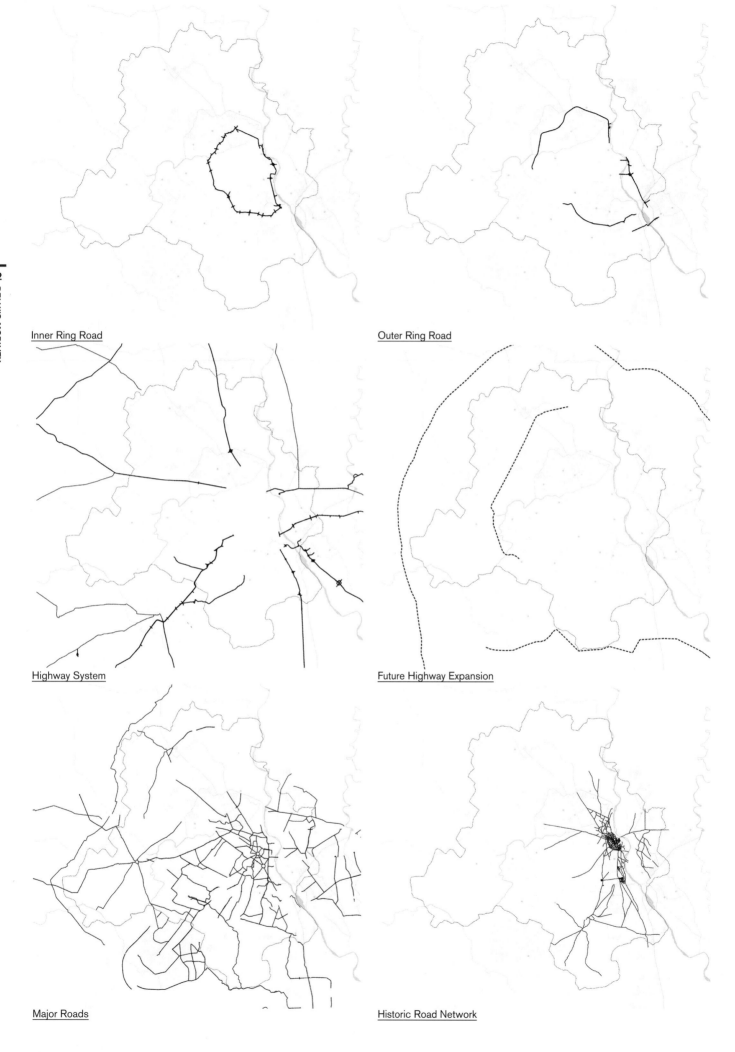

Inner Ring Road

Outer Ring Road

Highway System

Future Highway Expansion

Major Roads

Historic Road Network

National Rail Network

Bus Network

Metro System

Future Metro Expansion

Mobility Systems

A recent report commissioned by the Ministry of Urban Development predicts that without "adequate, comfortable and efficient public transport services and walking and cycling facilities", Delhi's dependence on cars will increase to intolerable levels. "Last mile connectivity", or getting travelers from the metro station to their doorstep, is necessary to convincing people to use public transportation. It is the responsibility of the entire system to see that every station—not just the marquis hubs that connect to the airport or bus depots—can safely and efficiently connect riders to the means of completing their journey. Generally the bus system is the focus of last mile connectivity analysis. In theory the bus system can respond more nimbly to customer demand, adjusting routes and bus stops in order to maximize customer satisfaction and usage. Yet this level of coordination does not exist. Additionally, nearly every rider is a pedestrian at some point, yet many footpaths are blocked by parked cars or other obstacles. Dedicated pedestrian pathways, as well as cycling lanes, are as beneficial for public safety as they are for enabling people with transportation options. Finally, it is important to consider personal safety when designing best journeys. Women in particular feel very vulnerable at many bus and metro stations, particularly at night. Care should be taken to improve lighting, visibility, and police surveillance for public transportation to insure they can confidently travel around the city.

1 - New Delhi Railway Station

2 - Ito Tilak Bridge

3 - Pul Bangash | Old Delhi Rail Station

4 - Inderlok | Ashok Park | Daya Basti

5 - Seelamp Ur

6 - Karkarduma | Anand Vihar

7 - Indira Gandhi International Airport

8 - Dwarka

Elevated Highway

Intermodal Transportation

Disconnected Infrastructure

Bridge Construction

Mobility Overlaps

Most travel in Delhi
utilizes multiple forms of
transportation - getting
to and from the bus or
the metro station involves
walking, driving, or hiring a
vehicle. Bus stops and metro
stations are not only points
of departure and arrival;
they are intermodal nodes
of activity where numerous
modes of transit converge.

Commuting Method

26% Foot

26% Bus

17% Motorcycle

13% Car

11% Bicycle

4%   Train / Metro

3%   Rickshaw

Commuting Distance

3km   Foot

15km Bus

11km Motorcycle

18km Car

9km   Bicycle

22km Train / Metro

15km Rickshaw

——— National Rail Network

●– – Metro Network + Stop

- - - - Bus Network

==== Future Highway

——— Primary Highway

——— Major Roads

///   Intermodal Node

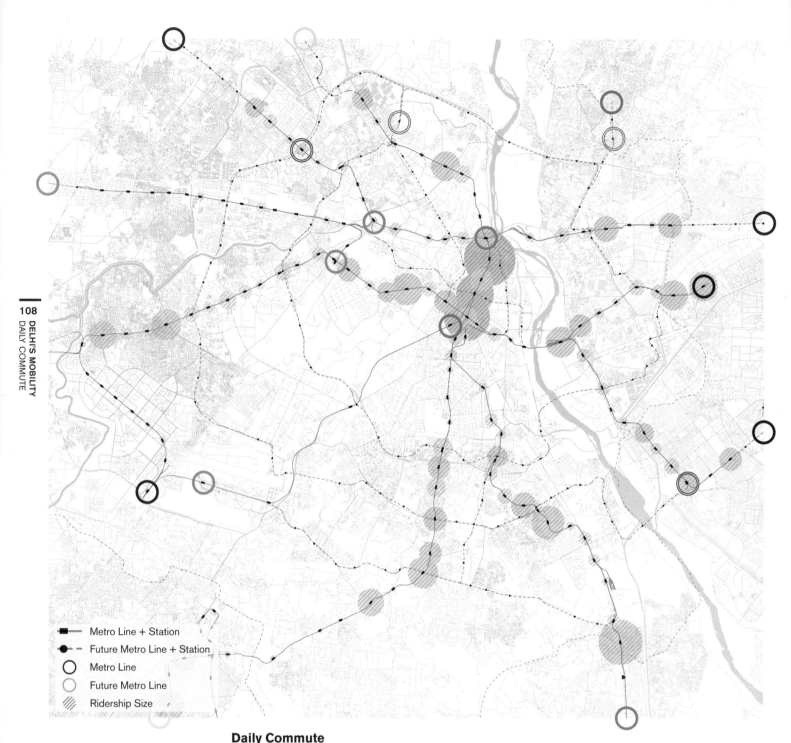

Metro Line + Station
Future Metro Line + Station
Metro Line
Future Metro Line
Ridership Size

Daily Commute

Line	Daily Ridership (avg)
Red	334,733
Yellow	831,258
Blue (3&4)	915,172
Green	91,100
Violet	197,610
Orange	20,000

Line	Line length (km)
Red	25.09
Yellow	49.00
Blue (3&4)	56.67
Green	18.46
Violet	40.34
Orange	22.70

Line	# of Stations
Red	21
Yellow	37
Blue (3&4)	51
Green	16
Violet	32
Orange	6

It is notoriously difficult to get to work in Delhi. Many people are stuck in traffic jams on a daily basis or must navigate roads on foot that are designed only for vehicular traffic. Add one disruption and an aggravation can turn into an ordeal. Yet over 75% of Delhi commutes are less than 10 km since jobs are decentralized in competing centers of gravity around the city. The many neighborhoods, offices, construction sites, and markets preclude the need to commute long distances, a scenario poor workers can ill afford. Most commutes feature multiple modes of travel–getting to and from the bus or the metro station involves walking, driving, or hiring a vehicle. Bus stops and metro stations are not only points of departure and arrival; they are nodes where numerous modes

of transit converge. One third commute by foot, bicycle or cycle rickshaw; over 40% commute by public transportation, and the Metro is slowly gaining a percentage of total commutes as new lines and stations are opened. Driving to work can be a miserable experience and it imposes large costs on the environment. Yet the number of drivers increases every year which caused the government to experiment in 2016 with odd-even car restrictions. While not a popular policy, these restrictions showed the public transportation system how to handle increased volume and forced commuters to learn how to travel by alternate means. These experiments and others like it can inform government strategies on how to incentivize commuters to choose public transportation.

Morning Commute

Waiting to Cross

Commercial Transport

Traffic Jam

New Metro Station

Yamuna Governance Structure

Various municipal, state and central government agencies govern and regulate the territory of the Yamuna and its drains and sub-drains. The complexity of Delhi's governance and the resulting difficulties of administrative coordination have played an important role in contributing to the degradation of Delhi's Yamuna. Surmounting the problems posed by Delhi's governance is essential to revitalizing the river and its tributaries.

Central Government
1. Central Ground Water Board
2. Central Pollution Control Board
3. Central Soil and Materials Research Station New Delhi
4. Central Water Commission New Delhi
5. Ganga Flood Control Commission (GFCC)
6. National Institute of Hydrology Roorkee
7. Upper Yamuna River Board
8. National Ganga River Basin Authority
9. Town and Country Planning Organization
10. Central Public Works Department
11. National Capital Regional Planning Board

State Government
12. Urban Development Division
13. Delhi Pollution Control Committee
14. Department of Irrigation and Flood Control
15. Public Works Department
16. Delhi State Industrial+Infrastructure Development
17. Forest Department

Municipal Government
18. New Delhi Municipal Council (NDMC)
19. Delhi Cantonment Board (DCB)
20. Municipal Corporation of Delhi (MCD)

Other Bodies
21. National Green Tribunal
22. The Electoral System
23. The World Bank
24. Supreme Court of India
25. NGOs
   - Yamuna Jiye Abhiyaan
   - Centre for Science and the Environment
   - Indian National Trust for Architecture and Cultural Heritage

Initiatives
26. National Mission for Clean Ganga (NMCG)
27. YAP-III (Yamuna Action Plan Phase III Funds)

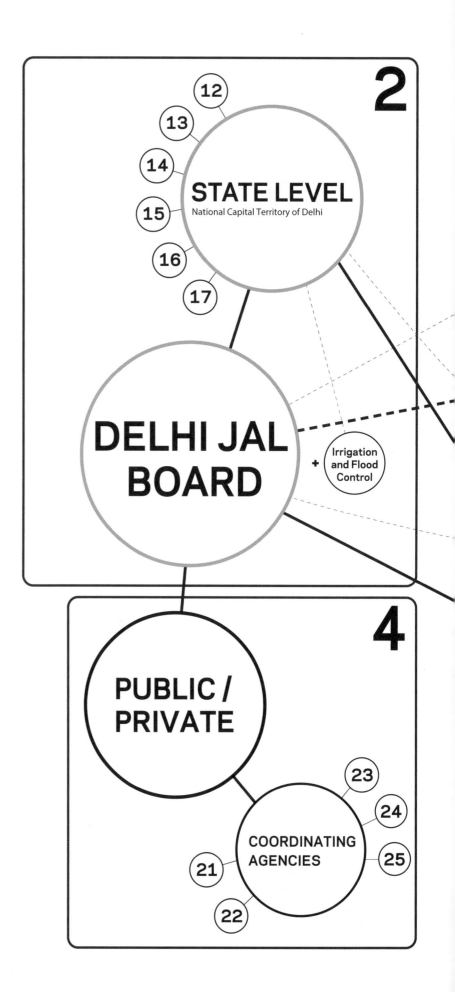

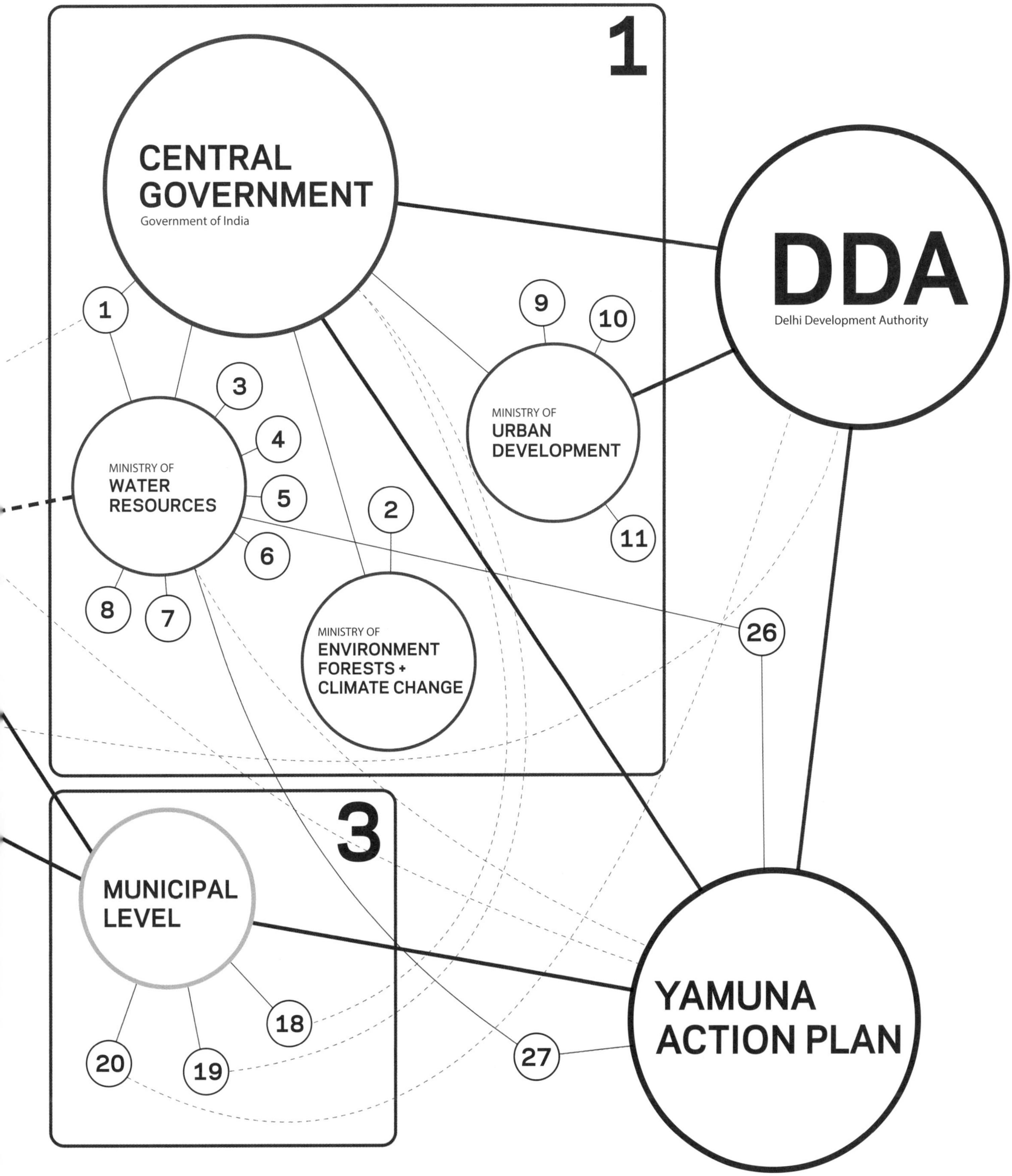

1

CENTRAL
GOVERNMENT
Government of India

DDA
Delhi Development Authority

(1)

(3)

(4)

(5)

(6)

(8) (7)

MINISTRY OF
WATER
RESOURCES

(9) (10)

MINISTRY OF
URBAN
DEVELOPMENT

(11)

(2)

MINISTRY OF
ENVIRONMENT
FORESTS +
CLIMATE CHANGE

(26)

3

MUNICIPAL
LEVEL

(18)

(20) (19)

(27)

YAMUNA
ACTION PLAN

DELHI'S GOVERNANCE AND EFFORTS TO REVITALIZE ITS YAMUNA

John Echeverri-Gent
Associate Professor, Politics
University of Virginia

Although the Yamuna River has historically been a vibrant center of social activity, culture, and biodiversity, it is now an environmentally degraded and socially neglected space in Delhi's ecological domain. The environmental degradation of Delhi's Yamuna has continued despite the government spending more than Rs. 20 billion over the last two decades to alleviate the problem.[1] Revitalizing Delhi's Yamuna is a formidable challenge because of the complexity of the problems that it entails. This essay demonstrates that the complex structure of Delhi's governing institutions is an important cause of the Yamuna's degradation, and surmounting the challenges posed by Delhi's governance is essential to revitalizing the river.

We begin by discussing the nature of Yamuna's degradation. Next, the essay describes the underlying causes contributing to the problem. It will demonstrate that Delhi's complex governance is a central cause of the Yamuna's degradation. Finally, the essay assesses the potential of different mechanisms to promote the coordination necessary to overcome the challenge of Delhi's complex governance.

I. The Nature of the Problem

The degradation of Delhi's Yamuna has three immediate sources. Diversion of the river's waters by upstream states and by Delhi itself has led to a drastic reduction of the Yamuna's natural flow in the Delhi area that undermines the river's capacity to dilute pollution, recharge local ground water levels, provide for biodiversity needs, and the social needs of people living in the vicinity of the river. Second, an 200 million litres of untreated or partially treated sewage[2], industrial effluents, and solid waste are discharged daily into the river, in effect, turning the riverbed into a sewage drain for many months during the year. Finally, the physical characteristics of the Yamuna's floodplain have been destroyed by numerous encroachments which, in addition to the dumping of solid wastes and unauthorized settlements, include state authorized metro complexes, bus depots, sports villages and facilities, crematoria, and cultural festivals. These encroachments have diminished the zone's capacity to channel flood water, recharge groundwater, and support biodiversity.

II. The Underlying Causes

The immediate sources of the Yamuna's problem are manifestations of two underlying causes with deep roots in Delhi's political economy. First, is Delhi's infrastructural deficit. The city's rapid population growth creates a formidable challenge to providing adequate infrastructure. From 1951 to 2017, the city's population grew from 3 million to a projected 19 million by March 2017.[3] India's capital has been unable to invest in the infrastructure necessary to properly service its proliferating population. Forty-nine percent of the Delhi's population lives in unauthorized colonies, slums and jhuggi-jhonpri clusters or squatters' settlements.[4] Though the Delhi Water/Jal Board (DWB) has expanded its coverage in recent years, one-quarter of Delhi's population remains without access to treated water.[5] According to one estimate, the DWB is able to provide just more than 40% of the city's per capita water needs.[6] Less than half the city's residents have yet to be connected to the sewage system,[7] and many of the existing sewers have caved in or are otherwise blocked.[8] According to expert, Isher Judge Ahluwalia, only 30% of Delhi's sewage is treated before it is discharged.[9]

Political impediments have limited the capacity of Delhi's Government of the National Capital Territory (GNCT) to finance the investments necessary to keep up with the city's population growth. The GNCT has failed to adequately tax what is perhaps India's most lucrative tax base with the highest per capita income of any Indian state. Consequently, the GNCT's own revenues as a proportion of GSP is lower than own revenue as a proportion of non-agricultural GSDP for most other states.[10] At the same time, the GNCT provides the highest per capita subsidies of any Indian state, and it has the lowest rate of recovery relative to the cost of its service.[11] Rather than being able to finance the infrastructure necessary to meet the needs of the rapidly growing city, the fiscal position of the Delhi municipal governments is characterized by persistent, large, and growing gaps between its revenues and expenditures.[12] The consequences of the fiscal gap can be seen in the DWB's budget. Though the funds for water supply and sanitation released to the DWB have grown by 28 percent from Rs. 13.4 billion to Rs 17.2 billion from 2007-08 to 2015-16, in real terms, after accounting for inflation, the value of its budget allocation has declined by more than 15 percent.[13]

The complexity of Delhi's governance and the resulting difficulties of administrative coordination the second factor contributing to the degradation of Delhi's Yamuna. As the map on page 112 shows, at least 26 different government agencies at four levels of governance have responsibilities affecting the condition of the Yamuna in the Delhi region.

One manner in which the complexity of governance affects the degradation of Delhi's Yamuna is that upstream governments divert the river's water before it arrives in Delhi. The governments of Haryana, Uttar Pradesh, Rajasthan and Himachal Pradesh redirect large amounts of water for irrigation and drinking above the Hathnikunj (Tajewala) barrage in Haryana. This a classic political economy problem in which these state governments are preoccupied in satisfying the demands of

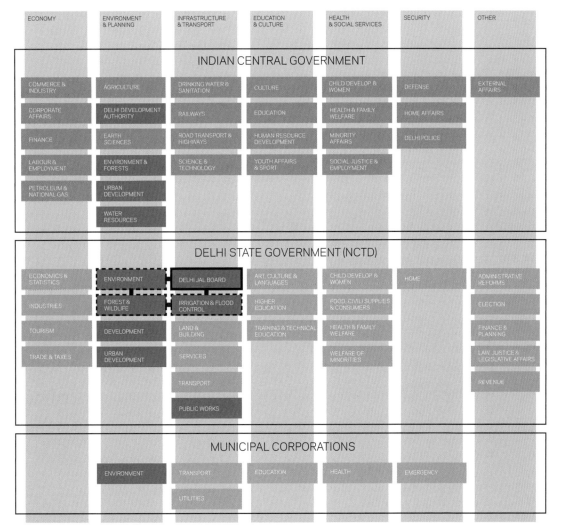

Figure 1

Delhi Governance Structure. Diagram adapted from lsecities.net

* Red highlights call out agencies which have operational authority over aspects of the Yamuna River and Delhi's drain system.
* The CEO of the Delhi Jal Board concurrently serves as CEO of Irrigation and Flood Control, Secretary of Environment, and Secretary of Forest and Wildlife.

powerful local constituencies at the expense of groups outside their jurisdiction. The problem is made worse because Delhi re-routs still more water above the Wazirabad Barrage through the Western Yamuna Canal in order to enhance the city's supply of drinking water. Some observers allege that Delhi does not get its fair share of the water despite a 1994 memorandum of understanding agreed to by the state and a 1998 order issued by the Supreme Court.[14] In any case, so much water is diverted that during much of the year, there is virtually no river flow. Increasing the river flow is essential for ameliorating the environmental degradation of Delhi's Yamuna.

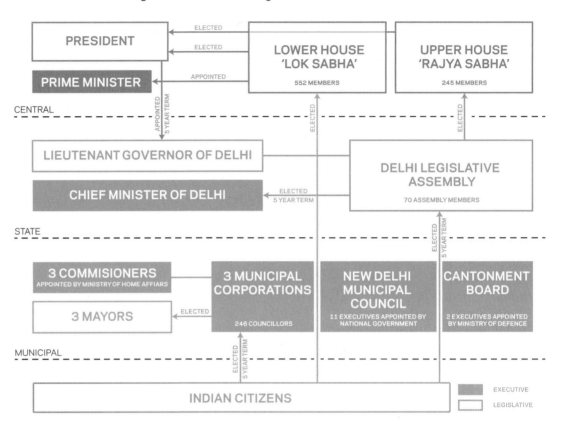

Figure 2

Delhi Governance Structure. Diagram adapted from lsecities.net

The division of the authority of elected officials into national, state, and municipal levels is another way in which the complexity of Delhi's governance contributes to the Yamuna's degradation. Throughout India, state governments have been reluctant to transfer buoyant sources of tax revenues to local governments. In recent years, fiscal tensions have been exacerbated by the fierce political rivalry between the Bharatiya Janata Party (BJP) which controls the national and municipal governments and the Aam Aadmi Party (AAP) which controls the GNCT located between the national and municipal governments. For instance, in each of the past three years, thousands of sanitation workers employed by at least one of the Delhi municipal corporations have gone out on strike after their wages were not paid. BJP municipal corporation leaders blamed the AAP-controlled GNCT for providing insufficient funds while AAP leaders of the GNCT suggested that the municipal corporations had wasted their funding and had failed to properly raise taxes.[15] An ongoing dispute between the DWB, the Delhi State Industrial Infrastructure Development Corporation, and Delhi's municipalities contributes to the inadequate regulation of industrial effluents.[16] Tensions also exist between the BJP-led central government and the GNCT as illustrated by Minister of Water Resources, Uma Bharti's charge that the AAP GNCT is delaying the implementation of plans to revitalize the Yamuna.[17] Part of the municipalities' weak fiscal position can be traced by to 2012 when Congress Party leader Sheila Dixit, as Chief Minister of the GNCT, decided to divide the Delhi Municipal Corporation into three separate corporations with the unstated goal of improving her party's chances of gaining access to power. Creating three municipalities tripled salary expenses for political officials and the upper echelons of municipal administration without increasing revenues for the already cash-strapped municipal government.[18]

Lack of coordination between the Delhi Development Authority (DDA), a central government agency responsible for planning and urban development in the Delhi region, and the DWB contributes to the ongoing capacity deficit for treating waste water. When the DDA plans and develops an area, it is responsible for including adequate infrastructure to meet the needs of that community. Often, its plans do not adequately account for population growth, and in some cases, it responds to political pressures to increase the ceiling for local floor area ratios. By the time that the DDA turns areas that it has developed over to the municipalities, the infrastructure is often inadequate to meet the needs of its population increasing the disparity between the waste generated by the population and the capacity to adequately process it.[19]

Delhi's complex governance also creates multiple regulators whose lack of coordination limits the effectiveness of efforts to protect the Yamuna. In March 2016, the Art of Living Foundation (AoL) chose the Yamuna river plane to hold its World Cultural Festival. The festival attracted 3.75 million people who viewed cultural performances on an immense stage spanning seven acres. According to an expert panel later constituted by the National Green Tribunal (NGT) to conduct a damage assessment, the event extended over 180 hectares. The panel found that the AoL's event degraded the flood plains topography, dissipated local water bodies and wetlands, and destroyed vegetation and biodiversity. It estimated that it would take ten years to restore the flood plan at a cost of more than Rs. 420 million. The festival was held despite that fact that in January 2015 the NGT had prohibited any new construction on the Yamuna flood plain under the Maily Se Nirmal Yamuna Revitalization Project, 2017 that it had ordered to rejuvenate the Yamuna. The AoL approached the DDA which reportedly initially denied permission to hold the festival on the Yamuna, but ultimately permitted the use of 24.46 hectares. A month before the festival, the NGT ruled that it was unable to ban the event, but it imposed a Rs. 5 million interim fine. The NGT, after receiving the report of the expert panel, is holding proceedings to determine if there should be an additional fine. Representatives of the AoL contest the findings of the expert panel's report. AoL leader Sri Sri Ravi Shankar declared that the AoL had obtained all the necessary permissions, and charged "If, at all, any fine has to be levied, it should be levied on the Centre and state governments and the NGT itself, for giving permission."[20]

III. Mechanisms of Coordination that Might Alleviate the Yamuna's Degradation

There are four mechanisms that have the potential to address the challenge of coordinating Delhi's complex governance to effectively alleviate the Yamuna's degradation. Extending the authority of key administrators across the boundaries of government agencies is a one strategy for administrative coordination. By the spring 2017, this approach has played an important role in addressing the challenges of administrative coordination in the GNCT. Keshav Chandra served as the Chief Executive of the Delhi Jal Board, Secretary of the Department of Irrigation and Flood Control, and Secretary, Environment and Forest, in Department of Environment. He is also serving as chairman of the Delhi Pollution Control Board, though he holds this position on an ad hoc basis. By exercising authority in these positions, he will play a key role in coordinating the efforts of these GNCT departments who play a key role in the efforts to vitalize Delhi's Yamuna. Nonetheless, coordination between the GNCT and the central government remains beyond the scope of this approach.

A second strategy involves creating administrative mechanisms to coordinate different government agencies and bridge the divide between different government levels. In 2007 a High Powered Committee for Yamuna River Development was constituted, and in 2010, it recommended the establishment of the Yamuna River Development Authority to coordinate the efforts to clean up the Yamuna by government agencies at the Central and GNCT levels.[21] Yet even during the period when the Congress part controlled both the central and Delhi governments, neither the High Powered Committee nor the YRDA succeeded in coordinating action to revitalize Delhi's Yamuna.[22] In August 2015, Delhi Chief Minister, Arvind Kejriwal and Union Water Resources Minister Uma Bharti announced that they had reached an agreement to forming a special purpose vehicle (SPV) to coordinate government efforts to revitalize the Yamuna.[23] To this date, the proposal remains still-born, an apparent victim of the central government's reluctance to fund the SPV and the political enmity between Kejriwal's Aam Admi Party and Bharti's Bharatiya Janata Party.[24] Nonetheless, establishing an SPV remains an attractive option, and the Delhi Water Board is promoting a new proposal to create an SPV named the Delhi Yamuna River Rejuvenation Corporation Ltd.[25]

In the context of these coordination problems, programs involving coordination among agencies at different governmental levels, such as the Yamuna Action Plans have not been successful.

Despite the fierce rivalry the Bharatiya Janata Party and the Aam Admi Party, the central and GNCT governments joined together to launch Phase 3 of the Yamuna Action Plan in May 2016. The new plan follows two earlier phases that achieved very limited success. Phase 3 consists of eight schemes including rehabilitating parts of the sewer system, enhancing the efficiency of sewage treatment plants, bringing in a garbage skimmer, and renovating Chhat Ghat where pilgrims worship alongside the river.[26] However, this "hardware approach" has critics who point out that among other things it fails to address the problem of waste coming from the almost 50 percent of Delhi's population that is outside of the sewage system.[27]

Judicial institutions, in particular, India's Supreme Court and the National Green Tribunal (NGT), comprise a third mechanism for coordinating government agencies and redressing the deficiencies in their efforts to protect Delhi's Yamuna. The Supreme Court has periodically issued rulings on efforts to revitalize the Yamuna ever since 1995 when it responded to public interest litigation by directing the Union Ministry of Forests and Environment to sanction sewage treatment plants for the river. In response to public interest litigation, the Supreme Court continues to intervene in an effort to make the government's efforts to ameliorate the Yamuna's degradation more effective. For instance, in February 2017, it ordered all industrial units in the Delhi area to have their primary effluent treatment plants operational within three months,[28] and it directed the DWB to draft a comprehensive report on the operation of interceptor sewage projects and sewage treatment plants.[29]

The NGT was established in 2010 as a forum that combines judicial, administrative, and technical expertise to address environmental matters. Usually in response to public interest litigation from NGOs, the NGT has issued many orders impacting efforts to revitalize Delhi's Yamuna, including penalizing religious groups for the environmental damages that their events have inflicted, imposing fines on individuals dumping garbage into the Yamuna, issuing orders requiring the improvement of STP efficiency, etc.[30] In response to a plea brought before it by the NGO, Yamuna Jiya Abhiyaan, the NGT authorized the Maily Se Nirmal Yamuna Revitalization Project, 2017–a promising initiative that mandates cooperation among the DWB, DDA, Ministry of Urban Development, and National Mission for Clean Ganga to curb pollution by banning on construction on the Yamuna's flood plain and setting up 15 sewage treatment plants. Implementation of the plan has been frustratingly slow with very little impact on the Yamuna as of the end of spring 2017. The NGT has repeatedly convened hearings on the plan and formed investigative committees in an effort to expedite its progress.

The Supreme Court and NGT–usually in response to public interest litigation–have made valuable contributions in ensuring that environmental interests are taken into account. Without their actions, these interests would likely remain mere externalities for powerful political groups and government agencies. These judicial institutions take actions that attempt to narrow the gap between policy objectives and policy outcomes that so often characterize policy implementation in India. However, they frequently face difficulties in spurring dynamic action by government agencies, and they have had limited success in promoting their coordination. Like all judicial institutions, the Supreme Court and NGT respond to problems rather than preventing them, and their agenda is limited by the capacity of social groups to secure effective legal representation.

India's democratic elections are the fourth mechanism that may help to overcome the coordination problems. The centrality of development issues in the 2014 general elections and the apparent support among the Delhi electorate for anti-corruption politics are two indications that elections might motivate government agencies to more effectively protect Delhi's Yamuna. At the same time, the mounting electoral power of privileged interests might lead to continued degradation of the Yamuna. Even if its political leaders are motivated to make serious efforts to revitalize the Yamuna, it is not clear that Delhi's governance institutions have the fiscal ability to provide the necessary infrastructure or the administrative capacity to manage it efficiently.

IV. Conclusion

Although policy authorities have attempted to ameliorate the degradation of Delhi's Yamuna for two decades, their efforts to alleviate the problem have met with limited success. The complex nature of the problem is an important reason for the shortcomings. Effective solutions require increased river flow; curtailing the dumping of sewage, industrial effluents, and solid wastes; and ending encroachments on the Yamuna's flood plain. The recent activism of NGO's, the judicial institutions, and more dynamic leadership both within the elected institutions and the government agencies raises hopes that efforts to revitalize Delhi's Yamuna a priority will be more successful. The government has allocated more resources to addressing the problem than ever before. However, revitalizing the Delhi's Yamuna will require not only a substantial investment of resources, but a multi-pronged effort coordinating agencies across multiple levels of the government. It will also require sensitivity to a range of political interests, including those groups without effective legal representation. The success of the most recent initiatives hangs in the balance.

Bibliography

1 I use a conservative estimate of the expenditures on the Yamuna from Neha Lalchandani & Jayashree Nandi, "Yamuna cleans up Rs 2000 crore from govt coffers in 22 years!" The Economic Times (February 23, 2017). Other estimates range as high as Rs. 44 billion. See Amit Anand Chaudhary, "Yamuna pollution: Supreme Court seeks report on sewage treatment plants," The Economic Times (February 21, 2017).

2 "AAP govt 200-cr-Yamuna riverfront-plan," Indian Express (October 27, 2016).

3 Planning Department, Government of NCT of Delhi, Economic Survey of Delhi 2016-17 p. 183. Available from http://www.delhi.gov.in/wps/wcm/connect/DoIT_Planning/planning/whats_new/economic+survey+of+delhi+2016+-+2017. Accessed on June 20, 2017.

4 This statistic was cited by India's Supreme Court. See Dhananjay Mahapatra, "Half of Delhi's population lives in slums," Times of India (October 4, 2012).

5 Economic Survey of Delhi 2016-17 p. 183.

6 Report of the Fourth Delhi Finance Commission, (Delhi, March 2013) pp. 214-15 available at http://delhi.gov.in/DoIT/DOIT/fdfc/DFC_Final_Report_2013.pdf. Accessed on August 8, 2016.

7 Report of the Fourth Delhi Finance Commission, (Delhi, March 2013) p. 56.

8 Om Prakash Mathur, "New Delhi, India," in Enid Slack and Rupak Chattopadhyay (eds.) Finance and Governance of Capital Cities in Federal Systems (Montreal: Queens University Press, 2009) p. 156.

9 Isher Judge Ahluwalia, "Cities at crossroads: When an open door policy is not enough," Indian Express (March 29, 2017).

10 Ibid., p. 156.

11 Om Prakash Mathur, "New Delhi, India," pp. 144-150.

12 The structure of Delhi's local urban government has always been complex. Governance occurred through the Delhi Municipal Corporation (DMC), the New Delhi Municipal Corporation, and the Delhi Cantonment Board until 2012 when the DMC was divided into three municipal corporations. For an insightful study of municipal finances in Delhi see, Simanti Bandyopadhya, "Local government finance: challenges in revenue raising at the Municipal Corporation of Delhi," Commonwealth Journal of Local Governance 16 (May 2015) pp. 60-84.

13 Author's calculations using DWB budget data from Economic Survey of Delhi 2016-17 p. 196 and data on the wholesale price index for all commodities from Reserve Bank of India, Handbook of Statistics on Indian Economy 2015-16, Table 40.

14 Whether or not Delhi is being treated equitably under the 1994 Upper River Yamuna Board Memorandum of Understanding and the 1998 Supreme Court order, the share set aside for Delhi is insufficient to meet Delhi's rapidly growing water needs in the new millennium. For opposition to the current arrangement see: Report of the Fourth Delhi Finance Commission pp. 50-54; and "Restoration and Conservation of River Yamuna: Final Report," submitted to the National Green Tribunal," 2013, p. 63. Available at: http://delhi.gov.in/wps/wcm/

connect/55a9380047b2199a9155d5bdc775c0fb/Final_Report_NGT-Yamuna_Restoration%2B%2811-4-2014%29.pdf?-MOD=AJPERES&lmod=-287594179. Accessed on August 8, 2016.

15 For instance, see: "Sanitation workers strike: AAP-BJP fight as Delhi stinks," Indian Express January 8, 2017; "East, North Delhi Municipal Corporations Call Off 16-Day Strike," NDTV (February 11, 2016); and Tarique Anwar, "Garbage politics 2.0: Delhi's sanitation workers to go on another strike from 26 June," First Post (June 20, 2015).

16 Report of the Fourth Delhi Finance Commission p. 186.

17 "AAP government sitting on plan to revive Yamuna, Says Uma Bharti," Times of India, 20 April 2017.

18 Ankita Sharma , "Delhi Polls: Delhi in Decay," Governance Now (April 16, 2017). Also see Arpula Singh, "MCD Trifurcation: A Failed Experiment, Or is There Hope Yet?" Huff Post (January 3, 2017) Accessed at http://www.huffingtonpost.in/apula-singh/mcd-trifurcation-a-failed-experiment-or-is-there-hope-yet_a_21646206/ on June 22, 2017.

19 Interview with Om Prakash Mathur, Institute of Social Sciences, New Delhi, July 20, 2016.

20 The best account of these events can be found in Sowmiya Ashok, "Hardlook: A look at the troubled waters of Yamuna floodplains one year after World Culture Festival," Indian Express (May 1, 2017).

21 "Yamuna development authority gets LG nod," The Times of India (July 31, 2010).

22 Nivedita Khandekar,"No Yamuna Authority Two Years After Panel Report," Hindustan Times (August 30, 2012).

23 "Centre, Delhi agree on legal entity to clean up Yamuna," The Times of India (August 9, 2015).

24 Shagun Kapil, "Kejri-Centre's clean Yamuna project going nowhere," Deccan Herald (February 12, 2016); and "Yamuna is dirty because Modi hates Kejriwal!" Governance Now (March 11, 2016).

25 Delhi Jal Board, GNCT of Delhi, "Creation of a Special Purpose Vehicle within the Yamuna River Development Authority for the effective Restoration and management of Yamuna River and its catchment," Delhi: (No date).

26 Damini Nath, "Yet another Yamuna action plan," The Hindu May 8, 2016.

27 Puja Bhattacharjee, "River Rejuvenation: And Unquiet Flows the Yamuna," Governance Now (May 16, 2016).

28 Samanwaya Rautray, "Get effluent treatment plants running in 3 months: Supreme Court diktat to industrial bodies," The Economic Times (February 24, 2017).

29 Amit Anand Choudhary, "Yamuna pollution: Supreme Court seeks report on sewage treatment plants," The Economic Times (February 21, 2017).

30 Ritam Halder, "2 new committees to oversee Yamuna cleaning," Hindustan Times (August 6, 2016);" "NGT meets govt agencies to discuss Yamuna revival plan," Hindustan Times (August 4, 2016); and NGT meet to check STP plan growth," The Times of India (August 3, 2016).

THE YAMUNA IN DELHI

Delhi's history is replete with accounts of the Yamuna as a generator of cultural and civic rituals; it was a public amenity that was considered sacrosanct. The God Krishna is depicted by the banks of the river and Mughal monuments celebrate the architectural union of land and water in profound expressions of buildings and gardens oriented towards the river. However, the advent of the new capital city by Sir Edward Lutyens and Herbert Baker began the process of dis-engagement with the river. It became a resource for water and no longer acknowledged the religious and secular rituals that were embedded in the historic life of the city. In colonial times New Delhi would rely on the water's commodification—an element to be piped, stored and dispensed from taps, without giving any architectural credence to the geography of its presence.

Neglect characterizes the present day city—it teems with a rapidly-increasing population, scant resources and even worse resource-management, and poor infrastructure. It lacks a holistic urban design that could accommodate the many levels of life that ought to co-exist with the river. In refusing to create a vision for this critical relationship between land and water, between habitation and ecology, New Delhi is in a very real emerging crisis—a rapid transition from a city without clean water for all its citizens to a city without any clean water at all.

Yamuna River

Satellite Images: Esri, Digital Globe, GeoEye,
Earthstar Geographies, CNES/Airbus DS, USDA,
USGS, AeroGRID, IGN and GIS User Community

1 - Unpolluted Yamuna and floodplain

2 - Floodplain Encroachment

The Dead Yamuna River

The Dead River

Over its lifetime, the Yamuna River has witnessed natural and human forces—at points hemmed in, dug up, or barricaded. Today, the river suffers in a critical state of degradation and at times is completely dead. Most of the Yamuna's original water flow is diverted far north of Delhi and the water that flows through Delhi today largely comes from drains. The depth the river averages 0.6 meters during non-monsoon periods only to widens considerably during the monsoon and reach an average depth of 2.5 meters. At its non monsoon depth, the water cannot move with enough force to flush out algae and sediment or even properly dilute the sewage pouring out of the drains. To do so would require far more of its original flow, meaning Delhi would have to allow more of its drinking supply to continue downstream, or Haryana and Uttar Pradesh would have to take less water out of the system via the Western and Eastern Yamuna Canals.

5 - Okhla Barrage

3 - Wazirabad Barrage and The Najafgarh Drain

4 - Old Delhi and Floodplain Encroachment

NEW DELHI IS IN A VERY REAL EMERGING CRISIS–A RAPID TRANSITION FROM A CITY WITHOUT CLEAN WATER FOR ALL ITS CITIZENS TO A CITY WITHOUT ANY CLEAN WATER AT ALL.

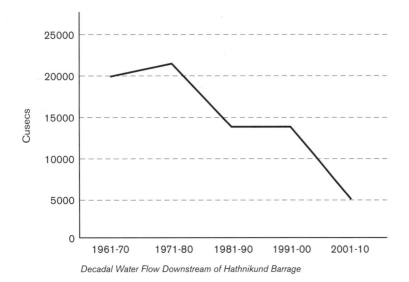

Decadal Water Flow Downstream of Hathnikund Barrage

The Yamuna Floodplain

As an increasing amount of water is diverted at the Hathnikund Barrage for the Western and Eastern Yamuna Canals the amount of water flowing downstream through the Yamuna has decreased; today much of the Yamuna is a dry river bed. In Delhi, during the eight months of the dry season, the Yamuna is fed mainly through a trickle of sewage and waste runoff from the city. As the city's water used increases dry season water levels in the river rise due to greater amounts of untreated water being dumped into the river. Consequently, flood waters are also rising during the monsoon season.

6th Century	—	Delhi Founded
16th Century ①	—	Humayun's Tomb Constructed
17th Century ②	—	Shahjahanabad and Red Fort constructed by Shah Jahan of the Mughal empire
1803	—	Delhi Falls to the British
1857	—	British quell the Delhi Rebellion
1890 ③	—	Civil Lines constructed by the British
1921 ④	—	Lutyens' New Delhi construction completed. City turns away from the river
1930 ⑤	—	Chandrawl WTP constructed
1955 ⑥	—	Major embankments constructed to prevent flooding, flood plain is narrowed
⑦	—	Wazirabad and Okhla Barrages constructed
⑧	—	Drains and Canals built, most sewage empties into the Yamuna River
1962 ⑨	—	Wazirabad WTP constructed
1975 ⑩	—	Development of Transyamuna, Noida, New Delhi, and Faridabad along the river bank
	—	Water treatment plants expanded in North Delhi
⑪	—	Slums develop near the Okhla Barrage
1990 ⑫	—	Okhla Bird Sanctuary Founded
2001 ⑬	—	Yamuna Bank Metro Station is built directly on the floodplain
⑭	—	DND Flyway Completed
2002 ⑮	—	Yamuna Biodiversity Park Founded
2004 ⑯	—	Signature Bridge Announced
2006 ⑰	—	Sonia Vihar WTP constructed
2010 ⑱	—	Commonwealth Games Village is built directly on the floodplain

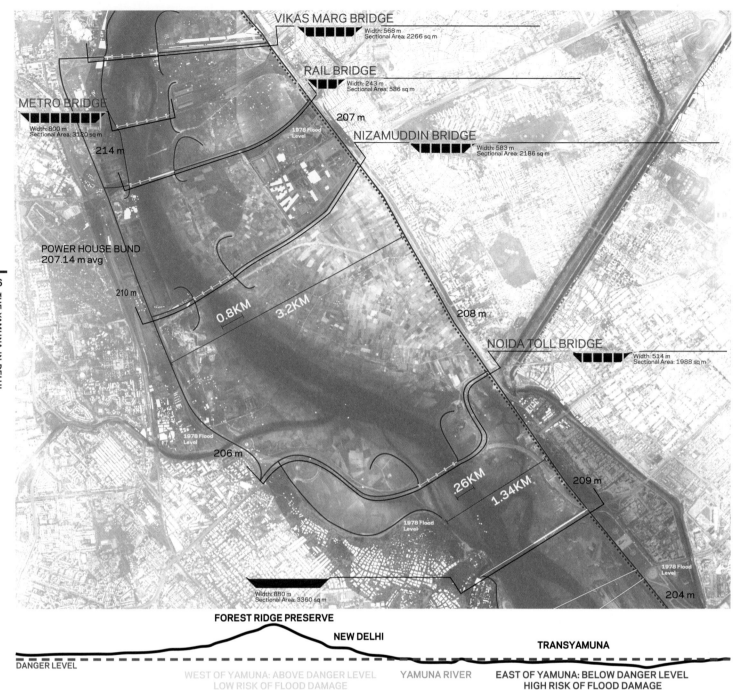

VIKAS MARG BRIDGE
Width: 568 m
Sectional Area: 2266 sq m

RAIL BRIDGE
Width: 243 m
Sectional Area: 586 sq m

METRO BRIDGE
Width: 800 m
Sectional Area: 3120 sq m

207 m

NIZAMUDDIN BRIDGE
Width: 583 m
Sectional Area: 2186 sq m

214 m

1978 Flood Level

POWER HOUSE BUND
207.14 m avg

210 m

0.8KM   3.2KM

208 m

NOIDA TOLL BRIDGE
Width: 514 m
Sectional Area: 1988 sq m

1978 Flood Level

206 m

.26KM   1.34KM

209 m

1978 Flood Level

1978 Flood Level

204 m

Width: 880 m
Sectional Area: 3360 sq m

FOREST RIDGE PRESERVE

NEW DELHI

TRANSYAMUNA

DANGER LEVEL

WEST OF YAMUNA: ABOVE DANGER LEVEL
LOW RISK OF FLOOD DAMAGE

YAMUNA RIVER

EAST OF YAMUNA: BELOW DANGER LEVEL
HIGH RISK OF FLOOD DAMAGE

Floodplain Encroachment

Yamuna River

Flood Impacted Infrastructure

Embankments

River Crossings

Bridges and other large infrastructures create obstructions in the river. This decreases the effective width of the floodplain and increases the speed of water during monsoon floods. This in turn taxes crossing structures, embankments, dredges the river bottom, and erodes riverbanks, accentuating the Yamuna's destruction.

During Mughal times, construction was constrained to the floodplain's high ground on rgw west bank. Since then, urban encroachment has expanded on both sides of the river. The encroachment of the river through the occupation of its natural terrain produces not only ecological damage but also potential hazards for population and basic

urban infrastructures. Following devastating floods in 1978, the Central Water Commission stated that the floodplain should really be kept clear of all barriers for a 5 km width alongside the river, despite the fact that for many years the widest portion of the floodplain measured only 3.5 km. Nevertheless, in 1999, the Delhi Metro Rail Corporation built a depot, a station, and an IT park right on the riverbed in the northeast. Subsequently the massive Akshardham Temple and its surrounding complex were constructed, followed by the Commonwealth Games Village, the Delhi Transco 16-hectare power station, another DMRC depot, yard, station, and most recently, a metro line at Yamuna Bank. Today, portions of the floodplain narrow to as much as 0.64 km.

HOW CAN THE YAMUNA RETURN TO ITS TRADITIONAL PLACE AS A CENTER OF URBAN LIFE?

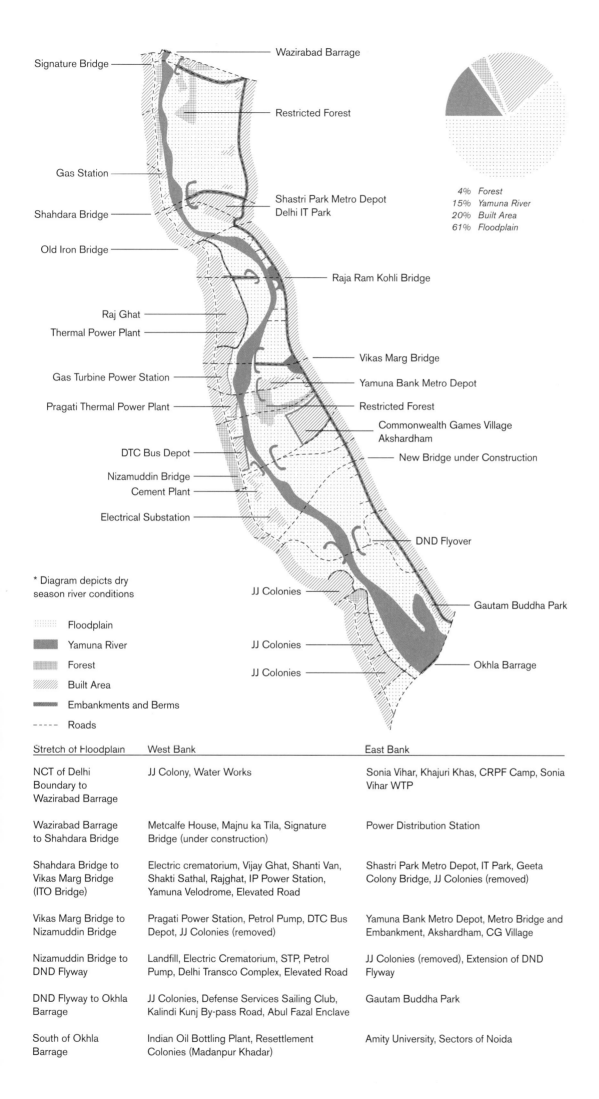

Signature Bridge
Wazirabad Barrage
Restricted Forest
Gas Station
Shastri Park Metro Depot
Delhi IT Park
Shahdara Bridge
Old Iron Bridge
Raja Ram Kohli Bridge
Raj Ghat
Thermal Power Plant
Vikas Marg Bridge
Gas Turbine Power Station
Yamuna Bank Metro Depot
Pragati Thermal Power Plant
Restricted Forest
Commonwealth Games Village
Akshardham
DTC Bus Depot
New Bridge under Construction
Nizamuddin Bridge
Cement Plant
Electrical Substation
DND Flyover
JJ Colonies
Gautam Buddha Park
JJ Colonies
JJ Colonies
Okhla Barrage

4%   Forest
15% Yamuna River
20% Built Area
61% Floodplain

* Diagram depicts dry
season river conditions

Floodplain
Yamuna River
Forest
Built Area
Embankments and Berms
Roads

Stretch of Floodplain	West Bank	East Bank
NCT of Delhi Boundary to Wazirabad Barrage	JJ Colony, Water Works	Sonia Vihar, Khajuri Khas, CRPF Camp, Sonia Vihar WTP
Wazirabad Barrage to Shahdara Bridge	Metcalfe House, Majnu ka Tila, Signature Bridge (under construction)	Power Distribution Station
Shahdara Bridge to Vikas Marg Bridge (ITO Bridge)	Electric crematorium, Vijay Ghat, Shanti Van, Shakti Sathal, Rajghat, IP Power Station, Yamuna Velodrome, Elevated Road	Shastri Park Metro Depot, IT Park, Geeta Colony Bridge, JJ Colonies (removed)
Vikas Marg Bridge to Nizamuddin Bridge	Pragati Power Station, Petrol Pump, DTC Bus Depot, JJ Colonies (removed)	Yamuna Bank Metro Depot, Metro Bridge and Embankment, Akshardham, CG Village
Nizamuddin Bridge to DND Flyway	Landfill, Electric Crematorium, STP, Petrol Pump, Delhi Transco Complex, Elevated Road	JJ Colonies (removed), Extension of DND Flyway
DND Flyway to Okhla Barrage	JJ Colonies, Defense Services Sailing Club, Kalindi Kunj By-pass Road, Abul Fazal Enclave	Gautam Buddha Park
South of Okhla Barrage	Indian Oil Bottling Plant, Resettlement Colonies (Madanpur Khadar)	Amity University, Sectors of Noida

+ 203 M

This water level during the monsoon is considered safe.

BECAUSE OF
CLIMATE CHANGE,
CURRENT STATISTICAL
CALCULATIONS ARE
UNDER SCRUTINY.
PREDICTIONS ARE
PROVING CHALLENGING
AND CHANCES OF
MASSIVE AND SUDDEN
RAINS ARE BECOMING
NOTABLY HIGHER.

+ 206 M

At this level, the Yamuna courses within the built city on the lower west bank beyond the informal settlement, and reaches higher embankments which are near capacity.

+ 204 M

At this stage, most of the low-lying areas are flooded and the water begin to spread into the city at gaps in the embankments. This level is considered the danger zone.

+ 205 M

The floodwaters submerge a major informal settlement on the lower west bank.

+ 207 M

In 1978, Delhi experienced the worst floor in its history at a record 207.49m level. The official death toll was 3,800.

+ 208 M

This mark represents the 100-year flood, defined as the 1% probability that the flood will occur in any given year. 100-year flood markers are common standards for design and construction. All current embankments are predicted to fail at this level.

THE CONSEQUENCES
OF STEADY FLOODPLAIN
ENCROACHMENT
ARE SEVERE. THE
EMBANKMENTS WILL
FAIL DURING A 100-YEAR
FLOOD EVENT, WIPING
OUT STRUCTURES BUILT
IN LOW LYING AREAS
OF THE FLOODPLAIN
AND INUNDATING EAST
DELHI WITH WATER.
THIS SCENARIO
IS UNAVOIDABLE
UNLESS SIGNIFICANT
INTERVENTIONS ARE
TAKEN TO RE-DESIGN
DELHI'S WATERWAYS.

Typical Yamuna Water Level

Normal Yearly Flood Zone
(+ 202 m)

Flooding Danger Level
(+ 204.8 m)

Level that all Embankments Fail
(+ 209 m)

Embankments

Flooded Buildings
(normal/danger/extreme)

Roads and Railroads
(flooded/unharmed)

Cart Paths
(flooded/unharmed)

Inaccessible Yamuna

Although the floodplain has been claimed for informal settlements and cultivation, the river's edge has not been utilized for formal use, public or private. The space is left as a dumping ground for the city's industry, solid waste, and energy infrastructures and almost fully occupied by heavily trafficked roads, railroads, large infrastructural developments, and informal settlements surrounding the polluted Yamuna. These infrastructures leave the river, once the center of urban life, largely inaccessible.

Yet devotees regularly find their way to formalize ghats to gather on the banks of the Yamuna to perform religious ceremonies. Despite government interdicts against throwing religious objects in the river, thousands gather at least twice a year to interact with the river by bathing and immersing statues and offerings. It is not at all uncommon for several people to drown in the course of these events, although police attempt to bar people from deeper waters and to rescue those in danger. These religious adherents are firm in their belief that the Yamuna is the main stage of Delhi, not "the topographical underbelly of the metropolis" as it has become in modern times.

Redevelopment plans for the waterfront have focused on concretizing the ghats, where the land and the river meet. But a reverence for the river, for its sacredness as well as its environmental significance for the ecological health of Delhi, might maximize the flourishing of the floodplains on both sides while still creating ample, safe space for religious observances to continue unimpeded.

Millennium Park Bus Depot

Train Tracks + Stations

Ring Road

Elevated Rail Bridge

Embankments

Power Station

Open Drains

TO NEW DELHI

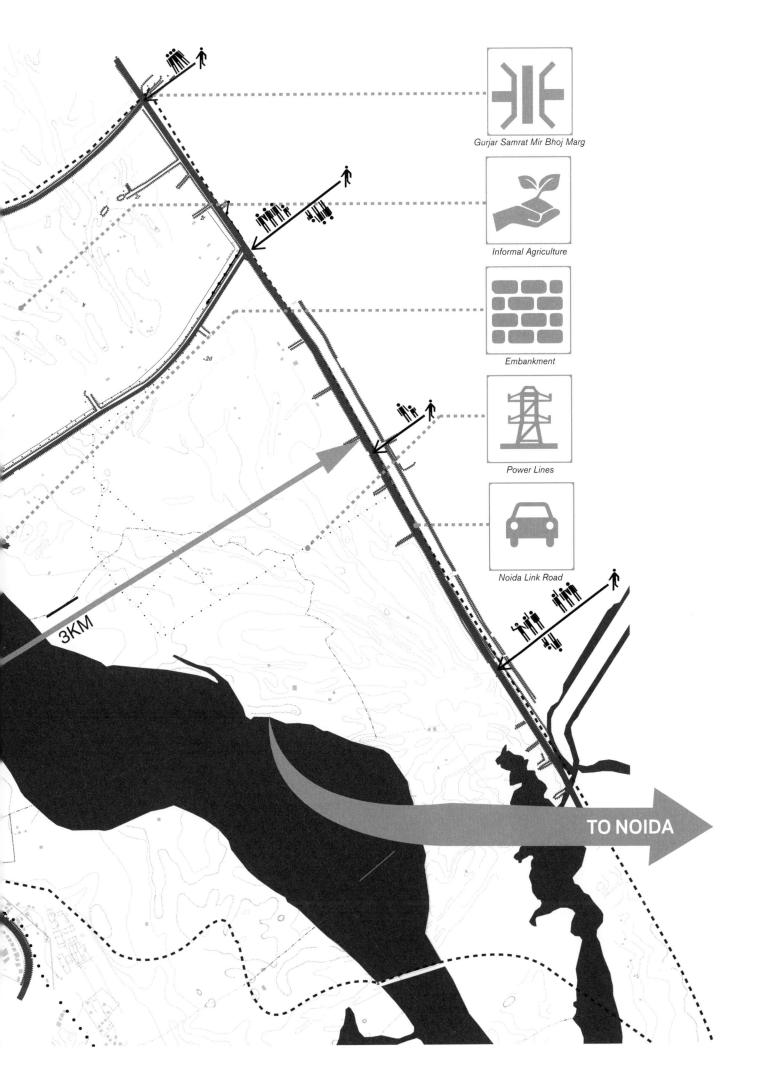

Gurjar Samrat Mir Bhoj Marg

Informal Agriculture

Embankment

Power Lines

Noida Link Road

3KM

TO NOIDA

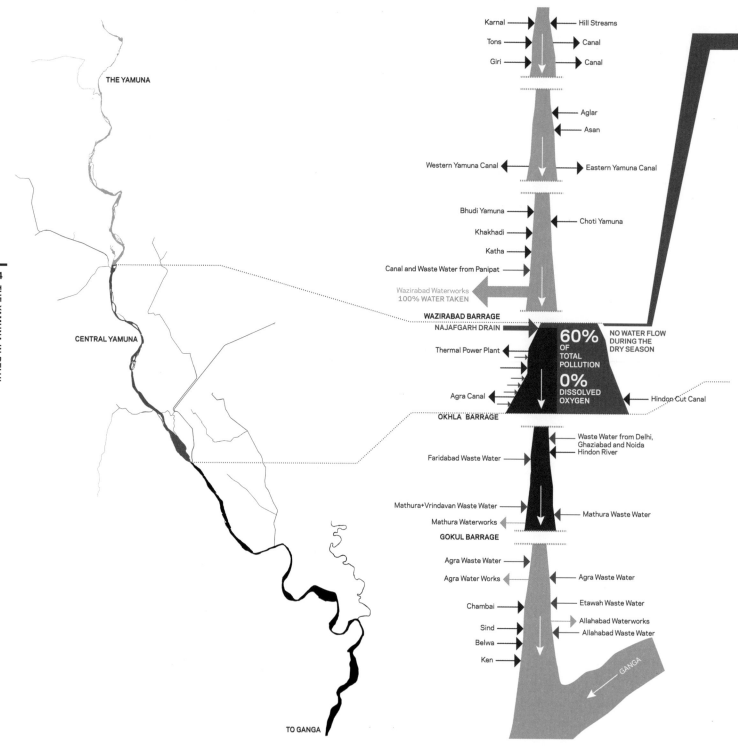

THE YAMUNA

CENTRAL YAMUNA

TO GANGA

Karnal — Hill Streams
Tons — Canal
Giri — Canal

Aglar
Asan

Western Yamuna Canal — Eastern Yamuna Canal

Bhudi Yamuna — Choti Yamuna
Khakhadi
Katha
Canal and Waste Water from Panipat

Wazirabad Waterworks
100% WATER TAKEN

WAZIRABAD BARRAGE
NAJAFGARH DRAIN

60% OF TOTAL POLLUTION

NO WATER FLOW DURING THE DRY SEASON

Thermal Power Plant

0% DISSOLVED OXYGEN

Agra Canal — Hindon Cut Canal

OKHLA BARRAGE

Waste Water from Delhi, Ghaziabad and Noida
Hindon River
Faridabad Waste Water

Mathura+Vrindavan Waste Water — Mathura Waste Water
Mathura Waterworks

GOKUL BARRAGE

Agra Waste Water
Agra Water Works — Agra Waste Water
Chambai — Etawah Waste Water
— Allahabad Waterworks
Sind — Allahabad Waste Water
Belwa
Ken

GANGA

The Cut and the Najafgarh Drain

Flowing 853 miles from the Himalayan Mountains to its confluence with the Ganges River, the Yamuna is the sole supplier of water for over sixty million people in India. Man-made pollution has rendered the Yamuna so inundated with human feces, industrial effluents, and irrigation chemical runoff that there is zero dissoluble oxygen content and no aquatic life in parts of the river that run through Delhi. As the population of India continues to increase, water pollution poses major risks for human health. During the dry season, when the Yamuna reaches Delhi at the Wazirabad Barrage, 100% of the natural flow of the river is cut. Sewage, wastewater, and trash from the Najafgarh Drain becomes the new flow. A quantitative relationship between Biochemical Oxygen Demand (BOD) load and the response in Dissolved Oxygen (DO) must be established for the Yamuna River near Delhi to accurately measure the health of the river. Typical qualitative models are not suitable for this situation because they can not calculate instances when dissolved oxygen becomes zero. Therefore, an enhanced BOD/DO model has been developed and tested with point source data from municipal, industrial, and urban drains.

1.6% (22km)
of the length of the Yamuna River is the Delhi segment, stretching from the Wazirabad to Okhla Barrage.

Organic Matter (BOD) Loads from Delhi Area Drains, May 2015

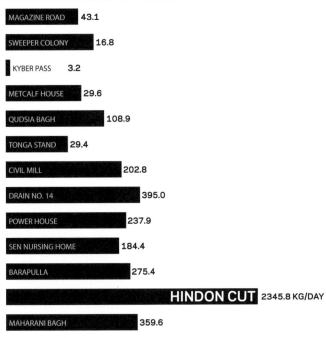

MAGAZINE ROAD	43.1
SWEEPER COLONY	16.8
KYBER PASS	3.2
METCALF HOUSE	29.6
QUDSIA BAGH	108.9
TONGA STAND	29.4
CIVIL MILL	202.8
DRAIN NO. 14	395.0
POWER HOUSE	237.9
SEN NURSING HOME	184.4
BARAPULLA	275.4
HINDON CUT	2345.8 KG/DAY
MAHARANI BAGH	359.6

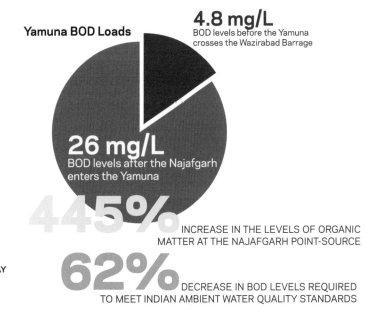

Yamuna BOD Loads

4.8 mg/L
BOD levels before the Yamuna crosses the Wazirabad Barrage

26 mg/L
BOD levels after the Najafgarh enters the Yamuna

445% INCREASE IN THE LEVELS OF ORGANIC MATTER AT THE NAJAFGARH POINT-SOURCE

62% DECREASE IN BOD LEVELS REQUIRED TO MEET INDIAN AMBIENT WATER QUALITY STANDARDS

Research Director: W. Lung, Professor of Civil and Environmental Engineering
Research Team: K. Carter, M. Grady, J. Johnson, E.McDuff, V. Tran, T. Zhang

100% OF YAMUNA WATER IS DIVERTED TO WAZIRABAD WATERWORKS

13.4 mg/L DISSOLVED O_2 PRIOR TO THE NAJAFGARH

OF TOTAL POLLUTION IN THE YAMUNA RIVER ORIGINATES FROM THE NAJAFGARH DRAIN

0.0 mg/L DISSOLVED O_2 AFTER THE NAJAFGARH

Satellite Images: Esri, Digital Globe, GeoEye, Earthstar Geographies, CNES/Airbus DS, USDA, USGS, AeroGRID, IGN and GIS User Community

As one of the most continuous linear systems of undeveloped space in the city, Delhi's urban waterways are a contested territory. A shortage of land in the urban core, combined with opportunistic infrastructure planning, has led to the layering of multiple infrastructures—including storm water, sewage, solid waste, electricity, and vehicular transportation—on top of the drain corridors. These infrastructure clogged urban arteries have in many cases precluded their use as public space, and caused adjacent neighborhoods to turn their backs to the drains. Only by providing a vision and sense of collective ownership for these drains can they be transformed to a source of ecological vitality and public space that they once knew.

—— Drains

Delhi's Drains

Before Delhi existed monsoon rains traveled down ridges and across plains, flowing into the Yamuna. Mughal architects only had to follow the resulting streams and rivers, installing tanks along their path, to store water for the dry months. Unlike sewer lines, which are designed to solve an urban problem, natural drains are an integral part of an ecosystem; if altered or removed the system can fall out of balance. A 1976 drainage map indicates 201 natural stormwater drains in Delhi. Yet, as the city grew, little attempt was made to preserve their function and drains became clogged with trash sludge. This impacts the city's ability to handle the torrential monsoon rains that occur during monsoon season. In a city full of people and concrete, a heavy rainfall can turn into a

disaster very quickly. Including artificial drains, there are around 1300 drains in Delhi, covering 1700 km. A thousand small storm drains flow into 22 main drains, most of which suffer from poor, broken, or absent lining, carrying a mixture of treated and untreated effluents into the Yamuna. Many settlements either lack a drain system or make due with cheaply built drains whose capacity is insufficient.

Waterlogged roads are common even for moderate downpours, and standing water causes the spread of waterborne diseases. Unfortunately, little can be done to remedy this situation without intense planning and coordination from numerous municipal bodies, government boards, and departments.

1 - Najafgarh Drain

2 - Mungashpur Drain Interceptor

3 - Najafgarh and Supplemental Drain Split

4 - Metro Green Line and National Railway

5 - Mahatma Gandhi Road

6 - Najafgarh and Supplemental Drain Confluence

7 - Wazirabad Barrage & Najafgarh Drain

*Satellite Images: Esri, Digital Globe, GeoEye,
Earthstar Geographies, CNES/Airbus DS, USDA,
USGS, AeroGRID, IGN and GIS User Community*

Najafgarh and Its Subdrains

Just as the Yamuna River bisects Delhi from north to south the Najafgarh Drain bisects Delhi from west to east. The Najafgarh serves as a continuous river of trash, sludge, sewage, and other effluents that bring adverse consequences to human habitation and the built environment.

For these reasons the Najafgarh is treated as a backyard to urban Delhi, but its wide banks and spacious open areas provide potential for a design that transforms the drain into a critical piece of public infrastructure. What is known as the Najafgarh Drain in Delhi is really the Sahibi River, originating near Jaipur in Rajasthan. An ephemeral river, it may run dry; but during the monsoon it is an important source of water in an arid region. In Delhi the Sahibi used to feed the Najafgarh Lake, which covered as much as 300 sq km. A natural shallow drain connected the lake to the Yamuna. The government decided in the 1960s to widen this natural drain and channel it, supposedly to prevent flooding from the lake. But the widening increased until the lake was no more. The lake bed became available for development, and the waterway became an liquid dump, collecting untreated sewage from tributary drains and depositing it all into the Yamuna just beyond Wazirabad, where the natural flow of the river is diverted. As Delhi continued to expand urban fabric engulfed the Najafgarh Drain.

1. Agricultural Land
2. Dwarka Water Treatment Plant
3. Gobind Singh Indraprastha University
4. Najafgarh Sewage Treatment Plant
5. Nilothi Sewage Treatment Plant
6. DDA Woodland Park at Hastsal
7. Nihal Vihar Park
8. Keshopur Park
9. Paschim Vihar District Park
10. Paschim Puri District Park
11. Chhatrapati Shivaji Park
12. Vir Savarkar Park and Herbal Garden
13. Karampura Industrial Area
14. Shastri Nagar District Park
15. Janak Vatika Park
16. Ashoka Garden
17. Gulabi Bagh Garden
18. Unassigned Space
19. Wazirabad Overlook

Najafgarh

Sewage Coverage: 10%
Sewage Generated: 7 MGD
Treatment Capacity: 5 MGD
Actual Treated: 1.5 MGD
Untreated Sewage: 5.5 MGD

Najafgarh Drain Neighborhoods

Because the Najafgarh Drain is so wide, and connections across it so few, it acts as a wall slicing Delhi apart. Like the Yamuna, the Najafgarh's smell and span reinforce boundaries and cause people and neighborhoods to turn away. Yet before Delhi, where the Najafgarh flows through rural Delhi, the drain still exists like a river, attracting birds and waterfowl. This atmosphere disappears as the drain approaches suburban Gurgaon where apartments rise precipitously over the waterway. The drain then rounds a sharp curve into the heart of Dwarka, the largest residential suburb in Asia. Fit into one bend is a large sewage treatment plant; in another, Guru Gobind Singh Indraprastha University. Opposite Dwarka is the mixed-income area Qutub Vihar, an industrial sector with considerable density. Bridges over the Najafgarh are spaced nearly 6 kilometers apart and prohibit people flowing between these neighborhoods. It is likely that the only people with much of a view of the water and its green borders are those who live in informal settlements on the drain edge and those whose high-rise apartments afford them a wide angle on the landscape. The most inviting stretch of the Najafgarh appears to be where it flows along the green campus of Delhi University. But by then dozens of tributary drains have filled it with domestic, industrial and agricultural waste. In the meantime it has brought little benefit to the neighborhoods it has crept behind, other than to carry away their sewage.

Dwarka

Sewage Coverage: 61%
Sewage Generated: 38.4 MGD
Treatment Capacity: 40 MGD
Actual Treated: 35 MGD
Untreated Sewage: 8.4 MGD

Keshopur

Sewage Coverage: 100%
Sewage Generated: 62 MGD
Treatment Capacity: 72 MGD
Actual Treated: 53.3 MGD
Untreated Sewage: 8.7 MGD

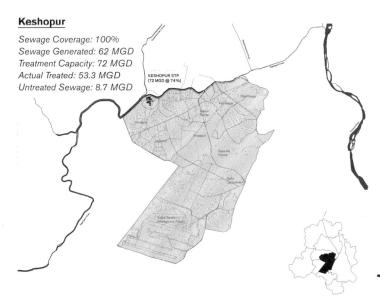

Nilothi

Sewage Coverage: 26%
Sewage Generated: 45 MGD
Treatment Capacity: 60 MGD
Actual Treated: 13.3 MGD
Untreated Sewage: 31.7 MGD

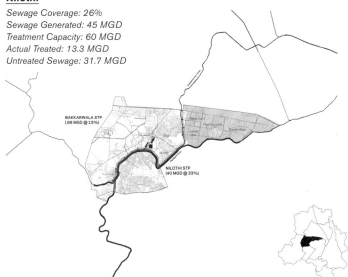

Rohini / Rithala

Sewage Coverage: 58.2%
Sewage Generated: 95 MGD
Treatment Capacity: 95 MGD
Actual Treated: 60 MGD
Untreated Sewage: 48 MGD

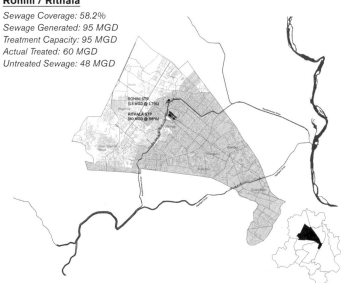

Coronation Pillar

Sewage Coverage: 49.5%
Sewage Generated: 55 MGD
Treatment Capacity: 30 MGD
Actual Treated: 19.2 MGD
Untreated Sewage: 35.8 MGD

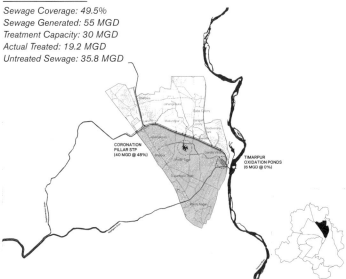

Delhi's Subdrain System

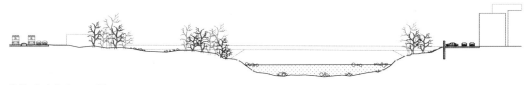

0. Typical drain condition.

1. Natural stream corridor.

2. Urban development begins to encroach.

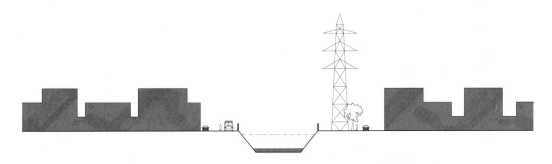

3. The sub-drain is channeled, increasing water velocity and disrupting ecosystems.

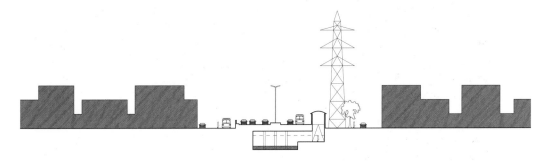

4. As urban land becomes more valuable the sub drains - existing linear corridors of
"open" land - becomes congested with multiple urban systems (energy, mobility, etc.).

Delhi's Nullahs

IF YOU LOOK BEYOND
THE WASTE AND IGNORE
THE SMELLS, DELHI'S
SUBDRAINS, OR NULLAHS,
BECOME A PASTORAL
LANDSCAPE. EXISTING
ALONGSIDE THE DENSITY
OF THE CITY THEY ARE
HIDDEN FROM VIEW,
OFFERING RESPITE AND
THE POTENTIAL FOR A NEW
SYSTEM OF GREEN PUBLIC
INFRASTRUCTURES WHICH
CONNECT THE CITY.

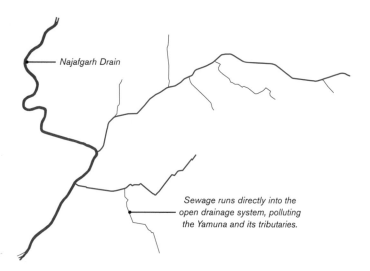

0 Original State

Najafgarh Drain

Sewage runs directly into the open drainage system, polluting the Yamuna and its tributaries.

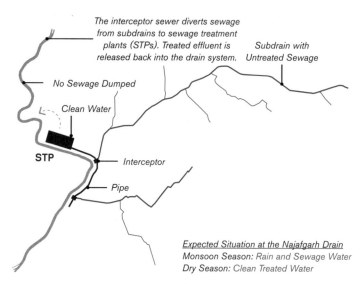

1 Primary Drain Catchment

The interceptor sewer diverts sewage from subdrains to sewage treatment plants (STPs). Treated effluent is released back into the drain system.

Subdrain with Untreated Sewage

No Sewage Dumped

Clean Water

STP

Interceptor

Pipe

Expected Situation at the Najafgarh Drain
Monsoon Season: Rain and Sewage Water
Dry Season: Clean Treated Water

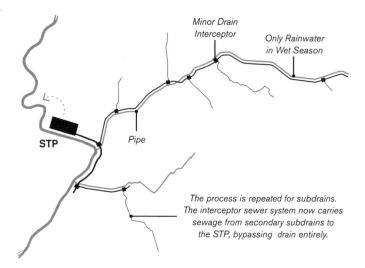

2 Sub-drain Catchment

Minor Drain Interceptor

Only Rainwater in Wet Season

STP

Pipe

The process is repeated for subdrains. The interceptor sewer system now carries sewage from secondary subdrains to the STP, bypassing drain entirely.

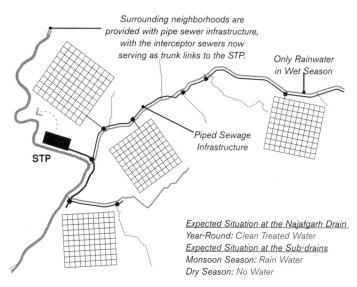

3 Complete Sewage Infrastructure

Surrounding neighborhoods are provided with pipe sewer infrastructure, with the interceptor sewers now serving as trunk links to the STP.

Only Rainwater in Wet Season

STP

Piped Sewage Infrastructure

Expected Situation at the Najafgarh Drain
Year-Round: Clean Treated Water
Expected Situation at the Sub-drains
Monsoon Season: Rain Water
Dry Season: No Water

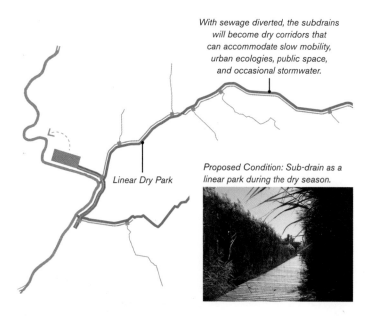

Dry Season Corridor

With sewage diverted, the subdrains will become dry corridors that can accommodate slow mobility, urban ecologies, public space, and occasional stormwater.

Linear Dry Park

Proposed Condition: Sub-drain as a linear park during the dry season.

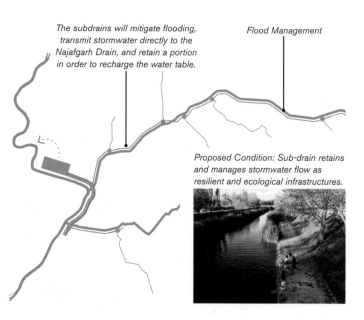

Monsoon Flow Management

The subdrains will mitigate flooding, transmit stormwater directly to the Najafgarh Drain, and retain a portion in order to recharge the water table.

Flood Management

Proposed Condition: Sub-drain retains and manages stormwater flow as resilient and ecological infrastructures.

The Interceptor Strategy

Delhi's urban waterways are contested territories where one must coordinate with up to six separate municipal agencies and private interests. The Delhi Jal Board is in the process of installing interceptor sewers along the subdrains to capture polluted water in the drain system and divert it to nearby sewage treatment plants. Piped sewage infrastructure will be installed in currently unsewered areas and the interceptor sewers will transport waste directly from buildings to treatment plants. This process of will effect 78 tributary drains that flow into the Najafgarh Drain and dramatically transform the function and character of the drain system. Subdrains will no longer contribute sewage to the Najafgarh, instead sewage treatment plants will become new urban springs, feeding the Najafgarh, and by extension the Yamuna, with treated effluent.

After interceptor implementation, sub-drains will revert to their natural function of handling stormwater and many will be dry channels for most of the year. Annual monsoons will require the subdrains to handle large volumes of water for short periods of time. Without a holistic urban design approach the new drain conditions will continue to be a major environmental and health hazard for millions of Delhi's inhabitants. The Najafgarh sub-drains need to be rethought as ecological linear parks during the dry season and designed to evacuate large amounts of storm water during the monsoon. The seasonal presence of water will create rich biodiversity corridors penetrating the city and connecting it with the Najafgarh River corridor.

WHAT WILL OCCUR DURING THE DRY SEASON? HOW CAN A DRAIN INTERVENTION STRATEGY PREVENT THE ACCUMULATION OF TRASH IN THE SUB-DRAINS WHEN THEY ARE NOT AT CAPACITY DURING THE MONSOON?

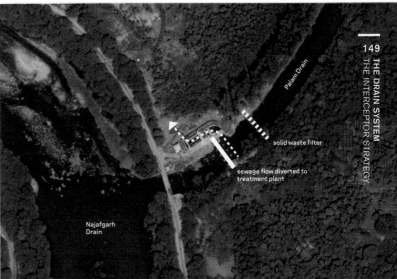

Palam Drain

solid waste filter

sewage flow diverted to treatment plant

Najafgarh Drain

build-up of solid waste is dredged daily

trash pickers from lowest castes salvage usable material

permeable barrier permits flow of liquid and small particulates

sewage diverted to Pappankalan STP via interceptor sewer

retractable barrier permits monsoon flow

THE REHABILITATION OF DELHI'S WATERWAYS REQUIRES A HOLISTIC APPROACH THAT CONSIDERS ALL OF THE CITY'S SYSTEMS IN CONJUNCTION.

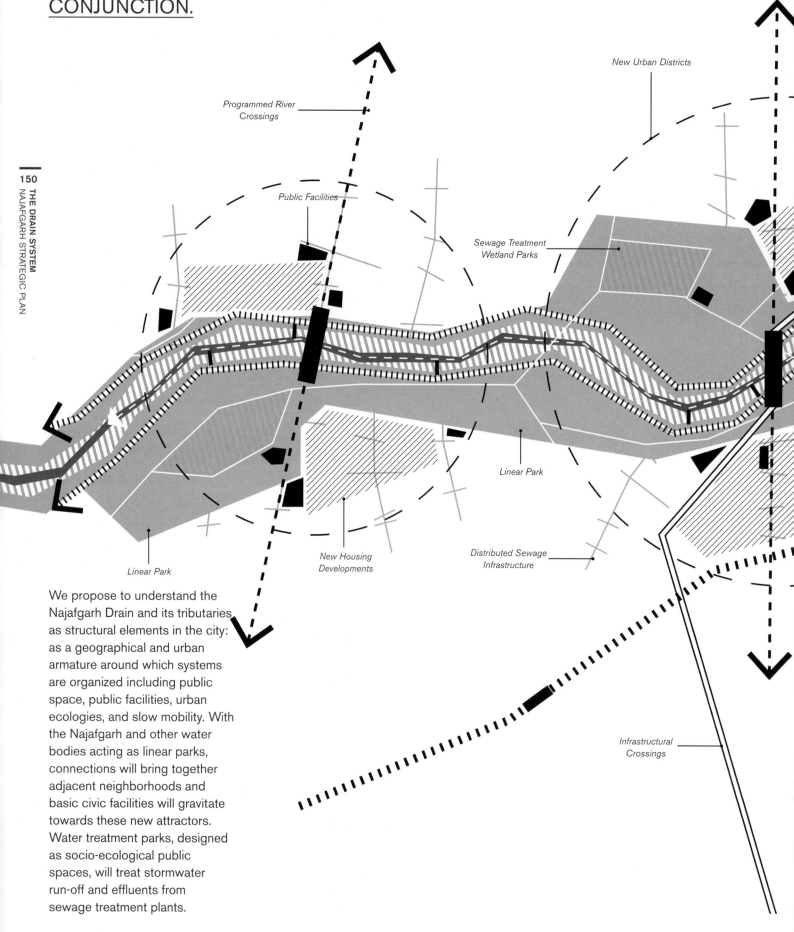

Programmed River
Crossings

New Urban Districts

Public Facilities

Sewage Treatment
Wetland Parks

Linear Park

Linear Park

New Housing
Developments

Distributed Sewage
Infrastructure

Infrastructural
Crossings

We propose to understand the Najafgarh Drain and its tributaries as structural elements in the city: as a geographical and urban armature around which systems are organized including public space, public facilities, urban ecologies, and slow mobility. With the Najafgarh and other water bodies acting as linear parks, connections will bring together adjacent neighborhoods and basic civic facilities will gravitate towards these new attractors. Water treatment parks, designed as socio-ecological public spaces, will treat stormwater run-off and effluents from sewage treatment plants.

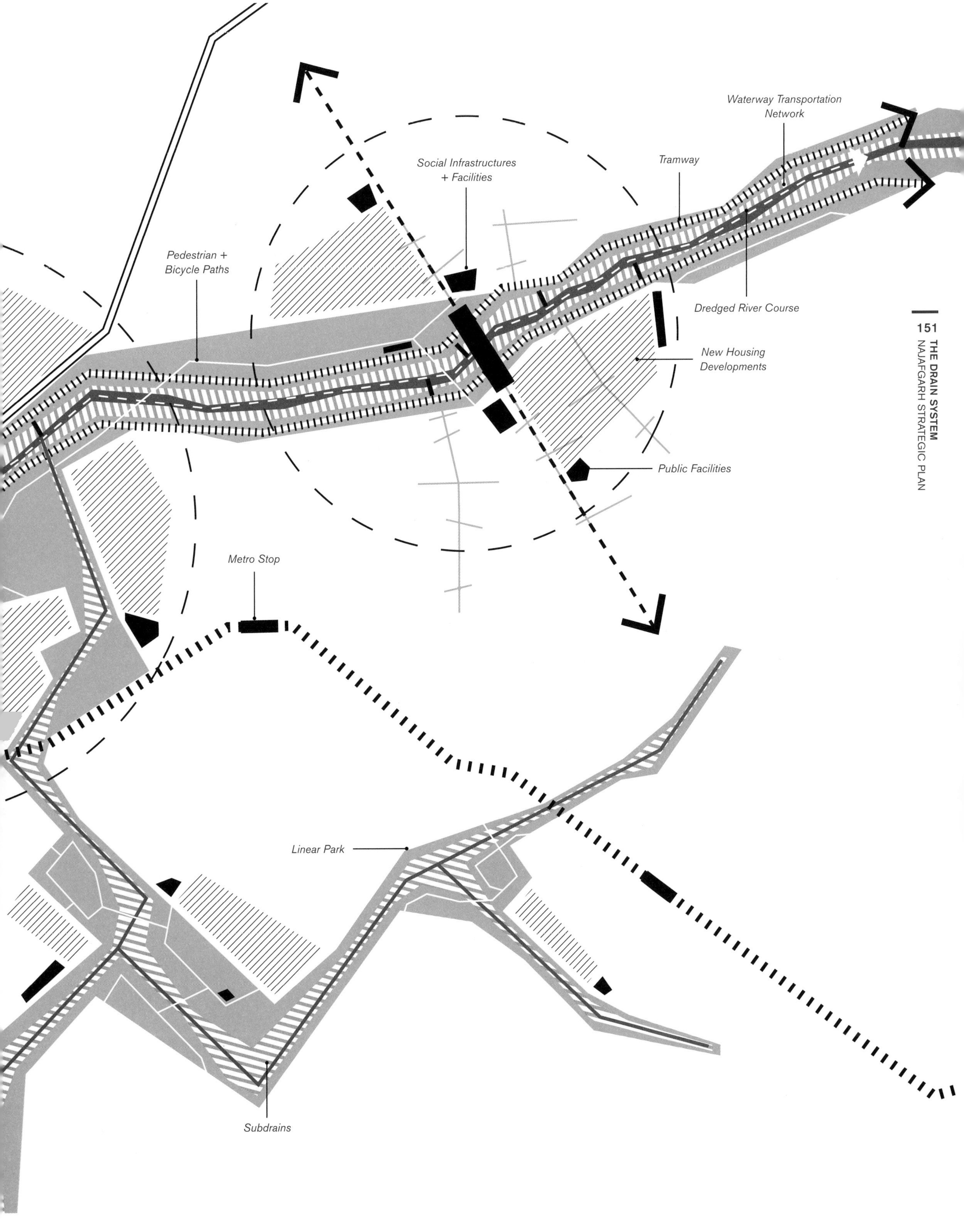

Waterway Transportation
Network

Social Infrastructures
+ Facilities

Tramway

Pedestrian +
Bicycle Paths

Dredged River Course

New Housing
Developments

Public Facilities

Metro Stop

Linear Park

Subdrains

A Vision of the Najafgarh

To conceptualize a new Najafgarh we start
by projecting ourselves back towards the
silver forest of origin, what it meant to expand
and settle there, cutting clearings, installing
grassland, and organizing the layout of the
water as the farmers did. By not establishing
a brutal picture of the site but rather allowing
the landscape to express its natural qualities,
the design embodies the story of a territory and
the relationship its inhabitants maintain with it.
Before occupation, the meander belonged to
the river, providing overflow space and natural

filtering through the vegetation, sheltering only
the most delicate areas. The original forest has
been reduced through the centuries to make
room for agriculture. This vision returns the
Najafgarh's landscape to its origin, allowing a
palette of vegetation to accentuate the park in
contrast to its urban context. In order to build
on agricultural land that is currently worked
and fertile, uses and modes of management
must be changed and irrigation ditches and
canals allowed to integrate with the existing
meander structure, organizing a living system.

THE PARK IS NOT AN
AUTONOMOUS OBJECT, CLOSED,
BUT A LANDSCAPE THAT REACTS
TO EVERYTHING AROUND IT.

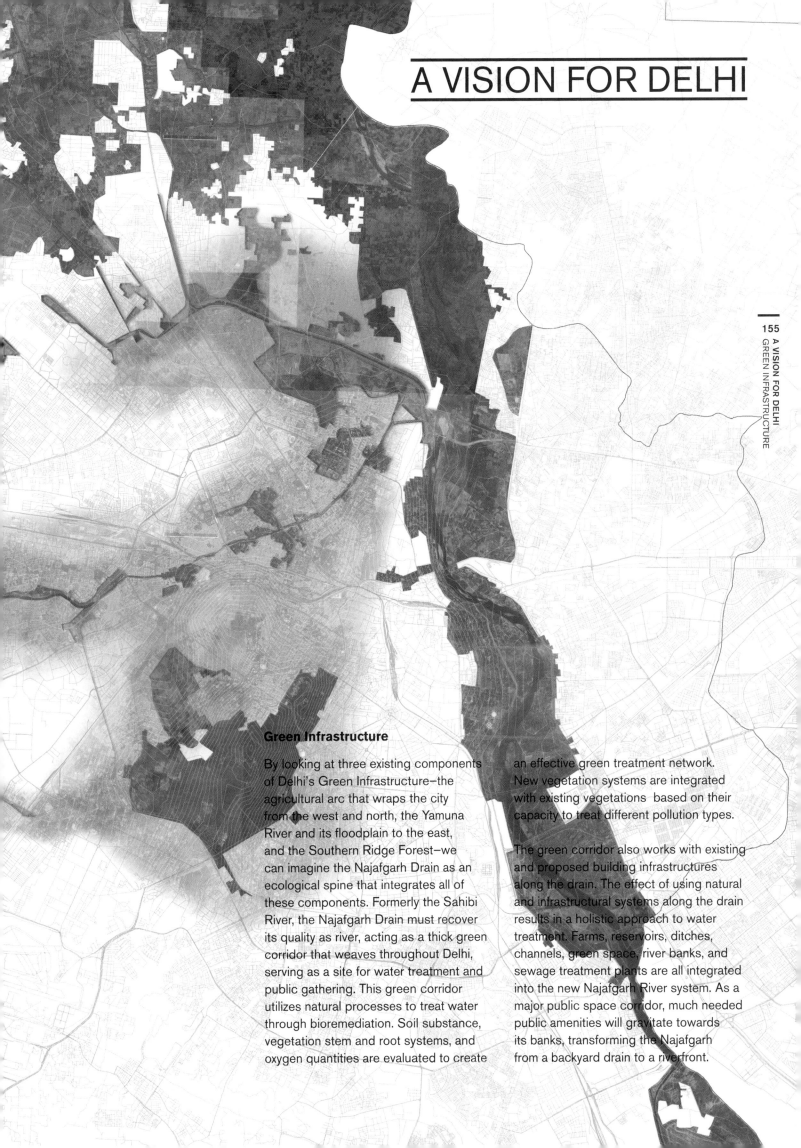

Green Infrastructure

By looking at three existing components of Delhi's Green Infrastructure—the agricultural arc that wraps the city from the west and north, the Yamuna River and its floodplain to the east, and the Southern Ridge Forest—we can imagine the Najafgarh Drain as an ecological spine that integrates all of these components. Formerly the Sahibi River, the Najafgarh Drain must recover its quality as river, acting as a thick green corridor that weaves throughout Delhi, serving as a site for water treatment and public gathering. This green corridor utilizes natural processes to treat water through bioremediation. Soil substance, vegetation stem and root systems, and oxygen quantities are evaluated to create

an effective green treatment network. New vegetation systems are integrated with existing vegetations based on their capacity to treat different pollution types.

The green corridor also works with existing and proposed building infrastructures along the drain. The effect of using natural and infrastructural systems along the drain results in a holistic approach to water treatment. Farms, reservoirs, ditches, channels, green space, river banks, and sewage treatment plants are all integrated into the new Najafgarh River system. As a major public space corridor, much needed public amenities will gravitate towards its banks, transforming the Najafgarh from a backyard drain to a riverfront.

Socioecological Strategic Plan

The plan integrates three primary layers into Delhi's urban fabric: critical ecologies, slow mobility, and public facilities. At a regional scale the corridor enables urban-agricultural symbiosis, promoting infrastructural and entrepreneurial relationships between Delhi's most urban regions and the agricultural crown at Delhi's edges. Within Delhi proper, the ecological network branches along former tributaries to include the Central Ridge Forest, sewage treatment wetland parks, city streets, and solid waste management. This new corridor receives, exchanges, filters, and processes this complex ecological matrix before emptying into the Yamuna floodplain, creating a clean and robust urban Delhi.

1. Restoration of the Najafgarh corridor as a linear continuous river park and shared public space

2. Socio-ecological water parks with green filters that treat the effluents of the sewage treatment plants

3. New public amenities located on the facade of the Najafgarh

4. Pedestrian, bike and tram mobility along the Najafgarh corridor with intermodal connections to the metro

5. Rejuvenation of the sub-drains as linear parks in the dry season and storm water drains in the monsoon season

6. Alternative decentralized waste and sewage treatment systems in areas without urban infrastructures

7. New transversal connections between neighborhoods across the Najafgarh

8. Agricultural parks connecting the citizens to their food sources to promote value and respect for the land

Facility Bridge Transverse Connection

Green Filters + Water Parks

Nilothi + Keshopur Sewage Treatment Plant

Sludge + Water Remediation Parks

Ramesh Nagar Subdrain Rejuvenation

Subhash Nagar Subdrain Rejuvenation

Decentralized Public Sewage Infrastructure

Ykaspur Subdrain Rejuvenation

Park Connection

Subdrain Seasonal Park

Hybrid Water + Energy Plant

Palam Subdrain Linear Park

Papankalan Hybrid Sewage Treatment Parks

Najafgarh-Palam Neighborhood Amenities

Green Filters and Water Parks

Najafgarh Agriculture Park Connection

Najafgarh Agriculture

INDIRA GANDHI
INTERNATIONAL AIRPORT

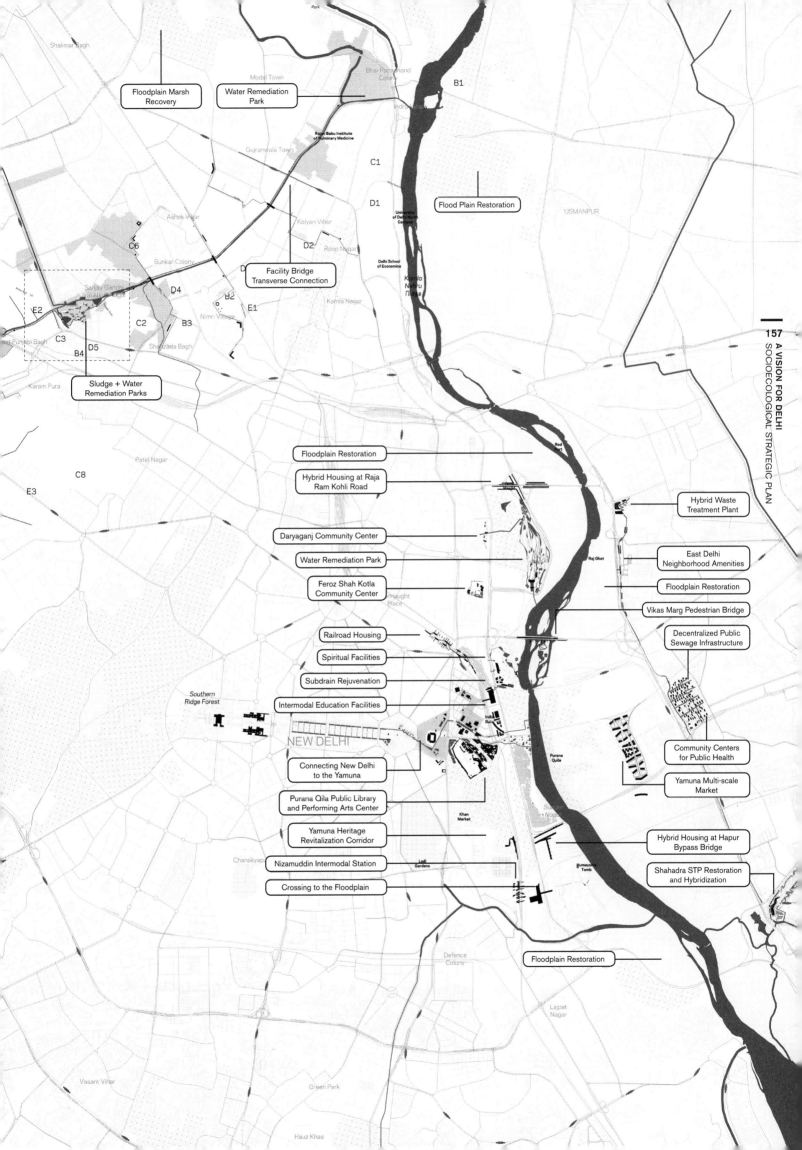

Floodplain Marsh Recovery

Water Remediation Park

B1

C1

D1

Flood Plain Restoration

USMANPUR

Facility Bridge Transverse Connection

D2

C6

D4

E2

B2

E1

C3

C2

B3

D5

B4

Sludge + Water Remediation Parks

C8

E3

Floodplain Restoration

Hybrid Housing at Raja Ram Kohli Road

Hybrid Waste Treatment Plant

Daryaganj Community Center

East Delhi Neighborhood Amenities

Water Remediation Park

Floodplain Restoration

Feroz Shah Kotla Community Center

Vikas Marg Pedestrian Bridge

Railroad Housing

Decentralized Public Sewage Infrastructure

Spiritual Facilities

Subdrain Rejuvenation

Intermodal Education Facilities

Southern Ridge Forest

Community Centers for Public Health

NEW DELHI

Connecting New Delhi to the Yamuna

Yamuna Multi-scale Market

Purana Qila Public Library and Performing Arts Center

Yamuna Heritage Revitalization Corridor

Hybrid Housing at Hapur Bypass Bridge

Chanakyapuri

Nizamuddin Intermodal Station

Shahadra STP Restoration and Hybridization

Crossing to the Floodplain

Floodplain Restoration

A MAP OF THE WORLD THAT DOES NOT INCLUDE UTOPIA

Rana Dasgupta
Novelist

"A map of the world that does not include Utopia," wrote Oscar Wilde, "is not worth even glancing at." Today, of course, we are realists, and Utopia has a bad name. But maps which show only what is can still seem sadly incomplete. Landscapes are replete, also, with what was and – which is our preoccupation here – what could be. If ever our hopes and dreams are to work their metamorphosis on reality, they first need to be well drawn.

A conversation I had a few years ago with an old man aroused in me hopes and dreams for the Yamuna River. Or, more precisely, for the relationship of that river to the city of Delhi, a relationship that has turned ruinous for conurbation and water body alike. The old man, now sadly deceased, was Anupam Mishra, a writer and environmentalist. The long walk we took together along the river was described in the last chapter of my book, Capital:

> The ... waterfront is an uncannily dead zone which the city's managers seem to have designated as a dumping ground. Behind the Secretariat building is a graveyard for retired ambulances, which are piled unceremoniously by the side of the road. There is a huge amount of masonry waste: unused paving slabs, sections of concrete pipe, and entire walls removed from the destroyed township, which are lent against each other like files on a shelf. A few hundred rusting steel chairs have been piled up on one patch of ground, a couple of storeys high.

> We are very close to the centre of the city but it as if its consciousness ends just short of the river. Delhi has its back to the water and only the roving underclass seems to come here, whose signs are everywhere: bedding in the bushes, discarded plastic bottles, human excrement, and the charred circles of cooking fires.

Like other relationships turned rotten, this one had a history, as Mishra explained. It had not always been so: the Mughals, after all, had built their city to look sensuously out on the river, and the waterfront was a pleasure zone of palaces and gardens. Significantly, the river was not the main source of their water. The reason they had been persuaded to build on this plain in the first place – and it was the same for a thousand years of previous settlers – was the abundance of ground water, a result of the run-off from the Aravalli Hills. The Mughal city was thick with wells, and also with their necessary corollary: man-made lakes and tanks which replenished what was drawn out by capturing rain and letting it seep down into the earth, rather than simply escape into the river. Paintings and engravings show a metropolis in a state of advanced hydraulic harmony: lush and verdant, it looks over a vast and voluptuous Yamuna.

The designers of the British city substantially changed this relationship to the river. First of all, they were determined to introduce a European-style water system, which required them to abandon ground water – which was why this place had been settled in the first place – and to take their water from the river, damming it upstream and running pipes into the city. Sewage pipes collected all the waste and dumped it back in the Yamuna downstream. This was a rude assault on a river that had long been embellished with delicate mythology and sensual ritual, and it turned it from a spectacle to a cistern. It also had the effect of gradually destroying the intricate system of wells and tanks which constituted the city's age-old water technology. During the course of the subsequent century, as Mishra explained on our walk, this turned to disaster.

The river rapidly ceased to be adequate for the city's water needs: Delhi's population is fifty times larger now than when the British built their system, while the Yamuna is the same size. So Delhi began to take water from other places. Now we have pipelines bringing water from the Ganges and Bhagirathi Rivers and from the Renuka Lake. Thousands of farmers have protested against Delhi taking their water.

Not only this, but we do not have the capacity to treat such large quantities of sewage. Our sewage systems were built to treat one river. Now three times this volume is coming into the system. This is why our sewage plants treat a smaller and smaller proportion every year. Most sewage now flows directly into the river. It is a poisonous brew, full of industrial effluent, and Delhi produces it on a monumental scale.

Now do you think our middle classes wish to pay the price of our present water shortage? Of course not. They wish to live free of any environmental context. That is the reward they expect from capitalism! They want to turn on their taps at any time and have water. The municipal supply, however, is heavily rationed, and provides water only for a few hours a day. So what do the middle classes do? They remember – they are good at history when they need to be! – that there is a rich supply of water under their feet. Over the last thirty years they have all dug private wells so they can pump out as much as they need. Every middle-class house has such a well, even though it is illegal. This water is completely unmonitored so of course the city's water authorities now have no idea how much sewage they need to build capacity for. And all this additional water also floods out into the Yamuna, raising the level still further.

But of course by now no one remembers the basic knowledge that governed Delhi's water management for a millennium: if you take water from the ground you have to replenish it. People are pumping water out of the ground for their baths and washing machines and swimming pools but they have not built a single water tank to recharge the ground supply. So Delhi's groundwater is also running dry. But let them not think about it! While it still comes out of the tap, let them pump away!

As a result of this, many areas of Delhi are now completely dry. Whole sectors of the city have run out of ground water and are supplied only by water trucks. There is a new five-star hotel that has no water: its water needs – baths, laundry, swimming pool, sauna – are all supplied by trucks which come at night in lines of a hundred or more. But while there is a way to spend oneself out of a problem, this city is curiously indifferent to that problem. Real-estate prices continue to rise even in areas where there is no water.

We often think that recent centuries have produced a lot of new knowledge. But this is because we are no longer equipped to recognise the knowledge of the past. I see modern times as one long history of forgetting. Even the kings are ignorant now of what every person who used to live in this place once knew."

Second, the British did not find the Yamuna beautiful. It was not a European-style river, consistent all year round, which could be walled in and enjoyed from riverside cafés and walkways. The Yamuna increased its volume many times during the monsoon, so it was impossible to wall it in: a great flood plain had to be left on either side, which was muddy and empty for much of the year. This they found visually unappealing – and "New Delhi" was built to face away from the river. The hydraulic appropriation of the river was compounded – made possible, even – by a breaking of sensual ties.

It is remarkable, today, how many people spend years in Delhi without ever laying eyes on the Yamuna. No one ever proposes an outing to the river, as is normal in so many other cities – and if they did it would not be clear how one would get there: the water is bizarrely difficult to find. This fact is of some use to the great numbers of Delhi's homeless, who are rebuffed from the city proper by all manner of stern regimes: the tracts of land by the Yamuna are so neglected that one can construct a residence there without much interference. But it is rough living, for that same reason, and even the poorest generally spurn it. Though space is frantically exploited in this heaving city of twenty millions, the spiny wasteland between the orbital road and the chemical river is largely deserted. The architectural orientation adopted by the British seems in fact to have led to mass riverine denial. On those occasions when people visit the river to deposit the ashes of loved ones, they proceed robotically with their ritual, as if the Yamuna had not become a stinking sewer.

This sewer stands at the centre of a vast and complex system of water supply and waste, for whose contemporary crisis it stands as the most conspicuous symbol. What I realized during my walk with Anupam Mishra was that the solution to this crisis would not come – though this is how the discussion generally begins – from innovations in technology or regulation. Such innovations would be necessary, of course; but they themselves depended on prior transformations that were sensual, conceptual – even philosophical. Delhi's older water systems, after all, were not shut away in some abstract, technological domain; they flourished because they were fully reflected in the life-worlds of individuals and communities. "Looking at a river, swimming in a river," Anupam pointed out, "these are the first stages of cherishing it. In Delhi, there used to be a great amount of life around the river – swimming, religious festivals, water games – but it has all come to an end. Think of religious immersion: it is not just superstition. It is a practice of water preservation. If our Prime Minister had to immerse himself in the Yamuna every year, it would be a lot cleaner than it is now."

Delhi had moved far away from such intimacy. The modern city was one which viewed nature less as idyll and more as savage threat, and, given the state into which the river had fallen, its citizens were quite content not to look at it. "Citizenship," anyway, was very much the issue – for Delhi was a divided place of enclaves, ghettos and stern hierarchies, and no public spaces, shared resources or common pleasures united its conflicted millions. Such division entered everywhere: each of its twenty-first-century engineering projects – the highways, Metro system, suburban extensions – seemed oblivious to the others. Delhi's people valued private accumulation (as they appreciated high walls and barbed wire): what other people could own or share was their own diminishment, and "public" goods – such as air and water – were terribly abused. Water, in fact, had turned into a general war of all against all: the propertied classes had given up on the public (river-sourced) supply and dug their own private wells – returning to the traditional groundwater but without acknowledging the old science of replenishment – and now they were each locked in an apocalyptic race against everyone else. Modern Delhi had many more reasons than the British not to wish to set eyes on the river: for its desecration brought to mind depths of unwanted shame and fear.

But the "hopes and dreams" I conceived that day derived from this realization: that the broken relationship between city and river was begun by architecture, and perhaps architecture could fix it again. "New Delhi" was built to face away from the Yamuna, which had therefore dropped out of the consciousness of a city that preferred not to see how it mutilated its old spirits. But the old rift could be bridged. Despite everything, the river basin was still epic: its great expanse – filled, after the rains, with rushing waters – could stop your heart when glimpsed, improbably, from the city's congested concrete. If it were possible to expose the city once again to the power of that spectacle which had animated for a millennium, Delhi would not carry on unchanged.

To overturn the very powerful legacy of the last century would require a forceful imagination. But the Mughal love for the Yamuna was still written into the city's architecture in certain places – such as the complex around Humayun's Tomb, which came within two hundred metres of the Yamuna flood plain. There was also the Delhi Zoo, which bordered the river, and the vast park created to memorialize Gandhi and other national figures. If one squinted at the map, a Utopia was already buried there, waiting to rise: why not interconnect these already-existing spaces, creating pedestrian and bike routes from the north to the south of the city, far from the clogged highways? Why not open these spaces to the river – many of them had been built thus – and make real provision for people of all backgrounds to use and enjoy it? Why not re-stitch, in short, all the myriad connections which bind cities to rivers everywhere, and let care for the river come later, as the inevitable result?

It was while I was in the grip of such imaginings that I first had conversations with Pankaj Vir Gupta and Iñaki Alday about the Yamuna River. I am very moved by the visions they and their students have since developed. I hope they will play a role in some true transformation of the broken relationship between this ancient river, and this upstart, reckless city.

To give a sense of what the river was, and can be again, here is what happened at the end of my walk with Anupam Mishra, which took us north of the city, beyond the dam, beyond the sewage pipes.

> We cross the hard soil. Bits of ancient pillars are lying half buried in the ground. We reach a cluster of small temples. And then, before us, is the Yamuna: blue, tranquil, magnificent.
>
> I gasp with the sight of it.
>
> "Yes," says Anupam sympathetically. "One can never believe that the river can be like this."
>
> This is not the black, sludgy channel we have been following all day. This is the primordial river, clear and fecund.
>
> We are in every sense, "before" Delhi. Before the river meets the city. Before the city was ever here.
>
> Boys paddle gleefully in the water. Families of moorhens glide across its surface. Rowing boats are moored at the river's edge, where you can see two metres to the bottom. In the middle of the river is a belt of golden reeds; the opposite bank must be a couple of kilometres away. Bright blue kingfishers chirp shrilly in the trees, which lean desirously over the water. A woman collects river water in a plastic canister.
>
> We sit down on the steps to look at the river. Nearby a group of men is playing cards under a peepul tree. One of them is a naked sadhu.
>
> We are in that altered soundscape of a river estuary, the sounds clear over the surface of the water. Birds call out across large distances.
>
> The horizon is open, and it is a relief. I realise how consumed my being has become by the internal drama of my dense adopted city. I have forgotten expansiveness. This megalopolis, where everything is vast, somehow offers little opportunity to see further than across the street. Everything is blocked off. Your eyes forget how to focus on the infinite.
>
> "I'm glad you could see this," says Anupam. "Now you realise why Delhi is here. It is one of the beautiful places of the earth."

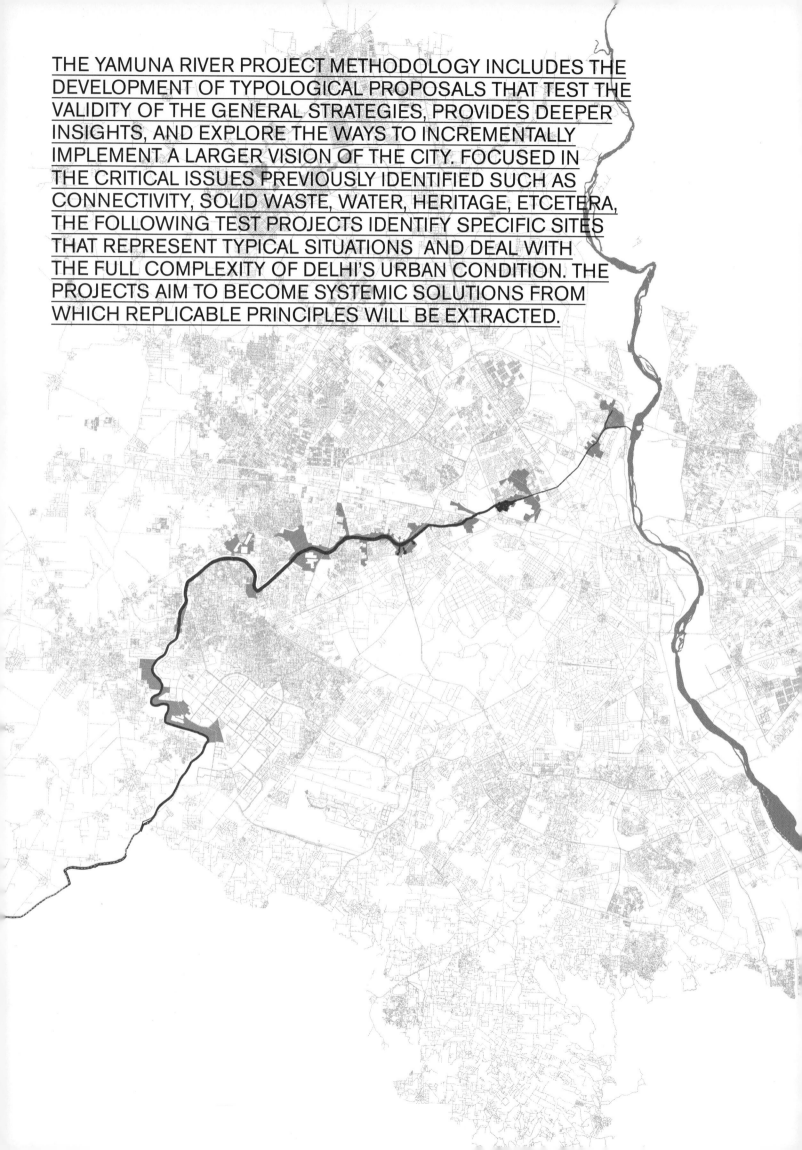

THE YAMUNA RIVER PROJECT METHODOLOGY INCLUDES THE DEVELOPMENT OF TYPOLOGICAL PROPOSALS THAT TEST THE VALIDITY OF THE GENERAL STRATEGIES, PROVIDES DEEPER INSIGHTS, AND EXPLORE THE WAYS TO INCREMENTALLY IMPLEMENT A LARGER VISION OF THE CITY. FOCUSED IN THE CRITICAL ISSUES PREVIOUSLY IDENTIFIED SUCH AS CONNECTIVITY, SOLID WASTE, WATER, HERITAGE, ETCETERA, THE FOLLOWING TEST PROJECTS IDENTIFY SPECIFIC SITES THAT REPRESENT TYPICAL SITUATIONS AND DEAL WITH THE FULL COMPLEXITY OF DELHI'S URBAN CONDITION. THE PROJECTS AIM TO BECOME SYSTEMIC SOLUTIONS FROM WHICH REPLICABLE PRINCIPLES WILL BE EXTRACTED.

NAJAFGARH DRAIN AS DELHI'S EAST - WEST SPINE

Following the thesis of the Yamuna River Project, that polluted water is the result of the urban inequality, we find that the Najafgarh Drain is not only the main source of pollution to the Yamuna but it also typifies many urban conditions found across Delhi. It connects the river with the agricultural belt and the rural nuclei, the peripheral urban villages and dispersed infrastructure, and the urban core of formal and informal fabric. The Najafgarh will be recovered as the major East-West socioecological urban structure of public space, ecology, and mobility.

As the main source of flow for the Yamuna in Delhi, the quality of Najafgarh waters present a critical environmental challenge. Sewage treatments plants become the new springs of the river, with water parks of public space providing tertiary treatment before releasing water to the drain and, eventually, to the Yamuna. Controlled areas will provide for 'ecological flow', allowing water to infiltrate the ground and recharge the water table to be reused for the city. The capillary network of drainage, now existing under severe urban pressure

and distortion, needs to be recovered and integrated into the riparian system of the Najafgarh Drain, returning its association to its former identity as the Sahibi River. In this process of restoration, the massive amounts of toxic sludge laying in the drain finds a new place and systems of remediation along the drain treat sludge and water without exporting toxicity to still undamaged land. The accommodation of dried and encapsulated sludge in new topographies creates parks and landscapes, giving a new identity to the flat banks of the drain.

The geographical continuity of the drain offers an opportunity to insert new modes of public transportation. Bicycle lanes and pedestrian paths for neighborhood mobility are intertwined with longitudinal public transportation in the banks—a new light train or tramway—and inside the permanent water flow, a boat line, with intermodal connections to metro and bus. This Najafgarh transportation connects several metro lines, completing the city's public mobility network, and offering opportunities for development and urban activity in these intermodal nodes.

The Drain Capillary System

As a necessary step towards revitalizing the Najafgarh Drain and the Yamuna River, this project proposes a continuous wetland park that acts as an urban capillary water system which treats agricultural and household waste water. The proposed system enhances the ability of adjacent landscapes to manage monsoon waters, replenish underground aquifers, and support agriculture, thus increasing food and water security for all of Delhi. As the park weaves through Delhi's residential neighborhoods, it provides a recreational area for play, open spaces for public gathering, and zones of respite from urban life. This landscape also educates Delhi's citizens on the process of recycling water through green infrastructure and processes of agricultural production, raising awareness around issues of agriculture, food, and water.

This urban project incorporates existing green spaces along the Najafgarh Drain and follows existing water flows from agricultural areas to create an integrated water treatment system. Existing watersheds through farms and neighborhoods are adapted to collect water and filter it through linear ponds or vegetative zones.

These ponds and vegetative zones then empty into stepped collection ponds which further treat the polluted water before it arrives in the Najafgarh. Each pond type has three conditions: dry, regular, and wet. Depending on their particular pollution levels and seasonal conditions, the ponds could support different types of recreational use while increasing accessibility to the drain and surrounding neighborhoods.

THE DRAIN CAPILLARY SYSTEM
JULY QIU

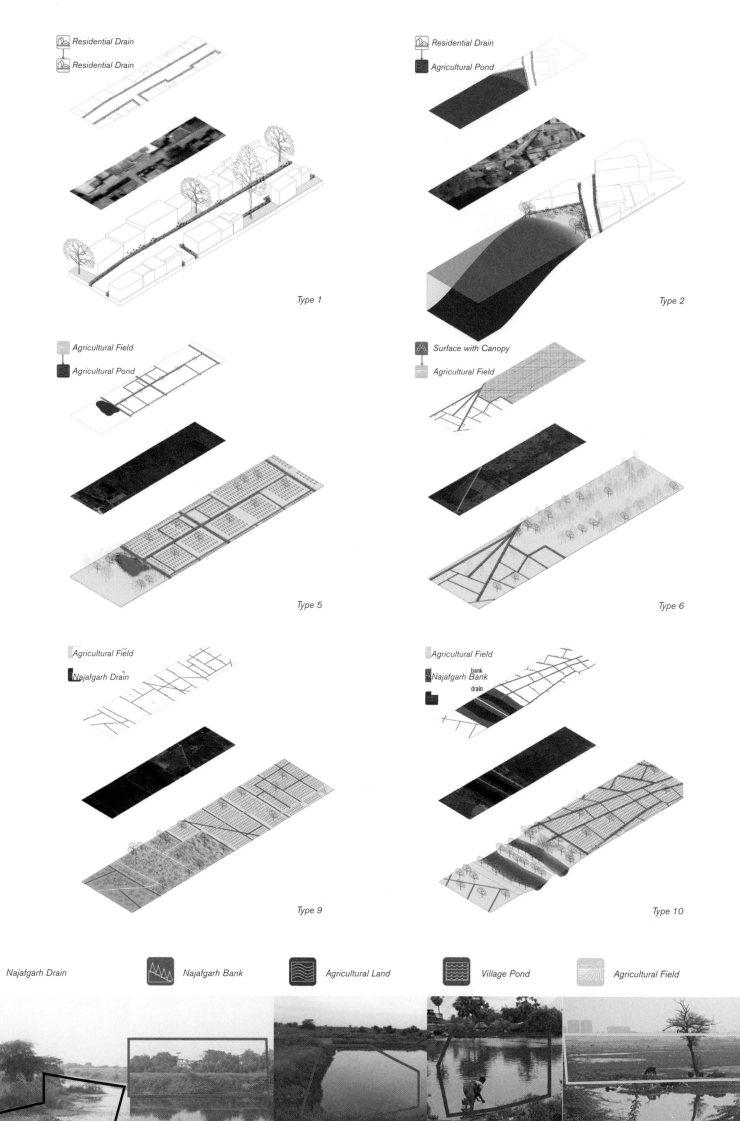

Residential Drain
Residential Drain

Type 1

Residential Drain
Agricultural Pond

Type 2

Agricultural Field
Agricultural Pond

Type 5

Surface with Canopy
Agricultural Field

Type 6

Agricultural Field
Najafgarh Drain

Type 9

Agricultural Field
Najafgarh Bank
bank
drain

Type 10

Najafgarh Drain   Najafgarh Bank   Agricultural Land   Village Pond   Agricultural Field

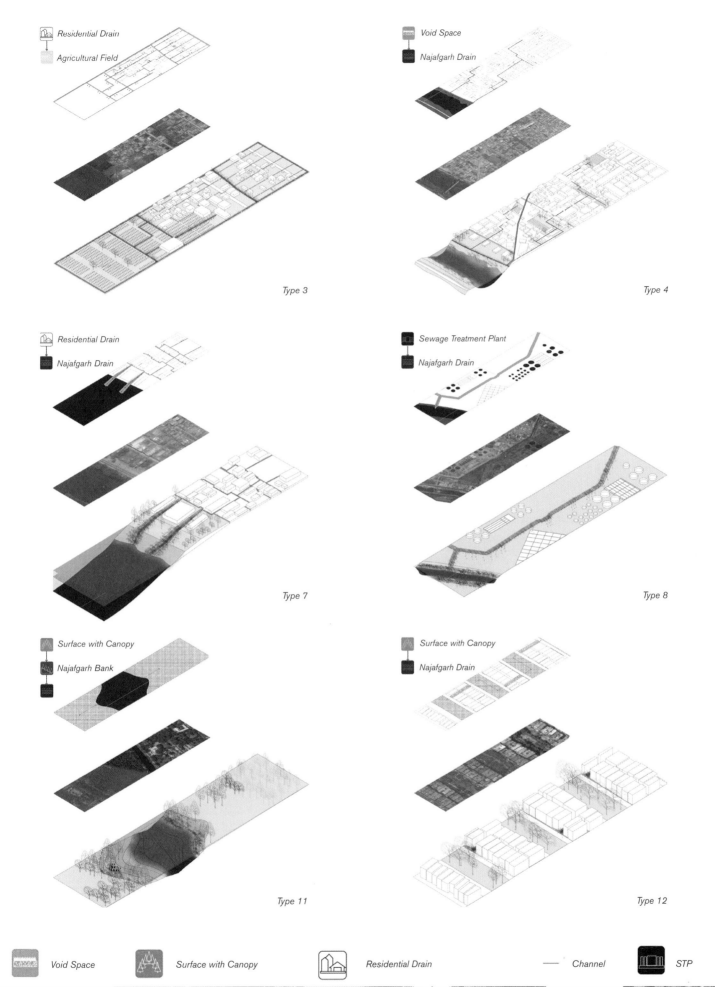

Residential Drain
Agricultural Field

Void Space
Najafgarh Drain

Type 3

Type 4

Residential Drain
Najafgarh Drain

Sewage Treatment Plant
Najafgarh Drain

Type 7

Type 8

Surface with Canopy
Najafgarh Bank

Surface with Canopy
Najafgarh Drain

Type 11

Type 12

Void Space   Surface with Canopy   Residential Drain   —— Channel   STP

The Najafgarh has potential to connect green infrastructures across the city.

Capillary Connections

Green Infrastructure

Najafgarh Drain

Ecological Corridor

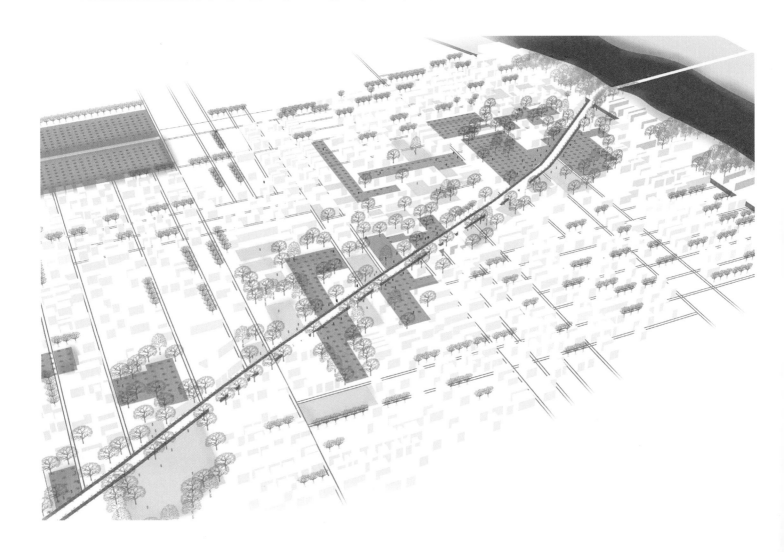

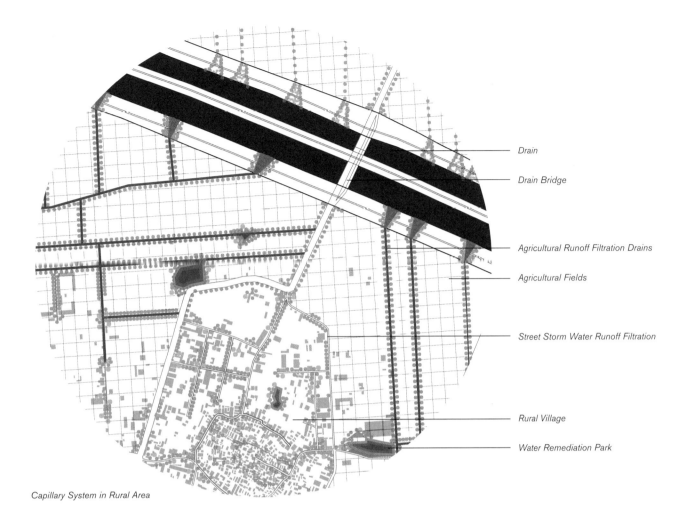

Drain

Drain Bridge

Agricultural Runoff Filtration Drains

Agricultural Fields

Street Storm Water Runoff Filtration

Rural Village

Water Remediation Park

Capillary System in Rural Area

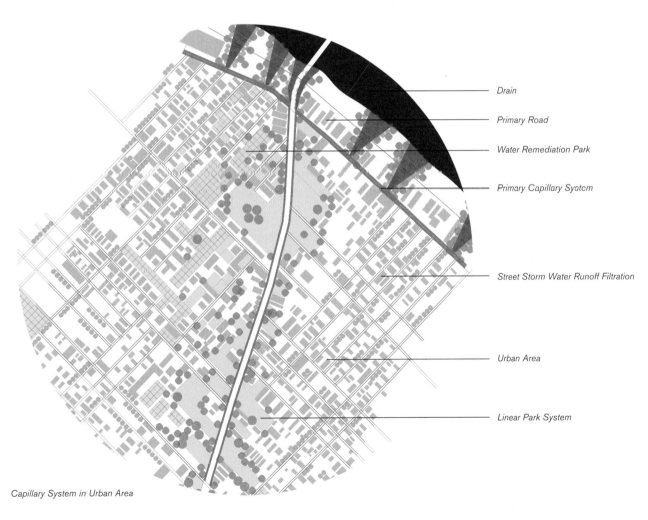

Drain

Primary Road

Water Remediation Park

Primary Capillary System

Street Storm Water Runoff Filtration

Urban Area

Linear Park System

Capillary System in Urban Area

WHAT IS KNOWN AS THE NAJAFGARH DRAIN IN DELHI IS REALLY THE SAHIBI RIVER, ORIGINATING NEAR JAIPUR IN RAJASTHAN. AN EPHEMERAL RIVER, IT MAY RUN DRY; BUT DURING THE MONSOON IT IS AN IMPORTANT SOURCE OF WATER IN AN ARID REGION. THE SAHIBI USED TO FEED THE NAJAFGARH LAKE, WHICH COVERED AS MUCH AS 300 SQ. KM.

Sludge Remediation Park

The Chhatrapati Ring Road Crossing typifies several major mobility crossings along the Najafgarh in which no intentional, urban-scale relationships exist. As a result, Delhi is structured from opposite ends. Additionally, this site features a typical "Najafgarh park," a well-used space that faces Delhi streets and turns its back to the drain. This project will utilize the waste created from the dredging of the Najafgarh to reshape the site into a more functional and ecological public space oriented toward the water.

The corridor construction initiates upstream, capturing downstream flows and deeply settled sludge. The dredging operation allows for a newly-contoured profile that creates a narrow channel for consistent flow through the dry season, wide and shallow banks for a robust riparian zone, and continuous slow mobility along the corridor. Sludge is dewatered on site and deposited on site in landfills that also receive other forms of waste from the corridor and greater Delhi.

The landfills and their surroundings are designed to become part of the urban fabric of Delhi. Along with the landfill operation, channels are cut across the Najafgarh flow to aid in drainage during and after construction. This transverse pattern of cuts and fills maintains ecological and urban connections between waterbody and city, combining urban-scale waste management with long-term views of public space and mobility.

Phase 1

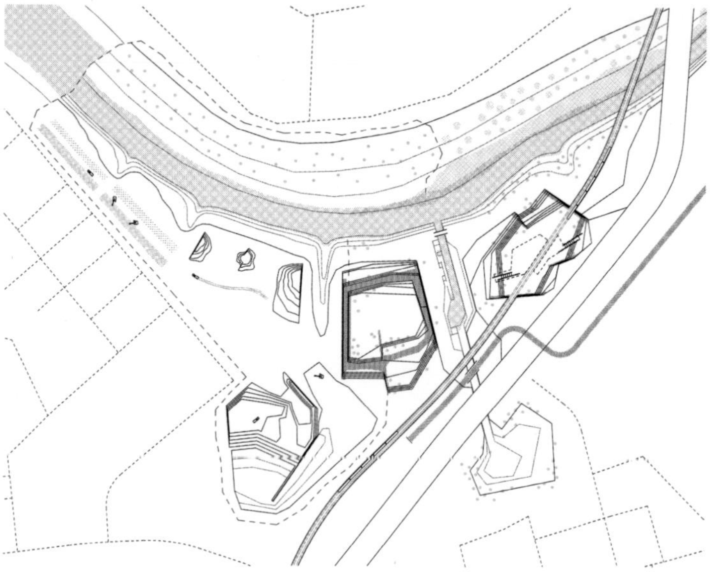

Phase II

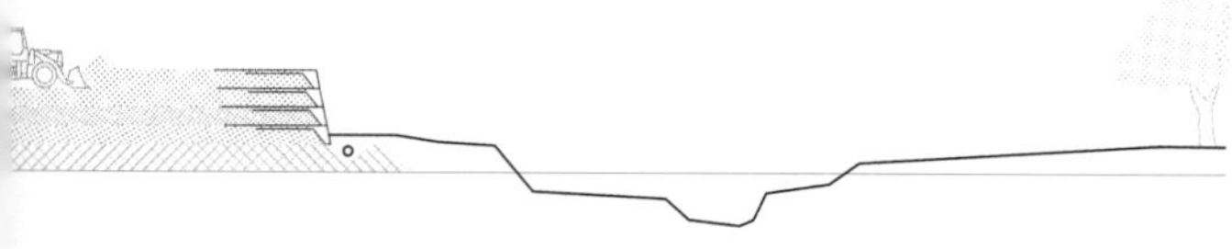

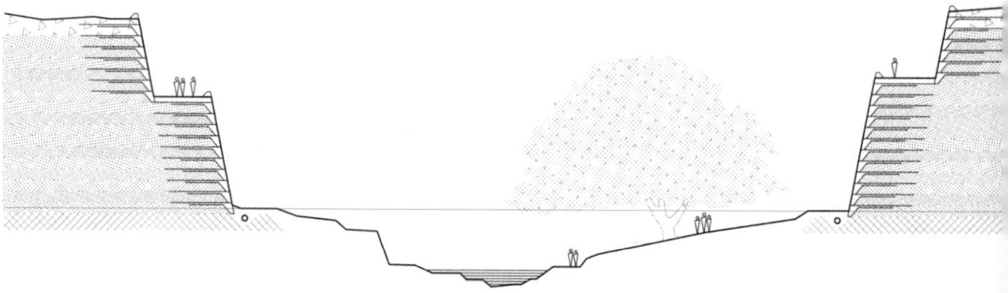

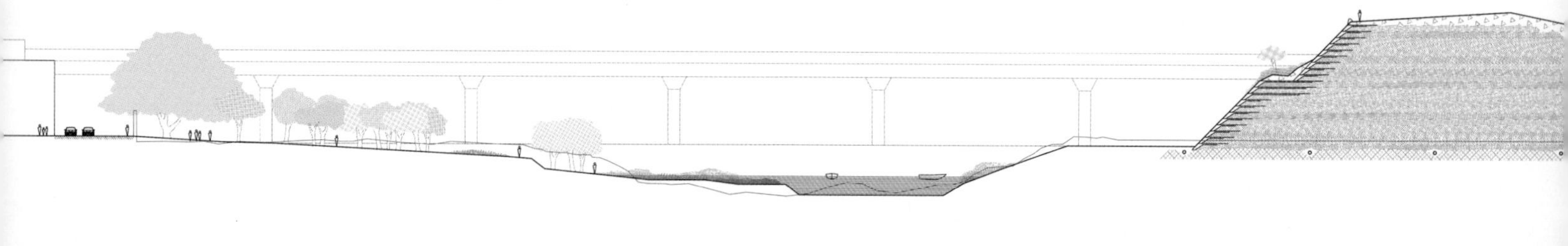

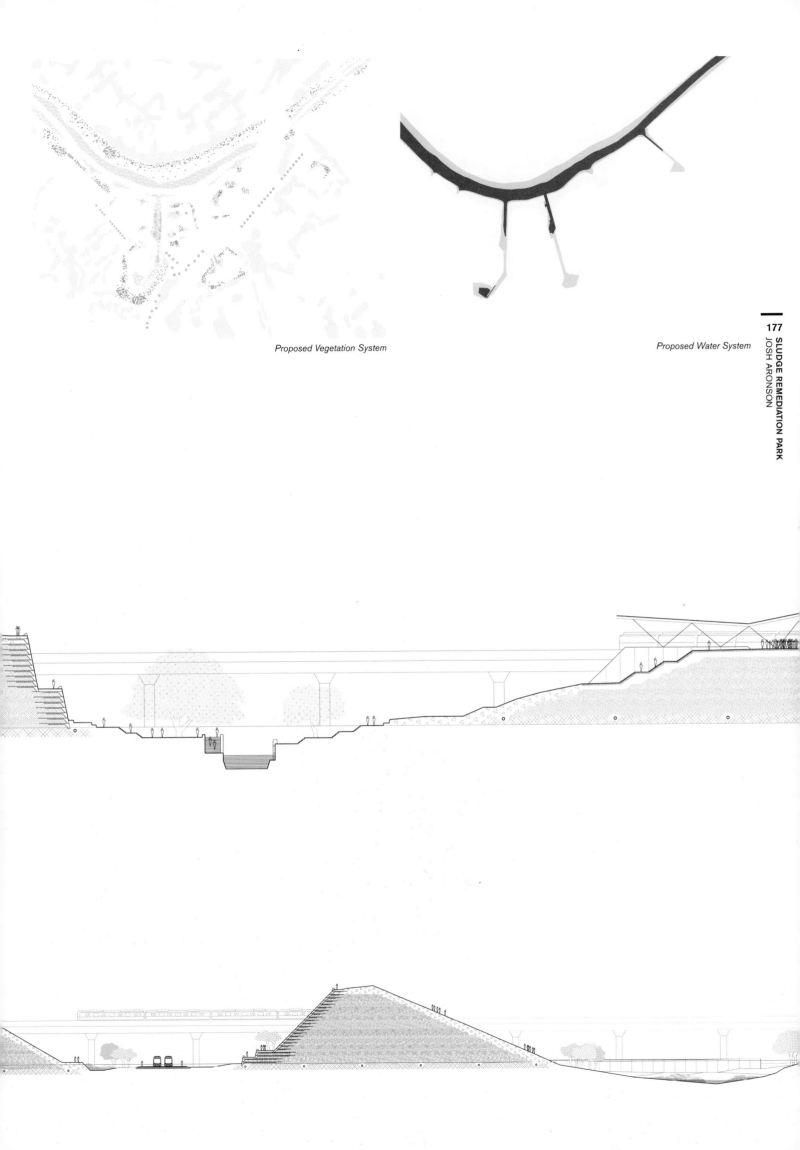

Proposed Vegetation System

Proposed Water System

DELHI'S SYSTEMS OF
STORMWATER AND WASTE
MANAGEMENT ARE INEXTRICABLY
EMBEDDED WITHIN THE URBAN
FABRIC OF EVERYDAY LIFE. CAN
THESE FACILITIES AND THEIR
BYPRODUCTS BE UTILIZED TO
PRODUCE NEW PUBLIC SPACES
IN THIS URBAN CONTEXT?

Water Remediation Park

Inderlok consists of a metro station intersecting the green and red lines, major roads, and a proposed tram line. An existing park is walled off from the metro station and residential neighborhoods, isolated from the urban context. Across from the metro station, a cluster of homes exists along the drain edge, just feet away from the water and sludge.

In the proposed strategy, the Inderlok Metro will be both pedestrian and vehicular accessible, providing a hub for people to gather. The cut and fill strategy will create a combination of green mounds and water pools made up of triangular pieces derived from the surrounding urban fabric. The Najafgarh water will pour into the park entrance as a channel for boats to meet the metro station. The water will flow underground into treatment pools scattered across the park and filter back out into the drain. The green mounds will vary in steepness and slope. Accessible from the ground plane, the mounds will afford a view of the surrounding landscape, which will function as a tree farm nursery for lost indigenous tree species. Proposed roads will no longer divide the park from the drain, but connect existing streets into a more fluid and safe system.

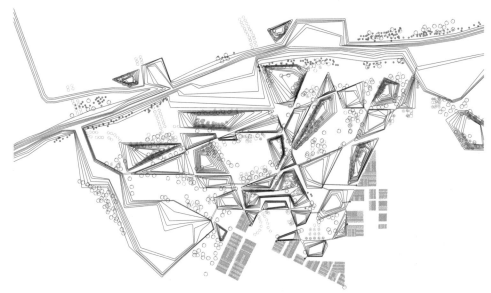

Proposed Wetland Vegetation Systems

Proposed Parkland Vegetation Systems

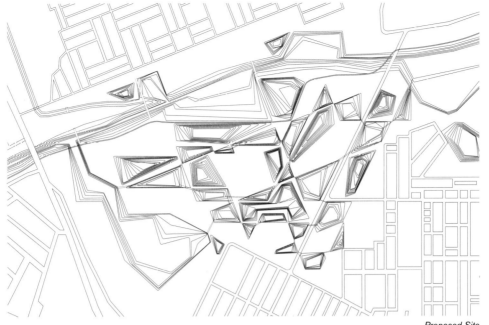

Proposed Site

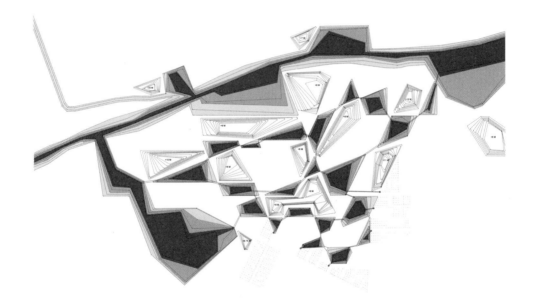

Proposed Monsoon Water Systems

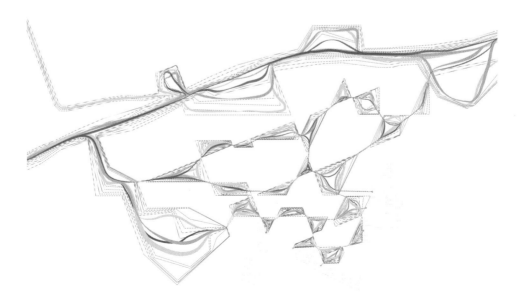

Proposed Dry Season Water Systems

SUBDRAINS AS LINEAR PARKS

The system of sub-drains of the Najafgarh-like the rest of tributaries of the Yamuna-are articulating elements between the drain as a new urban spine and the neighborhoods along it. This drainage system has evolved from geographical features across a forested and agricultural landscape to be canals under high urban pressure, loaded with raw sewage and trash. The implementation of the sewage interceptor strategy (pg 148) will transform channels of permanent flow in empty depressions for nine months of the year.

In order to avoid that the dry canals collect trash for nine months of the year—becoming a health hazard and causing massive floods due to a clogged storm water drainage system during the monsoon—it is necessary to apply a strategy of public space and ecology. For nine months, linear parks will create a network of space for leisure and slow mobility linking neighborhoods. Designed

to be compatible with seasonal change, for three months these linear parks will fulfill their hydrological function during the monsoon rains. Precedents of urban river recoveries in Spain (Zaragoza, Pamplona) show the advantages and viability of this strategy: hybridizing hydraulic infrastructures with public space. Together with this strategy, it will be necessary to uncap the larger sized covered sub-drains—such as the Palam—in order to secure social and ecological continuity through the new subdrain linear parks. Built structures, like walls and ramps, can be reused for pedestrian access, to manage water flows and store rainwater, and to support neighborhood facilities like shelters, public toilets, or laundry facilities. Sewage treatment plants and other hard urban infrastructures placed at the mouth of the sub-drains have the potential of being hybridized and transformed into mixed use public facilities with platforms for markets and events.

SUBDRAIN SEASONAL PARK
SOSA ERHABOR, ANDREW MORELL

1. DDA park
2. DG-2 park
3. District Park
4. Hastal Village
5. Hastal Phase II Park
6. JJ Colony
7. Krishi Apartments
8. Low Income Group (LIG) Housing
9. Middle Income Group (MIG) Housing
10. Najafgarh Drain
11. Proposed Housing
12. Shankar Garden
13. Shivam Apartments
14. Suryakiran Apartments
15. Uttam Nagar East Metro Station
16. Uttam Nagar Police Station
17. Veda Vyasa Dav Public School

Subdrain Seasonal Park

The current state of the Pankha Drain, located in Hastsal Village, causes physical harm to residents who surround it. To the east of the sewage-filled drain, informal housing conditions and neglected infrastructure undermine quality of life for this underserved portion of Delhi's population while the communities to the west of the drain enjoy improved living conditions. Acting as a buffer between the two communities, the Pankha Subdrain has an opportunity to stitch the communities together through a spine that organizes the urban fabric both laterally along the drain and longitudinally across the drain. As sub-drain remediation infrastructure is implemented, sewage will be removed and the drain will become seasonal, only filling with water during the monsoon months.

Hastsal Village is riddled with fragments of underutilized lots and parks. These spaces can be systematically organized into a larger, continuous park system by converting the now dry subdrain into a green passageway that runs from Uttam Nagar East to the Najafgarh Drain. This park system would provide safe passage for low income communities to access the metro station three kilometers away, create a framework for improved social housing for those displaced along the drain, act as a catalyst for economic stimulation, and clean waste water in a decentralized manner. A hybrid housing typology would anchor neighborhood systems organized along the newly designed park. The park spine would provide public space that varies seasonally in size and function due to controlled flooding while still connecting the existing transportation infrastructure to communities along the Najafgarh Drain.

Existing Landscape

Proposed Landscape

Existing Mobility System

Proposed Mobility System

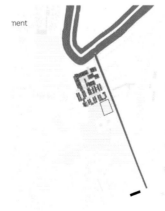

Existing Housing Development

Proposed Housing Development

Pankha Subdrain · Dry Season

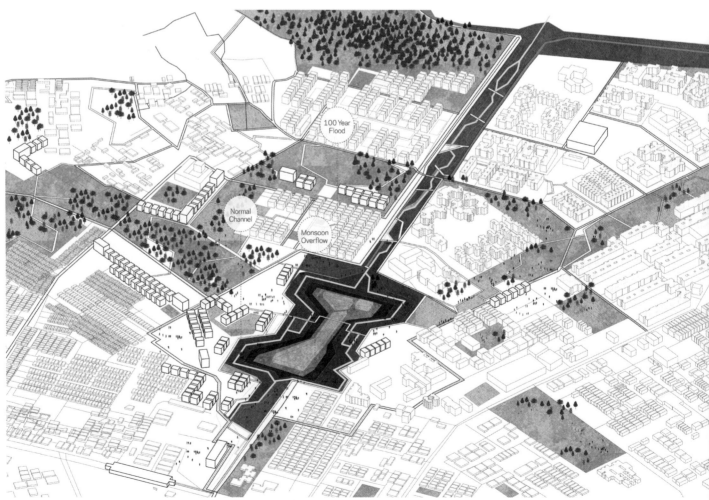

Pankha Subdrain · Monsoon Season

The slum populations along the Palam Drain are particularly vulnerable to flooding.

187 SUBDRAIN SEASONAL PARK
SOSA ERHABOR, ANDREW MORELL

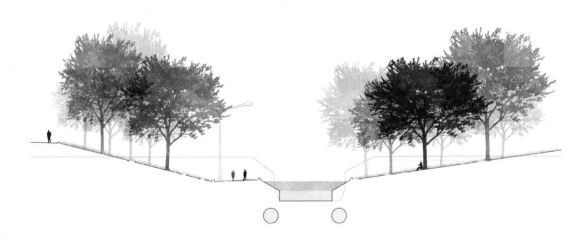

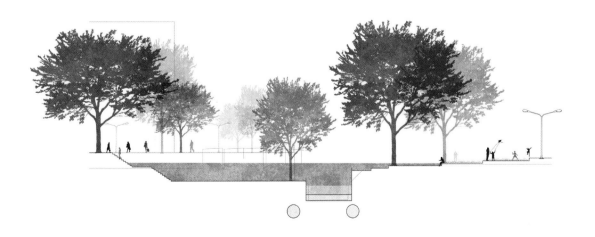

A THOUSAND SMALL STORM DRAINS FLOW
INTO 22 MAIN DRAINS WHICH CARRY A
MIXTURE OF TREATED AND UNTREATED
EFFLUENTS INTO THE YAMUNA. ESTABLISHED
BY THE MUGHAL EMPERORS AS A SYSTEM
OF STORM-WATER DRAINS, OR NULLAHS, THIS
SYSTEM NOW CREATES AN URBAN BACKYARD
OF STORM-WATER, HOUSEHOLD SEWAGE,
AND INDUSTRIAL WASTE THAT WINDS ITS WAY
THROUGH THE CITY.

Matiala

Dwarka

GURU GOBIND SINGH
INDAPRASTHA
UNIVERSITY

Metro - Blue Line

BGS INTERNATIONAL
PUBLIC SCHOOL

Dwarka

SRI VENKATESHWAR
INTERNATIONAL SCHOOL

PAPPANKALAN WETLAND PARK

DELTA OF DEATH

Subdrain Uncapping and Reuse

As one of the most continuous linear systems of undeveloped space in the city, Delhi's urban waterways are a contested territory.

A shortage of land in the urban core, combined with opportunistic infrastructure planning, has led to the layering of multiple infrastructures—including storm water, sewage, solid waste, electricity, and vehicular transportation—on top of the drain corridors. The clogging of these urban arteries has in many cases precluded their use as public space, and caused adjacent neighborhoods to turn their backs. The Palam Drain is a natural test site for an intervention in this urban system. On an average day, the Palam Drain carries 10 million gallons of untreated sewage and solid waste from surrounding settlements to the Najafgarh Drain and on to the Yamuna River. At 14 km, the Palam Drain is one of the longest tributary drains in the city, and it passes through a series of dramatically different social and spatial conditions: from the forested Delhi Ridge down through the headquarters of the Indian Army, passing through the city's largest contiguous informal settlement and the up-and-coming planned neighborhood of Dwarka on its way to the Najafgarh Drain.

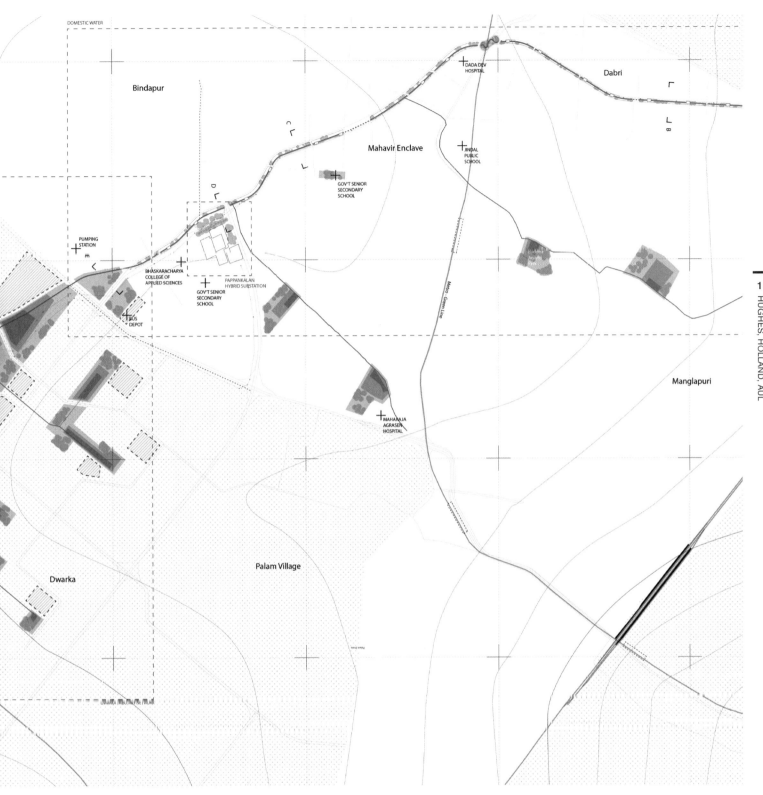

Bindapur

DOMESTIC WATER

Dabri

DADA DEV
HOSPITAL

Mahavir Enclave

JINDAL
PUBLIC
SCHOOL

GOV'T SENIOR
SECONDARY
SCHOOL

PUMPING
STATION

BHASKARACHARYA
COLLEGE OF
APPLIED SCIENCES

PAPPANKALAN
HYBRID SUBSTATION

GOV'T SENIOR
SECONDARY
SCHOOL

BUS
DEPOT

Manglapuri

MAHARAJA
AGRASEN
HOSPITAL

Palam Village

Dwarka

Palam Drain

Daylighting the Palam Drain

The project daylights the 5-km stretch of the Palam Drain currently capped by a six-lane road, adding landscape-based stormwater treatment systems, pedestrian and bicycle circulation, and a suite of public facilities to a busy corridor that serves a large lower-middle-class population.

The project establishes a new system of public space, allows for continuous pedestrian navigation, and makes habitable the city's infrastructural datum (approximately 4m below street level). It provides a respite from, and a new perspective on, the hyperactivity of a growing global megacity.

Making Oneself at Home in Public

The provision of clean water, and the activities that require it—including cooking, bathing, and using the bathroom—are often exclusively associated with the domestic realm. But in urban contexts such as Delhi, one cannot presume that piped infrastructure will deliver clean water to the interior of the home, nor discreetly remove dirty water from it. Instead, Delhi has developed social practices of procuring, using, and disposing of water in public, blurring the distinction between the domestic and the urban.

The architectural component of the Palam Drain daylighting project serves to harness and choreograph this public use of water, extending the domestic realm into the city. A series of twenty pavilions, an average of 200m apart, rise up from existing maintenance access structures, cantilevered out over the drain to maximize their square footage without impacting the ecological corridor below. They provide space for water treatment parks and public housing among other uses. The pavilions provide access to clean water in the form of public restrooms, water ATMs, and basins that can be used for washing and laundry. Rainwater harvesting and waste-treatment systems supplement piped connections to hard infrastructure, reducing the burden on the municipal system.

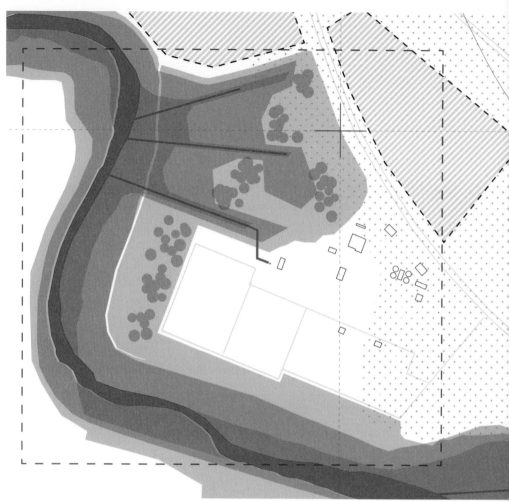

Pappankalan Wetland Park

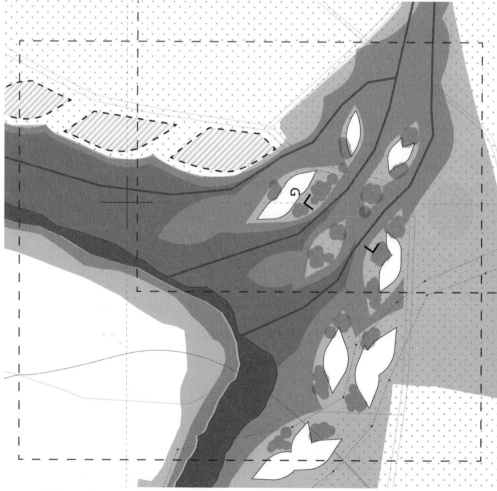

Recovered Subdarin Delta

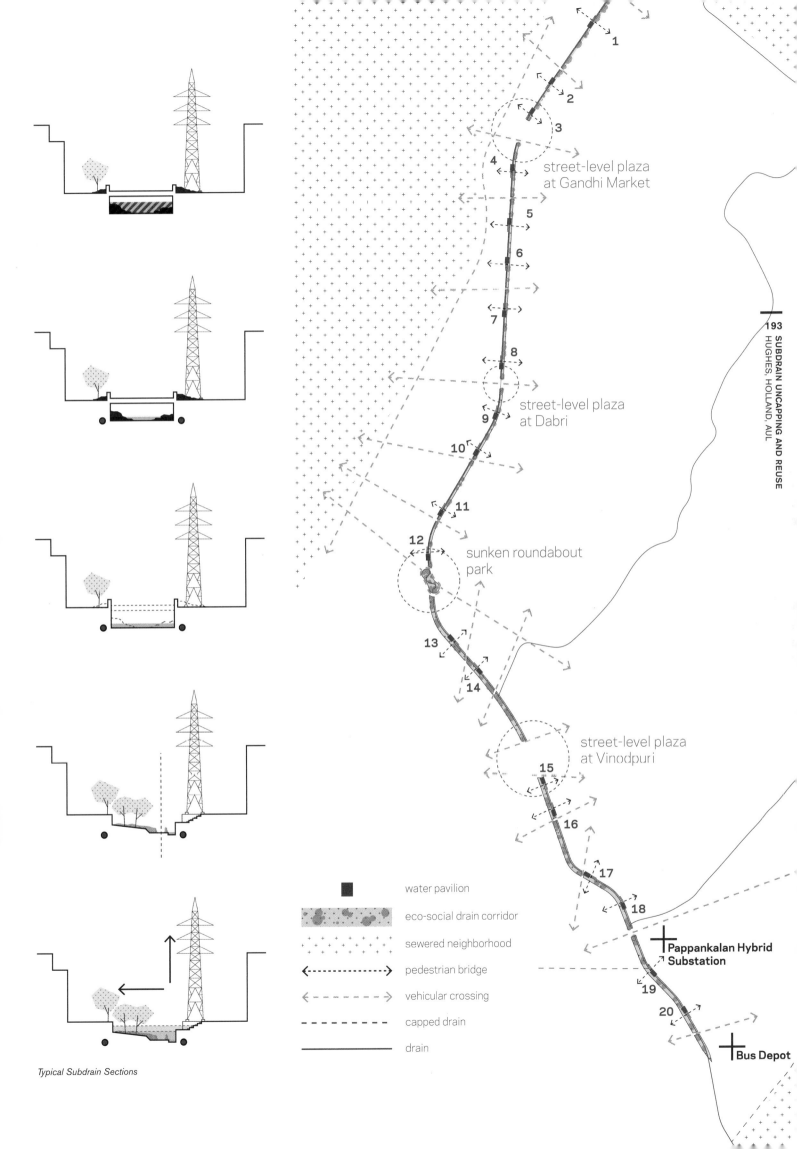

Typical Subdrain Sections

1

2

3

street-level plaza
at Gandhi Market

4

5

6

7

8

street-level plaza
at Dabri

9

10

11

12

sunken roundabout
park

13

14

street-level plaza
at Vinodpuri

15

16

17

18

Pappankalan Hybrid
Substation

19

20

Bus Depot

water pavilion

eco-social drain corridor

sewered neighborhood

pedestrian bridge

vehicular crossing

capped drain

drain

Subdrain Water Pavilion

The provision of clean water, and the activities that require it—including cooking, bathing, and using the bathroom—are often exclusively associated with the domestic realm. But in urban contexts such as Delhi, one cannot presume that piped infrastructure will deliver clean water to the interior of the home, nor discreetly remove dirty water from it. Instead, Delhi has developed social practices of procuring, using, and disposing of water in public, blurring the distinction between the domestic and the urban.

Moreover, the domestic sphere has in many cultures been constructed as a women's space, in contrast to the public realm, which is largely made for and by men. Access to safe and sanitary toilet facilities has been a recent focus of Indian women's rights groups, not least because having to leave the house to relieve oneself after dark leaves women vulnerable to assault.

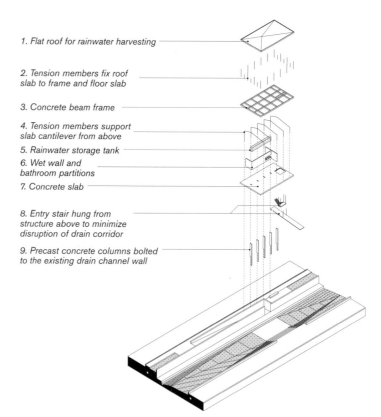

1. Flat roof for rainwater harvesting

2. Tension members fix roof slab to frame and floor slab

3. Concrete beam frame

4. Tension members support slab cantilever from above

5. Rainwater storage tank

6. Wet wall and bathroom partitions

7. Concrete slab

8. Entry stair hung from structure above to minimize disruption of drain corridor

9. Precast concrete columns bolted to the existing drain channel wall

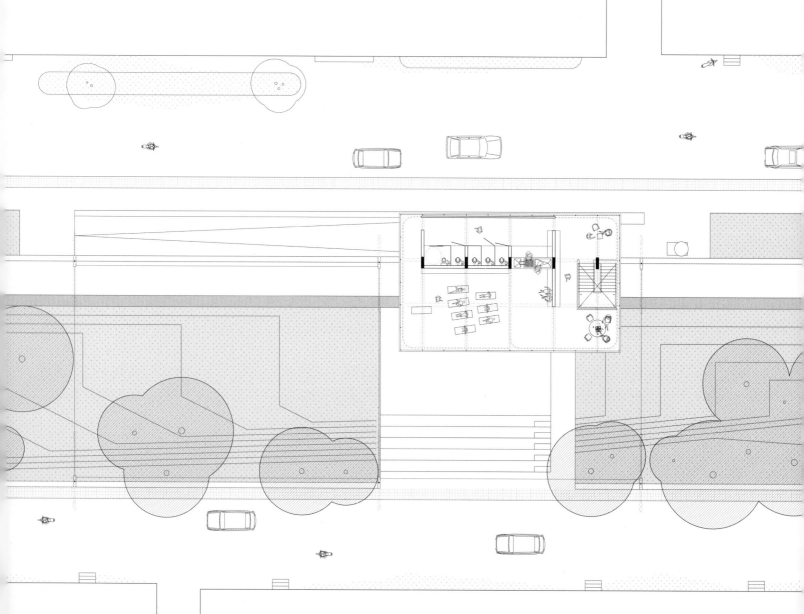

Daylighted Subdrain Park and Water Pavilion

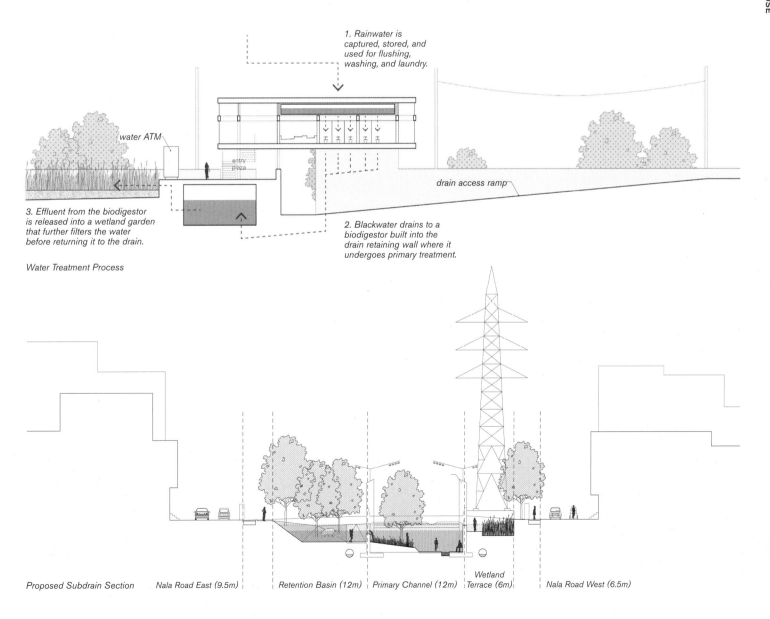

1. Rainwater is captured, stored, and used for flushing, washing, and laundry.

water ATM

entry plaza

drain access ramp

3. Effluent from the biodigestor is released into a wetland garden that further filters the water before returning it to the drain.

2. Blackwater drains to a biodigestor built into the drain retaining wall where it undergoes primary treatment.

Water Treatment Process

Proposed Subdrain Section   Nala Road East (9.5m)   Retention Basin (12m)   Primary Channel (12m)   Wetland Terrace (6m)   Nala Road West (6.5m)

THE NAJAFGARH SUB-DRAINS NEED TO BE RETHOUGHT AS ECOLOGICAL LINEAR PARKS DURING THE DRY SEASON, DESIGNED TO EVACUATE LARGE AMOUNTS OF STORM WATER DURING THE MONSOON. THE SEASONAL PRESENCE OF WATER WILL CREATE RICH BIODIVERSITY CORRIDORS PENETRATING THE CITY, CONNECTING IT WITH THE NAJAFGARH RIVER CORRIDOR.

EXISTING EXCHANGE OF GOODS

PROPOSED EXCHANGE OF GOODS

MANDI

60	SHOPS
46,500 m²	COVERED MARKET
26,000 m³	STORAGE
160 m	FROM FLOODPLAIN
5	ACCESS POINTS

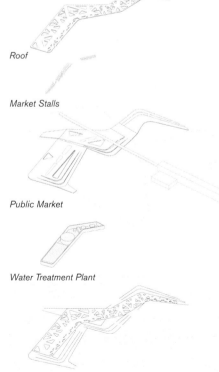

Roof

Market Stalls

Public Market

Water Treatment Plant

STP Restoration and Hybridization

The Shahdara Drain exists as a barren wasteland of black-water, sewage, contaminated soil, and trash. The proposed Shahdara Drain Restoration and Park serves to bring life back to the site. Situated in between dense urban fabric, this highly vegetated, open space offers an escape from Delhi's congested lifestyle. In order to remediate the water, the drain is reshaped into a meandering constructed wetland. The form allows phytoremediation, the mitigation of contaminated water through aquatic vegetation, to take place. This natural process eliminates the need for excavation and the disposal of chemicals, metals, and sludge to alternative sites. In addition, this intervention calls for the completion of the existing sewage treatment plant, which remains unfinished at the tip of peninsula. Improving the existing water quality allows this site to become a critical space between two densely populated areas—Vasundhara Enclave and Patparganj Industrial Area. Currently, Delhi's East Bank lacks program, amenities, and urban infrastructure. The project aims to bring prosperity and human experience to the site with the introduction of an expansive mandi. Elevated over the sewage treatment plant, this large-scale market creates a new ground plane over the drains. The platform acts as an undulating landscape that shelters high-intensity commercial activity and bridges select areas around the site with circulation ramps.

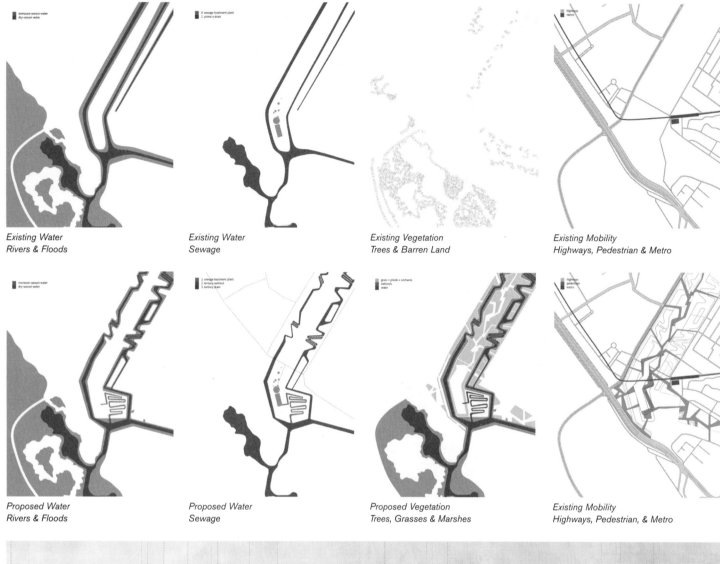

Existing Water
Rivers & Floods

Existing Water
Sewage

Existing Vegetation
Trees & Barren Land

Existing Mobility
Highways, Pedestrian & Metro

Proposed Water
Rivers & Floods

Proposed Water
Sewage

Proposed Vegetation
Trees, Grasses & Marshes

Existing Mobility
Highways, Pedestrian, & Metro

Proposed Native Vegetation

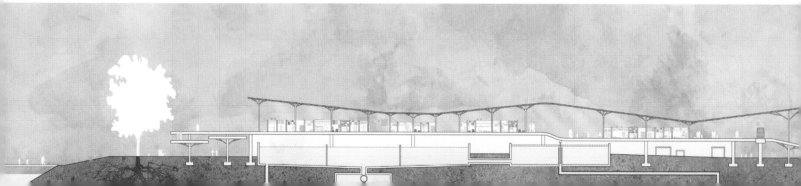

Shahdara Drain Market

Shahdara Drain Market and Wetland Park

THE JAL BOARD PROCESS
OF INSTALLING A SERIES OF
INTERCEPTOR SEWERS WHICH
WILL CAPTURE POLLUTED WATER
IN THE DRAIN SYSTEM AND DIVERT
IT TO NEARBY SEWAGE TREATMENT
PLANTS WILL ALLOW FOR THE
DRAIN SYSTEMS TO BE RECLAIMED
FOR NEW USES. HOW SHOULD
THESE SPACES BE DESIGNED?

DECENTRALIZED WASTE INFRASTRUCTURE

For multiple reasons, a number of critical urban infrastructures will need to be distributed and decentralized. The fabric of the urban villages—such as extremely dense Hastaal village by the Najafgarh—lacks a coherent and hierarchic street system that facilitates the insertion of large scale distribution or collection networks. The size of the megacity also suggests a polycentric strategy that keeps the infrastructure at a reasonable size and creates opportunities for redundancies in order to secure more resilient and flexible systems.

In unplanned urban villages of narrow streets and a random distribution of open spaces, small scale digesters and filters can be inserted to treat sewage locally, separate trash, and recover valuable materials for reuse. A network of small scale public spaces can perform as infrastructural devices that upgrade neighborhood services and connect to the drains and the social and ecological spines at the city scale.

Together with the permanent presence of raw sewage and trash in the streets of Delhi's urban villages, current landfills are one of the most acute crises, polluting water bodies and the air. Landfill remediation—mined, sealed and transformed into public parks—needs to be coordinated with new solid waste management systems and sorting facilities. Besides the physical structures, the remediation of Delhi's solid waste crisis will be dependent in behavioral changes sparked by communication, education, and respect for cultural practices. An essential part of this transition will be the respectful integration of the significant amount of population of all ages currently making their living in the fringes of the formal system.

Decentralized Public
Sewage Infrastructures

Hastsal Village is one of the most dense neighborhoods in Delhi. Accordingly, the area suffers many problems unique to its heavily cramped conditions. The area faces extremely limited public amenities such as schools, health clinics, police stations, and parks. Public amenities that are provided are heavily walled off and disconnected from the surrounding neighborhoods. Because of this limited visual and physical accessibility, public space, including the Najafgarh, is often used as a dumping ground for trash and sewage. Another result of limited public space is an increase in the importance and function of the street. As a shared common space, the street is used for

recreational, economical, and social functions in addition to transportation. Despite the importance of the street, however, the infrastructure, specifically water infrastructure, is very poorly maintained, unable to handle seasonal flooding, sewage, or drinking needs of the people it services. This project restores the community's relationship to the Najafgarh Drain by redesigning the street. In addition to introducing new public amenities, the streets will create decentralized systems that process sewage, storm water, and trash. Streets are programed depending on their scale and function. Small-scale streets will receive public restrooms

and small trash collection systems. The public restrooms will be serviced by decentralized septic tanks that filter gray water through biofiltration parks located along the street or in available empty lots. Trash, the majority of which is recyclable or compostable, will be separated and used to service small green spaces and community gardens that can grow crops for people or animals. For larger-scaled streets, public infrastructure will also increase in scale and hybridity while still integrating into the decentralized waste treatment systems. This proposal results in a networked park system through which treated water will eventually flow to the Najafgarh Drain.

Existing Empty Spaces and Parks

Decentralized Sewage Network

Decentralized Waste Process

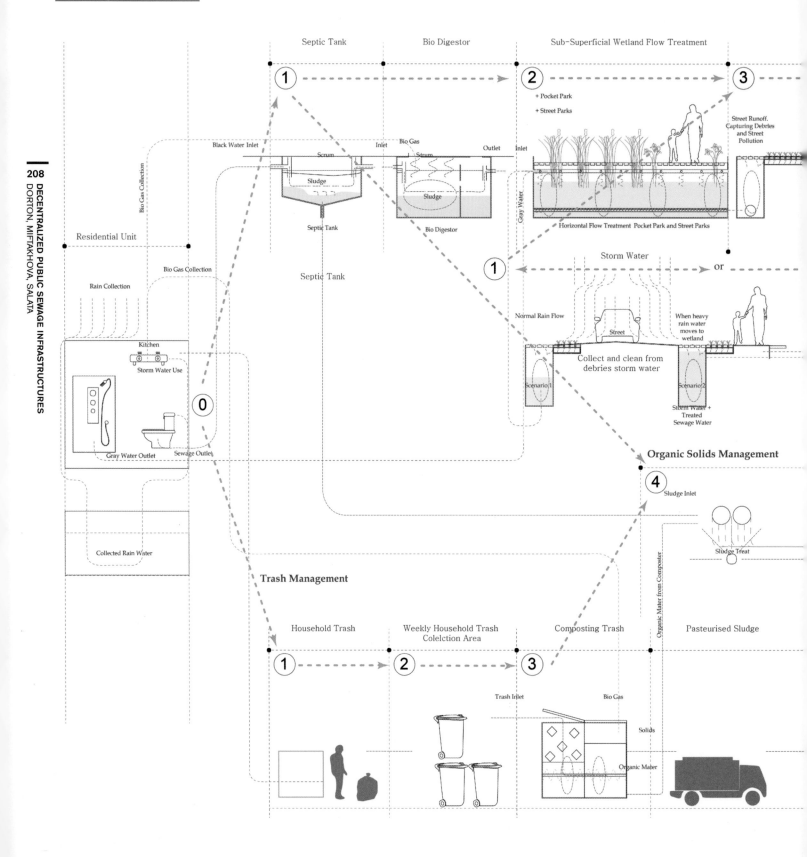

Septic Tank

Bio Digestor

Sub-Superficial Wetland Flow Treatment

+ Pocket Park
+ Street Parks

Street Runoff.
Capturing Debries
and Street
Pollution

Black Water Inlet

Bio Gas

Inlet

Strum

Outlet

Inlet

Scrum

Sludge

Sludge

Gray Water

Septic Tank

Bio Digestor

Horizontal Flow Treatment Pocket Park and Street Parks

Bio Gas Collection

Residential Unit

Septic Tank

Storm Water

or

Bio Gas Collection

Normal Rain Flow

When heavy
rain water
moves to
wetland

Rain Collection

Street

Kitchen

Storm Water Use

Collect and clean from
debries storm water

Scenario 1

Scenario 2

Storm Water +
Treated
Sewage Water

0

Organic Solids Management

Gray Water Outlet

Sewage Outlet

4

Sludge Inlet

Collected Rain Water

Sludge Treat

Trash Management

Organic Mater from Composter

Household Trash

Weekly Household Trash
Colelction Area

Composting Trash

Pasteurised Sludge

1

2

3

Trash Inlet

Bio Gas

Solids

Organic Mater

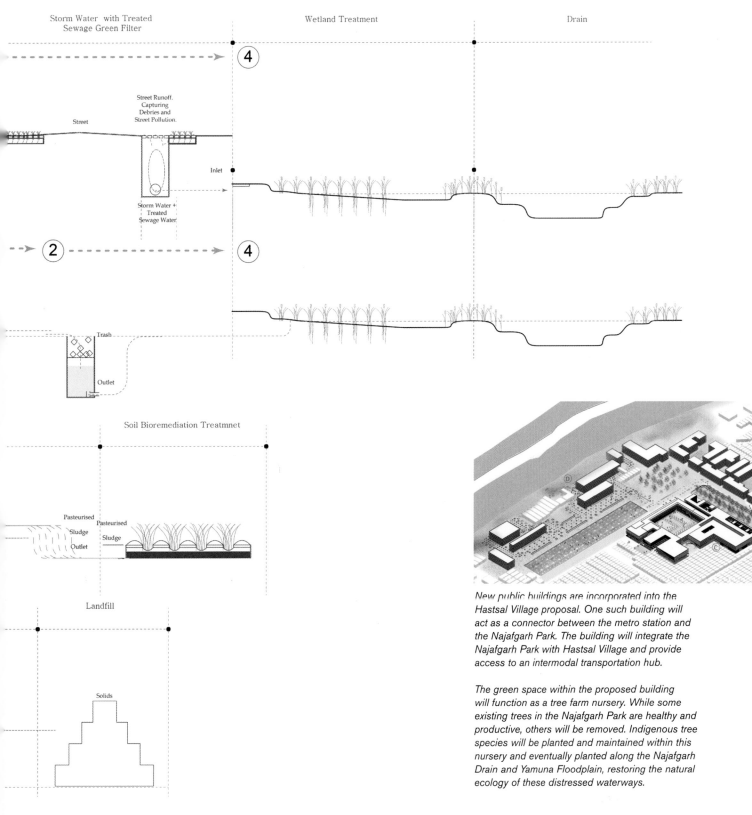

Storm Water with Treated
Sewage Green Filter

Wetland Treatment

Drain

④

Street

Street Runoff.
Capturing
Debries and
Street Pollution.

Inlet

Storm Water +
Treated
Sewage Water

②

④

Trash

Outlet

Soil Bioremediation Treatmnet

Pasteurised
Sludge

Pasteurised
Sludge

Outlet

Landfill

Solids

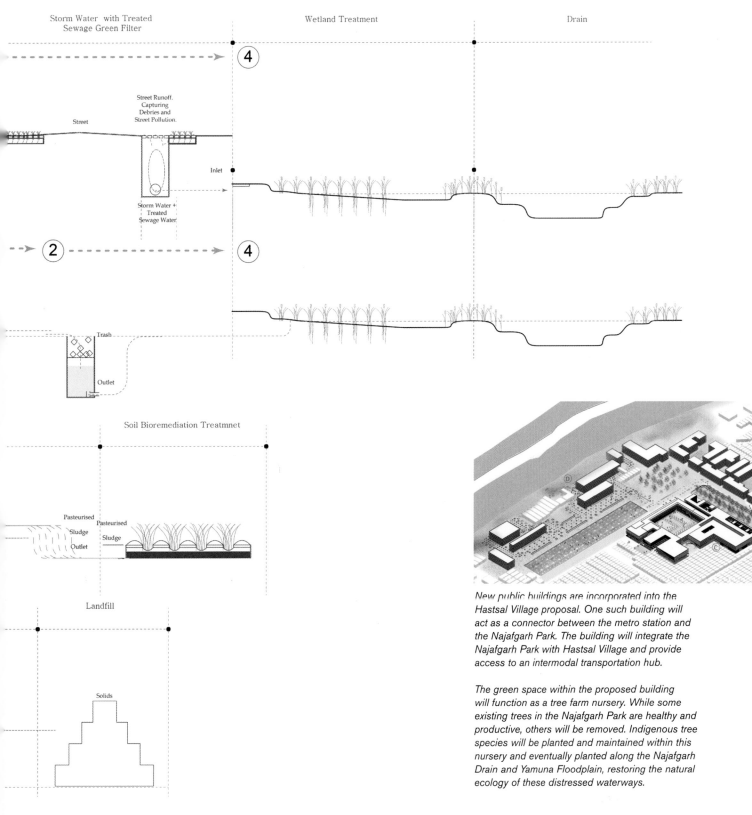

New public buildings are incorporated into the
Hastsal Village proposal. One such building will
act as a connector between the metro station and
the Najafgarh Park. The building will integrate the
Najafgarh Park with Hastsal Village and provide
access to an intermodal transportation hub.

The green space within the proposed building
will function as a tree farm nursery. While some
existing trees in the Najafgarh Park are healthy and
productive, others will be removed. Indigenous tree
species will be planted and maintained within this
nursery and eventually planted along the Najafgarh
Drain and Yamuna Floodplain, restoring the natural
ecology of these distressed waterways.

THE AMOUNT OF WASTE GENERATED DAILY HAS OVERWHELMED THE CAPACITY OF DELHI'S INFRASTRUCTURE. UNCOLLECTED WASTE ENDS UP IN INFORMAL LANDFILLS–OFTEN EMPTY LOTS, ROADSIDES, OR THE DRAIN SYSTEM. THE ANSWER MAY LIE IN DECENTRALIZING TREATMENT AND PRIORITIZING DEVELOPMENT OF SPECIALIZED WASTE PROCESSING SITES.

Waste Collection and Landfill Remediation

This urban project addresses Delhi's dysfunctional waste management system and the tolls it enacts on the city's population. In particular, focus is on the gigantic, problematic Bhalswa "landfill" which currently towers 50m above its surroundings. In reality, this "landfill" is a dumping ground because it is unlined, contaminating groundwater aquifers, and emits uncaptured methane gas which burns uncontrollably, thus significantly contributing to the city's toxic levels of air pollution and severely compromises the health of surrounding communities.

Through this project, waste is no longer considered something to ignore or hide, but is instead utilized as a resource vital for the city's operation, prosperity, and ecological health. A zero-waste management system is proposed which re-imagines Delhi's waste management system. Waste separation is prioritized;

compostables, recyclables, construction waste, industrial waste, and household waste are collected and treated according to their own specifications, allowing them to be treated effectively while maximizing their potential ecological and social value. This new network is composed of two parts. The Sorting Complex - a hybridization of the waste economic industry that contains with housing, training, and educational opportunities for Delhi's informal waste pickers which protect their livelihoods and provide better living conditions. Landfill Parks - a series of public parks that result from landfill mining and reclamation.

This project reclaims the landfill to form a new typology which eliminates current pollutants and supports ecological functions, introduces a variety of public spaces and facilities, and provides new recreation opportunities.

Construction Timeline

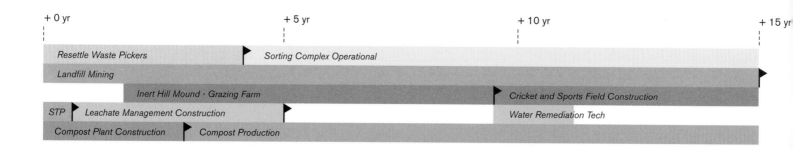

+ 0 yr   + 5 yr   + 10 yr   + 15 yr

Resettle Waste Pickers	Sorting Complex Operational
Landfill Mining	
Inert Hill Mound - Grazing Farm	Cricket and Sports Field Construction
STP ▸ Leachate Management Construction	Water Remediation Tech
Compost Plant Construction ▸ Compost Production	

Site Plans

1. Parking Lots
2. Water Treatment Plant
3. Compost Plant
4. Mobile Screening Plant
5. Sports Field
6. Playground
7. Cricket Stadium
8. Forest Theater
9. Forest Valley
10. Overlook Bridge
11. Forest Trail
12. Market Corridor
13. Water Remediation
14. Entrance Plaza
15. Pond Plaza
16. Grazing Farms
17. Bhalswa Diary Village
18. Supplementary Drain

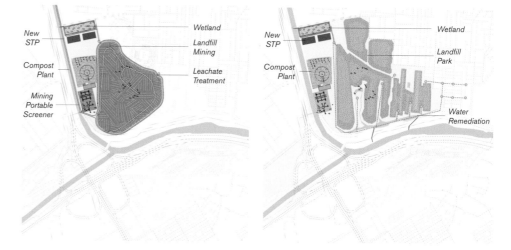

New STP · Compost Plant · Mining Portable Screener · Wetland · Landfill Mining · Leachate Treatment

New STP · Compost Plant · Wetland · Landfill Park · Water Remediation

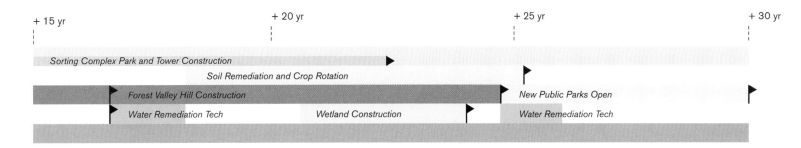

| | + 15 yr | + 20 yr | + 25 yr | + 30 yr |

Sorting Complex Park and Tower Construction

Soil Remediation and Crop Rotation

Forest Valley Hill Construction

New Public Parks Open

Water Remediation Tech

Wetland Construction

Water Remediation Tech

18. Supplementary Drain
19. Wetland
20. Residue Management
21. Plastic Sorting
22. Aluminum Sorting
23. Glass Sorting
24. Pre-Sorting
25. Sorting Factory
26. Paper Sorting
27. Green Belt
28. Social Housing
29. Waste-Built Hill Park
30. Herb Garden
31. Phytoremediation
32. Mixed-Use Tower
33. Waste Collecting Points
34. Urban Village
35. Pedestrian Corridor

Compost Plant
Landfill Park
Wetland Park

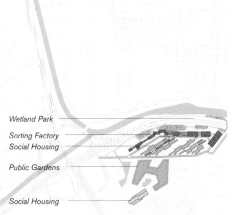

Wetland Park
Sorting Factory
Social Housing
Public Gardens
Social Housing

Landfill Mining Process

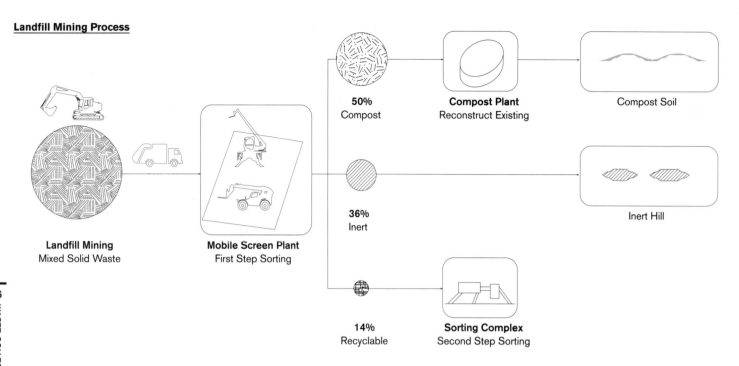

Landfill Mining
Mixed Solid Waste

Mobile Screen Plant
First Step Sorting

50%
Compost

Compost Plant
Reconstruct Existing

Compost Soil

36%
Inert

Inert Hill

14%
Recyclable

Sorting Complex
Second Step Sorting

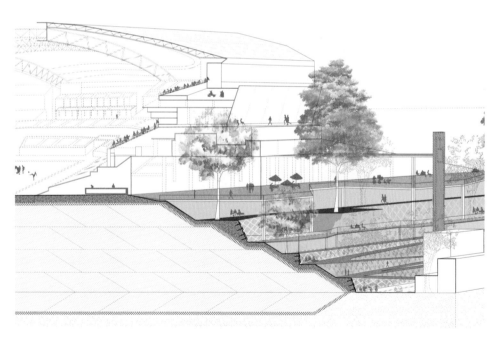

Landfill Park

The Bhalswa Landfill transformation will take 20 years to complete. Because of the extreme health hazards posed by the landfill adjacent slums will be relocated before remediation can take place. Next, landfill mining begins and mobile screening plants are deployed to sort the mined landfill waste. Recyclable and compostable waste is removed to be processed elsewhere on site; remaining waste is then relocated on site to form new waste-built hills that take advantage of the latest landfill technology and contribute to groundwater treatment. Eventually, the entire landfill is mined and the area is transformed into a landfill park, offering public amenities and recreational options while contributing to the ecological health of the Bhalswa region.

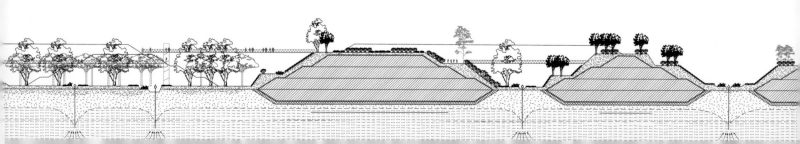

+ 0 yr

Drain

Bhalswa Landfill

High Polluted Area / Relocate Slum

+ 3 yr

Inert Waste

Mixed Waste

Landfill Mining

Drain

Mobile Screening Plant

Waste-Built Hill + Compost Soil

Groundwater Treatment Pump

+ 10 yr

Waste-Built Hill (North Side)

Landfill Mining

Drain

Mobile Screening Plant

Groundwater Treatment Pump

+ 15 yr

Waste-Built Hill + Compost Soil

Drain

Mobile Screening Plant

Landfill Mining

Groundwater Treatment Pump

+ 20 yr

Waste-Built Hill + Compost Soil

Drain

Groundwater Treatment Pump

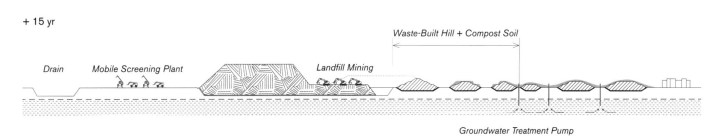
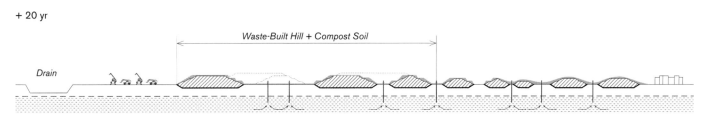
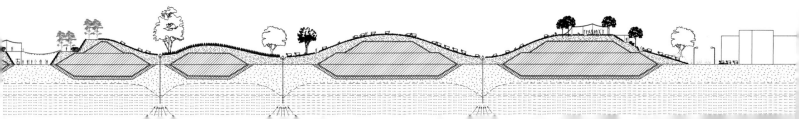

Sorting Complex Process

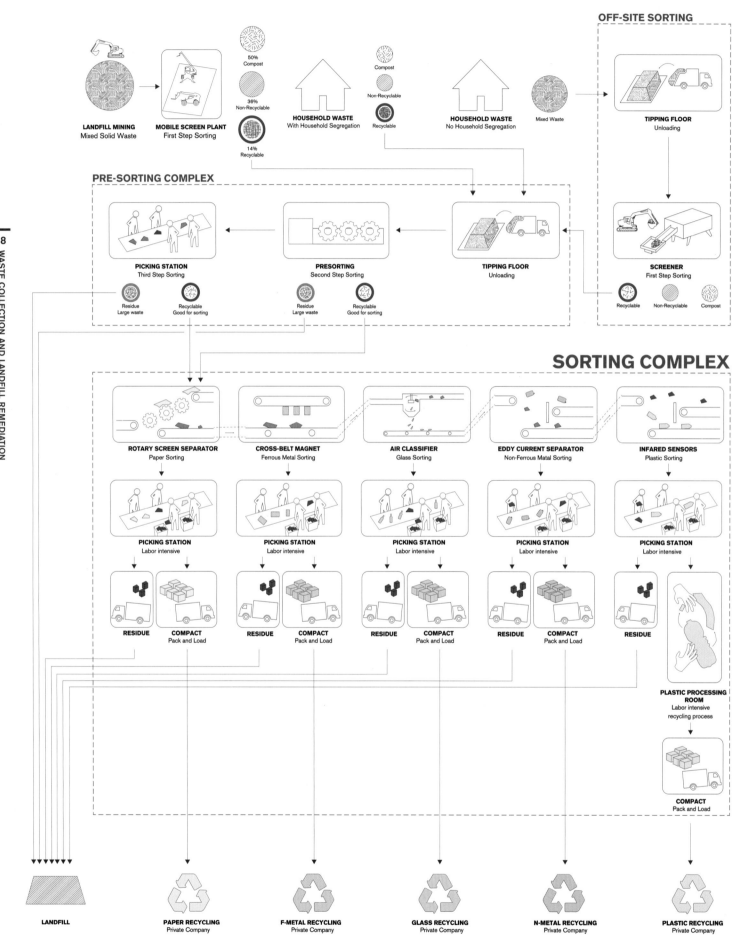

OFF-SITE SORTING

LANDFILL MINING
Mixed Solid Waste

MOBILE SCREEN PLANT
First Step Sorting

50%
Compost

36%
Non-Recyclable

14%
Recyclable

HOUSEHOLD WASTE
With Household Segregation

Compost

Non-Recyclable

Recyclable

HOUSEHOLD WASTE
No Household Segregation

Mixed Waste

TIPPING FLOOR
Unloading

SCREENER
First Step Sorting

Recyclable

Non-Recyclable

Compost

PRE-SORTING COMPLEX

PICKING STATION
Third Step Sorting

Residue
Large waste

Recyclable
Good for sorting

PRESORTING
Second Step Sorting

Residue
Large waste

Recyclable
Good for sorting

TIPPING FLOOR
Unloading

SORTING COMPLEX

ROTARY SCREEN SEPARATOR
Paper Sorting

CROSS-BELT MAGNET
Ferrous Metal Sorting

AIR CLASSIFIER
Glass Sorting

EDDY CURRENT SEPARATOR
Non-Ferrous Matal Sorting

INFARED SENSORS
Plastic Sorting

PICKING STATION
Labor intensive

PICKING STATION
Labor intensive

PICKING STATION
Labor intensive

PICKING STATION
Labor intensive

PICKING STATION
Labor intensive

RESIDUE

COMPACT
Pack and Load

RESIDUE

COMPACT
Pack and Load

RESIDUE

COMPACT
Pack and Load

RESIDUE

COMPACT
Pack and Load

RESIDUE

PLASTIC PROCESSING ROOM
Labor intensive
recycling process

COMPACT
Pack and Load

LANDFILL

PAPER RECYCLING
Private Company

F-METAL RECYCLING
Private Company

GLASS RECYCLING
Private Company

N-METAL RECYCLING
Private Company

PLASTIC RECYCLING
Private Company

Pre-sorting Complex   *Paper Sorting*   *Glass Sorting*

Sorting Complex - Segment A

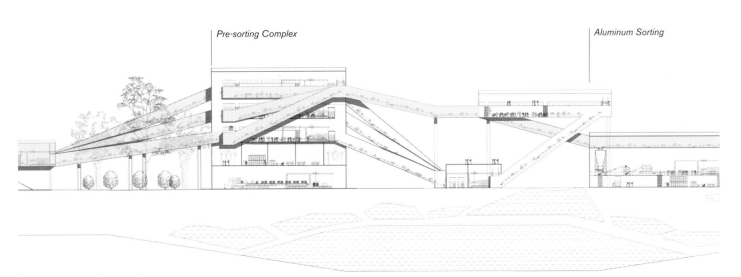

Pre-sorting Complex   *Aluminum Sorting*

Sorting Complex - Segment B

Plastic Sorting   *Residue Management*

Sorting Complex - Segment C

UNPLANNED GROWTH HAS TAKEN PLACE
WITHOUT SEWAGE PIPES—WASTE WATER
RUNS THROUGH THE STREETS TO OPEN
DRAINS. BETWEEN FOUR AND FIVE MILLION
INHABITANTS, MORE THAN 25% OF DELHI'S
POPULATION, ARE NOT CONNECTED TO THIS
BASIC INFRASTRUCTURE AND TREATMENT
PLANTS ARE HIDDEN FROM THE PUBLIC EYE.

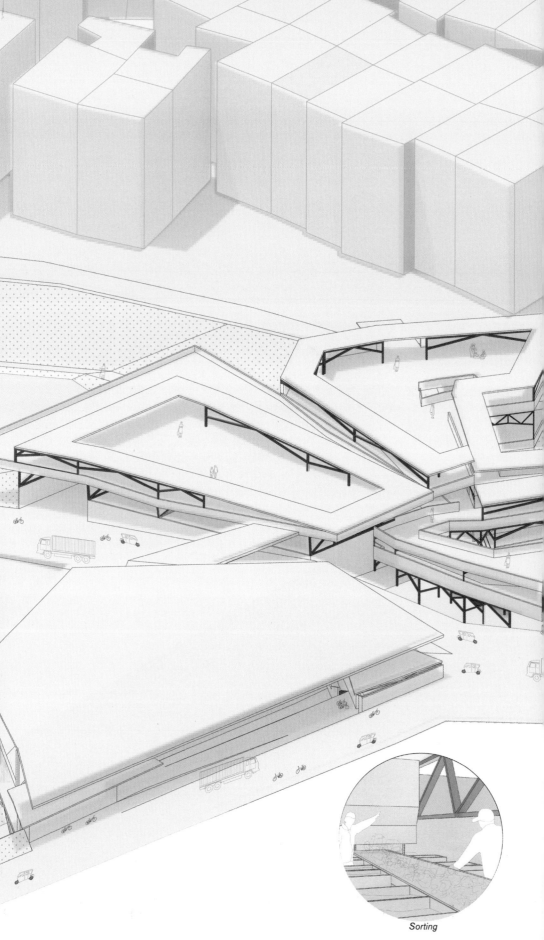

Hybrid Waste Treatment Plant

How can "informal" settlements be empowered to support change? Within the context of Delhi, the Yamuna River was once a powerful resource to the city. Now, the tributaries have been coated in concrete and filled with trash and effluent, and the river is running black. This is a large scale issue—one of the largest pollutants of the Yamuna River and the greater environmental systems of Delhi is solid waste.

Centralized collection and disposal systems hinder improvements to the existing system of landfills since Delhi has simply run out of space for their expansion. Decentralized waste management infrastructure will allow the waste system to operate more effectively and provide opportunities to support novel forms of public amenities such as schools and training centers. Placing new waste management and community facilities along the drains allows these hybrid infrastructures to act as a catalyst for revitalizing existing social and culture structures.

The site chosen is located at the edge of one of the largest slums of Delhi. The project captures the settlement's waste before it exits the area and provides support to local workers who utilize the informal waste collection cycle as their livelihood. By incorporating educational resources into the new waste treatment facility, community engagement in the informal waste process increases, helping to alleviate inefficiencies. Additionally, as workers become part of a stronger economy, education and job training skills provide new opportunities, and child care and health services provide support to the needs of working families.

Sorting

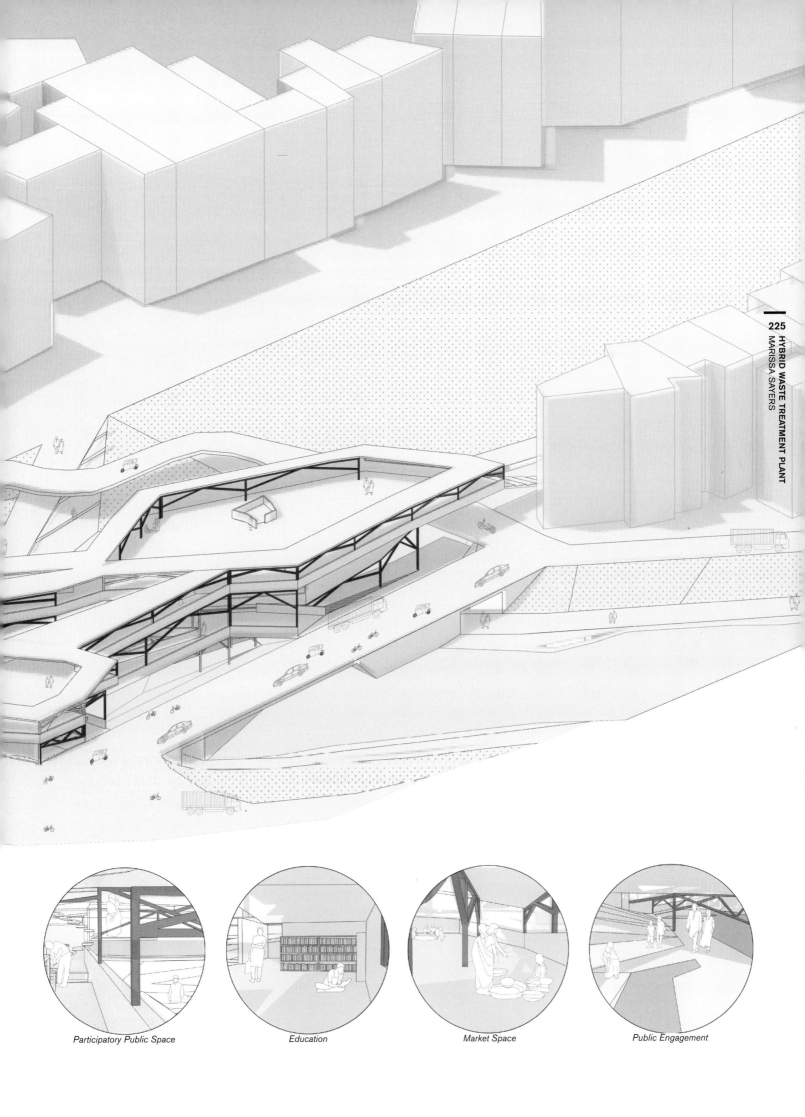

Participatory Public Space

Education

Market Space

Public Engagement

Phase 1 - Initiation
Goals: Remove ragpickers from the terrible landfill conditions to a safe working environment

Phase 2 - Capacity Increase
Goals: Increase the efficiency of the process and share new skills

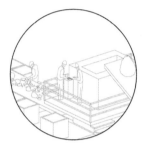 

Phase 3 - Public Addition
Goals: Provide new spaces for the community to gether for learning and sharing

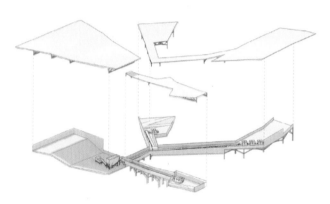

Phase 4 - Landscape
Goals: Provide clean open space where people can interact with the environment

Phase 5 - Expansion
Goals: Adapt the facilities as needs change over time t provide for the evolving society around it The structure can be expanded by adding structure to the initial armature

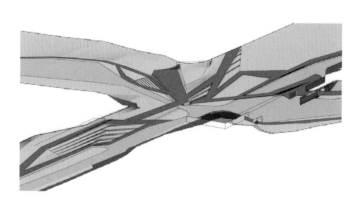

Metals Processing

The metals processing is partnered with a workshop where the metals and other construction type materials can be reused by the residents of the community to produce new things. This gives them space to create, meet needs at home, and sell.

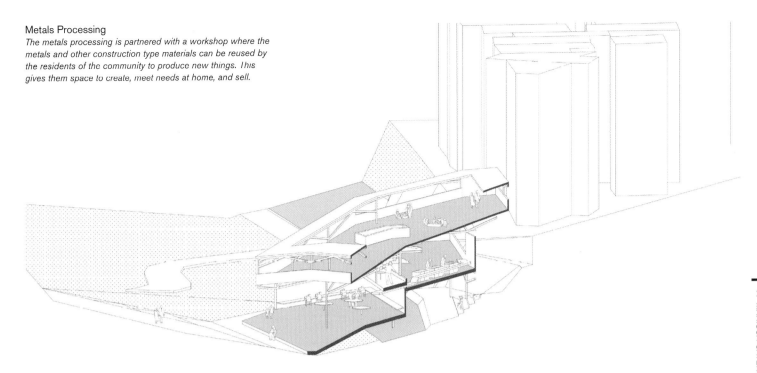

Plastics Processing

The plastics recycling is partnered with a technology space which allows people to have access to the internet and space to collaborate with others. the wall between the two programs is not closed off, instead people are able to see and hear the process.

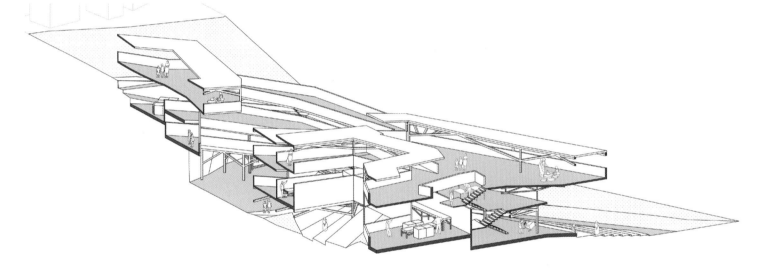

Paper Processing

The paper processing is partnered with a lending library and book making area. People from the community come here to read, and exchange books with each other. There is also a space to make their own books for reading, drawing, and sharing ideas.

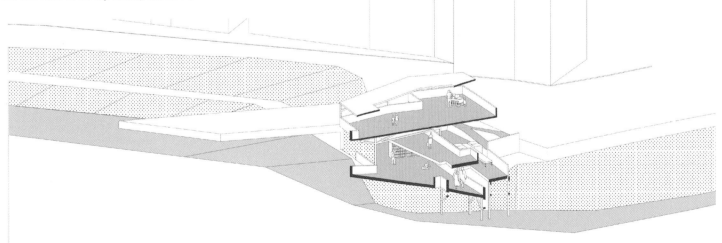

THE YAMUNA RIVER COMMONS

The Yamuna and its floodplain is re-envisioned as Delhi's big commons, the next major public space operation since the construction of New Delhi. Instead of wide avenues and bare axes, today's monumentality is linked to the scale of ecology and welcomes the entire, highly diverse, population of the megacity.

Transparency and accessibility to the Yamuna, its floodplain, and its tributaries is the first step towards the recovery of the river and Delhi's ecology. We reconcile the urgent need of re-stitching cultural and social narratives together with the physical presence of Delhi's backbone in the daily life of its inhabitants. The cleansing of waters will only take place if taken back to the public sphere, under the close watch of the people.

British New Delhi did not know how to relate to a seasonal river. Reconnecting the city to the water is a long overdue public space operation that will integrate major heritage sites now isolated in the city, revitalize the Pragati Maidan convention area, and finally give people access to the river. New basic public facilities at the scale of the neighborhood, the city, and the nation are linked to the fringe of the floodplain. Currently, several critical urban infrastructures are using the floodplain as an empty backyard. Power plants, electrical substations, cement and gas plants are currently destroying the riparian ecologies and the social value of the Yamuna while being at severe risk of destruction by floods at any given year. There needs to be a plan for their progressive removal and relocation—timed to their obsolesce—with the appropriate strategy for restoration instead of the current abandonment of 'infrastructural cadavers'.

In their place, cultural amenities, markets, educational or spiritual spaces, are opportunities to construct a urban buffer and tune the relations between Delhi's population and their Yamuna. Designed as an integral part of the living system of the Yamuna, this new urban façade will be resilient to floods and compatible with the river ecologies.

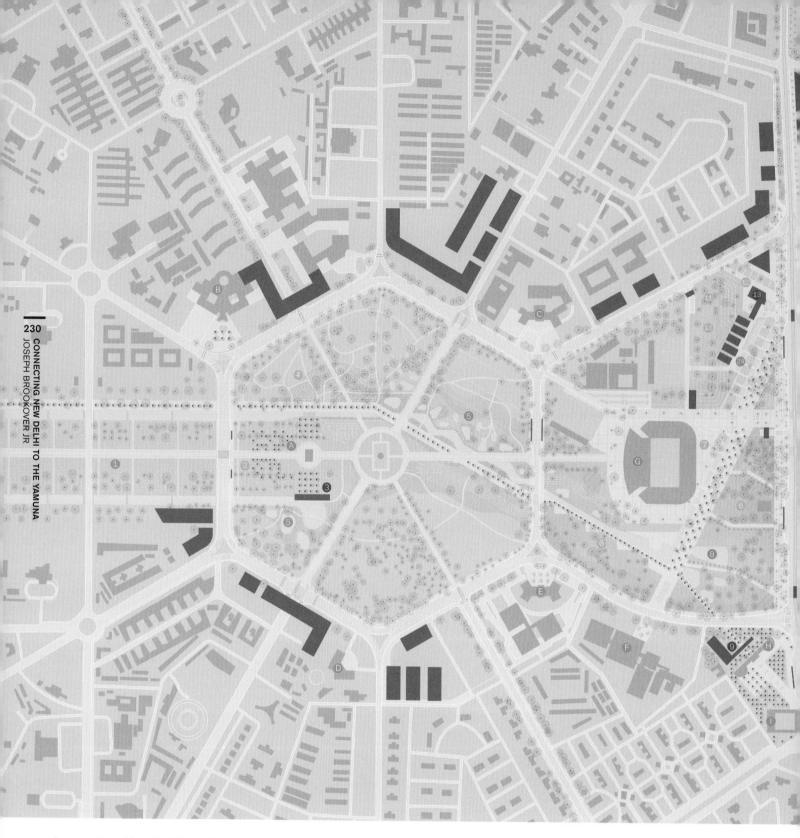

Connecting New Delhi to the Yamuna

The explosive development of Delhi after Imperial British rule began a process of expansion away from the Yamuna River highlighted by a frayed urban fabric and lack of a shared social identity.

The centrally located government zone, Lutyens' Plan, epitomizes this physical and psychological divide; it is the continuation of a political power structure which resists moments of reflection and shared identity necessary for the development of a cohesive society, leading to issues of growth, waste, water, health, war,

and oppression. The project looks to create a situation in which a shared identity can emerge. It begins through an analysis of the city by transect, not zone, seeking to reveal the latent identity of the urban fabric and speculating on new adjacencies. Research of the existing conditions shows a segmented urban fabric that restricts pedestrian movement and limits usable public space. Walking the site reveals disconnects along the axis from the Yamuna, past Pragati Maidan and Purana Qila, between the National Stadium and India Gate park.

Urban Interventions

1. Water Remediation
2. "Forest" - Manas Wildlife Sanctuary
3. Cultural Center
4. "Mountains"
5. "Wetlands" - Keoladeo
6. "Plains"
7. "Desert"
8. "Lakes"
9. Cultural Center
10. "Plateau" - Kass Plateau
11. Flower Field
12. Orchard
13. Cultural Center
14. "Mountains"
15. Cultural Center

16. Mangrove Tank - Sundarbans National Park
17. Pragati Maidan Market
18. "Coast"
19. New Expo Center & Mixed Use Development
20. Urban Forest
21. "Wilderness" - Western Ghatts
22. Cultural Center

Existing Context & Collaborations

A India Gate
B Hyderabad House
C Government Building
D Bikaner House
E National Gallery of Modern Art
F Delhi High Court
G Major Dhyan Chand National Stadium

H Old Gate of Purana Qila
I Masjid Khairu Manzil Mosque
J Purana Qila
K India Trade Commission
L Pragati Maidan Expo Center
M Craft Museum
N National Science Center Museum
O Performing Arts Center - Joey Laughlin
P Pragati Maidan Community College - Fuhou Zhang
Q Indraprastha Housing Community - Cristina Castillo
R Trans-Yamuna Housing - Eric Barr
S Yamuna Tower housing - Donna Ryu
T Yamuna Floodplain Redevelopment - Abby Sandberg
U Yamuna Floodplain Redevelopment - Aaron Bridgers
V Pragati Maidan Expo Center

New Building
Existing Building
Softscape
Hardscape

India Gate Biodiversity Park

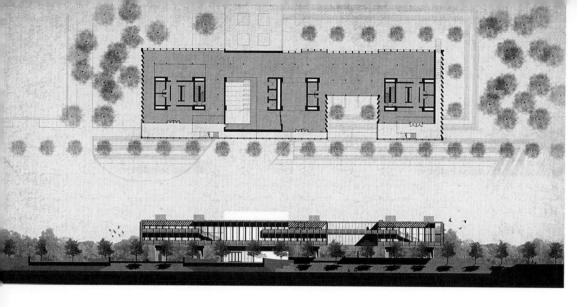

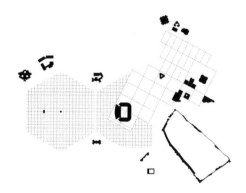

1. Analysis
Existing Built Fabric
Organization & Proximity

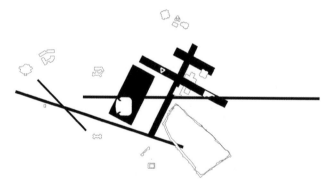

2. Speculation
Existing Transects
Connections & Order

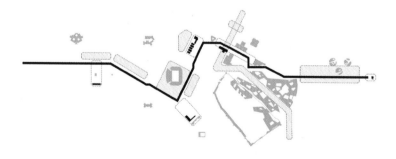

3. Site Structure
Proposed Urban Transects
Pedestrian Transects & Reinforcing Zones

The city and its sacred river are disconnected, walled off internally and from each other, resulting in oppressive unused space often guarded by barbed wire, guard posts, and visible paramilitary.

The project stitches together existing fabric and proposed projects through the introduction of new systems which reorient the city to its history and culture, connect to nature, establish democratic space and allow for a new memory to emerge through moments of recognition between individuals.

A new urban forum of public space and cultural institutions is founded: a Cultural Transect for an Independent India. Along this forum Indian history and identity can be experienced through a sequence of events representing the many ancient forms and landscapes found across diverse regions of India.

The forum allows citizens to envision a network between the past, present, and future, nature and city, culture, education, and the arts, creating a shared democratic space. A shared cultural identity emerges over time through moments of recognition and shared experience of a free people.

Existing Infrastructure
Buildings & Mobility & Water

Existing & Demo Infrastructure
Buildings

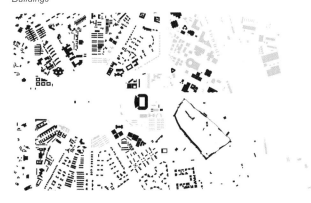

Existing Mobility Infrastructure
Walls & Pedestrian & Vehicular

Proposed Mobility Infrastructure
Pedestrian & Vehicular

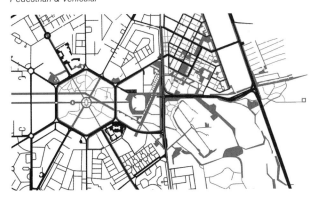

Ecology
Water Systems

Ecology
Vegetation Systems

CONNECTING NEW DELHI TO THE YAMUNA
JOSEPH BROOKOVER JR

Existing & Proposed Infrastructure
Buildings

Proposal
Cultural Transect

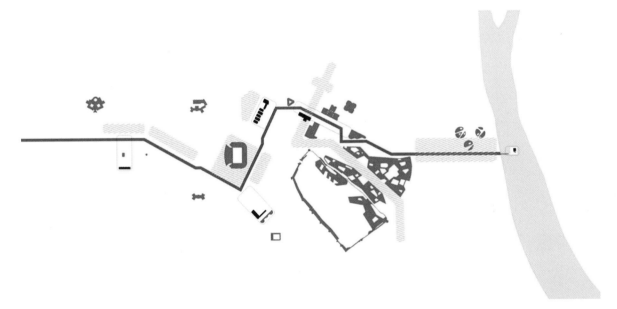

Proposal
Cultural Transect

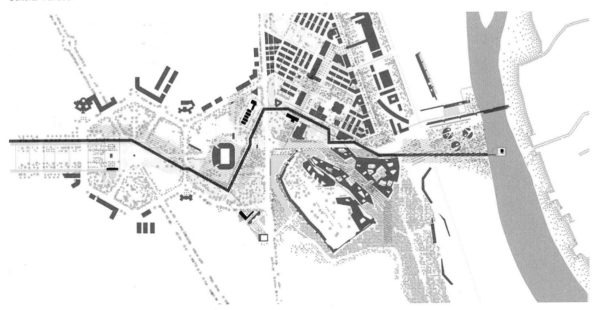

FOR CENTURIES, THE RIVER AND ITS
FLOODPLAIN HAVE SERVED AS A
CENTRAL FIXTURE IN THE DAILY LIFE
OF DELHI'S INHABITANTS–PERHAPS
ONE DAY THE YAMUNA WILL BE
RETURNED TO ITS PROPER ROLE.

Intermodal Education Facilities

This project transforms the Anna Narga district from a desolate piece of land into a mixed-use center with multiple programs built around and on top of a revived bus station. In the future, this project will provide one of the best educational resources in Delhi in addition to various public spaces located around the center for the citizens of Delhi. At the same time, connections and accessibility improvements are created to relink this site with surrounding city blocks in every direction.

The site of this project is located in the center of Delhi, surrounded by a few very important city blocks of municipal and public buildings. However this site, basically occupied by railways, drainage, slums, and an obsolete bus depot, has become a great gap in the city,

blockading accessibility between different areas. According to early research, most primary schools are located in the periphery areas of Delhi. The periphery lacks diverse public resources while the city center has little educational resources but some of the best public resources in the city. Instead of removing the obsolete bus depot and the existing buildings, the proposed school is built on an added roof over the bus station and the abandoned buildings are renewed to become dormitories for students. A rooftop park and an activity center will form a bridged connection between Pragati Maidan, the floodplain landscape parks, and metro station. To the north and the south, the project also connects mixed-use housing and the proposed university with dynamic public spaces.

LONG CONSIDERED A SACRED RIVER, TODAY THE YAMUNA FACES CONTINUOUS STRESS FROM DELHI'S URBAN EXPANSION. THE NAJAFGARH DRAIN ACCOUNTS FOR OVER 60% OF TOTAL POLLUTANTS IN THE RIVER, AND WITHOUT SUBSTANTIAL INTERVENTION THE NAJAFGARH DRAIN WILL CONTINUE TO DUMP WASTE INTO THE YAMUNA, RENDERING THE RIVER DEAD.

Spiritual Facilities by the River

The Indraprastha Floodplain sits unoccupied, covered in fragments of defunct infrastructure. Ground cover creeps over unused rail lines that once carried coal and fly ash. Public access to the site is difficult and completely severs the people from the river. Despite it being a former industrial span, the landscape has been returned over to nature. The green that reclaims the floodplain hosts wildlife: butterflies, cows and peacocks. Where people can access the river, spiritual ceremonies provide a sense of healing to the space.

Currently, the strategy to mitigate flooding of the Yamuna River is to block water from entering the site completely. This cuts off the site's accessibility to the river, while the drain runs directly into the river. The proposed drainage strategy follows a new soil remediation park to come to a sewage treatment plant. From here, any gray water is redirected to a series of filtration beds and active wetlands throughout the site. In recovering the Yamuna floodplain for the people, an especially spiritual reconciling occurs at the proposed cremation grounds. Cremation in India is a fact of everyday life, with wooden pyres lining the river to best situate the soul for release from the deceased. In this new model for cremation grounds, people are confronted with loss and their own mortality in a space that celebrates the Yamuna, a sacred river. The Indraprastha Cremation Grounds are meant to provide for those two realms of mourning: those who depart and those who will return.

Site Process

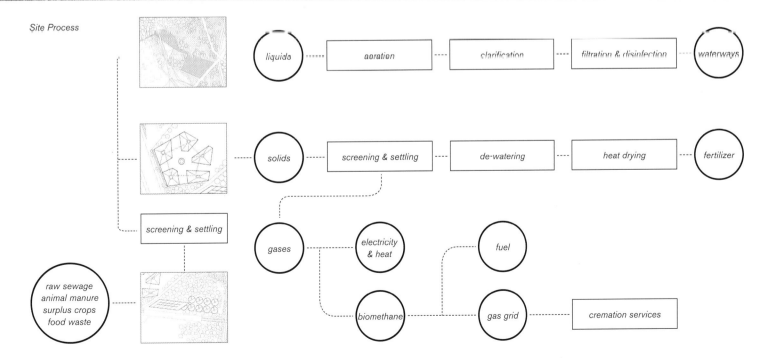

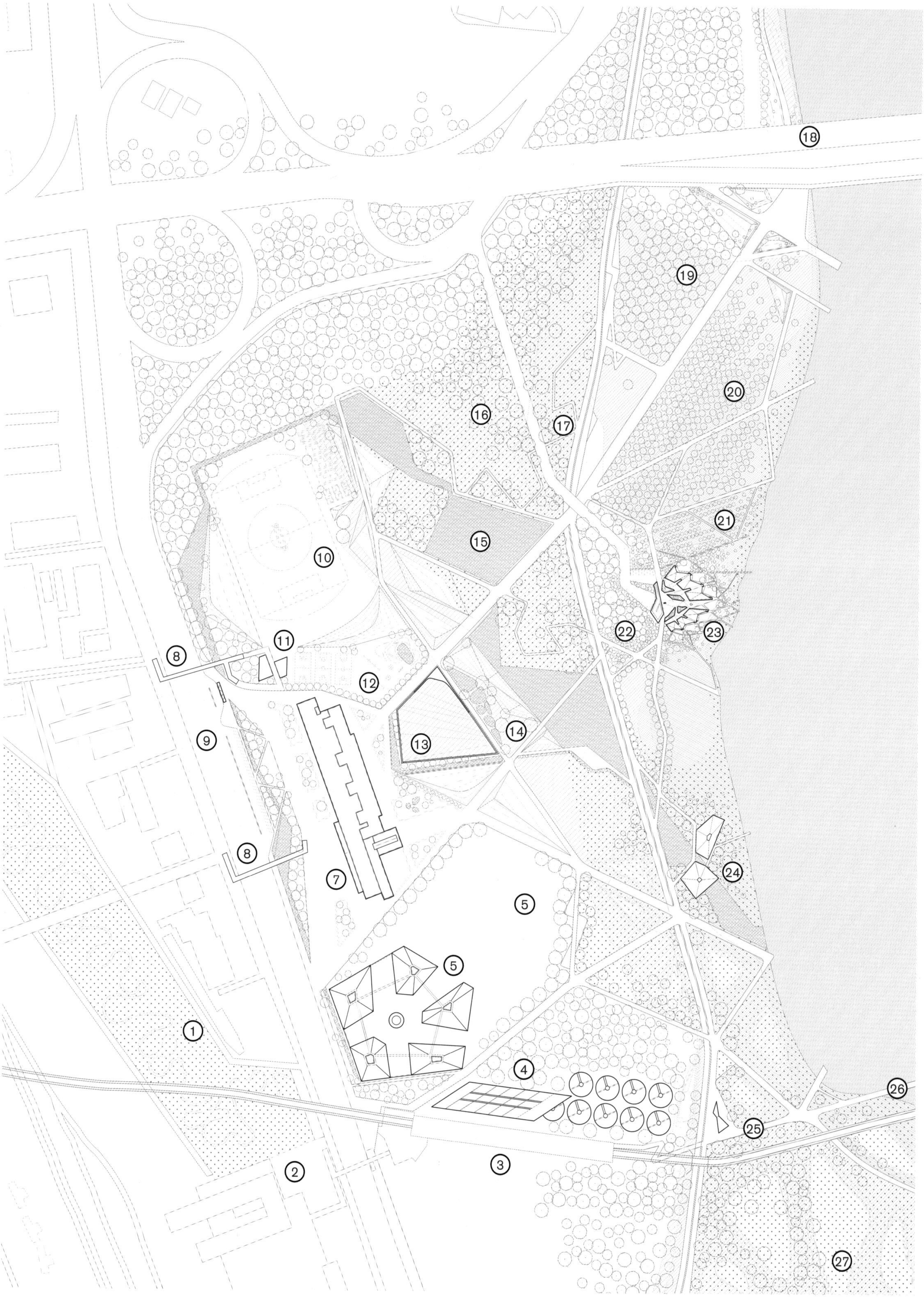
1
2
3
4
5
5
7
8
8
9
10
11
12
13
14
15
16
17
18
19
20
21
22
23
24
25
26
27

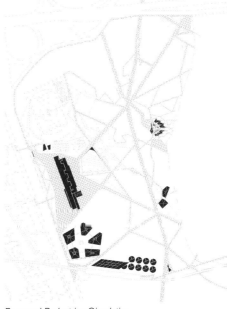

Existing Pedestrian Circulation

Proposed Pedestrian Circulation

1. Sen Nursing Home Drain
2. Pragati Maidan Community College
3. Existing Metro Station
4. Sewage Treatment Plant
5. Biomass Digester
6. Lawn
7. New Yamuna Bazaar
8. Pedestrian Bridge
9. Bus Stop
10. Recreation Fields
11. Field Equipment
12. Playground
13. Amphitheater
14. Recreation Pools
15. Drain Filtering Beds
16. Active Wetlands
17. Bicycle and Rickshaw Path
18. Vikas Marg Pedestrian Bridge
19. Neem Forest
20. Mango Orchard
21. Sandalwood Forest
22. Raised Pedestrian Path
23. Indraprastha Cremation Grounds
24. Public Baths
25. Restroom Pavilion
26. Bridge to Seasonal Island
27. Riparian Forest and Wetland

Existing Drain

Proposed Drain

Construction Process

A. Charred Wood Louvers

Charred wood louvers are angled to shed rain while filtering natural light into the space below. The char of the material reflects this light and creates a glowing effect within the roof.

B. Steel Truss

A chimney is suspended from a steel truss, the chimney acting as a keystone. Gravity loads are transferred from the center out to the four corners.

C. Charred Wood Cladding

The underside of the roof is clad with narrow charred wood boards, spaced regularly to filter light. The upward angle of the ceiling directs heat in and around the chimney to combat heat loss. Additionally, the material echoes traditional Hindu cremation ceremonies that use wooden pyres.

D. Stainless Steel Chimney

The suspended chimney hangs above the dais that performs as the focal point during the ceremony and cremation. The chimney's telescoping mechanics allow the bottom to lift during the ceremony and close during the cremation.

E. Masonry Dais

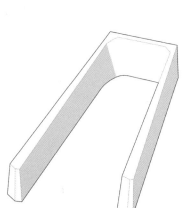

During the ceremony and cremation the body rests on a ceramic retort base set within a masonry dais. Under the ceramic tiles, a removable tray collects ashes as the body is cremated.

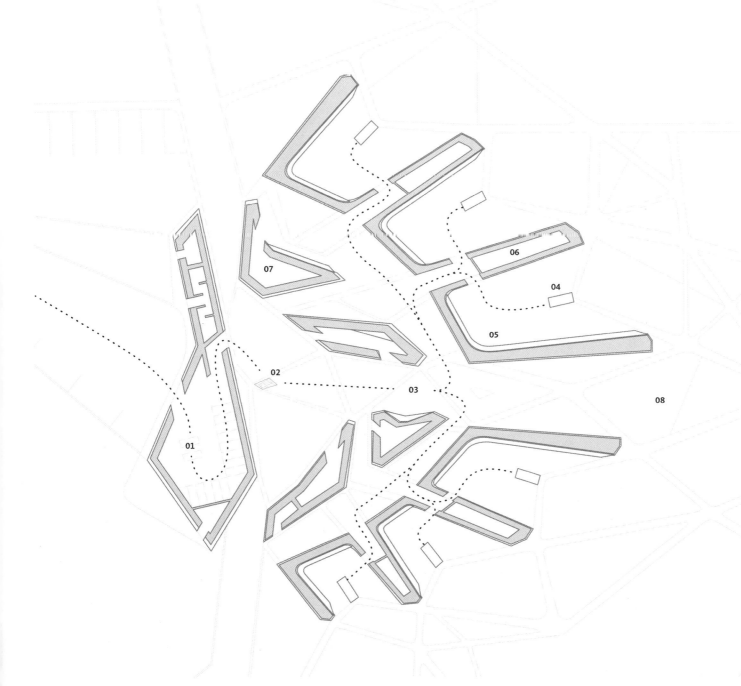

Procession through Circulation

01 Grounds workers or family cleanse and prepare the body for the ceremony.

02 A family member, often the eldest son, collects a flame that will be used to light the cloth over the deceased.

03 The procession crosses over the dry gravel beds that act as seasonal rivers, taking on water during the monsoon.

04 Family and friends gather around the dais, adorning the deceased with flowers and spices. Chants are spoken while circling the body.

05 A family member will start the cremation fire by lighting the cloth draped over the deceased. The retort or chimney is closed and attendees remain until the cremation has finished.

06 Ash is collected from the dais and is stored temporarily for two days while it completely cools.

07 The ashes are further processed to reduce any remaining bone and remove other debris.

08 Once the family collects the ashes, ideally, they are sprinkled in the River Yamuna.

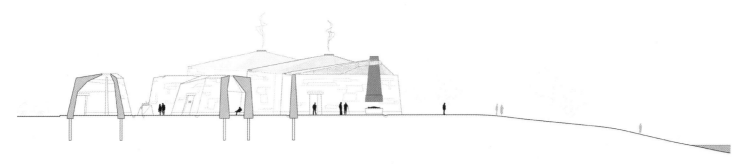

IN THE HEART OF DELHI, LARGE
SWATHS OF UNDEVELOPED
LAND REST BETWEEN MOBILITY
SYSTEMS, DRAINS, AND LARGE
URBAN INTERVENTIONS. THESE
AREAS PRESENT OPPORTUNITIES
FOR NEW PUBLIC SPACES AND
SOCIAL INFRASTRUCTURES.

The Yamuna Multi-scale Market

A disconnection between producers and consumers in New Delhi's food distribution system results in high food-price inflation and harvest spoilage. The flow of food, from production to distribution, and the commodification of food products can be an influential driver of social, environmental, and economic systems; this project focuses on how an architectural intervention can increase cultural identity and optimize accessibility, and reinforce the connection between spaces of production and distribution in New Delhi by introducing a new food distribution center on the banks of the Yamuna.

Modern technology and industrial agricultural practices have radically transformed traditional mixed farming methods to large-scale monoculture farming. The inefficiency of the food distribution system in India is responsible for high food-price inflation—which produces estimated losses worth $10 billion due to spoilage—and unequal access to markets for small farmers. Food stocks travel indirect journeys from countryside to city through several government markets and are handled by five or six middlemen before reaching consumers; over one third of produce is lost every year due to spoilage. This causes price increases of as much as five hundred percent from the time food is sold by the producer to when it reaches the consumer.

The project focuses on strengthening community and cultural identity in conjunction with improved access to market venues for producers and consumers. Design interventions will

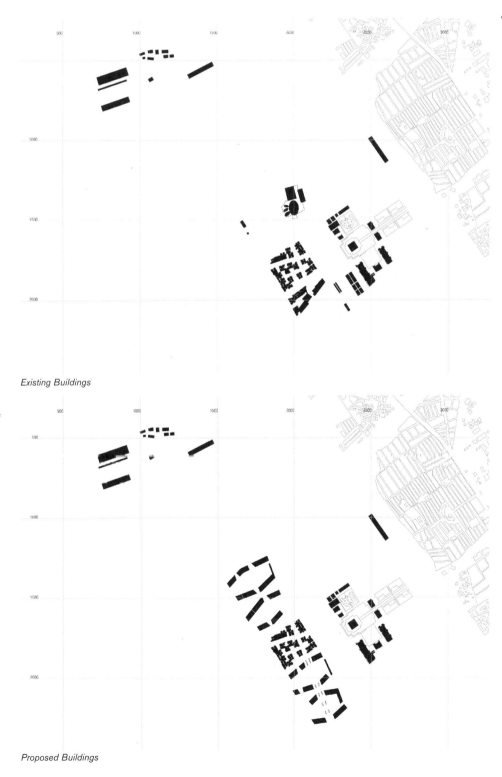

Existing Buildings

Proposed Buildings

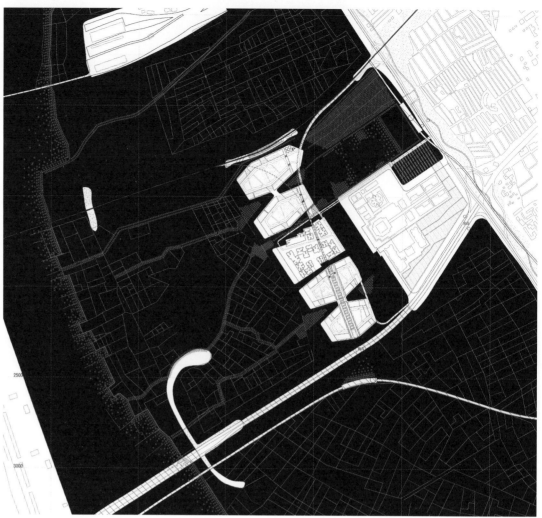

100 Year Flood Level

include spaces for food distribution, production, and consumption at strategic access points in the city. In densely urbanized and rapidly growing cities, public space is essential to support cultural life. A clear example of space that has multiple uses and improvisational activities, equitable access, and a strong cultural identity is the Indian maidan. It is characterized by a vast open ground for a diverse spectrum of urban life and activity, including markets, sporting events, and religious gatherings. Historically in Delhi, the dry Yamuna riverbed served as a maidan and offered respite from within the enclosure of the city. The need for a common place that is set apart from the territory of urban sprawl continues to be important today. However, in modern Delhi many public spaces are increasingly developed in ways that prevent impromptu gathering and collective engagement.

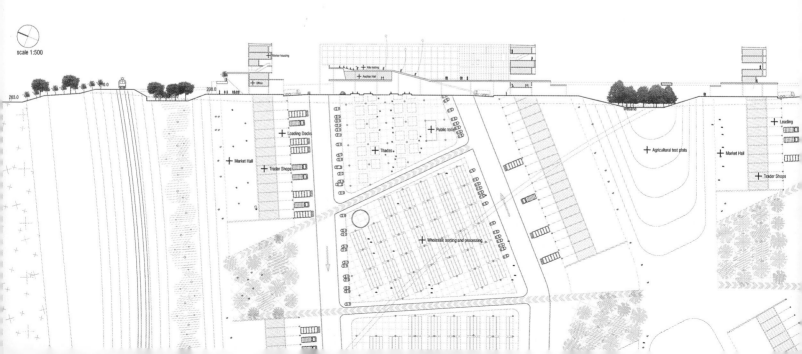

scale 1:500

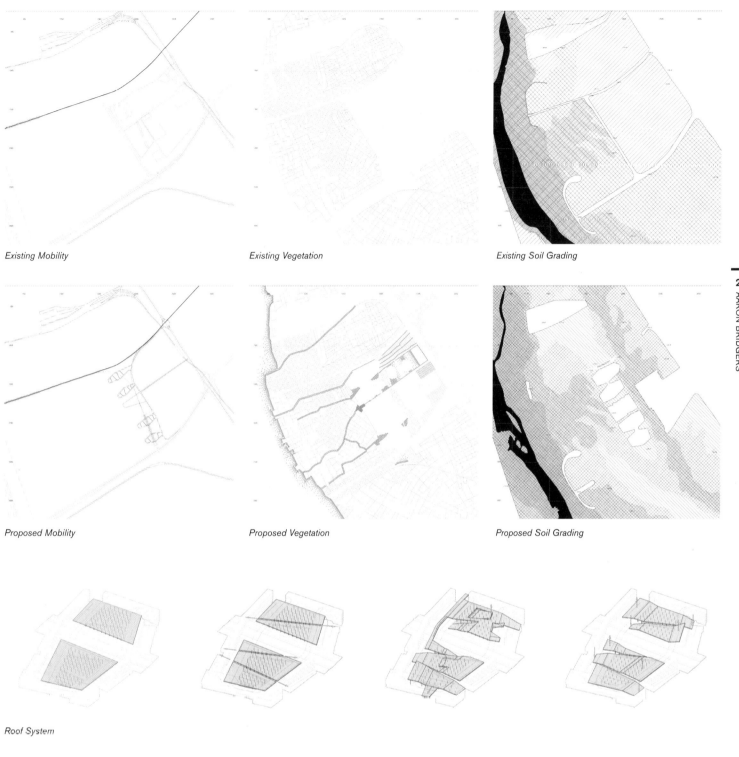

Existing Mobility

Existing Vegetation

Existing Soil Grading

Proposed Mobility

Proposed Vegetation

Proposed Soil Grading

Roof System

Yoga Field

Test Kitchen

208.0

203.9

208.0

+ Existing housing

+ Existing housing

+ Existing housing

Public toilet

+ Trader Shops

+ Existing housing

+ Existing housing

Secondly, this project will propose new ways to connect spaces of food production with distribution in New Delhi by reinterpreting the maidan for the 21st century. Modern advances in international food transportation have allowed for food to be grown at far distances from where it is purchased, which has had an enormous impact on how food is produced and consumed. For those who are able to afford it, the long distance food system offers exceptional choice and variety. Yet this distance between production and consumption often displaces local cuisine, is heavily reliant on fertilizers, and enables monocrop agricultural practices. Global food movements such as "Slow Food" and "Urban Agriculture" seek alternatives to the current food system, instead proposing an ecological alternative to the fast-paced efficiency of the current food system.

Finally, the project will focus on how new and re-purposed infrastructural systems can be used to increase equitable food distribution in the city. This new food distribution center will promote a revitalized use of existing infrastructures at the bridges and intermodal transit stations along the river. The leftover space along the Yamuna River's edge is a critical asset to the city which, coupled with food systems, can be a major driver for cultural, economic, and environmental change for the exploited Yamuna floodplain.

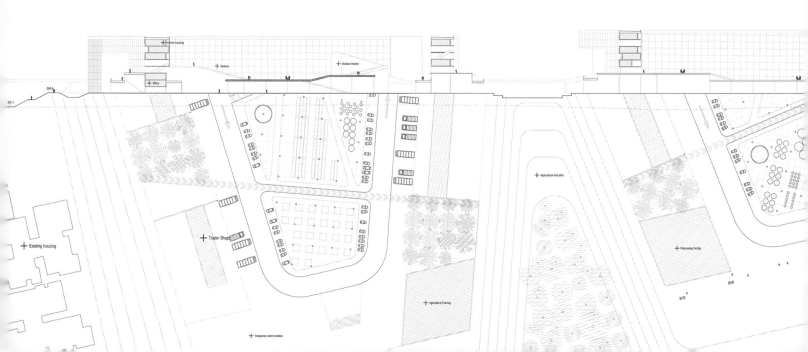

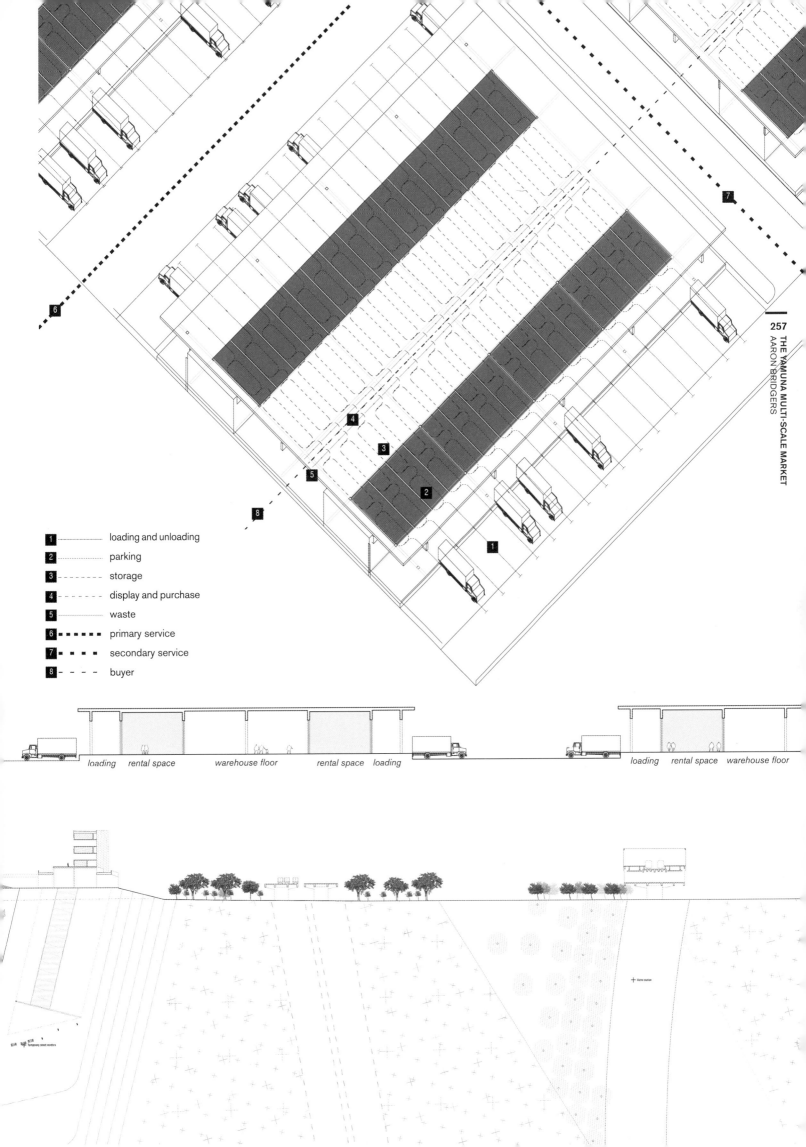

1 .... loading and unloading
2 .... parking
3 - - - - - - storage
4 - - - - - display and purchase
5 .... waste
6 ▪▪▪▪▪▪▪ primary service
7 ▪ ▪ ▪ ▪ secondary service
8 - - - - buyer

loading rental space   warehouse floor   rental space loading

loading rental space warehouse floor

THE YAMUNA FLOODPLAIN RECOVERY

The Yamuna floodplain will be shared by all constituencies, human and non-human. The river and its seasonal floods need the space to release their energy, recharge the water table, irrigate and fertilize the soil, and maintain and foster riparian ecologies. Inserted among the riverbanks, forests are grown on remediated soil and irrigated with clean water, and agriculture fields are cultivated to continue to locally feed part of the population.

The best stewards of this complex ecological mosaic will be Delhi's population; they also play a role in fostering a rich urban ecosystem. The size of the floodplain–three kilometers wide in some points–requires a new understanding of ecological and dynamic public space. The design of hybrid ecosystems, intertwining fields, people, forest and wetlands, is thought as a mosaic. The variations in this socioecological and productive matrix take into account the transitions from the edge of the city to the continuously shifting line of the Yamuna waters.

Although the riverbank is not the place to clean the massive amount of raw sewage coming through the drains–this needs to be a progressive process throughout the city's hard and soft infrastructures–there are a number of remnant flows and local remediation requiring water parks in which the processes of cleaning waters is part of a social public space.

Currently, the Yamuna is completely walled off by fences, highways, and railroads. Historically, as all over the world, river corridors have been used as corridors for mobility and transportation, taking advantage of their relentless continuity and soft slopes. In Delhi, the banks of an ignored Yamuna were the perfect location for railroads, used at the same time as bonds against floods, which cut off access from the city to the floodplain. A systematic strategy for permeating the roads and railroads can solve problems of local flash floods caused by lack of water's access to natural drainage, as well as generate opportunities for social amenities for the local communities such as schools, community centers, primary health care facilities, and women's shelters.

These barriers have segregated from the floodplain not only people and neighborhoods, but also natural marsh and lake systems, now abandoned meanders of a once lively and fluctuating Yamuna. Today, marshes are receding due to urban encroachment, the dumping of debris, and a lack of fresh waters formerly brought by a myriad of streams.

Besides, the scarce water that does feed the marshes comes heavily polluted, accompanied by trash, bringing with it the loss of health and biodiversity. These factors cause marshes to be perceived as a negative space without value. Marsh restoration starts with fresh water from the new 'springs'–the sewage treatment plants purified effluent–and integrating them with the surrounding urban fabric through delicate gradations. This is a novel way to recuperate ecosystems that are no longer able to survive as natural and pristine ecological islands, even though they are still very much needed for the health and diversity of our contemporary hybrid natural environment.

Floodplain Restoration

The Yamuna floodplain is an extremely fragile and polluted zone that has been exploited for far too long. Goals for future development of the floodplain include regenerating the floodplain area for flood control and biodiversity conservation with the creation of a restricted forest and wetland ecosystem Construction in any form is banned by the government up to 500m from both sides of the river's course. Since 1977, the main river channel has been greatly reduced while emergence of informal slum communities increased. Now nearly 4,000 acres of land on the floodplains is occupied illegally.

Agriculture is prevalent on both sides of the Yamuna floodplain. During the dry season, the majority of the river shrinks, leaving the catchment area ideal for farming. It is illegal to farm on the floodplain since fertilizer runoff is a main source of contamination in the Yamuna River. The soil is also contaminated by industrial waste and untreated raw sewage coming from the 22 drains that enter the Yamuna basin.

There are three growing seasons: Kharif (July-October), Rabi (October-March) and Zaid (April-June). A majority of the land is sown more than once in a calendar year. While production yields have increased due to technological advancements, losses due to inadequate storage and transportation remain static at 10%, enough to feed an estimated 118 million people a year.

Various irrigation schemes have been developed to ensure continual food security. Ponds, tanks and rainwater meet the rest of the irrigation needs. We propose any further agriculture on the floodplain be made legal so that it can be regulated to reduce pollution. The northern and southern floodplain will remain as traditional agriculture, irrigated with canals sourced directly from the Yamuna and allowed to flood during monsoon season. The proposed agriculture between Gurjar Samrat Mihir Bhoj Marg Bridge and the Indraprastha Metro Station will be accessible to public use, serving as community gardens or as educational prototypes.

1. Restore River Access

The north and southern parts of the site are for traditional (privately owned) agriculture while the central part is accessible by the public.

The farmland can be appropriated for community gardens walking/bike trails provide opportunities for recreation, fishing, bird watching and ceremonial practices.

2. Forest Design Operation

1: Line public access points with trees to provide shade
2: Border agriculture plots and irrigation canals to prevent soil erosion
3: Use vegetation to spur bacterial growth for bioremediation
4: Allow a natural buffer to thrive at the river's edge (10-50m)
5: Create patches of forest for interior species to thrive

3. Water Flow

1: Raw sewage and municipal water treated away from the floodplain in a water treatment facility
2: Involves separating solid waste
3: Water flows along the six canals of sub-surface wetlands
4: Canals run through the agriculture plots to irrigate and recharge groundwater
5: Water flows into wetlands for treatment before entering the Yamuna

4. Agriculture

Existing agriculture is expanded to provide food for more families. Canals from the Yamuna are directed through the plots for irrigation. One Acre (of wheat) needs 1,791 gallons of water per year. Total acreage of agriculture on the floodplain would consume 1,684,386 million gallons of year.

New Agriculture: 449 acres

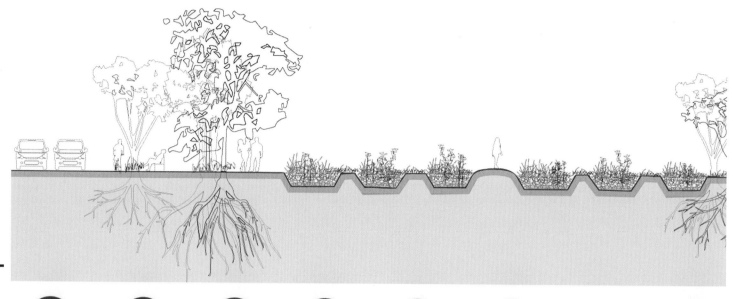

BAUHINIA PURPUREA:
PUPLE ORCHID

KIGELIA
AFRICANA

FICUS RACEMOSA:
INDIAN FIG

ZIZYPHUS
NUMMULARIA

BROAD
LEAVED CATTAIL

INDIAN GRASS

ULOTRICHALES

DIATOMS
-METAL TOXICITY
BIOINDICATORS

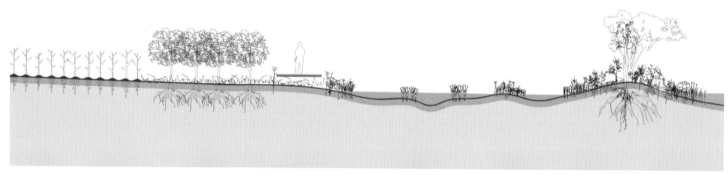

SOYBEANS

MANGO TREE

T/TR: SYZYGIUM CUMINI:
JAMBUL

SCHOENOPLECTIELLA
ROYLEI

COMMELINA BENGHALENSIS:
BENGHAL DAYFLOWER

FIMBRISTYLIS
DICHOTOMA

WATER HYSSOP

LEMNA PERPUSILLA:
DUCK WEED

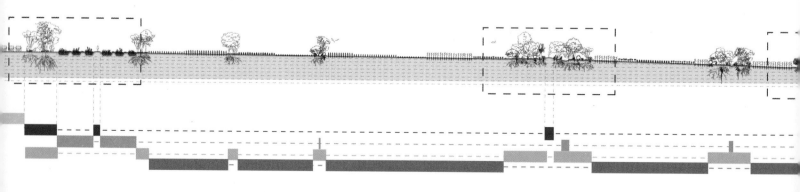

DESMIDS

AZADIRACHTA INDICA:
INDIAN LILAC

RANUNCULUS SCELERATUS:
CELERY-LEAVED BUTTERCUP

BOMBAX CEIBA:
RED SILK COTTON TREE

CARISSA SPINARUM:
BUSH PLUM

SACCHARUM BENGALENSE:
SUGAR CANE

EHRETIA LAEVIS

AILANTHUS EXCELSA:
INDIAN TREE OF HEAVEN

ENTEROLOBIUM BARINENSE
CARDENAS AND RODRIGUEZ

CORDIA DICHOTOMA

COMMELINA UNDULATA:
LONG LEAVED DAYFLOWER

CYPERUS
BULBOSUS VAHL

EAST INDIAN
HYGROPHILA

WATER HYACINTH

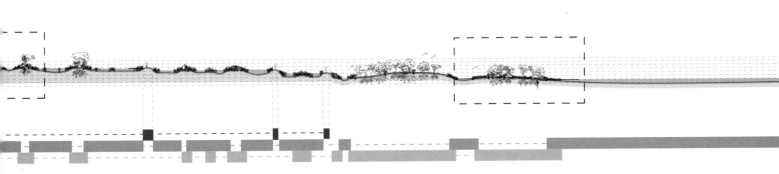

THE YAMUNA FLOODPLAIN, AT AN ESTIMATED 8,100 HECTARES, IS AN EXTENSION OF THE RIVER AND SUPPORTS ECOLOGICAL COMMUNITIES AND BIODIVERSITY WITHIN THE AREA. THIS SENSITIVE ZONE IS HOME TO A VARIETY OF BIRDS AND FISH AND IS AN IMPORTANT GROUND WATER SOURCE FOR THE CITY. HOWEVER, MANY UNAUTHORIZED ACTIVITIES ON THE FLOODPLAIN, INCLUDING SLUM DWELLINGS AND ILLEGAL AGRICULTURE, HAVE PLACED THE AREA IN JEOPARDY.

Floodplain Marsh Recovery

Jahangirpuri Marsh typifies the landscape that used to make up Delhi's floodplain before these natural ecologies gave way to urban expansion. Today, the marsh is one of the critical ecosystems that remains in Delhi but it is facing serious issues such as waste dumping, marsh drying, and decreased water quality. In recent decades, informal settlements have encroached upon the marsh, resulting in a dramatic decrease of its land area. The marsh is separated from the surrounding communities by a 2.5 meter wall in an effort to "protect the marsh." In reality, this wall removes the marsh from the city and public consciousness, turning it into a backyard for which no one is responsible. As a result, the marsh is disconnected from the area's natural watersheds, its edges are used as dumping grounds, and its interior has be claimed to dump excess from the sewage treatment process.

The Coronation Pillar Sewage Treatment Plant (STP) borders the marsh and is considered a main source of pollution for the marsh. This STP, with a capacity of over 40 MGD, collects sewage from nine communities along the marsh and either treats this sewage, returning treated effluent to a small drain which flows to the Yamuna, or directs sewage to the Supplementary Drain as dirty water containing solid waste and dissolved pollutants (which also then flows to the Yamuna). Additionally, biogas is produced as a byproduct of the sewage treatment process. The Coronation Pillar STP releases this biogas into the marsh without any treatment—the marsh's ecology is not respected, it is simply treated as a buffer to protect the community from toxic pollutants.

This project proposed to recover the marsh by treating it as a productive resource and ecological zone for the city; integrating the marsh with the surrounding community instead of using walls to isolate and "protect" it.

A hybrid sewage treatment system is proposed to provide water to the marsh necessary to restore marsh decay and sustain a healthy ecosystem. Constructed wetlands and bioremediation are used to treat semi-clean sewage from the STP and recharge surrounding water bodies and aquifers. Eventually, treated effluent will be directed to the Supplementary Drain in order to provide the Najafgarh and Yamuna with clean water. The restored marsh will incorporate new public spaces along its edges, allowing public access and encouraging ecological stewardship for students and the surrounding community.

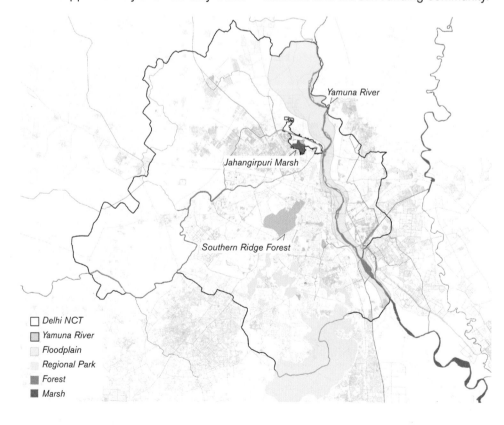

☐ Delhi NCT
◻ Yamuna River
▫ Floodplain
▫ Regional Park
▪ Forest
■ Marsh

1. Community Center
2. Visitor Center
3. Overlook Deck
4. STP Walk
5. Riparian Path
6. Entry Plaza
7. Detention Pond
8. Path
9. School Street Entrance
10. Camping Zone
11. Marsh Access
12. Rain Garden
13. Playground
14. Kitchen Garden
15. Picnic Zone
16. Shallow Area
17. Central Protected Marsh
18. Naini Lake
19. Rainwater Cascade
20. Lagoon
21. Tree Walk
22. Woodland
23. Ecological Restoration
24. Constructed Wetland
25. Coronation Lake
26. STP Visitor Center
27. Reservoir
28. Sewage Treatment Ponds
29. Research Center
30. Fishing

1807

1964

FLOODPLAIN MARSH RECOVERY
XIAONIAN SHEN

2001

2012

2017

C&D con-
struction-
waste

Metro
Facilities

Supplementary Drain (to Yamuna River)

STP effluent

Metro
Station

Coronation Pillar
Sewage treatment
plant

Coronation Park

Abandoned
STP

Debris

Jahangirpuri Marsh

Naini
Lake

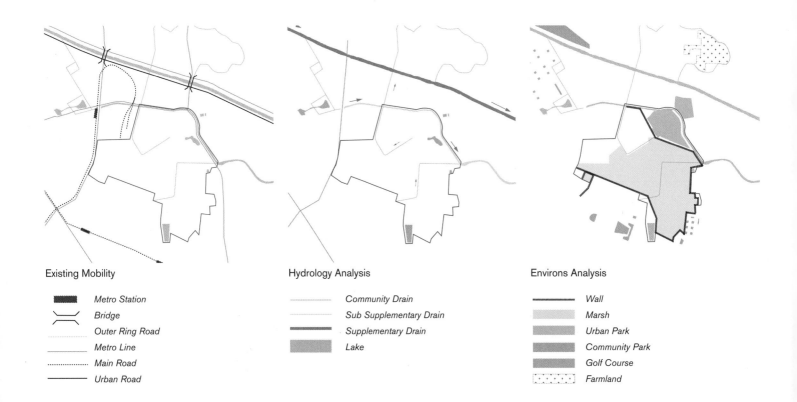

Existing Mobility

▬	Metro Station
⊢⊣	Bridge
⋯⋯	Outer Ring Road
——	Metro Line
⋯⋯⋯	Main Road
——	Urban Road

Hydrology Analysis

⋯⋯⋯	Community Drain
⋯⋯⋯	Sub Supplementary Drain
——	Supplementary Drain
▬	Lake

Environs Analysis

▬▬▬	Wall
▬	Marsh
▬	Urban Park
▬	Community Park
▬	Golf Course
⋮⋮⋮	Farmland

Marsh Remediation

The natural ecosystem is rapidly disappearing from the Jahangirpuri marsh due to urban encroachment and depleted aquifers. Adjacent communities are walled off and disconnected. Flora across many strata: understory, shrub, weed, herb, and aquatic are required to fully restore the march ecosystem.

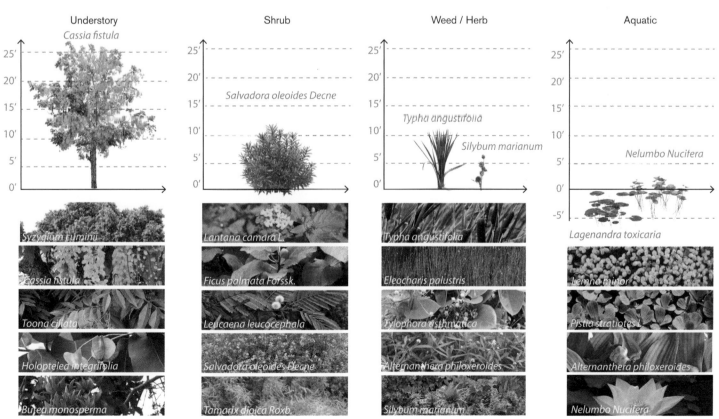

Understory
Cassia fistula
Syzygium cumini
Cassia fistula
Toona ciliata
Holoptelea integrifolia
Butea monosperma

Shrub
Salvadora oleoides Decne
Lantana camara L.
Ficus palmata Forssk.
Leucaena leucocephala
Salvadora oleoides Decne
Tamarix dioica Roxb.

Weed / Herb
Typha angustifolia
Silybum marianum
Typha angustifolia
Eleocharis palustris
Tylophora asthmatica
Alternanthera philoxeroides
Silybum marianum

Aquatic
Nelumbo Nucifera
Lagenandra toxicaria
Lemna minor
Pistia stratiotes L.
Alternanthera philoxeroides
Nelumbo Nucifera

Sewage treatment plant
(sewage resource)

treating sewage flo

Existing Land Use

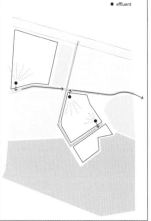

Existing Sewage Flow

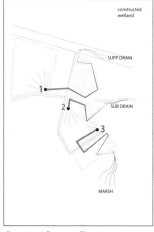

Proposed Sewage Flow

STP Spring Park

An abandoned STP on site is transformed into a public park where visitors can learn about the sewage treatment process. Constructed wetlands capture runoff from existing drains and give second life to the marsh by allowing it to naturally treat effluent from nearby communities. A segment of these constructed wetlands is designed to accommodate future STP expansion and diverts treated effluent to the Supplementary Drain. Public parks are provide access and social amenities.

Lagenandra toxicaria
(native water purify plant)

Floodable microtopography
roots help degrade organic matter

treated flow to reservoir →

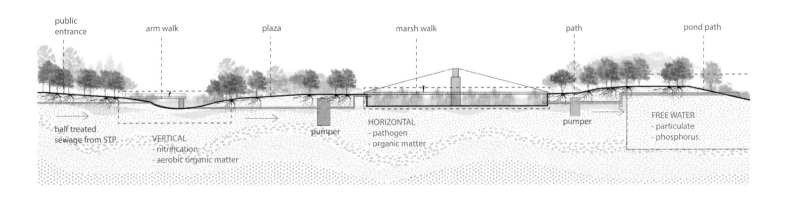

public
entrance   arm walk   plaza   marsh walk   path   pond path

half treated
sewage from STP   VERTICAL   pumper   HORIZONTAL   pumper   FREE WATER
                    -nitrification   -pathogen   -particulate
                    -aerobic organic matter   -organic matter   -phosphorus

Lagenandra toxicaria
(native water purify plant)

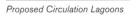
Proposed Circulation Lagoons

Feed Marsh with Treated Water

Restore Marsh Habitat

Ecological Loop

Bolstered by a clean water supply, key native plant species are introduced to restore the marsh ecosystem. Not only does this restoration introduce diverse vegetation types from different stratas, but it also creates sanctuaries for migratory birds and other forms of wildlife. An elevated skywalk offers a path that separates visitors from the ground level in order to minimize disturbance to the marsh ecosystem. Bird watching towers create observation points along the path.

Indian dragonfly
ecology health indicator species

Bird watching tower
for ecology research observation

ated sewage flow

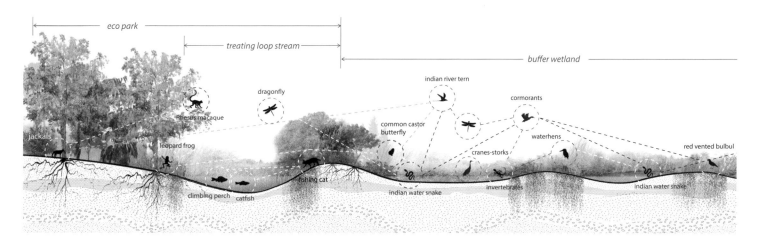

eco park

treating loop stream

buffer wetland

indian river tern

dragonfly

cormorants

common castor
butterfly

rhesus macaque

waterhens

jackals

cranes-storks

red vented bulbul

leopard frog

indian water snake

fishing cat

invertebrates

indian water snake

climbing perch   catfish

Chilli Pepper

Curry Leaves

Existing Marsh Edge

Remove Wall, Create Public Space

Storm-water Management

Marsh Edge and Public Space

The new marsh edge will provide multi-use public space for the surrounding communities and divert and treat storm-water runoff in infiltration ponds. After treatment, clean effluent will be reused as irrigation water on site for public gardens and for educational purposes. Various space are provided for playgrounds, outdoor education for children, and plazas for public gathering during traditional festival. People are able to access and cross the marsh through access bridges.

filtration pond
(stormwater management)

Lemongrass

Spear Mint

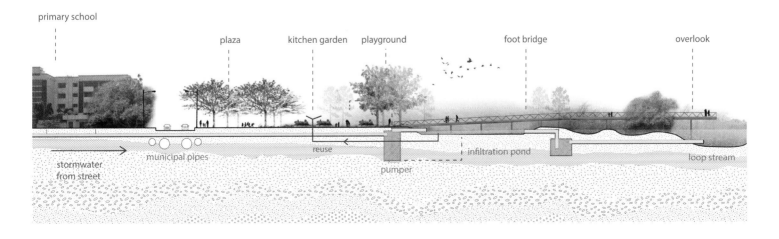

primary school

plaza   kitchen garden   playground   foot bridge   overlook

stormwater
from street   municipal pipes   reuse   pumper   infiltration pond   loop stream

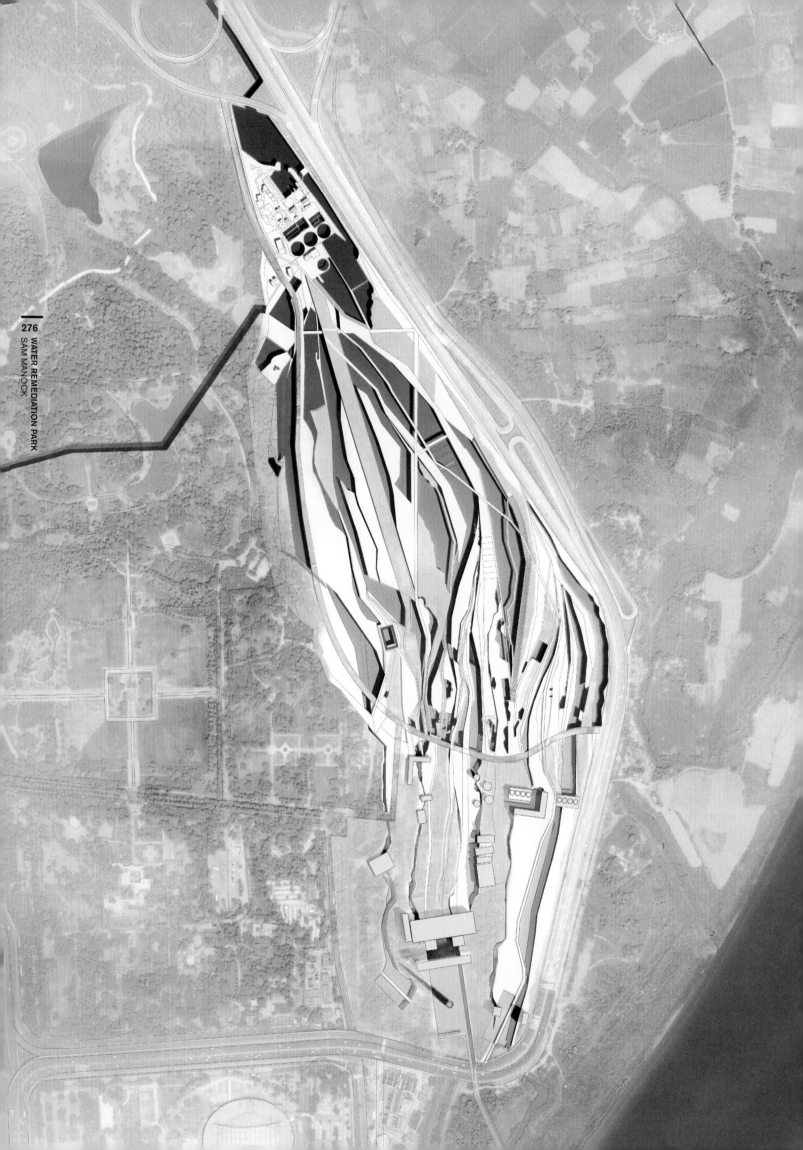

Water Remediation Park

On the site of the decommissioned Raj Ghat coal power plant and its dry ash field, this project acts as a unifying catalyst between people and water. Reallocating the contaminated water from open drains and sewage systems that cross its perimeter, water is initially treated at the northernmost point of the site and then filtered across over 750m of plants and ponds. This constructed landscape simultaneously treats over 100,000 m³ of water daily and almost triples the available accessible public space. Pedestrian paths traverse the entire site, and a tuk-tuk and small vehicle path winds its way from the Indraprastha Housing Community to the south and up through the Interchange Housing directly north. The purified water flows from the site end and pool at the southern end of the 1150m-long site, flowing in, around, and even through a new Modern Culture and Arts Center. Using the bones of the old thermal plant as a framework, this project preserves its massive cooling tower as a marker and a reminder of the old. By placing it in a reflecting pool of the collected water, the tower is not only duplicated in length by its reflection, but uses its infrastructure to help replenish the groundwater supply underneath it.

The Modern Culture and Arts Center is organized as a series of pavilions, surrounded by pools that are meant to be welcoming and unrestrictive, flowing freely and closely incorporated with the movement of people.

Just as the now-dry baolis historically served as architectural testaments to the importance of water, this project allows the people of Delhi to celebrate their modern artistic and cultural heritage while also obtaining a sense of pride, clarity, and closeness with the water that built their city.

Crossing to the Floodplain

This project contributes to revitalization efforts around Humayun's Tomb to create a Utilitarian Public Space. The Public Space, an Educational and Ecological Park, becomes an urban catalyst and nexus within the fabric of the city to strengthen and improve the flows and connections of the site. The park acts as a mediator between human, infrastructural, and natural systems to create an asset for the city, while also addressing and improving the health of the Yamuna River and New Delhi's water systems.

By claiming space for the public and by creating and reinforcing connectivity, this project defines Humayun's Tomb and its surrounding area as a prominent urban structure that not only serves the tourist, but the city as a whole with the aim to improve both human and environmental health.

roof surface

direct sunlight excluded by

valleys between buildings

Urban Facade

Ecological Park

Education Center

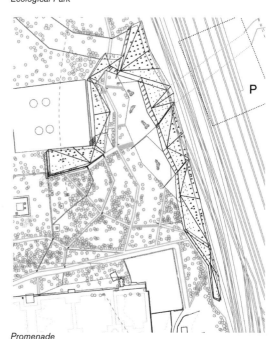

Promenade

rain

water directed to riparian wetland

water from roof directed to retention pools

summer wind from south-east

site terraces direct water to riparian wetland

cross ventilation under canopy

circulation

air intake in mechanical room brings air down to labyrinth

labyrinth to pre-cool and preheat air for HVAC

cistern for collected rainwater

on-site grey water

hot water

boiler connection

city water main

on-site potable water

heat recovery system with grey water system

hot water cylinder

pump feed to toilets in public restrooms

Necessity of Public Space

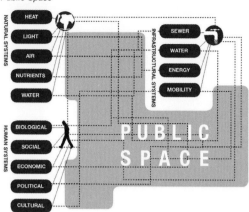

Human & Environmental Health

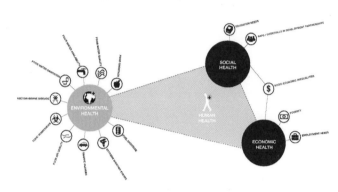

Human & Environmental Health

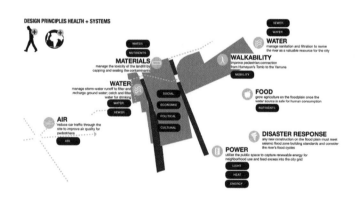

Roof Diagrams

Typical structural bay

*Roof plane folds to
divert rainwater*

*Gutters at seams
collect rainwater*

*Ridges direct excess water
to ecological park*

*Geometry expands and contracts
based on circulations flows*

Site Plan

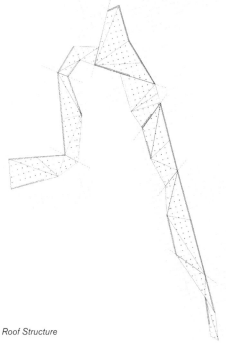

Roof Structure

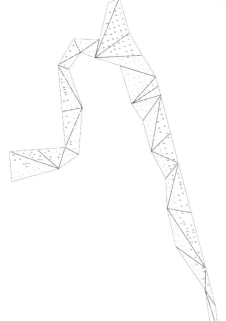

Roof Plan

SOCIAL HOUSING

Delhi's rapid growth has made the task of providing enough housing an impossible challenge. Of course, the most vulnerable population suffer most from the lack of proper housing, inhabiting informal housing and slums without basic living conditions and services. Without provision of drinking water, their sewage is not accounted for and ends up in the Yamuna after running through streets, canals, and drains. For a significant change in the condition of the drains and the river to occur tackling the housing and domestic infrastructures crisis is required.

The urgency of providing proper housing to millions of Delhi's inhabitants becomes even more critical with the expected growth by ten million new inhabitants (United Nations, Department of Economic and Social Affairs, Population Division, 2014). Delhi already has areas of extreme density (up to ten times more than compact cities as Barcelona), and is sprawling without control or a planned strategy and therefore without infrastructure, transportation, or preservation of green coverage.

Housing Delhi's population requires the development of new typologies in the domestic space and, even more importantly, in unit aggregations and the construction of neighborhoods. At the same time, existing urban voids offer unusual opportunities. Significant areas of land along infrastructures are now unused, such as the railroad corridors cross Delhi, and create barriers of vacant space. Similarly, major avenues are designed as interstate roads with vast fringes along the sides which are ideal for collecting trash and informal temporary occupations. Rethinking these vast negative spaces along infrastructures provides opportunities for housing and for the creation of a new urbanity, civic continuity, and enhanced safety.

The process of upgrading and providing basic services to the unplanned urban villages require a long term strategy. Some of these neighborhoods are today located in floodable areas, including the floodplain of the Yamuna. While new locations are identified and prepared for safe housing nearby, temporary shelters, above the level of the monsoon waters can be planned and built. Solid bases with storage, basic infrastructures, and facilities for farming can act as foundations for seasonal shelters made of zero ecological footprint materials such as bamboo.

HYBRID HOUSING AT HAPUR BYPASS BRIDGE
ERIC BARR

Hybrid Housing at Hapur Bypass Bridge

New Delhi's housing deficit parallels its incredible population growth. With a large percentage of migrants relocating from impoverished rural villages, most are unable to afford planned housing and must resort to informal settlements. These slums lack even basic amenities and foster unsanitary living conditions that fall well short of humane. Only 24 percent of the urban population lives in planned colonies; 76 percent lives in these substandard housing areas. Many are homeless. In a mega-city of 19 million people, this is a social crisis on an unprecedented scale.

Hapur Bypass is the first in a series of super-bridge communities that respond to the city's major infrastructural deficiencies—unregulated agriculture, sanitation, waste management, commercial dysfunction, and lack of housing—by proposing a radically different model for social housing. By densifying the current bridges into cultural centers of activity, a new nexus will link the city's east and west divisions together and re-establish the Yamuna as the beating heart of the city.

Delhi's lowest echelon has found refuge on the floodplain. Slum-dwellers use the land illegally for agriculture, growing poisoned crops to sell within the city's informal markets. This social sub-condition goes unnoticed, however, because the river is physically inaccessible. In fact, the only place where the river is even visible is from atop the city's bridges. Trans-Yamuna focuses on one of these bridges as the site for a new public territory that will rehabilitate the ecoregion and re-center New Delhi upon the once-sacred Yamuna River.

The proposed Hapur Bypass project offers a new prototype of living and communal

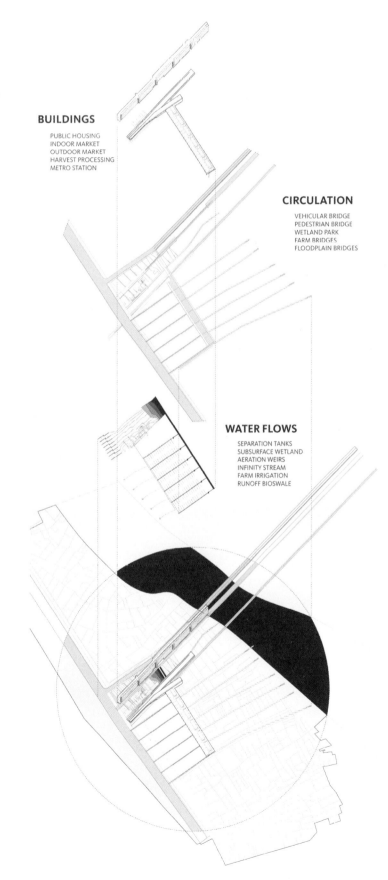

BUILDINGS

PUBLIC HOUSING
INDOOR MARKET
OUTDOOR MARKET
HARVEST PROCESSING
METRO STATION

CIRCULATION

VEHICULAR BRIDGE
PEDESTRIAN BRIDGE
WETLAND PARK
FARM BRIDGES
FLOODPLAIN BRIDGES

WATER FLOWS

SEPARATION TANKS
SUBSURFACE WETLAND
AERATION WEIRS
INFINITY STREAM
FARM IRRIGATION
RUNOFF BIOSWALE

gathering. With its existing twin-bridge structure, one road hosts vehicular traffic while the other converts into a new pedestrian promenade. Here, commercial agoras combine with vertical housing villages, industrial-harvesting facilities, and a metro station to form a hybridized urban block. Hapur Bypass also creates a new maidan that encourages social interaction between all citizen classes, a trend that has faded with the stepwells of old. The project is a new riparian destination, both urban and agrestal, integrating unobtrusively with the volatile monsoon floodplain. The land is relinquished back to the Yamuna, seasonal floods rush uninhibited, and the lush plains are optimized to an agrarian state of production.

This new community weaves everyday cultural routines around an interactive subsurface constructed wetland, which filters city runoff and landfill leachate before it can contaminate the river. Water purification becomes visible through stepped basins, and clean water emerges to irrigate the surrounding agriculture. Harvested food is sold at the community's market, and through this cycle inhabitants understand the site, its natural systems, and their own position within the landscape.

The project adapts to its subtropical locale through a series of simple design and orientation strategies. The linear structure positions itself along an east-west axis, exposing a southern scrim of operable photovoltaics to direct solar radiation. This both mitigates heat gain and converts Delhi's high solar insulation into electricity for the affordable housing

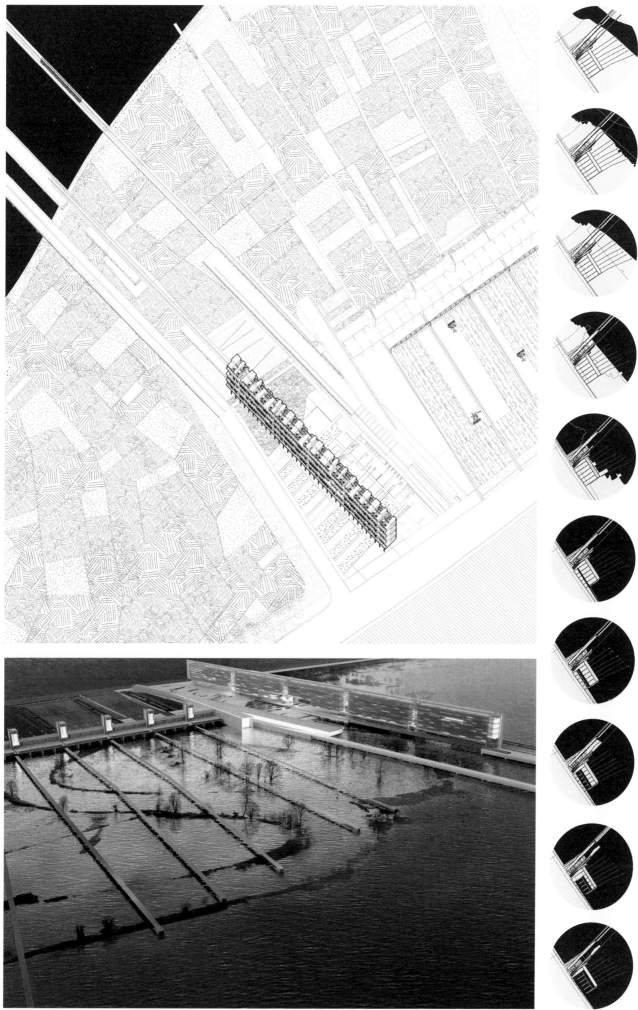

Flood-able Infrastructure during monsoon season

units. The building also employs vegetation and louvers along the south facade for shading.

The entire housing block is elevated six meters off of the floodplain. Located above local obstructions, each unit receives a consistent airflow for cross-ventilation. The superblock is comprised of 50m2 linear apartment units that span the entire width of the building; each unit has large apertures on the north and south facades that simultaneously vent the interiors and provide uninhibited views to the city's riparian ecozone. This strategy works well for the hot and dry climate that persists for eight months of the year.

The housing superstructure supports three economic tiers of apartment units. Some tenants will be able to afford air conditioning; others will not. To accommodate these various income levels, tenants will have the option of adding an indoor air unit to their apartment. Up to nine apartments can link their ductless wall mounts to an outdoor condenser located on the building's roof. Quiet, compact, and capable of dehumidifying without a water tank, these air conditioners can supplement thermal comfort when passive ventilation just isn't enough. This period will typically be during the monsoon autumn months, when humidity spikes. This project can be constructed in phases and in different aggregated densities contributing to its prototypical and site adaptability.

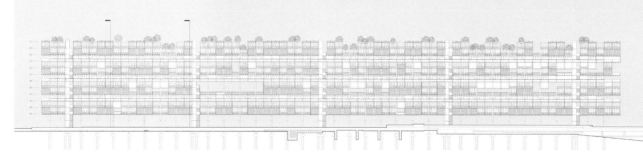

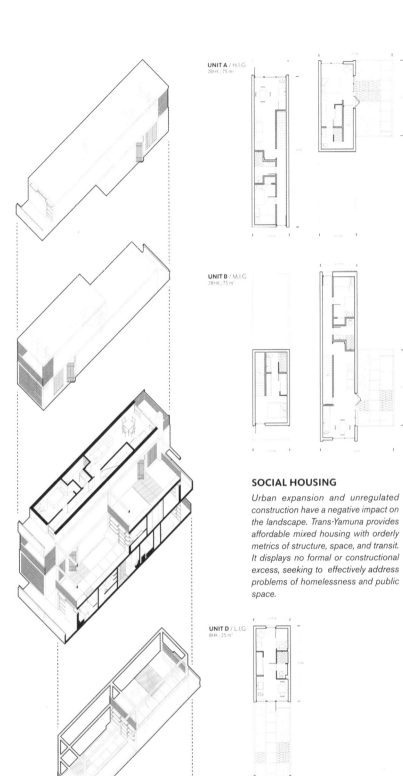

UNIT A / H.I.G
2BHK ; 75 m²

UNIT B / M.I.G
2BHK ; 75 m²

SOCIAL HOUSING

Urban expansion and unregulated construction have a negative impact on the landscape. Trans-Yamuna provides affordable mixed housing with orderly metrics of structure, space, and transit. It displays no formal or constructional excess, seeking to effectively address problems of homelessness and public space.

UNIT D / L.I.G
BHK ; 25 m²

UNIT C / L.I.G
2BHK ; 50 m²

N

ITS EMBANKMENTS CONSTANTLY MODIFIED, PERIODICALLY CROSSED BY BRIDGES, AND LINED BY LARGE ELECTRICAL AND WATER RELATED INFRASTRUCTURES, THE YAMUNA IS TREATED AS A PLACE WITHOUT SIGNIFICANCE, BYPASSED AND OUTRIGHT IGNORED. CAN INTERVENTIONS UTILIZE THESE EXISTING CONDITIONS TO TRANSFORM THE YAMUNA'S RELATIONSHIP WITH DELHI'S INHABITANTS?

HYBRID HOUSING AT RAJA RAM KOHLI BRIDGE
YUSHAN

Hybrid Housing at Raja Ram Kohli Bridge

Some estimates find that more than 70% of people in Delhi live in substandard housing. Often, Delhi deals with its increasing population by employing the "solution" of relocating the urban poor to colonies in rural areas. However, this is not an ideal solution. Due to relocation people are severed from established communities and suffer long travel distances to work. This project seeks to hybridize underutilized infrastructures in Delhi, such as highway overpasses, to provide social housing communities with easy access to transportation.

New affordable housing communities should focus on creating affordable living spaces that are located near public amenities. The Raja Ram Kohli Bridge is an ideal place for this type of project. The existing bridge links Delhi's Old City on the west bank of the Yamuna, and Geeta Colony on the east bank, two of the most crowded slums in Delhi The bridge thus forms a substantial connection to two urban centers. Natural ventilation and sound attenuation drive the organization of the housing units which are elevated above the floodplain to allow seasonal monsoon waters to flow freely.

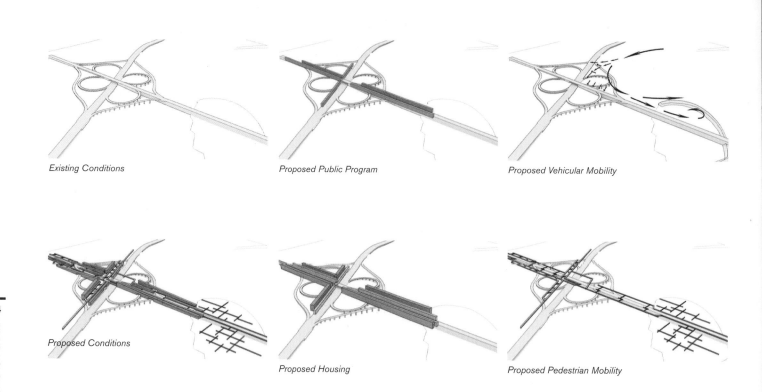

Existing Conditions

Proposed Public Program

Proposed Vehicular Mobility

Proposed Conditions

Proposed Housing

Proposed Pedestrian Mobility

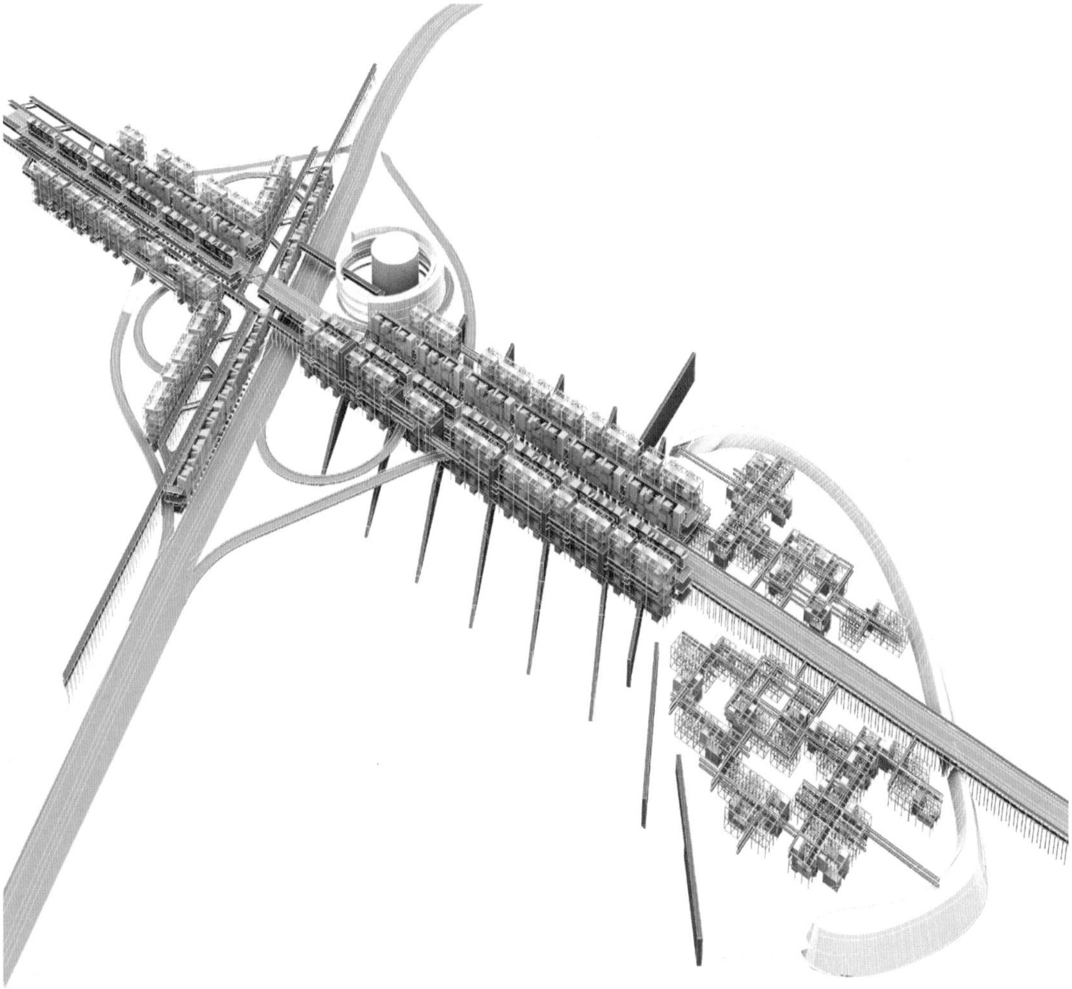

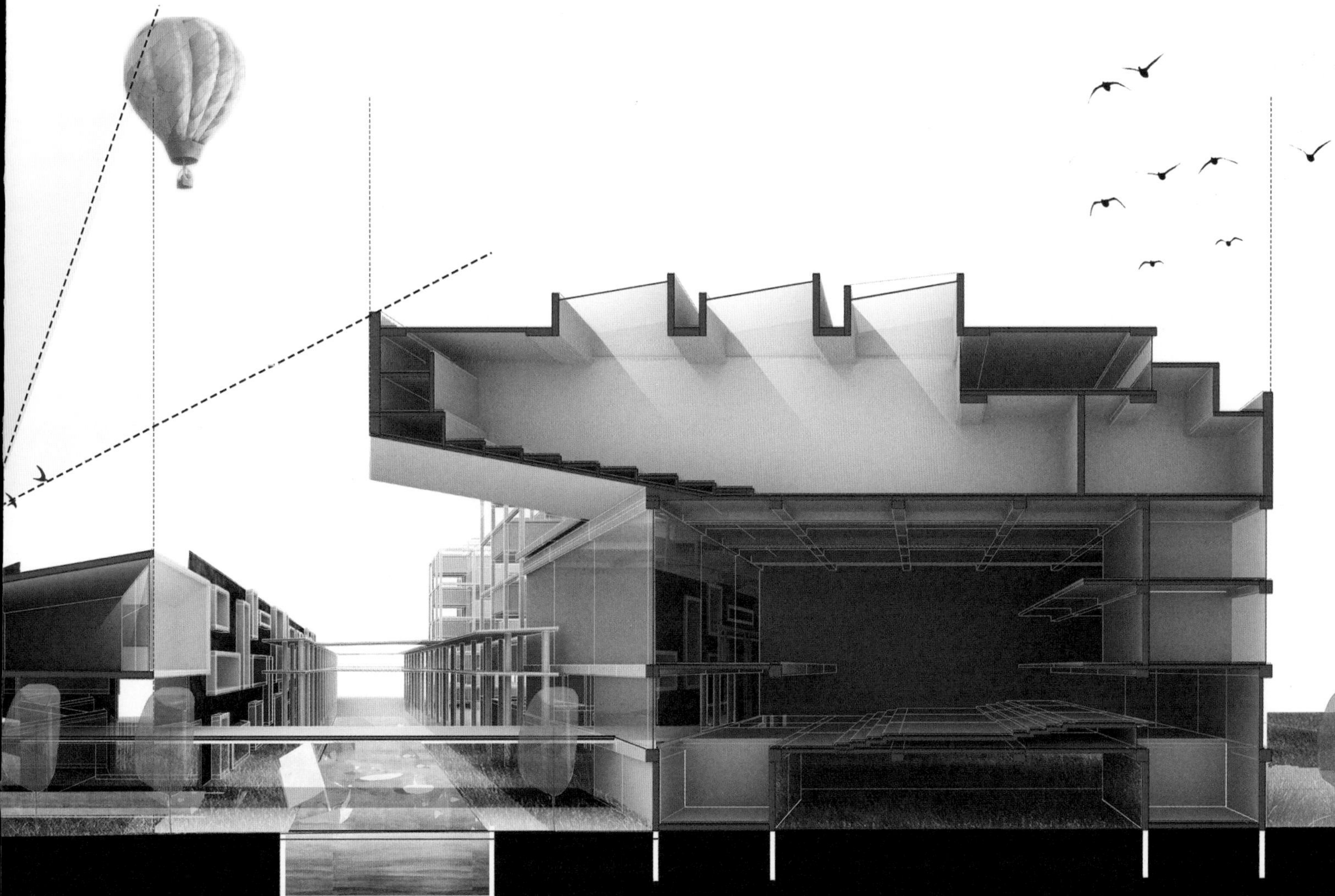

MOST TRAVEL IN DELHI UTILIZES MULTIPLE FORMS OF TRANSPORTATION—GETTING TO AND FROM THE BUS OR METRO STATION INVOLVES WALKING, DRIVING, OR HIRING A VEHICLE. BUS STOPS AND METRO STATIONS ARE NOT ONLY POINTS OF DEPARTURE AND ARRIVAL; THEY ARE INTERMODAL NODES OF ACTIVITY WHERE NUMEROUS MODES OF TRANSIT CONVERGE.

Railroad Housing Network

The Tilak Bridge, north of the Pragati Maidan Development, represents a crucial mobility link between the northern and southern sections of New Delhi. The surrounding urban context, devoid of usable pedestrian access, is currently a physical barrier, severing the existing heritage corridor. This project seeks to link the underutilized regional rail station and two metro stations while also incorporating a new affordable housing development along the regional rail embankment. By creating a new residential hub interwoven with an intermodal station, a new node is created that facilitates pedestrian access to the surrounding urban projects and the Yamuna River, creating a truly

intermodal transport system at this critical juncture of infrastructure.

In addition, Mathura Road, one of the busiest secondary roads in the city, will be reconfigured to include a new tramway system, filling in the gaps untouched by the metro system. This new cross-section will create not only more efficient vehicular travel but safer pedestrian and bicycle access throughout the city in order to allow for the reduction of car-based travel. The Intermodal Housing Network represents a critical piece of the city's rapidly developing, yet fragmented, transport network and has the capacity to re-stitch the city's highly dense urban fabric.

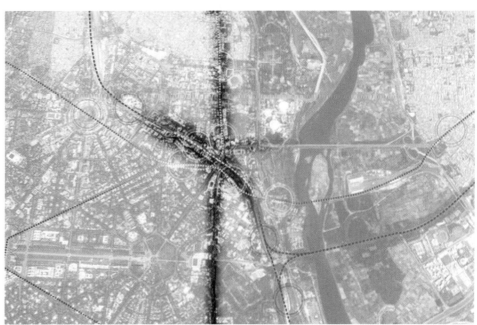

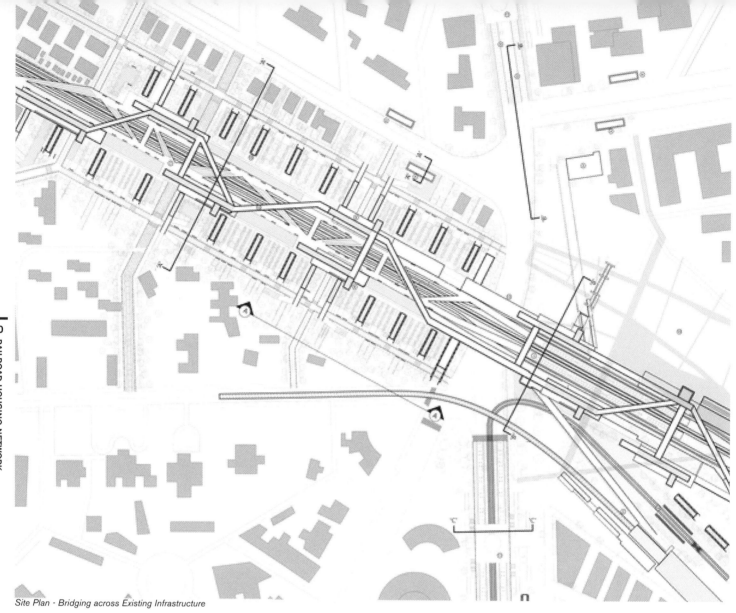

Site Plan - Bridging across Existing Infrastructure

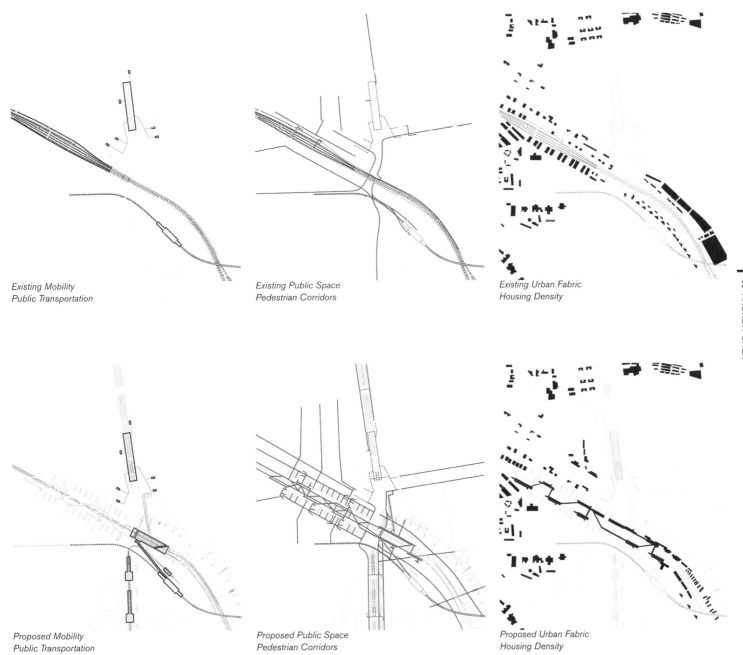

Existing Mobility
Public Transportation

Existing Public Space
Pedestrian Corridors

Existing Urban Fabric
Housing Density

Proposed Mobility
Public Transportation

Proposed Public Space
Pedestrian Corridors

Proposed Urban Fabric
Housing Density

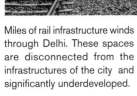

Miles of rail infrastructure winds through Delhi. These spaces are disconnected from the infrastructures of the city and significantly underdeveloped.

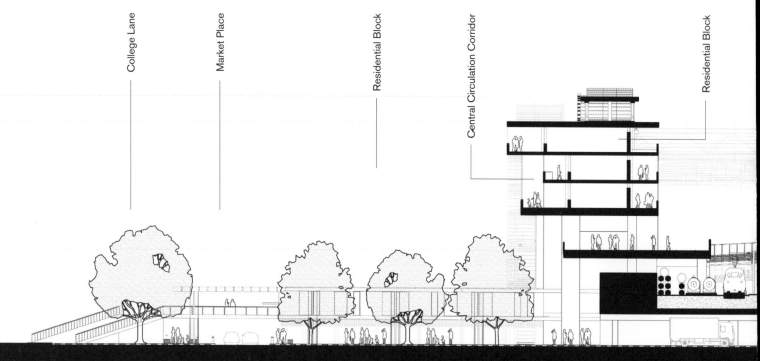

College Lane

Market Place

Residential Block

Central Circulation Corridor

Residential Block

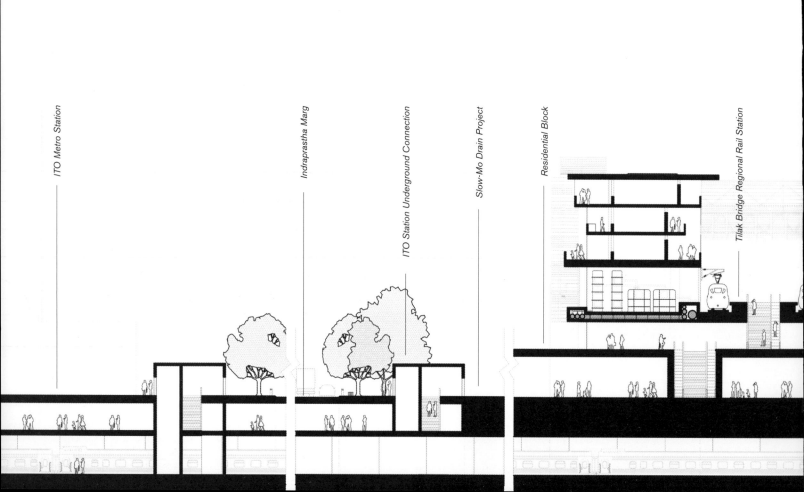

ITO Metro Station

Indraprastha Marg

ITO Station Underground Connection

Slow-Mo Drain Project

Residential Block

Tilak Bridge Regional Rail Station

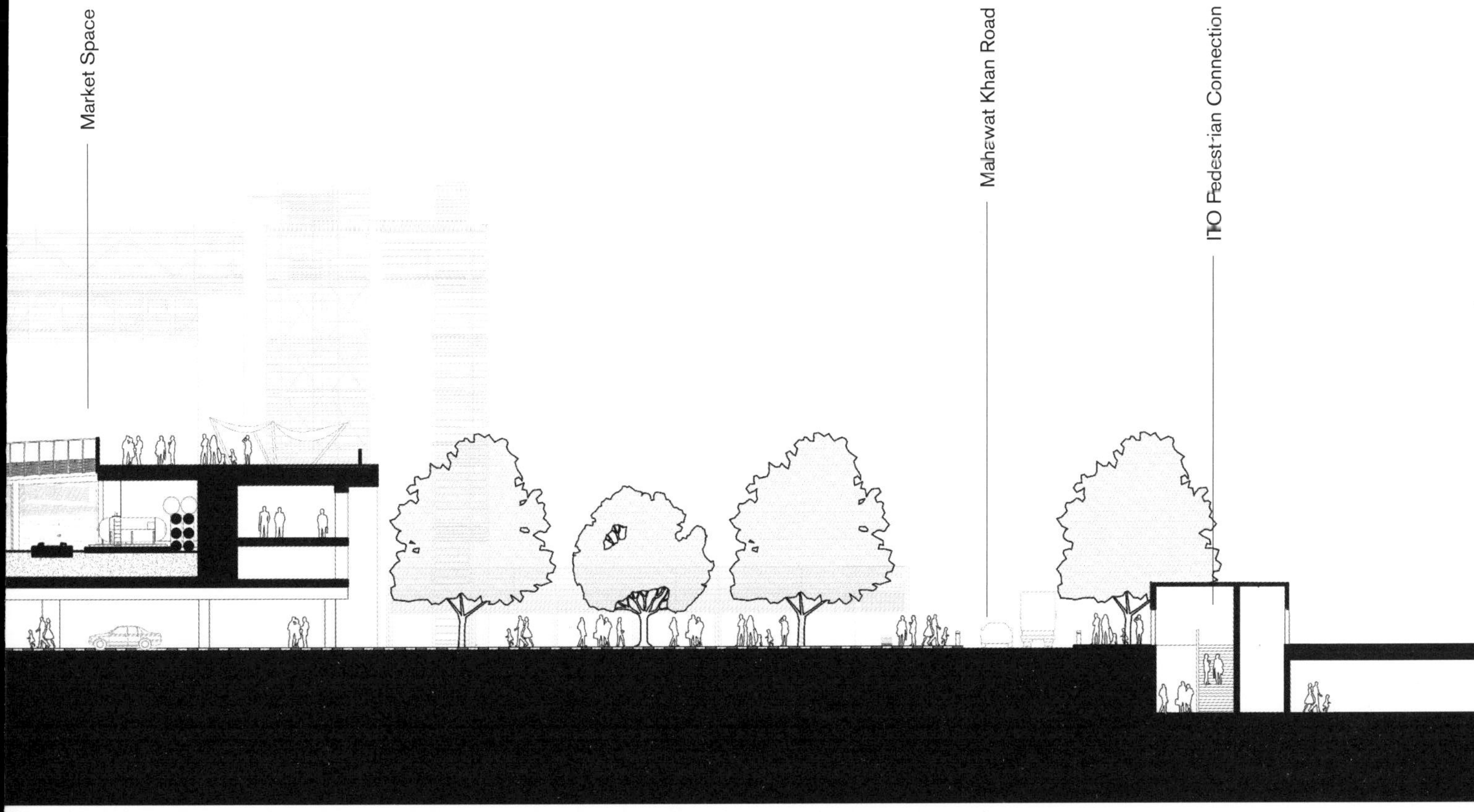

Market Space

Mahawat Khan Road

ITO Pedestrian Connection

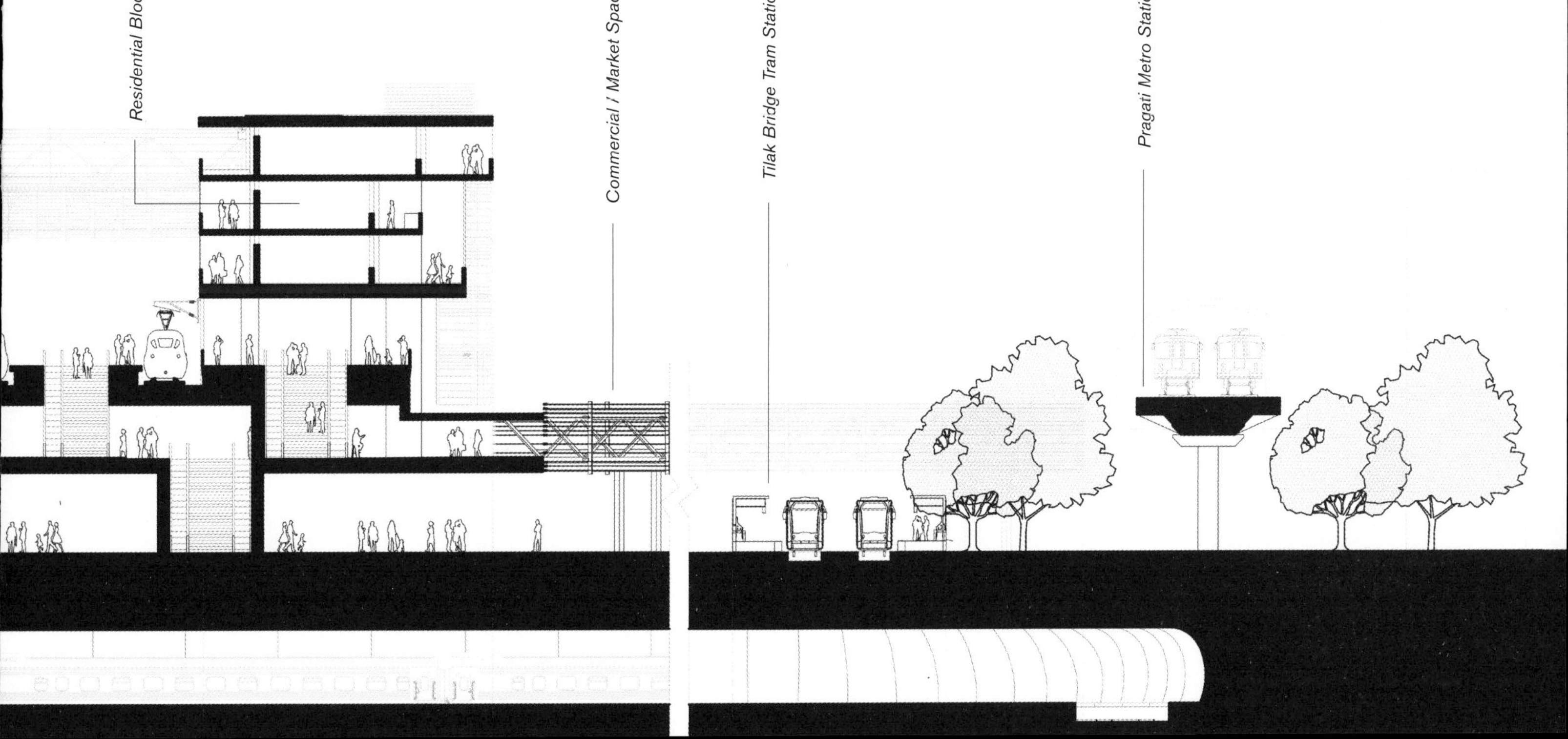

Residential Block

Commercial / Market Space

Tilak Bridge Tram Station

Pragati Metro Station

ALTHOUGH THE FLOODPLAIN HAS
BEEN CLAIMED FOR INFORMAL
SETTLEMENTS AND CULTIVATION,
THE RIVER'S EDGE HAS NOT BEEN
UTILIZED FOR FORMAL USE, PUBLIC
OR PRIVATE. THE SPACE IS LEFT
AS A DUMPING GROUND FOR THE
CITY'S INDUSTRY, SOLID WASTE, AND
ENERGY INFRASTRUCTURES.

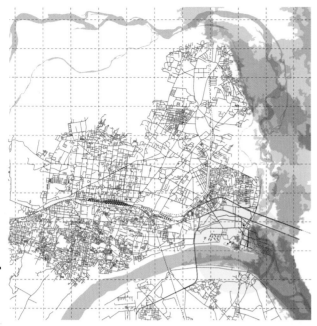

82.0m - Typical Seasonal Flooding

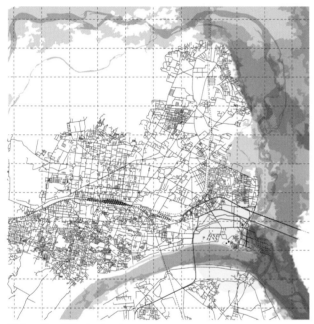

83.5m - Flood Warning Levels

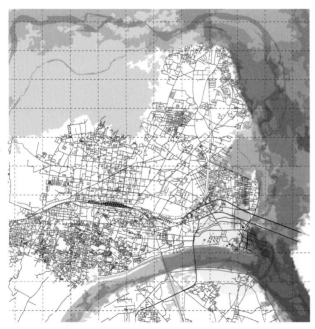

84.5m - Flood Danger Levels

Floodplain Temporary Shelter

In India, monsoon floods are a chronic problem between the months of June and September, an occurrence familiar to local residents. Due its geography, the Yamuna River suffers extreme impacts from yearly monsoon floods which cause unavoidable damage to many thousands of informal households – submerging villages, washing away crops, destroying roads, disrupting power and phone lines. Residents are left marooned for days while others must flee to provisional relief camps without access to the basic needs of daily life: food, clean water, and shelter.

The result of this floodplain habitation is a non-permanent urban configuration: people occupy the land or migrate to other locations depending on seasonal variances. Residents of these informal settlements remain a legitimate and productive category of urbanism and highlight a critical duality between ecology and structure. The fertile lands in the floodplain service their daily life as an economic and spiritual resource by contributing to the city's food stores while providing immediate access to the river for prayer and sacred offerings.

This project proposes a situation in which residents of informal settlements are able to remain on the land that secures their livelihood, provides necessary urban amenities for dignified and quality living, and withstands the cyclical four-month monsoon flooding. In contemporary and global urbanism, it is becoming more evident that in order for cities to be sustainable, they need to accommodate living situations that are characterized by states of temporary flux in structure, scale, and ecology rather than being anchored solely to static material configurations.

This project proposes to accommodate such realities. First, the project establishes a series of storage facilities capable of withstanding monsoonal floods while providing for the essential necessities of clean water and food that are often scarce during flood events. Flexible, low-skill, and easily replicated construction methods that utilize a bamboo mega-structure allow for phased construction as urban populations continue to grow. The project incorporates mixed-use programs such as affordable housing, communal dining, schools, and community centers which are essential for vibrant urban life.

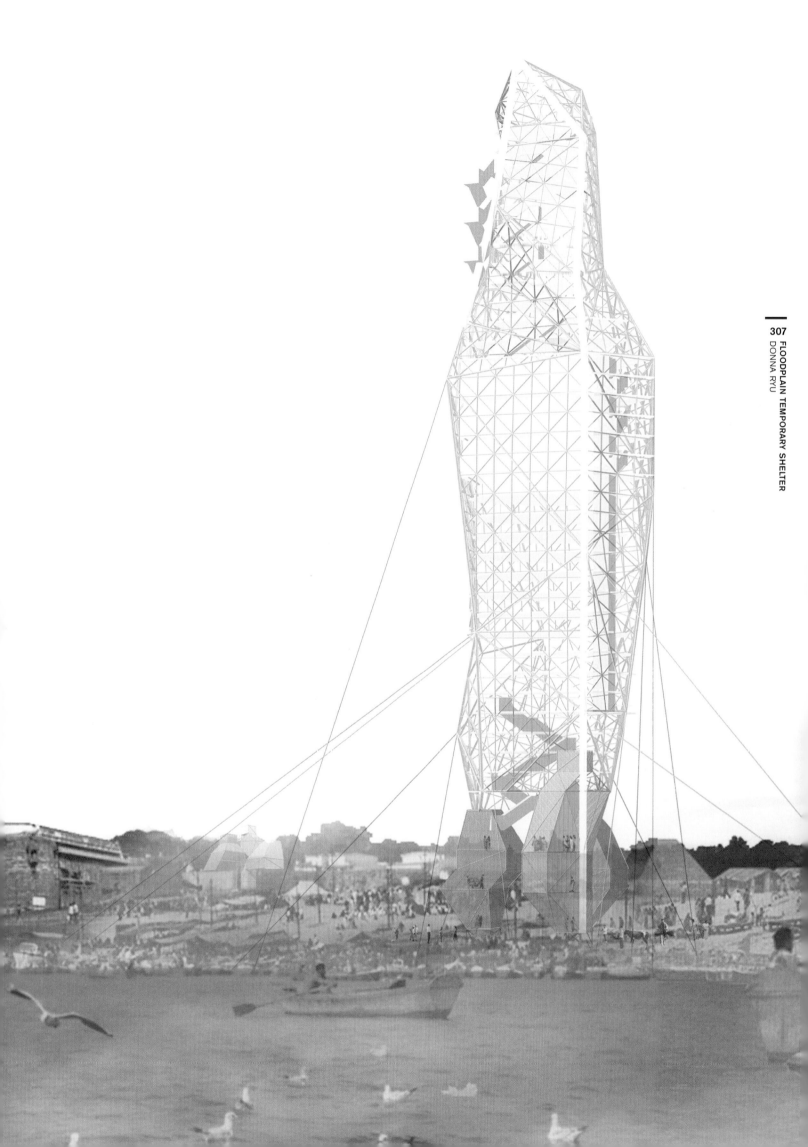

Existing Municipal Water Tank

1/4 mile (10 min. boat ride)

Existing Municipal Water Tank

Yamuna River

B.S.3594 Flood Disaster Extents

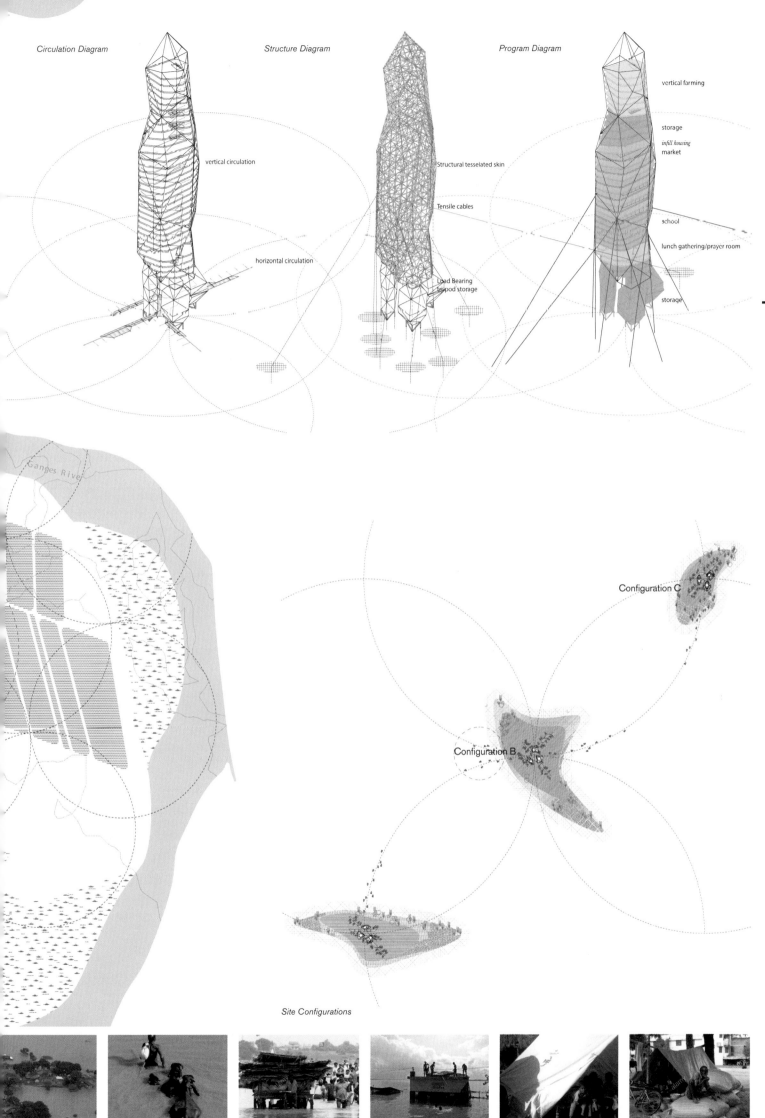

Circulation Diagram

vertical circulation

horizontal circulation

Structure Diagram

Structural tesselated skin

Tensile cables

Load Bearing
Tripod storage

Program Diagram

vertical farming

storage
infill housing
market

school

lunch gathering/prayer room

storage

Ganges River

Configuration C

Configuration B

Site Configurations

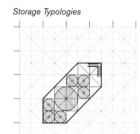

Total Volume: 66,400 cubic square feet
Total Tons: 1,481 T

 (1) 21'-0" diameter
@ 5 floors
Metric Tons: 371 T

(6) 10'-6" diameter
@ 3 floors
Metric Tons: 1,110 T

Waste capacity: 88,488 people
Water capacity: 4,777 people
Grain capacity: 41,684 people

Total # of people served:
4,777 people

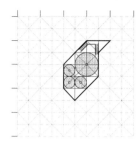

Total Volume: 41,500 cubic square feet
Total Tons: 926 T

(1) 21'-0" diameter
@ 5 floors
Metric Tons : 371 T

(3) 10'-6" diameter
@ 3 floors
Metric Tons : 555 T

Waste capacity: 55,327 people
Water capacity: 2,987 people
Grain capacity: 26,063 people

Total # of people served:
2,987 people

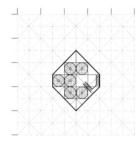

Total Volume: 49,800 cubic square feet
Total Tons: 1,110 T

(0) 21'-0" diameter
@ 5 floors
Metric Tons : 0`

(6) 10'-6" diameter
@ 3 floors
Metric Tons :1,110 T

Waste capacity: 66,321 people
Water capacity: 3,580 people
Grain capacity: 31,242 people

Total # of people served:
3,580 people

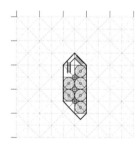

Total Volume: 49,800 cubic square feet
Total Tons: 1,110 T

(0) 21'-0" diameter
@ 5 floors
Metric Tons :0

(6) 10'-6" diameter
@ 3 floors
Metric Tons :1,110 T

Waste capacity: 66,321 people
Water capacity: 3,580 people
Grain capacity: 31,242 people

Total # of people served:
3,580 people

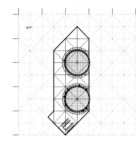

Total Volume: 33,200 cubic square feet
Total Tons: 742 T

(2) 21'-0" diameter
@ 5 floors
Metric Tons :742 T

(0) 10'-6" diameter
@ 3 floors

Waste capacity: 44,334 people
Water capacity: 2,393 people
Grain capacity: 20,884 people

Total # of people served:
2,393 people

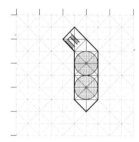

Total Volume: 33,200 cubic square feet
Total Tons: 742 T

(2) 21'-0" diameter
@ 5 floors
Metric Tons :742 T

(0) 10'-6" diameter
@ 3 floors
Metric Tons :0

Waste capacity: 44,334 people
Water capacity: 2,393 people
Grain capacity: 20,884 people

Total # of people served:
2,393 people

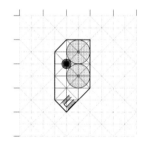

Total Volume: 33,200 cubic square feet
Total Tons: 742 T

(2) 21'-0" diameter
@ 5 floors
Metric Tons : 742 T

(0) 10'-6" diameter
@ 3 floors

Waste capacity: 44,334 people
Water capacity: 2,393 people
Grain capacity: 20,884 people

Total # of people served:
2,393 people

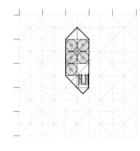

Total Volume: 41,500 cubic square feet
Total Tons: 925 T

(0) 21'-0" diameter
@ 5 floors
Metric Tons :0

(5) 10'-6" diameter
@ 3 floors
Metric Tons : 925 T

Waste capacity: 55,268 people
Water capacity: 2,983 people
Grain capacity: 26,050 people

Total # of people served:
2,983 people

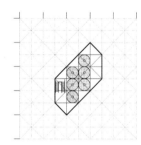

Total Volume: 49,800 cubic square feet
Total Tons: 1,110 T

(0) 21'-0" diameter
@ 5 floors
Metric Tons :0

(6) 10'-6" diameter
@ 3 floors
Metric Tons :1,110 T

Waste capacity: 66,321 people
Water capacity: 3,580 people
Grain capacity: 31,242 people

Total # of people served:
3,580 people

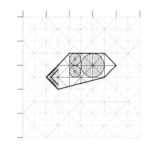

Total Volume: 33,200 cubic square feet
Total Tons: 741 T

(1) 21'-0" diameter
@ 5 floors
Metric Tons : 371 T

(2) 10'-6" diameter
@ 3 floors
Metric Tons : 370 T

Waste capacity: 44,274 people
Water capacity: 2,390 people
Grain capacity: 20,856 people

Total # of people served:
2,390 people

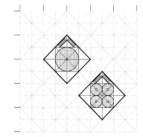

Total Volume: 74,700 cubic square feet
Total Tons: 1,111 T

(1) 21'-0" diameter
@ 5 floors
Metric Tons : 371 T

(4) 10'-6" diameter
@ 3 floors
Metric Tons :740 T

Waste capacity: 66,381 people
Water capacity: 3,583 people
Grain capacity: 31,270 people

Total # of people served:
3,583 people

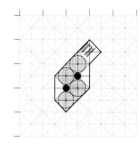

Total Volume: 66,400 cubic square feet
Total Tons: 1,484 T

(4) 21'-0" diameter
@ 5 floors
Metric Tons : 1,484 T

(0) 10'-6" diameter
@ 3 floors
Metric Tons : 0

Waste capacity: 88,668 people
Water capacity: 4,787 people
Grain capacity: 41,768 people

Total # of people served:
4,787 people

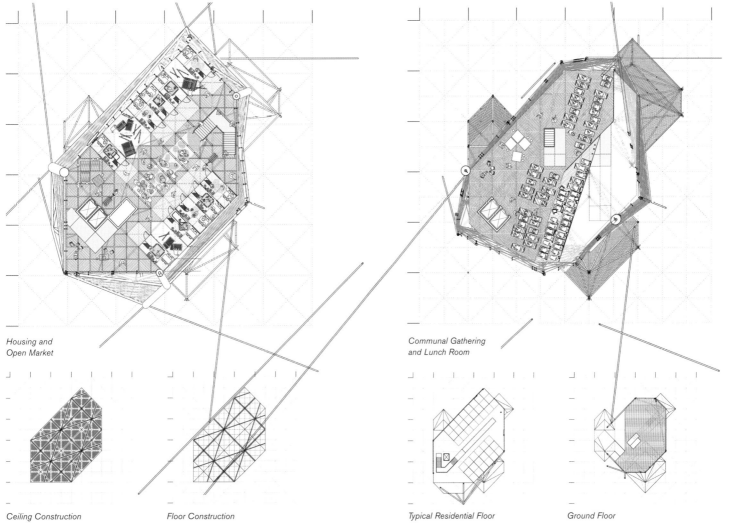

Housing and
Open Market

Communal Gathering
and Lunch Room

Ceiling Construction

Floor Construction

Typical Residential Floor

Ground Floor

Flood Water Simulations

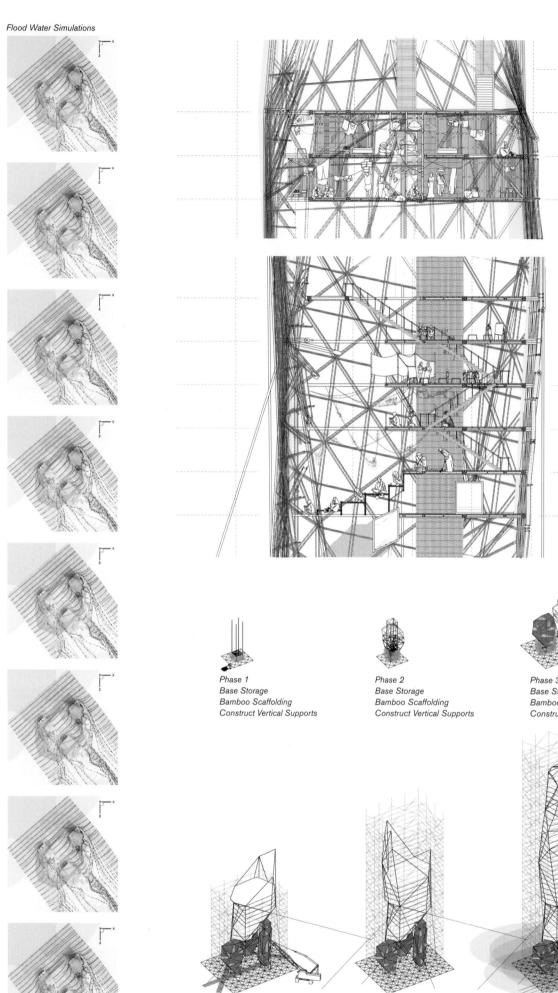

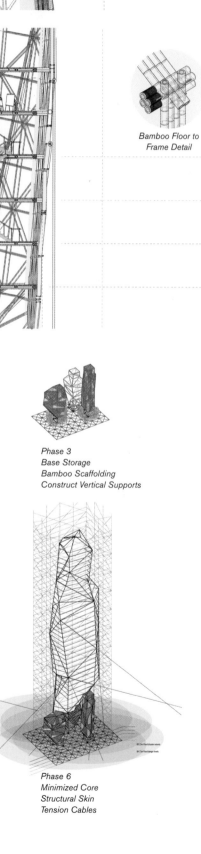

312
FLOODPLAIN TEMPORARY SHELTER
DONNA RYU

*Bamboo Wall
Partion Detail*

*Bamboo Floor to
Frame Detail*

Phase 1
Base Storage
Bamboo Scaffolding
Construct Vertical Supports

Phase 2
Base Storage
Bamboo Scaffolding
Construct Vertical Supports

Phase 3
Base Storage
Bamboo Scaffolding
Construct Vertical Supports

Phase 4
Minimized Core
Structural Skin
Tension Cables

Phase 5
Minimized Core
Structural Skin
Tension Cables

Phase 6
Minimized Core
Structural Skin
Tension Cables

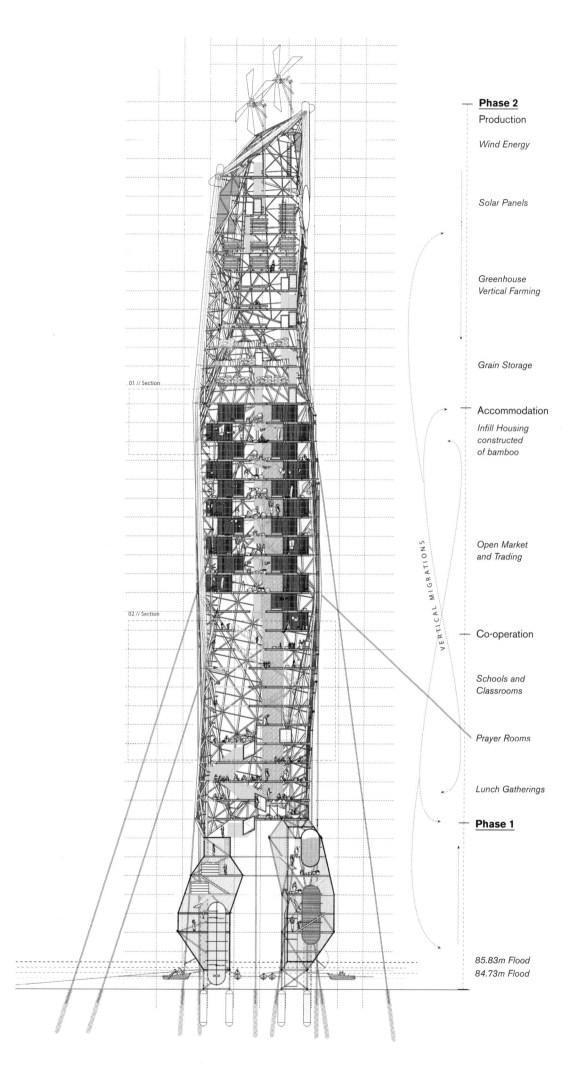

Phase 2

Production

Wind Energy

Solar Panels

Greenhouse Vertical Farming

Grain Storage

Accommodation

Infill Housing constructed of bamboo

Open Market and Trading

Co-operation

Schools and Classrooms

Prayer Rooms

Lunch Gatherings

Phase 1

VERTICAL MIGRATIONS

01 // Section

02 // Section

85.83m Flood
84.73m Flood

HYBRID INFRASTRUCTURES

As in most other cities across the globe, infrastructure is designed with a single logic, supposedly optimum for a single use, without consideration of their urban context and without care for the livelihood of adjacent areas. These infrastructural bubbles become severe interruptions of Delhi's fragile urbanity. Focused inwards, infrastructure creates problematic areas of friction with the zones of extreme density around them. This is true for power plants and electrical substation, but also for other urban elements that have traditionally created urban fabric in other cities, such as bridges or transportation stations.

Currently, the scarce bridges that cross the Yamuna have lengths between one and three kilometers, and are designed for only vehicular traffic. Their relation with the city fabric creates significant areas of empty and marginal space among highways, intersections, and overpasses, and lack any idea of urbanity. The fences and empty service space along bridges make the Yamuna almost invisible even while crossing it. Besides offering opportunities for placing housing that creates neighborhoods in areas of contact with the city, the current vehicular bridges allow for the insertion of pedestrian and bicycle lanes, with enough space for social interaction, and for markets and ramps that provide platforms to access the water.

Delhi's busy train stations require a large amount of poorly used space for inefficient and often dangerous intermodal connections with buses, cars and rickshaws. In stations like Nizamuddin, the chaos of buses and cars makes it impossible to reach a portion of the floodplain specially damaged by industrial occupation.

This neglected space is an opportunity for rethinking intermodal connections, creating areas of new centrality, and facilitating pedestrian continuity within the city and with the Yamuna.

Vikas Marg Pedestrian Bridge

The Vikas Marg Pedestrian Bridge serves as an east-west connection across the Yamuna River and redefines the common bridge infrastructure. More than just a transportation artery from one riverbank to the other, the project introduces new ways in which Delhi's citizens can engage and access the Yamuna River. The project combines both functional and leisure components that cater to the experience and safety of the pedestrian.

Paths allow bikers to travel safely off the main motorway and informal market spaces and seating areas enliven the atmosphere within to mimic what already happens on the streets. Docks on the river create opportunity for boat rentals, outdoor pools, island accessibility, and ceremonial practices. A covered canopy structure isolates the pedestrian space from the two motorways that flank it. Canvas shades are hung on steel

framework, creating a dynamic play of light and shadow while protecting people from Delhi's harsh climate. By converting the bridge into a productive space, pedestrian space, which are normally treated as an afterthought throughout the city, become a central focus of daily activity. Pedestrian activity brings new life to the Vikas Marg Bridge, transforming it into a new destination point along the Yamuna River.

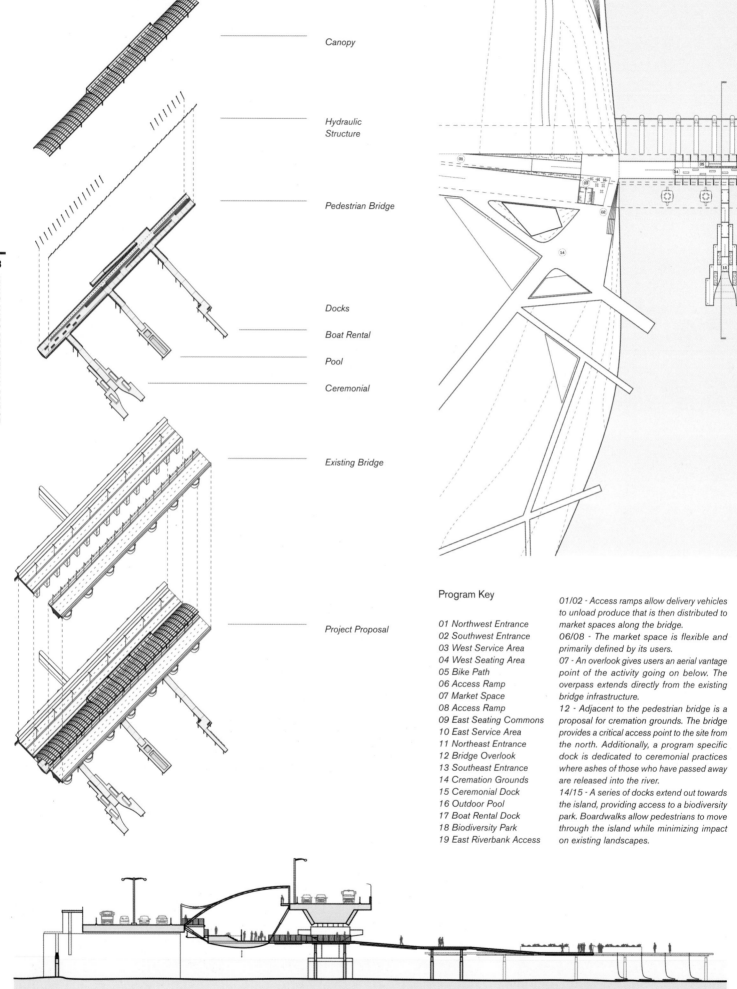

Canopy

Hydraulic
Structure

Pedestrian Bridge

Docks

Boat Rental

Pool

Ceremonial

Existing Bridge

Project Proposal

Program Key

01 Northwest Entrance
02 Southwest Entrance
03 West Service Area
04 West Seating Area
05 Bike Path
06 Access Ramp
07 Market Space
08 Access Ramp
09 East Seating Commons
10 East Service Area
11 Northeast Entrance
12 Bridge Overlook
13 Southeast Entrance
14 Cremation Grounds
15 Ceremonial Dock
16 Outdoor Pool
17 Boat Rental Dock
18 Biodiversity Park
19 East Riverbank Access

01/02 - Access ramps allow delivery vehicles to unload produce that is then distributed to market spaces along the bridge.
06/08 - The market space is flexible and primarily defined by its users.
07 - An overlook gives users an aerial vantage point of the activity going on below. The overpass extends directly from the existing bridge infrastructure.
12 - Adjacent to the pedestrian bridge is a proposal for cremation grounds. The bridge provides a critical access point to the site from the north. Additionally, a program specific dock is dedicated to ceremonial practices where ashes of those who have passed away are released into the river.
14/15 - A series of docks extend out towards the island, providing access to a biodiversity park. Boardwalks allow pedestrians to move through the island while minimizing impact on existing landscapes.

Dry Season

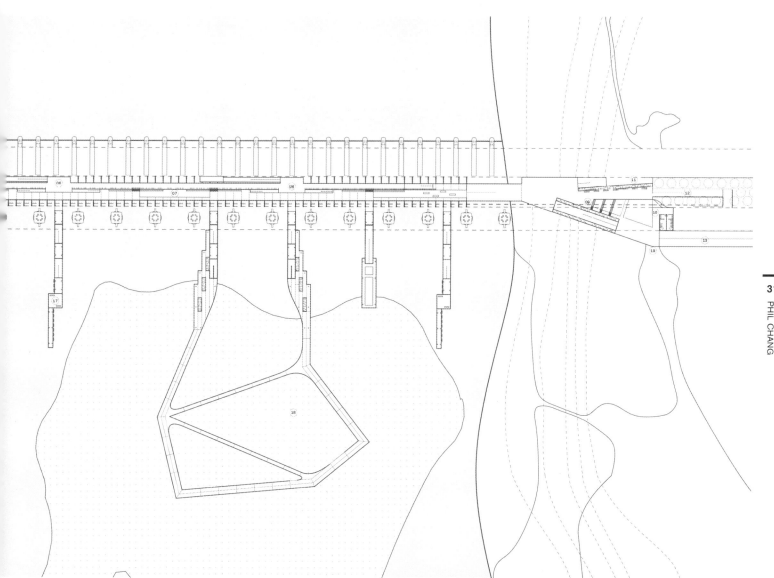

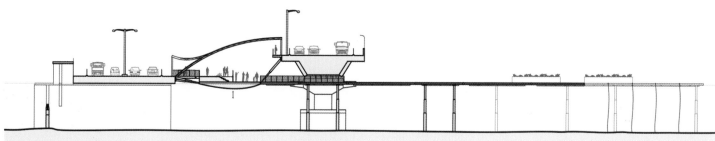

Monsoon Season

BRIDGES AND STREETS IN DELHI HAVE BEEN BUILT FOR A SINGULAR PURPOSE, TO MEET HIGH TRAFFIC DEMANDS. THIS DEMAND CREATES EXTREMELY CONGESTED TRAFFIC THAT IS UNSAFE AND INEFFICIENT WHILE IGNORING THE PEDESTRIAN. CAN BRIDGES AND STREETS BE ADAPTED FOR MULTIPLE USES?

Ground Level Plan

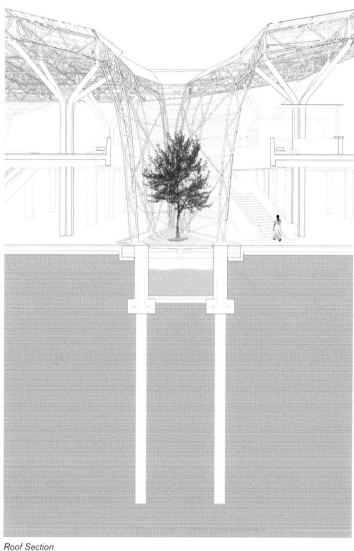

Roof Section

Nizamuddin Railway Station

Delhi is a city of extreme contrast and diversity with little place for a middle ground or commons. Situated along the Yamuna River, this intermodal station not only addresses the disconnect between the city of New Delhi and the Yamuna River, but also the localized disconnect where distance, lack of cohesion, and congestion separate two, soon to be three, transportation lines.

The flows of people, transportation, and ecological systems, in their separation and coming together, inform the layout of the site both horizontally and vertically.

There are essentially two ground conditions of the station: one for the circulation of people and transportation, and the other, above, for the circulation of the elements-water, light, and air.

The project seeks to accommodate the diversity of needs of Delhi's citizens by functioning as a place of common ground. An expansive open space acts as a connective tissue in between the stations defined by the column grid, canopy structure, skylights, and smaller enclosures. Within this space opportunity for flexible movement and circulation

as well as flexible program is possible. The regular structure is broken by moments where vertical circulation is necessary to access the transportation lines and other amenities below.

At these irregularities, the roof folds and punctures the ground. Reacting to the flows of people, the roof provides access and serves as a way-finding device for connections to the bus terminal and metro station. The roof also provides chimneys for ventilation, light wells for the underground spaces, and collection points to remove water from the site.

Site Strategy

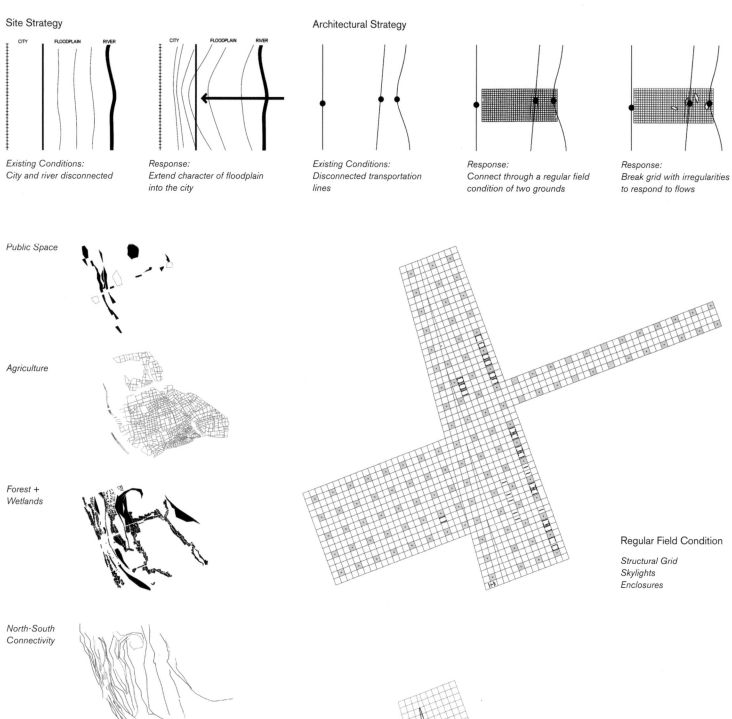

Existing Conditions:
City and river disconnected

Response:
Extend character of floodplain
into the city

Architectural Strategy

Existing Conditions:
Disconnected transportation
lines

Response:
Connect through a regular field
condition of two grounds

Response:
Break grid with irregularities
to respond to flows

Public Space

Agriculture

*Forest +
Wetlands*

*North-South
Connectivity*

Water

All

Regular Field Condition

Structural Grid
Skylights
Enclosures

Irregular Field Condition

Vertical Circulation
Wayfinding
Ventilation
Light
Water Collection

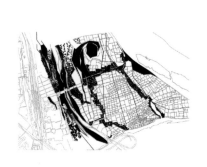
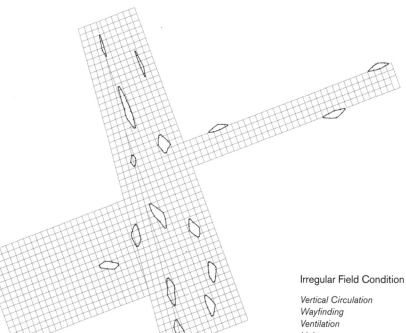

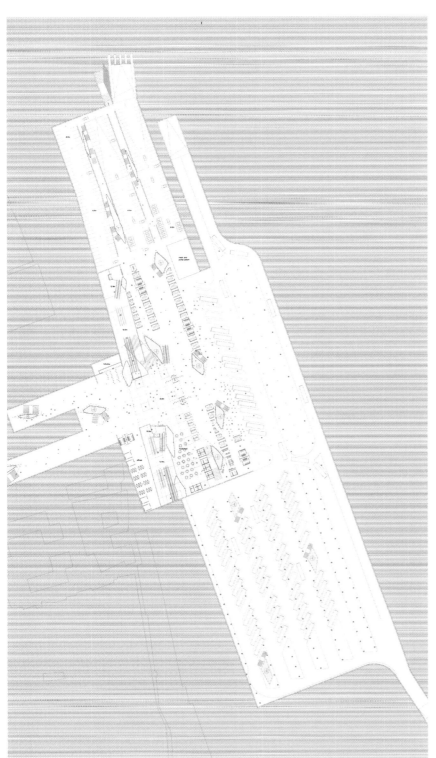

Lower Level Plan

325

NIZAMUDDIN INTERMODAL STATION
MICHELLE STEIN

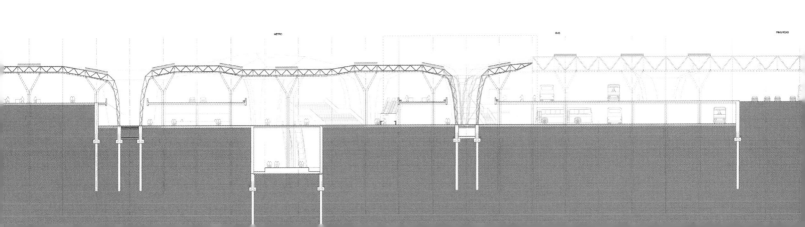

Railroad to Floodplain Connection

Hazrat Nizamuddin Railway Station bisects two worlds: Nizamuddin East Colony, a complex of big homes, private gardens and clean pavement, and the neighborhood of Sari Kale Khan, a shanty city of densely-occupied streets and dirt roads. The axis of railway tracks is a stark barrier between these realities and this is manifested in the subdued assets of the station: two pedestrian bridges. The station boasts no additional public amenities, only these passages that allow access to the platforms. Ways to enter the station from the west are obstructed by walls and traffic and the eastern entrance faces consistent vehicular and pedestrian congestion. People cross here to reach commuter trains or shortcuts to western parts of the city. Travelers aiming to board long distance trains are in the minority.

This proposal increases access to both sides of the track and stitches together the dueling urban fabrics. Six new bridges connect each neighborhood with the other while also offering access to Millennium Park, the metro, and the renewed Yamuna River cultural corridor. A marketplace, commercial stores, restaurants, and artist galleries anchor these bridges on the west edge, drawing wealthier residents to the center for recreation and workers to a place of opportunity. The canopy system of water catchment connects these enclaves sustainably. Hazrat Nizamuddin Station is transformed from a bridge sitting between two cities into a city of bridges.

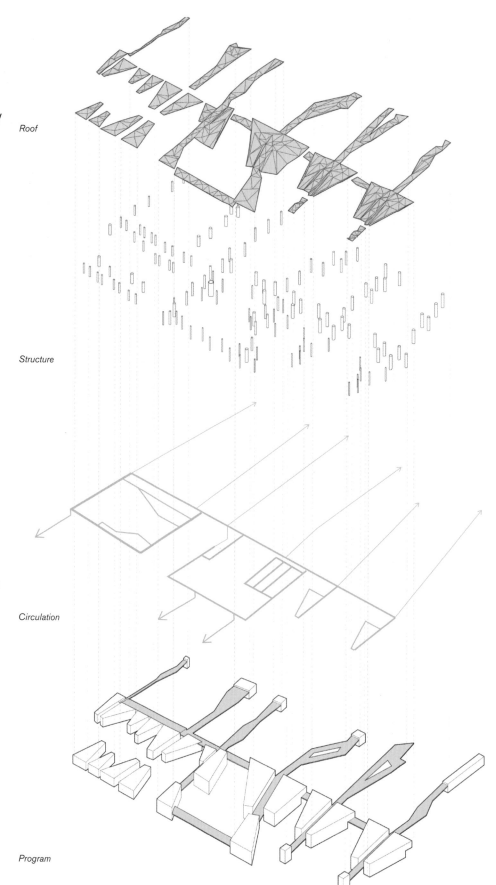

Roof

Structure

Circulation

Program

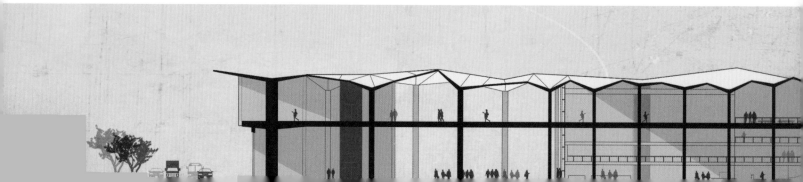

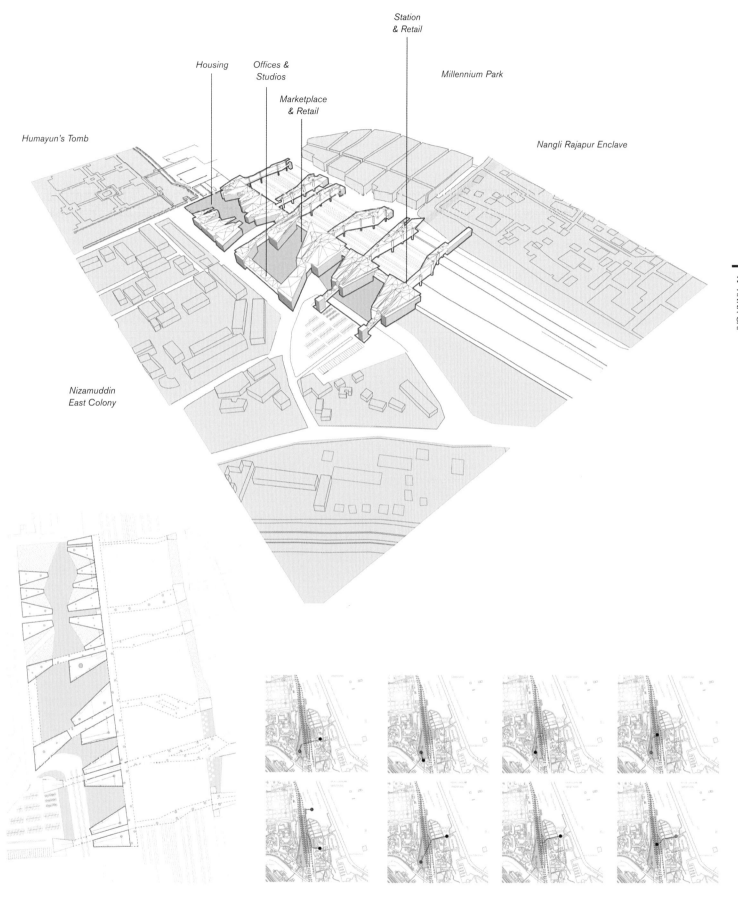

Humayun's Tomb

Housing

Offices &
Studios

Marketplace
& Retail

Station
& Retail

Millennium Park

Nangli Rajapur Enclave

Nizamuddin
East Colony

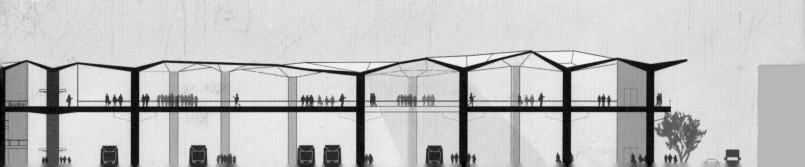

NEIGHBORHOOD PUBLIC AMENITIES

Entire areas of Delhi, especially urban villages and informal settlements, lack not only water and sanitation infrastructure, but also basic public amenities such as schools, primary care, community centers, toilets, laundry facilities, and safe spaces for women and children. A systematic program to insert amenities into these places is essential in order to provide for basic services while acting as a catalyst for urban improvement.

In Delhi, almost every space is used, or misused, for multiple activities. Building in this culture, synergic programs need to be combined in opportunistic ways to provide services and generate nodes of local activity that are clearly perceived as the commons for the community. Every intervention should link interior and the exterior spaces as local 'urban projects', include decentralized infrastructures as needed, and participate in solving the always present problems of discontinuity and lack of accessibility.

In some cases—such as Daryaganj—the former floodplain lays walled off and a few meters below the extremely dense neighborhood, completely disconnected and tagged as—derelict—park. Tackling all these deficiencies holistically, architecture is synergized with public space and mobility to offer hybrid solutions with new streets that offer market space, a programmed park, and a system of buildings able to provide needed social programs.

Multiple vacant and misused spaces along roads and drains are opportunities for the insertion of public amenities that restore and properly use the waterways, creating urban facades. Continuity and connectivity in the city minimizes marginality and increases safety. In some cases, the space of opportunity can be a bridge over the drain in itself.

The generic vehicular bridge, designed as a mere road most often without proper sidewalks, can be hybridize with any necessary social program. 'Building-bridges' are historically present in many places across the world, and new versions will strategically solve acute necessities in Delhi's neighborhood

In the dense urban villas, without infrastructure or large vacant lots for development, the insertion of decentralized sanitation will require small operations of reconstructing a few homes. This can be combined with the creation of small local public spaces, replacement housing, and basic public amenities. A block by block strategy is an option for incremental and low impact surgery in order to upgrade and improve the living conditions that results in minimum social disturbance and displacement.

Park and Community Centers

Housing is a necessity that, in Delhi, consistently fails to meet the needs of a growing population. More often than not, the solution to providing affordable shelters is to construct massive apartment towers which, while standing at over twenty stories tall with thousands of single to multi-occupant units, still fail to provide basic facilities and amenities.

The Daryaganj neighborhood exists as a relic of British imperialism that lacks any defined urban character. What were once elegant art-deco homes are now shells that provide shelter to thousands of people, and stores and shops have wedged into the last available spaces on the street. Those who cannot fit between buildings and fences are pushed to the very edge of the neighborhood, in informal settlements that border a four-meter tall wall.

The Daryaganj Park and Community Center addresses these issues by constructing a new urban promenade that connects Daryaganj to Raj Ghat on the Yamuna Floodplain. By bridging outwards from the dense city and creating new mobility corridors and access points, congestion and housing issues are alleviated. The city street, which before was overcrowded and unclear, is brought back into daylight, and affordable, easily constructed, and aesthetically light housing blocks rest on top of a new park that retains and mitigates excess water while providing a quiet, shaded ecological expanse.

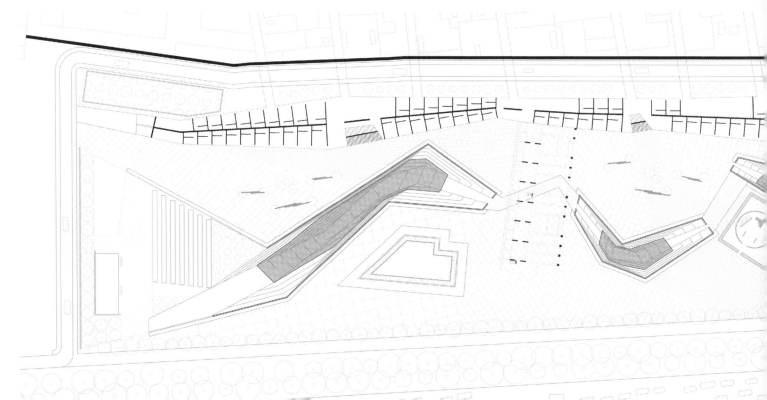

Sectionally, the barrier of the city transforms into a new urban promenade with shops, markets, and stores programmed underneath a tapered slab. The housing units are lifted above the ground plane, allowing for continuous circulation underneath the building.

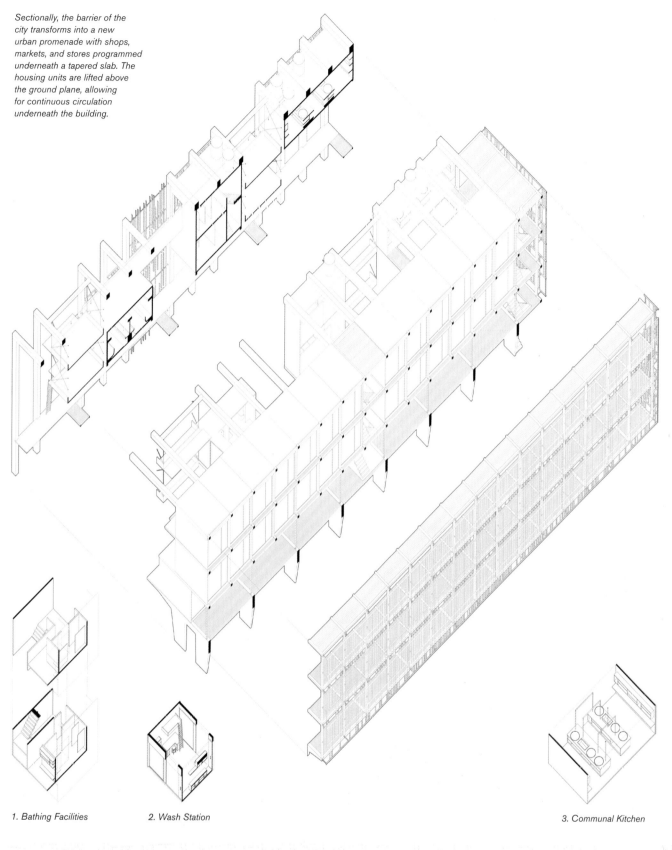

1. Bathing Facilities

2. Wash Station

3. Communal Kitchen

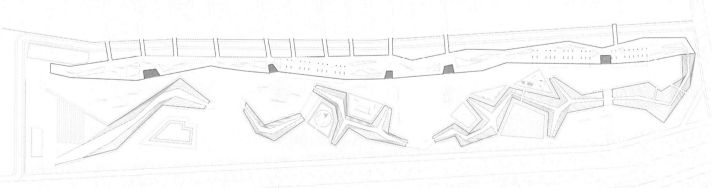

LEFTOVER SPACES THAT RUN PARALLEL TO HIGHWAYS ARE OFTEN OVERLOOKED AND IMPROPERLY PLANNED. COMPRISED OF INFORMAL HOUSING AND PARKING LOTS, THE RESULT IS A PHYSICAL BARRIER BETWEEN NEIGHBORHOODS THAT ARE DISCONNECTED FROM THE CITY AS A WHOLE.

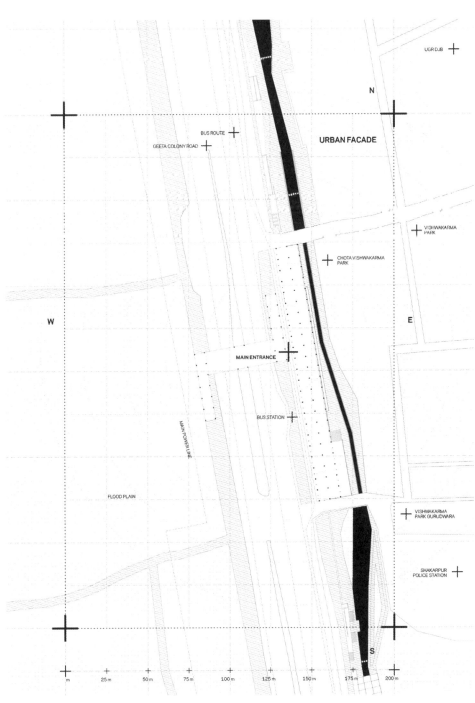

Women's Shelter and Laundry Facilities

Laxmi Nagar is a dense neighborhood in East Delhi bordering the Yamuna Floodplain This neighborhood is well known for its roadside shopping and Tuesday markets. However, residents are disconnected from the floodplain due to the eight lane Geeta Colony Road which forms a physical barrier between parks and housing colonies of Laxmi Nagar and several other neighborhoods in East Delhi.

This project reconnects East Delhi to the Yamuna Floodplain, reshaping the urban fabric for a more cohesive and connected "Urban Facade." Towards this end, a new 7.5 km linear park is developed along the highway for pedestrian use and for enhancement of existing markets along the neighborhood's edge. In addition, 13,000 units of social housing are proposed, addressing Delhi's housing shortage and contributing to a vibrant urban life along the linear park. The project also adds over 100,000 sqm of public facilities such as toilets, laundry facilities, and community centers. Finally, this project redevelops the drains that run through the edge by daylighting the water with the introduction of hardscapes and softscapes which treat and control the flow of water.

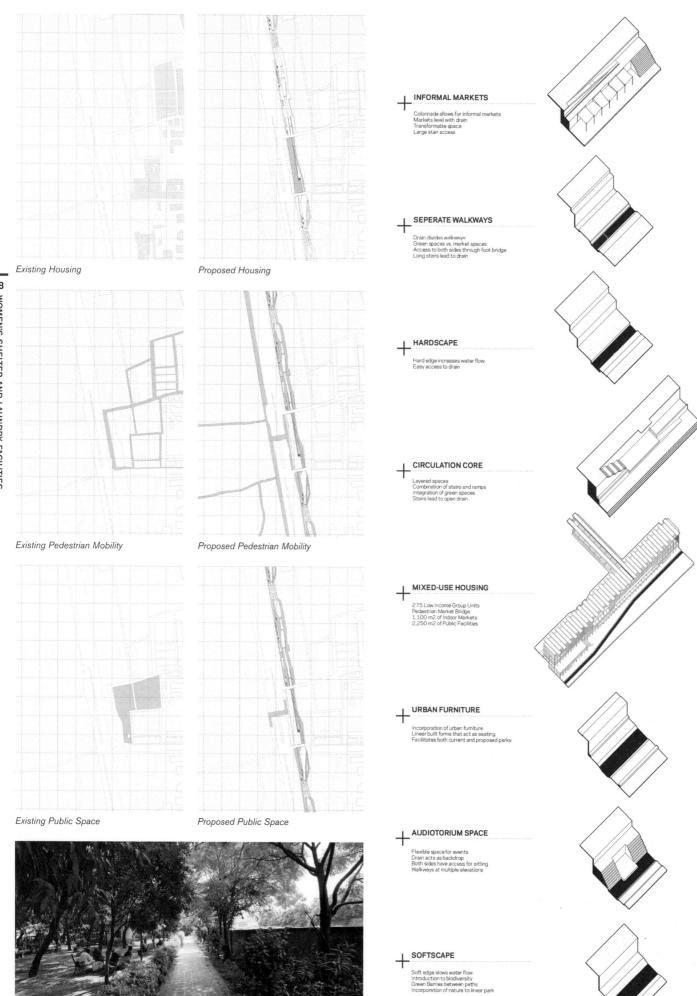

Existing Housing

Proposed Housing

Existing Pedestrian Mobility

Proposed Pedestrian Mobility

Existing Public Space

Proposed Public Space

INFORMAL MARKETS

Colonnade allows for informal markets
Markets level with drain
Transformable space
Large stair access

SEPERATE WALKWAYS

Drain divides walkways
Green spaces vs. market spaces
Access to both sides through foot bridge
Long stairs lead to drain

HARDSCAPE

Hard edge increases water flow
Easy access to drain

CIRCULATION CORE

Layered spaces
Combination of stairs and ramps
Integration of green spaces
Stairs lead to open drain

MIXED-USE HOUSING

275 Low Income Group Units
Pedestrian Market Bridge
1,100 m2 of Indoor Markets
2,250 m2 of Public Facilities

URBAN FURNITURE

Incorporation of urban furniture
Linear built forms that act as seating
Facilitates both current and proposed parks

AUDIOTORIUM SPACE

Flexible space for events
Drain acts as backdrop
Both sides have access for sitting
Walkways at multiple elevations

SOFTSCAPE

Soft edge slows water flow
Introduction to biodiversity
Green Barries between paths
Incorporation of nature to linear park

Public Facility Bridges

This project proposes a series of new bridges across the Najafgarh Drain which address issues of pedestrian mobility and a lack of public amenities by connecting urban neighborhoods on either side of the drain.

Many existing bridges cross the Najafgarh Drain serving the city's transportation needs. But these bridges are infrequent and are built to primarily serve vehicular transportation. As a result, the drain acts as a major barrier between neighborhoods on either side of the drain, limiting pedestrian connectivity and access to public services and amenities.

The Najafgarh provides many locations for new bridges, not for transportation needs, but to act as social amenities and connectors. The bridges connect existing social infrastructures (such as parks, schools, universities, and hospitals) on either side of the drain and act as catalysts for the drain remediation process, creating a network of parks and social services which strengthen the idea of the Najafgarh as a new green, urban corridor serving Delhi.

Research centers, schools, civic centers, markets, sports facilities, and intermodal connectors are all potential uses of these new bridges in order to stitch the neighborhoods together on each side of the Najafgarh. The bridges integrate into the new linear park along the Najafgarh Drain and contribute to its presence in everyday public life by providing public bathrooms, gardens, public wifi access, co-working spaces, bike repair stations, and gyms.

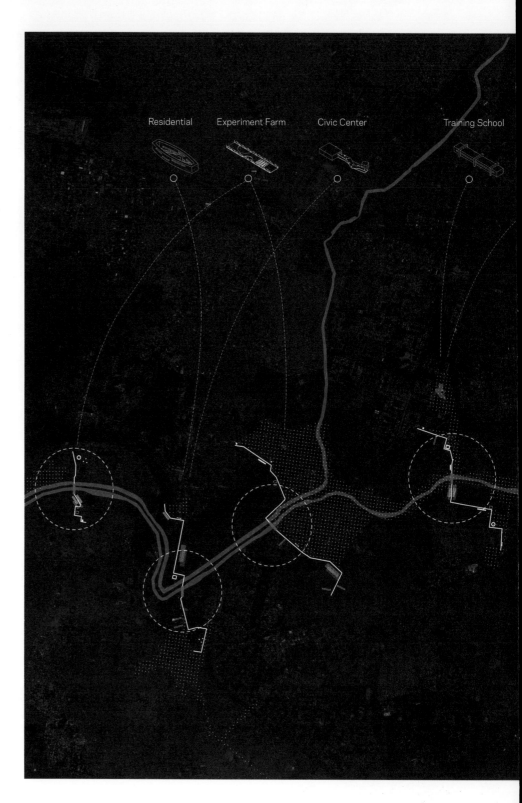

Residential   Experiment Farm   Civic Center   Training School

Proposed Building Footprints

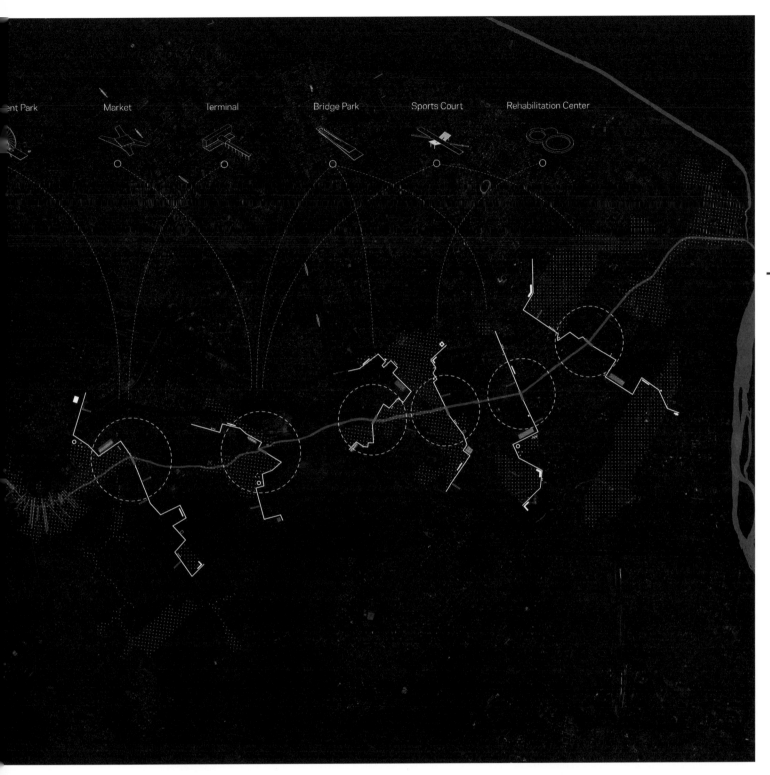

ent Park Market Terminal Bridge Park Sports Court Rehabilitation Center

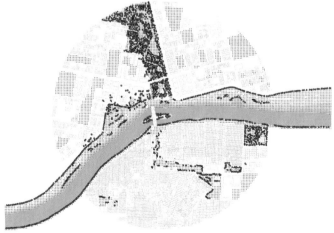

Proposed Vegetation

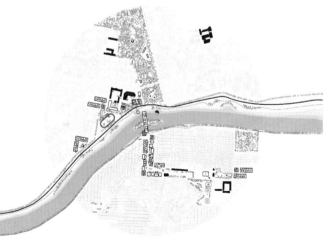

Combined

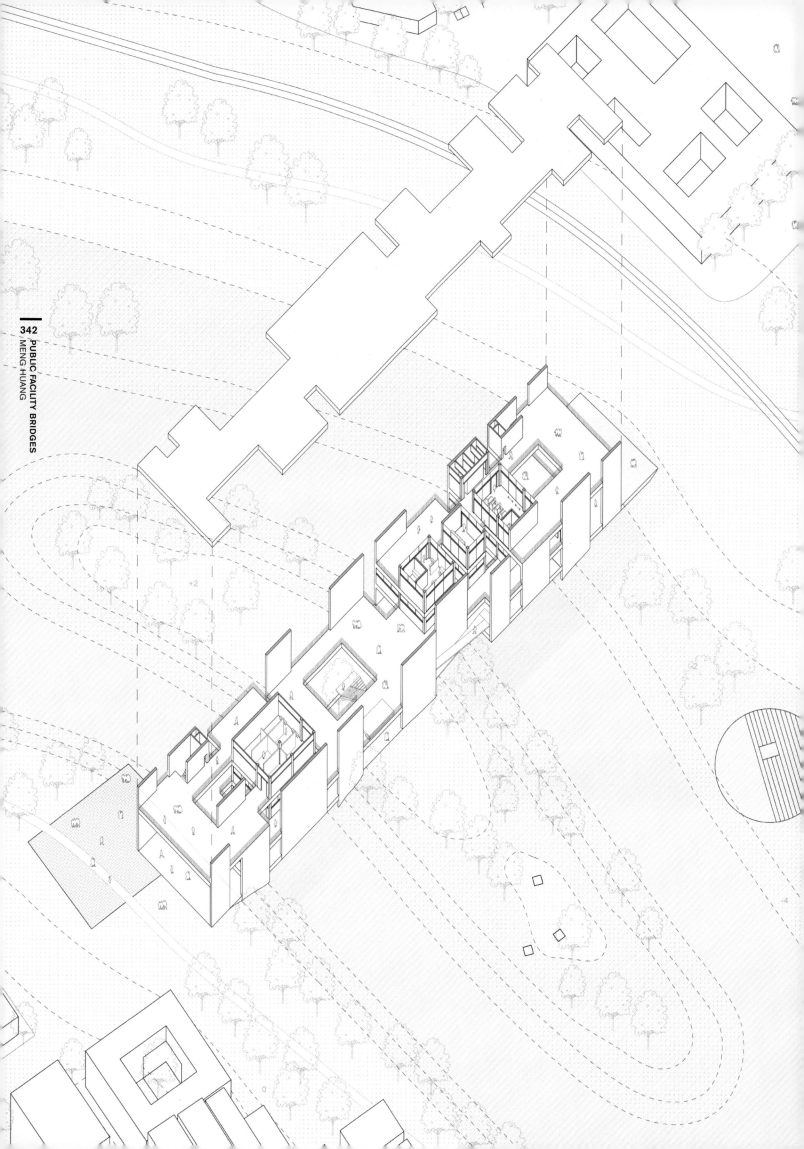

Existing Urban Fabric

Punctuated Intervention

Diffuse Equipment

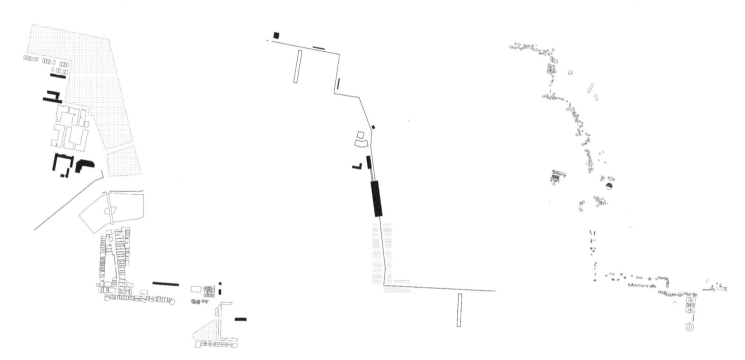

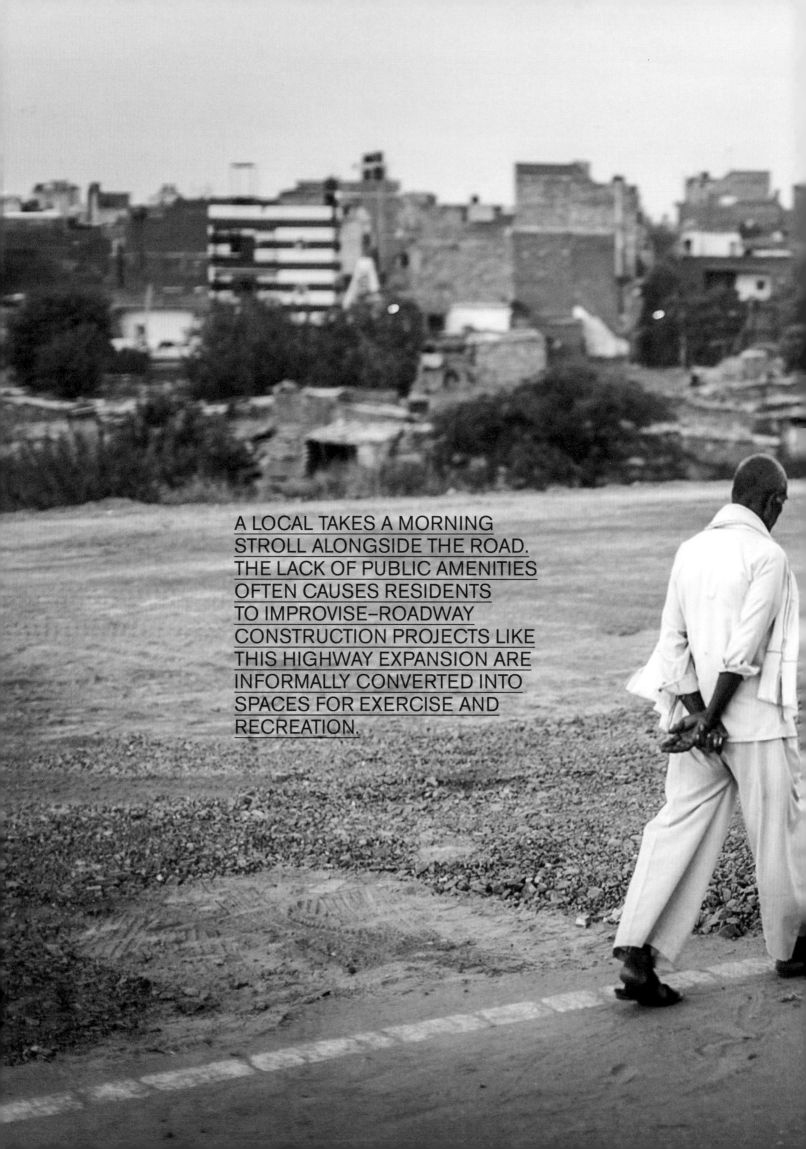

A LOCAL TAKES A MORNING STROLL ALONGSIDE THE ROAD. THE LACK OF PUBLIC AMENITIES OFTEN CAUSES RESIDENTS TO IMPROVISE—ROADWAY CONSTRUCTION PROJECTS LIKE THIS HIGHWAY EXPANSION ARE INFORMALLY CONVERTED INTO SPACES FOR EXERCISE AND RECREATION.

Community Centers for Public Health

This project is located in Ganesh Nagar in East Delhi, a dense neighborhood which offers no public space for its residents. As in most informal neighborhoods in Delhi, there is a drain running along the neighborhood which carries untreated effluent directly into the Yamuna River.

The project proposes to remove some of the housing in the neighborhood and relocate the displaced tenants into a new apartment building on site which also hosts public services such as schools, clinics, youth centers, exhibition centers, and markets. A new public plaza is also created which provides open air gathering space and wetlands to form a decentralized water treatment system which provides clean water to the neighborhood. Water is cleaned on site and used by the local residents but will also eventually flow to the Yamuna and contribute to the cleansing of the river. This will contribute to not only providing the neighborhood with clean water and services but also ensures that gardens located in the new public spaces are cultivated with clean water. This project serves as a prototype that can be applied to many dense neighborhoods on the river's edge in East Delhi.

Existing Public Space

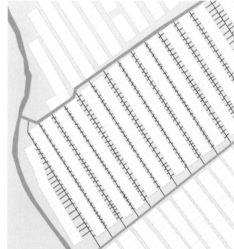

Existing Sewage Systems

Proposed Public Space

Proposed Sewage Systems // Proposed

A. Housing
B. Septic Tank
C. Leach Beds
D. Bioremediation
E. Water for Public Use
F. Piped Water Connection

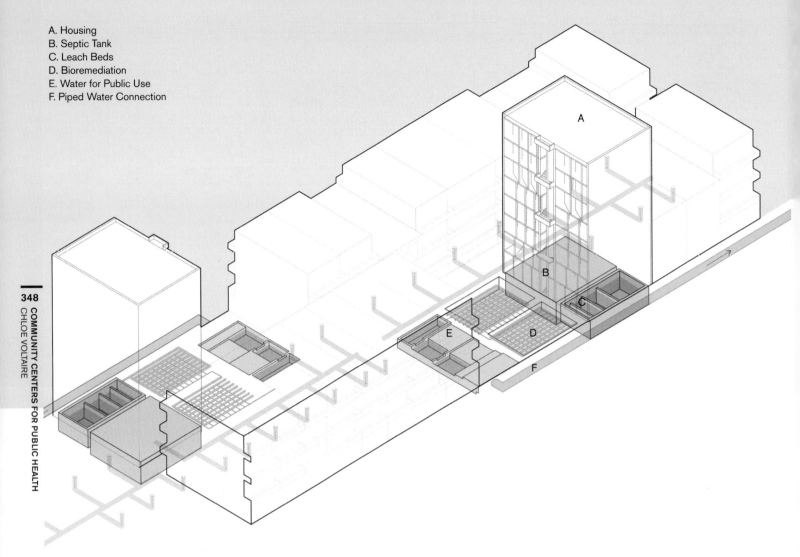

Bioremediation Process

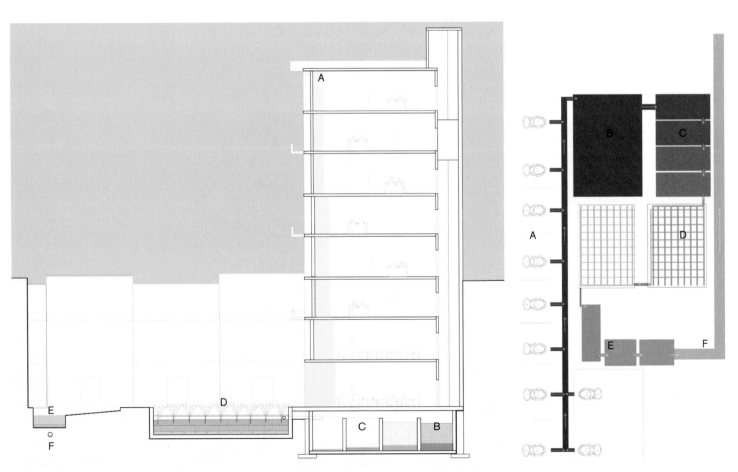

HERITAGE REVITALIZATION

Architectural heritage makes Delhi one of the most extraordinary capitals in the world. Still, most of it has severe dysfunctions in maintenance and accessibility. A visitor cannot walk between heritage sites due to a complete disconnection. Parallel to the Yamuna, an extraordinary heritage route could connect the Red Fort with Humayun's Tomb, crossing Feroz Sha Kotla, Purana Qila, and Sunder Nursery. In the in between, the route will connect sarais, tombs, and other historic monuments in Delhi's zoo or hidden in the urban fabric. The legacy of Mughal, Lodi, and other dynasties becomes intertwined with British and modern architecture, creating a public space with continuous latent potential.

An entire urban design strategy can be based on just conceiving Delhi's rich heritage as an urban spine, synergic with the main Yamuna commons. A continuity of pedestrian and public space is essential to its success. The reconsideration of accessibility should be linked to the former, as well as the integration of adjacent neglected spaces. But together with these basic urban strategies, the programmatic use of many of these extraordinary

heritage sites needs to be adjusted. Some sites should just be restored and made accessible, with complementary facilities added in the side, as in Humayun's Tomb. In some others, the site itself should incorporate new lively programs to revitalize monuments and also serve the city. This strategy has proven to provide for the recovery and maintenance of significant monuments in Europe and other continents, but even more important, to reconnect them with a city's contemporary inhabitants, becoming essential parts of people's life and identity.

Medium scale sites such as Feroz Sha Kotla, already very intimately linked to a specific community, can incorporate amenities to serve these communities, such as schools and community centers. Major scale monuments like Purana Qila, surrounded by bus depots and other empty spaces, have the potential of becoming major facilities at the national level, commensurate to the importance and footprint of the monument itself. A national public library and performing arts center is one of the programmatic examples explored which brings back to life the extraordinary historic potential of the national capital of India.

Purana Qila Public Library
and Performing Arts Center

As an extension of a new cultural corridor along the Yamuna, the new Public Library and Performing Arts Center of Delhi brings relevance and accessibility to Purana Qila, the dilapidated old fort in the center of the capital. This new public facility is situated as an expansion of the fort wall which historically was used as programmed space necessary to the functioning of the fort. Situated in contrast to the historic private library of Humayun above, this new democratic library offers opportunity for all the citizens of Delhi

to gain access to knowledge through digital, physical, and personal interfaces. Additionally, the center provides the visitor with a new experience of the fort itself as historical artifact.

The center's spatial qualities are defined by material qualities such as transparency and opaqueness, lightness and darkness, integration with the landscape as well as protection from Delhi's climate. Bringing a new relevance to the fort is crucial for the preservation of this historic monument.

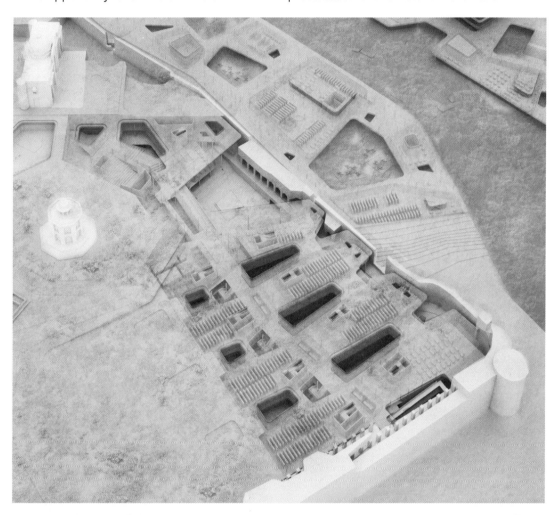

Site Plan

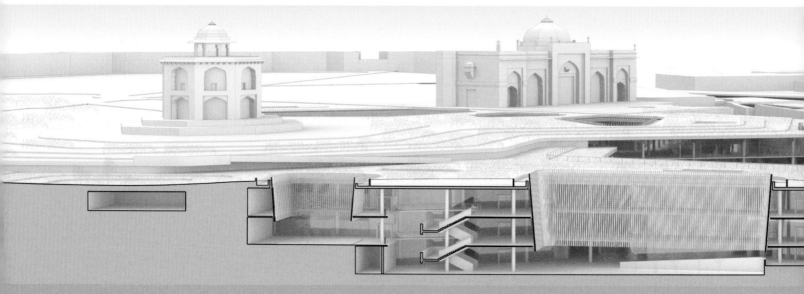

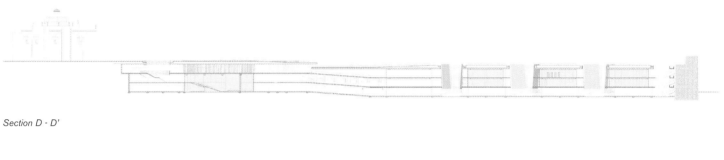

Section D - D'

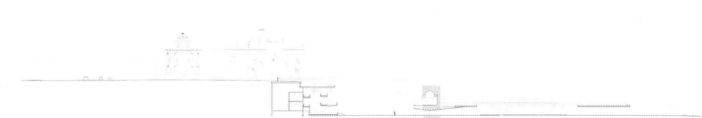

Section C - C'

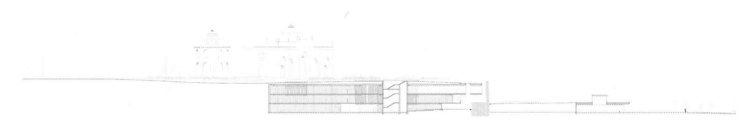

Section B - B'

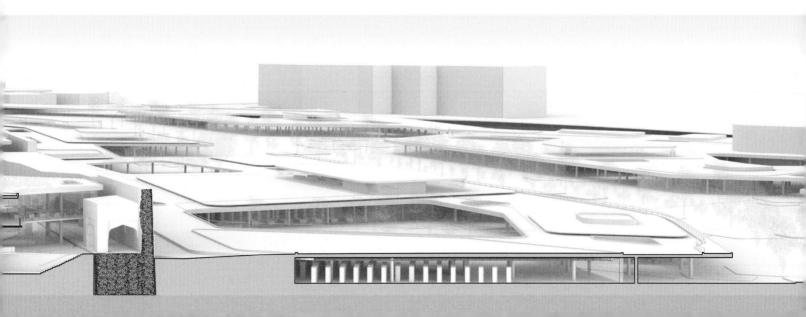

CENTURIES OLD MONUMENTS
ALONG THE YAMUNA RIVER CREATED
A NEW RIVERFRONT GARDEN
TYPOLOGY. MANY OF THOSE
MONUMENTS, IN VARIOUS STATES OF
PRESERVATION, CAN STILL BE FOUND
TODAY ALONG THE REMNANTS OF
THE HISTORIC YAMUNA MEANDER.

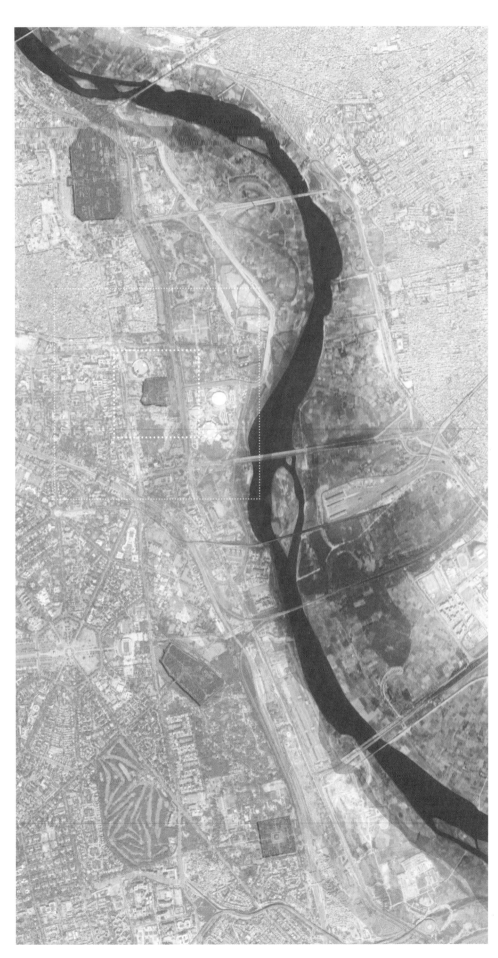

Feroz Shah Kotla Community Center

Built in the 14th century by Shah Feroz Shah Kotla Tughlaq, this citadel is the fifth of seven historic cities of Delhi and the first to be constructed along the banks of the Yamuna River. While the river has since changed its course, the fort still aligns with a series of monuments that once shared this edge including the Red Fort, Purana Qila, and Humayun's Tomb. This project intends to draw attention to the Feroz Shah Kotla monument before it recedes behind weeds and ad hoc construction. Yet it is not enough to merely convert this fort into a museum. While the fort may be under-appreciated by most of Delhi, the site is still very much alive and animated by the Muslim community that finds solace in and around its walls. This project intends to elevate this minority and reconnect them to the larger city of Delhi by constructing a community center within the walls of the fort. Through restrained and sensitive architecture, this project respectfully asserts that a monument is not a curious novelty from the past, but the foundation of a city. The Feroz Shah Kotla Community Center insists on the coexistence of paradoxes, between a community and the city, the temporal and the eternal, and the past and the present.

EPILOGUE

Keshav Chandra
Former CEO Delhi Jal Board

Rivers don't die quickly. A stream of water that nurtures civilizations loses its life only because civilizations fail to fulfill their obligations towards it. The Yamuna, which found a place in the Hindu pantheon is today living the curse of an insensitive economic development of several decades. Delhi, which built many empires on the banks of this river over centuries, is at its wit's end today to see the moribund state of its life-giver.

Where has the city gone wrong? In the last four decades when Delhi broke its shackles and started to emerge as an economic giant, slow growing hinterland fueled the influx of population to the unprepared city. Delhi was continually found wanting to cope with this humongous in-migration. Scores of new settlements mushroomed in a totally unplanned manner, severely compromising the essential services meant for safe and healthy urban living. Wastewater generated by thousands of unplanned colonies found its way to the river through more than two hundred natural drains crisscrossing the city. Not only the Yamuna became terminally polluted, but also the entire hydrology of the city feeding the river became toxic.

Endeavors to rejuvenate the ailing Yamuna have been undertaken in the past in the name of the Yamuna Action Plan I, II, and III. However, these action plans failed to translate into the intended objective to clean the river and had an almost negligible impact on the overall hydrology of the city. The reason behind this glaring failure is more than apparent. All these plans tried to situate the solution in the realm of stark engineering projects ignoring the important urban planning aspect altogether. While increasing volumes of sewage were brought to the newly build wastewater treatment plants, the aggregated hydrology of the city remained completely untouched. Today the glaring reality that urban planning needs to be resurrected and given the center stage in the river cleaning effort has become evident. At the same time, it is also apparent that the gargantuan task of cleaning the river along with the entire hydrology can't be handled by any one institution alone. It needs to collaborate, co-operate and bring in the expertise unavailable to the city agencies locally.

The Delhi Jal Board has realized the immense potential in collaborations with local and global expert institutions. It has signed a Memorandum of Understanding with the University of Virginia - a globally acclaimed research institution, with an outstanding urban expertise. This partnership has infused a new and refreshing dimension to the river cleaning effort. Delhi's largest watershed - the Najafgarh Drain and its basin, have been selected for the intensive scrutiny and detailed planning. This book illustrates some of the chosen projects from a gamut of a vast array of projects which emerged as a product of this planning exercise. The untiring effort of Professor Iñaki Alday, Professor Pankaj Vir Gupta, students and faculty at the University of Virginia, Shri Radheahyam Tyagi, Shri V K Gupta, Shri Vikram, Ms. Mriganka Saxena, and officers of the Delhi Jal Board has made this fabulous book a reality. A sure and certain step is afoot, and we all hope that this journey will stop only when the Yamuna gets its turtle back in its waters.

REFERENCES

01 DELHI'S URBAN HISTORY

History of a Settlement   02-03

Text:

Delhi Tourism. "Lal Kot or Qila Rai Pithora". Accessed July 6, 2017. http://www.delhitourism. gov.in/delhitourism/aboutus/quila_rai_pithora.jsp.

Menon, A. G. Krishna. Forward. *Maps of Delhi, by Pilar Maria Gurerrieri*, ix-xxix. New Delhi: Niyogi Books, 2017.

Nath, V. "Planning for Delhi". *Geojournal,* 29.2 (February 1993). 171-180. Accessed July 6, 2017. http://www.jstor.org/stable/41125163?seq=1#page_scan_tab_contents

Pilar Maria Guerrieri. *Maps of Delhi*. New Delhi: Niyogi Books, 2017.

Ray, Aniruddha. *Towns and Cities of Medieval India: A Brief Survey*. New Delhi: Manohar Publishers, 2015.

Singh, Patwant. "Sir Edwin Lutyens and the Building". *Icon*. The World Monuments Fund. Winter 2002, 38-43. Accessed July 6, 2017. https://www.wmf.org/sites/default/files/article/pdfs/pg_38-43_new_delhi.pdf

Tankha, Madhur, "The Discovery of Indraprastha". *The Hindu*, March 11, 2014. Accessed July 6, 2017. http://www.thehindu.com/news/cities/Delhi/the-discovery-of-indraprastha/article5772895.ece.

The Divine India. "The Feroz Shah Kotla Fort". Updated, November 11, 2016. Accessed July 6, 2017. http://www.thedivineindia.com/feroz-shah-kotla-fort/5810.

Diagrams and Images:

"City of Delhi Before the Siege". 1858. Wikipedia. Accessed June 26, 2017. https://en.wikipedia.org/wiki/Old_Delhi#/media/File:Delhi-lond-illust-1858.jpg. (Original image sourced from DELHI, 1857 provided by Prof. Emerita Frances Pritchett, Columbia University in Sept 2013).

White, F.S. "Sketch of the Environs of Delhi". National Archives of India, 1807.

Mughal Delhi   08-09

Text:

Asher, Catherine B. "Sub-Imperial Palaces: Power and Authority in Mughal India". *Ars Orientalis*, 23 (1993). 281-302. Accessed July 7, 2017. http://www.jstor.org/stable/4629454.

Koch, Ebba. "Mughal Palace Gardens from Babur to Shah Jahan". *Muqarnas*, 14 (1997). 143-165. Accessed July 7, 2017. http://www.jstor.org/stable/1523242

Ray, Aniruddha. "Shahjahanabad (Delhi)". *Towns and Cities of Medieval India: A Brief Survey*. 290-313. New Delhi: Manohar Publishers, 2015.

Diagrams and Images:

Martin, R.M. "View of Delhi from the River Showing the King's Palace". 1860. Accessed July 9, 2017. http://www.columbia.edu/itc/mealac/pritchett/00routesdata/1600_1699/redfortdelhi/redfortdrawings/redfortdrawings.html

Weller, Edward. "Plan of Delhi and its Environs". The Weekly Dispatch. Duke Street, Bloomsbury. 1857. Accessed September 19, 2017. http://www.columbia.edu/itc/mealac/pritchett/00maplinks/colonial/wellermaps/delhi1857/delhi1857.html. (Original image sourced from DELHI, 1857 provided by Prof. Emerita Frances Pritchett, Columbia University in Sept 2013).

Post Mughal Delhi   10-11

Daigrams and Images:

"Delhi from the Ridge Camp". Illustrirte Zeitung, November 14 1857. Accessed June 26, 2017. http://www.columbia.edu/itc/mealac/pritchett/00maplinks/colonial/rebellion1857/zeitungview/zeitungview.html (Original image sourced from DELHI, 1857 provided by Prof. Emerita Frances Pritchett, Columbia University in July 2007).

Wood, Evelyn. "Plan of the Seige of Delhi". *Our Fighting Services*, 492. London, New York (etc.): Cassel, 1916. Accessed September 19, 2017. https://en.wikipedia.org/wiki/File:Plan_of_the_Siege_of_Delhi_-Our_fighting_services_-_Evelyn_Wood_pg492.jpg

Yamuna as Goddess and Icon   12-15

Text:

Sinha, Amita, and D. Fairchild Ruggles, "The Yamuna Riverfront, India: A Comparative Study of Islamic and Hindu Traditions in Cultural Landscapes". *Landscape Journal* 23.2 (2004). 141-152.

Viennot, Odette. Les Divinités Fluviales Ganga et Yamuna: *Aux Portes des Sanctuaires de l'Inde; Essai D'évolution D'un Thème Décoratif*. Paris, 1964.

von Stietencron, Heinrich. *Ganga und Yamuna: Zur Symbolischen Bedeutung der Flussgöttinnen an Indischen Tempeln*. Wiesbaden, 1972.

Diagrams and Images:

"Leaf from a Bhagavata Purana series". The Cowherd Women of Vraja Observing the Vow of Katyayani. India, The Delhi-Agra region, perhaps Mathura, ca. 1520 – 1530. Opaque color on paper The Fralin Museum of Art The University of Virginia Museum purchase with Curriculum Support Fund 1994.11.

"Leaf from a portfolio by Ghulam Ali Khan". (fl. 1817-55). The Red Fort of Delhi from the Yamuna River. Inscribed "View of the Palace Buildings of the Shah Boorj, Summer Boorj, and Ussud Boorj from the Eastern or river face." India, Company Style, Delhi,

c. 1852-54. Watercolor on paper. Sold at Bonham's London, 23 Apr 2013, Lot 352. Present location unknown. Photograph courtesy Bonham's, London.

"The River Goddess Yamuna and Attendants". India, Rajasthan, circa 800 Sculpture Red sandstone Los Angeles County Museum of Art From the Nasli and Alice Heeramaneck Collection, Museum Associates Purchase (M.79.9.10.2a)

"Venugopala". The work of Ustad Hasan (active ca. 1750-1770). India, Rajasthan, Bikaner. Dated V.S 1823/ A.D. 1766. Opaque color and gold on paper. Private Collection. Ex-Maharaja of Bikaner Collection.

British New Delhi   16-17

Diagrams and Images:

Hall, E. E. "Rashtrapati Bhavan Looking East". The Lutyens Trust, c. 1920. Accessed June 21, 2017. http://www.lutyenstrustexhibitions.org.uk

"India Gate in 1940s." Digital Image. *39 Absolutely Iconic Photos from India's Past that Every Indian Must See*. Accessed June 21, 2017. http://www.folomojo.com

"Lutyens' Delhi". Centre for South Asian Studies, University of Cambridge. Accessed July 6, 2017. http://sites.asiasociety.org/princesandpainters/design-of-delhi-edwin-lutyens.

"Lutyens' Projected Imerial Delhi". *Encyclopedia Britannica*, 11th ed. 1910-12. Accessed July 7, 2017. http://www.columbia.edu/itc/mealac/pritchett/00maplinks/modern/delhimaps/britannica1910.jpg

Modern Evolution of Delhi   18-19

Text:

Government of National Capital Territory of Delhi, "Housing and Urban Development," in Economic Survey of Delhi, 2012-2013. Access May 30, 2017. http://delhi.gov.in/DoIT/DoIT_Planning/ES2012-13/EN/ES_Chapter14.pdf

Hashmi, Sohail. "Delhi 1803-2012: A Brief Biography." *KAFILA: Ten Years of a Common Journey*, March, 5 2012. Accessed June 30, 2017. https://kafila.online/2012/05/03/ten-in-one-delhi-1803-2012-5-2/

Verma, Deepti. "Indraprastha: The Capital of Pandavas." *India Opines*, March 1, 2014. Accessed June 30, 2017. http://indiaopines.com/indraprastha-capital-pandavas/

Urban Evolution   20-21

Text:

Bhaduri, Amita, et. al. "On the Brink: Water Governance in the Yamuna River Basin in Haryana". *Delhi: Peace Institute Charitable Trust*, 2010.

Delhi Jal Board. "Delhi Water Conservation Act, 2016". Accessed June 22, 2017. http://www.delhi.gov.in

Hashmi, Sohail. "Delhi 1803-2012: A Brief Biography." *KAFILA: Ten Years of a Common Journey*, March, 5 2012. Accessed June 30, 2017. https://kafila.online/2012/05/03/ten-in-one-delhi-1803-2012-5-2/

Kumar, Sanjay. "Changing Electoral Politics in Delhi: From Caste to Class". New Delhi: Sage Publications, 2013.

Middleton, L. and S. M. Jacob. "Census of India, 1921". *Digital Repository of Gokhale Institute of Politics and Economics*. 1923. http://dspace.gipe.ac.in/xmlui/handle/10973/18931

Moraes, Frank R. "Jawaharlal Nehru". *Encyclopedia Britannica*. Last Modified May 7, 2017. https://www.britannica.com/biography/Jawaharlal-Nehru

Office of the Registrar General & Census Commissioner, India. "Census Tables 1941". Accessed June 23, 2017. http://www.censusindia.gov.in/Census_And_You/old_report/Census_1941_tebles.aspxq

Sundaram, K.V., Vaddipart Lova Surya Prakasa Rao, Vernon Ram. "Delhi". *Encyclopedia Britannica*. Last Modified April 20, 2017. https://www.britannica.com/place/Delhi

Verma, Deepti. "Indraprastha: The Capital of Pandavas". Accessed June 30, 2017). http://indiaopines.com/indraprastha-capital-pandavas/

Diagrams and Images:

Delhi. "Patterns of Growth". *LSECities*. Accessed July 09, 2017. https://lsecities.net/media/objects/articles/patterns-of-growth/en-gb/

Government of National Capital Territory of Delhi, "Demographic Profile," in Economic Survey of Delhi, 2012-2013. Accessed May 30, 2017. http://delhi.gov.in/DoIT/DoIT_Planning/ES2012-13/EN/ES_Chapter%202.pdf

Spatial Growth of Delhi (1950-2014). Nair, Shalini. "NCR Urbanisation". *The Indian Express*, September 12, 2015. Accessed July 12, 2017. http://indianexpress.com/article/india/india-others/ncr-urbanisation-delhi-remains-the-epicentre/

Statistical Abstract of Delhi 2016. Government of National Capital Territory of Delhi. Accessed June 14, 2017. http://www.delhi.gov.in/wps/wcm/connect/f508bc8046667b0e9cf6bcf5a4ed47e7/Stattistical+Abstract+of+Delhi+2014.pdf

Delhi's Exponential Expansion   22-23

Text:

Population Foundation of India and Population Reference Bureau, "The Future Population of India: A Long Range Demographic View," August, 2007. Accessed on May 30, 2017. http://www.prb.org/pdf07/futurepopulationofindia.pdf.

Delhi 2021 Masterplan   26-27

Images:

"Master Plan for Delhi 2021". Master Plan, January 19, 2007. Accessed September 13, 2017. http://delhi-masterplan.com/zonal-plans-mpd-2021/land-use-plan/

02 DELHI'S URBAN LAYERS

Continental Climate   30-31

Diagrams and Images:

Bhalme, H. N., D. A. Mooley, and S. K. Jadhav. "Fluctuations in the Drought/Flood Area over

Table 1:

Major historical climate crises - water

1. 1943 - Tamil Nadu Very heavy rainfall in Madras.
2. 1994 - Kerala 209 human lives lost. Crop worth Rs. 144.500 cores damaged. Public utility worth Rs. 105 cores damaged.
3. 1988 - Assam 167 persons died. 25,000 hectares of crops damaged.
4. 1930 - Maharashtra Damage to agriculture and property was extensive.
5. 1965 - Andhra Pradesh. Severe flooding.
6. 1981 - Rajasthan Abnormally heavy rain caused flooding in Jaipur, Tonk, Nagaur and Sawai Madhopur. Extensive damage to property and loss of lives reported.
7. 1927 - Gujarat. Flood Water rose to about 7m. high in Sabarmati river.
8. 1927 - Orissa. Severe flooding of Baitarni, water rose to height of 21m. at Akhyapada. Cuttak town cut off from rest of the country for 7 days.
9. 1988 - Andhra Pradesh Assam 109 people died. Paddy crop in 3 lakh hectares completely damaged.
10. 1979 - Saurashtra and Kutch Severe flooding in Rajkot. 2000 - Andhra Pradesh Hyderabad
11. 131 persons died. Hyderabad flooded. Many areas under 3m of water. Paddy, chilly crop worth hundreds of cores damaged.
12. 1982 - Orissa. Severe flooding hit Mahanadi, damage to crops, property and loss of lives reported.

13. 1880 - NW Uttar Pradesh 150 persons lost their lives.
14. 1900 - West Bengal 60-80 cm. rain during 20-22 Sept. causing severe flooding.
15. 1926 - Madhya Pradesh Severe flooding of Narmada and Mahanadi.
16. 1964 - Karnataka Vijaywada was under 3 m. deep water.
17. 1961 - Bihar. Extensive damage to agriculture and property.
18. 1955 - Punjab. Thousands of people evacuated due to severe flooding in rivers of Uttar Pradesh and Punjab. Near Delhi, flood water rose to danger level. Death toll was about 1500.

Table 2:

Major historical climate crises - temp

1. 1983 - 100 million impacted Tamil Nadu, West Bengal, Kerala, Rajasthan, Karnataka, Bihar, Orissa
2. 1972 - 50 million impacted Rajasthan, Himachal Pradesh, and Uttar Pradesh
3. 1987 - 300-500 million impacted Whole of eastern and northwestern India
4. 1979 - 200 million impacted Eastern Rajasthan, Punjab, Himachal Pradesh,and Uttar Pradesh.
5. 2000 - 100 million impacted Rajasthan, Gujarat, Orissa, Andhra Pradesh, and Madhya Pradesh
6. 1982 - 100 million impacted Rajasthan, Punjab, and Himachal Pradesh
7. 1992 - no figures available Rajasthan, Orissa, Gujarat, Bihar, and Madhya Pradesh

India and Relationships with the Southern Oscillation". *Monthly Weather Review* 111, no. 1 (September 24, 1983): 86-94. Accessed June 19, 2017. doi:10.1175/1520-0493(1983)111<0086:fitdao>2.0.co;2.

Dube, R.K., and G.S. Prakasa Rao. "Extreme Weather Events over India In The Last 100 Years." *The Journal of India Geophysical Union* 9, no. 3 (July 2005): 173-87.

Kailasa, Nathan K. "Drought Profile: Haryana State in North India." *Drought Network News*, 1994.

Menon, Meena. "Maharashtra Drought Man-made: Analysis." *The Hindu*, June 13, 2016. Accessed June 19, 2017. http://www.thehindu.com/news/national/other-states/maharashtra-drought-manmade-analysis/article4577079.ece.

Ranil, Samud. "Drought in India Before and After Independence." *My India*, February 11, 2017. Accessed June 19, 2017. http://www.mapsofindia.com/my-india/india/drought-in-india-before-and-after-independence.

Saini, Shweta, and Ashok Gulati. "El Nino and Indian Droughts - A Scoping Exercise". *Delhi: Indian Council for Research on International Economic Relations*, 2014.

Dr. Somasunder, K., "All India area weighted monthly, seasonal and annual rainfall (in mm) from 1901-2015, 1901-2015." India Meteorological Department version. *Distributed by The Ministry of Earth Sciences, Government of India.* https://data.gov.in/catalog/rainfall-india

Dr. Somasunder, K., "Monthly, Seasonal and Annual Maximum Temperature in India from 1901 to 2015, 1901-2015". India Meteorological Department version. *Distributed by The Ministry of Earth Sciences, Government of India.* https://data.gov.in/catalog/rainfall-india

Dr. Somasunder, K., "Monthly, Seasonal and Annual Minimum Temperature in India from 1901 to 2015, 1901-2015". India Meteorological Department version. *Distributed by The Ministry of Earth Sciences, Government of India.* https://data.gov.in/catalog/rainfall-india

Monsoon   32-33

Text:

Collier, W.; Webb, R. H. "Floods, Droughts, and Climate Change." *University of Arizona Press.* November 2002

Kumar, Vijay. "Delhi's Monsoon Woes—the Need for a Scientifically-developed Drainage Master Plan." Accessed June 23, 2017. https://worldwide.dhigroup.com/presences/xpxx/india/news-archive/delhis-monsoon-woes-the-need-for-a-scientifically-developed-drainage-master-plan

Rana, Preetika. "Monsoon Lands, Floods Delhi Airport." *The Wall Street Journal*, June 17, 2013. Accessed June 23, 2017. https://blogs.wsj.com/indiarealtime/2013/06/17/monsoon-lands-floods-delhi-airport/

Vikram Soni, Shashank Shekhar, and Diwan Singh, "Environmental flow for Monsoon Rivers in India: The Yamuna River as a Case Study," https://arxiv.org/pdf/1306.2709.pdf, (June 5, 2017).

Diagrams and Images:

Dube, R.K., and G.S. Prakasa Rao. "Extreme Weather Events over India In The Last 100 Years." *The Journal of India Geophysical Union* 9, no. 3 (July 2005): 173-87.

Dr. Somasunder, K. "Yearly and Seasonal Frequency of Cyclones and Depressions, 1901-2015." India Meteorological Department version. *Distributed by The Ministry of Earth Sciences, Government of India.* https://data.gov.in/catalog/rainfall-india

Delhi's Geology   34-35

Text:

Sarkar, Aditya; Shakir, Ali; Suman, Kumar; Shashank, Shekhar: and SV, Rao. "Groundwater Environment in Delhi, India." *Groundwater Environment in Asian Cities: Concepts, Methods and Case Studies.* Chapter: 5, edited by Sangam, Shrestha; Vishnu, Prasad Pandey; Binaya, Raj Shivakoti; and Shashidhar, Thatikonda. 77-108. Elsevier, 2016.

Diagrams and Images:

Craig J. Wandrey and Ben E. Law. "Map Showing Geology, Oil and Gas Fields and Geologic Provinces of South Asia Edition 2". *U.S. Geological Survey Open File Report.* Issue OFR-97-470-C. Denver, Colorado. U.S. Geological Survey, Central Energy Resources Team. 1999. http://geology.cr.usgs.gov/energy/WorldEnergy/OF97-470C/index.html

Danielson, J.J., and Gesch, D.B. "An enhanced global elevation model generalized from multiple higher resolution source datasets". *International Archives of the Photogrammetry, Remote Sensing and Spatial Information Sciences*, v. XXXVII, Part B4, Beijing, 2008. p. 1,857–1,864.

"World Geologic Maps." World Petroleum Assessment - World Geologic Maps: *USGS, Energy Resources Program.* May 12, 2017. Accessed June 21, 2017. https://energy.usgs.gov/OilGas/AssessmentsData/WorldPetroleumAssessment/WorldGeologicMaps.aspx.

Lehner, B., Grill G. "Global river hydrography and network routing: baseline data and new approaches to study the world's large river systems." *Hydrological Processes*, 27.15: 2171–2186. 2013. Accessed June 22, 2017.

Historic Bundhs and Baolis   36-37

Text:

"Fish Culture in Undrainable Ponds: A Manual for Extension." *Food and Agriculture Organization of the United Nations: Fisheries and Aquaculture Department.* Accessed June 4, 2017. http://www.fao.org/docrep/003/T0555E/T0555E08.htm

Jain-Neubauer, Jutta. "The Stepwells of Delhi." *INTACH Delhi Chapter.* Accessed June 27, 2017. http://wgbis.ces.iisc.ernet.in/biodiversity/sahyadri_enews/newsletter/issue52/bibliography/the-Stepwells-of-Delhi.pdf

John, Shobha. "Medieval Bundhs May Hold Key to Water Problem." *The Times of India*, August 19, 2001. Accessed June 4, 2017. http://timesofindia.indiatimes.com/city/delhi/Medieval-bundhs-may-hold-key-to-water-problem/articleshow/1915375056.cms

Diagrams and Images:

Datta, Ragan. "Baolis of Deli." May 10, 2017. Accessed October 17, 2017. https://rangandatta.wordpress.com/2017/05/10/baolis-step-wells-of-delhi/

Yamuna River Canal System   40-41

Text:

Badhuri, Amita. "Two States, a Canal, and a River." *India Waterportal*, May 17, 2016. Accessed June 19, 2017. http://www.indiawaterportal.org/articles/two-states-canal-and-river

Jain, Sharad K., Pushpendra K. Agarwal and Vijay P. Singh. "Hydrology and Water Resources of India." *Water Science and Technology Library 57* (2007). Springer Science & Business Media, 2007.

Diagrams and Images:

Water Resources Information System of India. Accessed June 25, 2017. http://www.india-wris.nrsc.gov.in/wrpinfo/index.php?title=Main_Page

Water Treatment Plants   42-43
Text:
"Department of Delhi Jal Board." *Delhi Government Portal.* Accessed July 9, 2017. http://
    www.delhi.gov.in/wps/wcm/connect/doit_djb/DJB/Home/About+Us
"Quality Control Setup of Delhi Jal Board." *Delhi Government Portal.* Accessed October 3,
    2017. www.delhi.gov.in/wps/wcm/connect/.../DTQC.doc?MOD=AJPERES
Diagrams and Images:
"Department of Delhi Jal Board." *Delhi Government Portal.* Accessed July 9, 2017. http://
    www.delhi.gov.in/wps/wcm/connect/doit_djb/DJB/Home/About+Us

Drinking Water Delivery   50-51
Text:
"DJB Plans Piped Water for All by 2017" *The Times of India*, August 30, 2016. Accessed
    June 27, 2017. http://timesofindia.indiatimes.com/city/delhi/DJB-plans-piped-water-
    for-all-by-2017/articleshow/53918563.cms
Government of the National Territory of Delhi. "Schedule of Water Tankers." Last
    Updated April 7, 2017. http://www.delhi.gov.in/wps/wcm/connect/DOIT_DJB/djb/
    our+services1/schedule+of+water+tankers
Nandi, Jayashree. "Groundwater, Half of Supply." *The Times of India*, June 17, 2012.
    Accessed June 27, 2017. http://timesofindia.indiatimes.com/city/delhi/Groundwater-
    half-of-supply/articleshow/14112566.cms?referral=PM
"Report of the Controller and Auditor General of India on Social Sector (Non-PSU) for
    the Year Ended 31 March 2012." Government of National Territory of Delhi (2013).
Sethi, Aman. "At the Mercy of the Water Mafia." *Foreign Policy.* Accessed June 27, 2017.
    http://foreignpolicy.com/2015/07/17/at-the-mercy-of-the-water-mafia-india-delhi-
    tanker-gang-scarcity/
Diagrams and Images:
"2 - Water Supply Situation Analysis." *Harvard University Department of Physics.* Accessed
    July 9, 2017. http://users.physics.harvard.edu/~wilson/arsenic/conferences/Feroze_
    Ahmed/Sec_2.htm
"Radial Well - Radial Well Service Provider, Supplier, Trading Company, Bhubaneswar,
    India." Audio Visual Equipment Supplier in Odisha, Professional Audio Visual Systems
    Suppliers, India. Accessed July 9, 2017. http://electrotechs.tradeindia.com/radial-
    well-1854576.html

The Economics of Water: A Programmatic Outlook   52-55
Text:
Briscoe, J., 2011, "Invited Opinion Interview: Two Decades at the Center of World Water
    Policy," *Water Policy*, 13, p. 147-160.
Briscoe, J., 1997, "Managing Water as an Economic Good: Rules for Reformers," *Water
    Supply"* 15, 4, Yorkshire, p. 153-172.
Debaere, P. and A. Kurzendoerfer, 2017, "Decomposing U.S. Water Withdrawal since
    1950," *JAERE*, forthcoming.
Debaere, P., "The Global Economics of Water: Is Water a Source of Comparative
    Advantage", *American Economic Journal: Applied Economics*, April, p. 32-48.
Global Water Intelligence, 2014, *Global Water Market 2014*, Oxford, UK.
Griffin, R., 2016, "Water Resource Economics", *MIT Press*, Cambridge.
Hardin, G., 1968, "The Tragedy of the Commons," *Science*, 162, p. 1243-1248.
Hoekstra, A., and M. Mekonnen, 2012, "The Water Footprint of Humanity", Proceedings of
    the National Academy of Science, April, p. 3232-3237.
Olmstead, S., 2003, "Water Supply and Poor Communities: What's Price Got to Do with
    it?," *Environment: Science and Policy for Sustainable Development*, 45:10, p. 22-35.
Johansson, R., Tsur, Y., Roe, L., Doukkali, R., and A. Dinar, 2002, "Pricing Irrigation Water:
    A Review of Theory and Practice," *Water Policy*, 4, p. 173-199.
Rogers, P., de Silva, R., and Bhatia, R., 2002, "Water is an Economic Good: How to Use
    Prices to Promote Equity, Efficiency, and Sustainability," *Water Policy*, 4, p. 1- 17.
Whittington, D., W. Hanemann, C. Sadoff, and M. Jeuland, 2008, "The Challenge of
    Improving Water Sanitation Services in Less Developed Countries", in: Whittington,
    D., W. Hanemann, C. Sadoff, and M. Jeuland, *Foundations and Trends in
    Microeconomics*, Vol. 4, p. 469-609.

Groundwater Pollution   56-57
Text:
Bhaduri, Amita and Bhim Singh Rawat. "Alarm Bells Ring for Delhi's Groundwater." *India
    Waterportal*, January 25, 2016. Accessed June 21, 2017. http://www.indiawaterportal.
    org/articles/alarm-bells-ring-delhis-groundwater.
Lal Seth, Bharat. "Delhi Groundwater, A Deadly Cocktail: CGWB Report." *Down to Earth*,
    April 22, 2013. Accessed June 20, 2017. http://www.downtoearth.org.in/news/delhi-
    groundwater-a-deadly-cocktail-cgwb-report--40863.
Nandil, Jayashree. "Water Table Dropping Fast in 'Critical" South Delhi Areas." *Times of
    India*, May 5, 2015. Accessed June 20, 2017. http://timesofindia.indiatimes.com/city/
    delhi/Water-table-dropping-fast-in-critical-south-Delhi-areas/articleshow/47168437.
    cms.
"Study on Groundwater Recharge in NCT Delhi." Accessed June 20, 2017. http://
    naturalheritage.intach.org/wp-content/uploads/2017/02/Study-Ground-water-
    recharge-NCTDelhi.pdf
Diagrams and Images:
Dash, Ch Jyotiprava & Sarangi, Arjamadutta & Singh, D.K.. (2010). "Spatial variability of
    groundwater depth and quality parameters in the National Capital Territory of Delhi."
    Environmental Management. 45. 640-650. Accessed June 27, 2017. https://www.
    researchgate.net/publication/260230590_Spatial_variability_of_groundwater_depth_
    and_quality_parameters_in_the_National_Capital_Territory_of_Delhi
"Quality Control Setup of Delhi Jal Board." *Delhi Government Portal.* Accessed October 3,
    2017. www.delhi.gov.in/wps/wcm/connect/.../DTQC.doc?MOD=AJPERES

Drains and the Sewage System   58-59
Diagrams and Images:
"Department of Delhi Jal Board." *Delhi Government Portal.* Accessed July 9, 2017. http://
    www.delhi.gov.in/wps/wcm/connect/doit_djb/DJB/Home/About+Us

Sewage and Water Systems   60-61
Diagrams and Images:
"Department of Delhi Jal Board." *Delhi Government Portal.* Accessed July 9, 2017. http://
    www.delhi.gov.in/wps/wcm/connect/doit_djb/DJB/Home/About+Us

Population Density and Demographics   66-67
Text:
Bagga, Bhuvan. "Rich Man's Capital: Delhi's Per Capita Income is Three Times the
    National Average and Residents are on a Spending Splurge." *Daily Mail*, April 27,
    2012. Accessed June 20, 2017. http://www.dailymail.co.uk/indiahome/indianews/
    article-2136360/Rich-mans-capital-Delhis-capita-income-times-national-average--
    residents-spending-splurge.html
Burdett, Ricky. "A Tale of Four World Cities: London, Delhi, Tokyo and Bogotá Compared."
    The Guardian, February 11, 2015. Accessed June 21, 2017. https://www.theguardian.
    com/cities/2015/feb/11/tale-four-cities-london-delhi-tokyo-bogota-data
Lahiri, Tripti. "Delhi Journal: The Luytens Legacy." *The Wall Street Journal*, December 29,
    2011. Accessed June 21, 2017. https://blogs.wsj.com/indiarealtime/2011/12/29/
    delhi-journal-the-lutyens-legacy/?mg=prod/accounts-wsj
"Report: Delhi Per Capita Income is Triple the National Average." *Asia Times*, May 16,
    2017. Accessed June 20, 2017. http://www.atimes.com/article/delhi-per-capita-
    income-triple-national-average/
Diagrams and Images:
2011 Census of India. *Governmnet of India.* Accessed April 7, 2017. http://www.
    censusindia.gov.in/2011census/hlo/HLO_Tables.html

Housing   68-69
Text:
Government of National Capital Territory of Delhi, "Housing and Urban Development."
    in Economic Survey of Delhi, 2014-2015. Accessed June 9, 2017. https://
    openbudgetsindia.org/dataset/1aae6a29-a044-4dac-b4aa-250443754a3d/
    resource/15736f26-9d5d-4edc-9075-0257a697ae46/download/economic-survey--
    -housing-and-urban-development.pdf
Ishtiyaq, M. and Sunil Kumar. "Typology of Informal Settlements and Distribution of Slums
    in the NCT, Delhi." Journal of Contemporary India Studies: Space and Society.
    Hiroshima University, 2011. Accessed June 21, 2017. http://home.hiroshima-u.ac.jp/
    hindas/PDF/2010/Ishtiyaq_and_Kumar(2011).pdf
King, Julia. "Unthinking Housing for the Urban Poor." *Incremental Cities*, Septemeber 18,
    2012. Accessed June 16, 2017. https://incrementalcity.wordpress.com/2012/09/18/
    unthinking-housing-for-the-urban-poor/
Diagrams and Images:
Ishtiyaq, M. and Sunil Kumar. "Typology of Informal Settlements and Distribution of Slums in
    the NCT, Delhi." Journal of Contemporary India Studies: Space and Society. Hiroshima
    University, 2011. Accessed June 21, 2017. http://home.hiroshima-u.ac.jp/hindas/
    PDF/2010/Ishtiyaq_and_Kumar(2011).pdf
King, Julia. "Unthinking Housing for the Urban Poor." *Incremental Cities*, Septemeber 18,
    2012. Accessed June 16, 2017. https://incrementalcity.wordpress.com/2012/09/18/
    unthinking-housing-for-the-urban-poor/

Agriculture   72-73
Text:
Anima, P. "While the River Heals." *Business Line.* Accessed June 7, 2017. http://www.
    thehindubusinessline.com/blink/know/while-the-river-heals/article7460273.ece
Kornstein, Samuel and Paul Artiuch. "Sustainable Approaches to Reducing Food Waste in
    India." *MIT Independent Activities Period Research Project.* Accessed June 6, 2017.
    http://web.mit.edu/colab/pdf/papers/Reducing_Food_Waste_India.pdf
Kuma Rai, Raveendra, Alka Upadhyay, C. Shekhar P. Ojha, and Vijay P. Singh. "The Yamuna
    River Basin: Water Resources and Environment." *Dordrecht: Springer Science
    Business Media B.V.*, 2012.
Kumar, Ashok. "India's Livestock Population Down." *OneWorld South Asia.* Accessed
    June 6, 2017. http://southasia.oneworld.net/news/india2019s-livestock-population-
    decreases-by-3.33-census#.WTaE6xjMzGI
Diagrams and Images:
2010 - 2011 Agriculture Census of India. *Department of Agriculture and Cooperation.*
    Accessed October 14, 2017. http://agcensus.nic.in/document/agcensus2010/
    agcen2010rep.htm

Food Distribution Network   74-75
Text:
Bajaj, Vikas. "As Grain Piles Up, India's Poor Still Go Hungry." *The New York Times*, June
    7, 2012. Accessed June 6, 2017. http://www.nytimes.com/2012/06/08/business/
    global/a-failed-food-system-in-india-prompts-an-intense-review.html
Te Lintelo, Dolf, Fiona Marshall and D.S. Bhupal. "Peri-urban agriculture in Delhi, India."
    Food and Agriculture Organization of the United Nations. Accessed June 21, 2017.
    http://www.fao.org/docrep/004/y1931m/y1931m02.htm
"The Prospects for Liquid Air Cold Chains in India." *Birmingham Energy Institute.* University
    of Birmingham. Accessed 6, 2017. http://www.birmingham.ac.uk/Documents/news/
    The-prospects-for-liquid-air-cold-chains-in-India.pdf

"Transporting Grains for Northeast Begins." *Dhaka Tribune*, June 9, 2013. Accessed June 6, 2017. http://archive.dhakatribune.com/bangladesh/2013/jun/09/transporting-food-grains-northeast-india-bangladesh-begins

Public Facilities - Education   76-77

Text:

"Girl Education Ranked High in Delhi, Kerala, TN." India Today, March 10, 2015. Accessed June 21, 2017. http://indiatoday.intoday.in/education/story/girl-education/1/423118.html

Jha, Deepak. "An Untold Story- Delhi's Silent Education Revolution And Why We Should Take Note." T*he Political Funda*, April 28, 2016. Accessed June 22. 2017. http://thepoliticalfunda.com/Social/Detail/An_Untold_Story_Delhi's_Silent_Education_Revolution_And_Why_We_Should_Take_Note144

Kalra, Aparna. "Why India's Richest State Cannot Hire Enough Teachers." *India Spend*, January 14, 2017. Accessed June 22, 2017. http://www.indiaspend.com/cover-story/why-indias-richest-state-cannot-hire-enough-teachers-47765

Pandey, Priyanka. "8,000 New Classrooms by July This Year." *The Pioneer*, April 4, 2016. Accessed June 22, 2017. http://www.dailypioneer.com/city/8000-new-classrooms-by-july-this-year.html

Tsujita, Yuko. "Deprivation of Education: A Study of Slum Children in Delhi, India." Commissioned for the *EFA Global Monitoring Report* 2010. 2009. Accessed May 30, 2017.http://unesdoc.unesco.org/images/0018/001865/186592e.pdf

"Statistics of School Education, 2010-2011." *Government of India*, 2012. Accessed May 30, 2017. mhrd.gov.in/sites/upload_files/mhrd/files/SES-School_201011_0.pdf

"Steady Rise in Literacy Rate Among Delhi's SC Population." *Economic Times*, June 24, 2015. Accessed June 21, 2017. http://economictimes.indiatimes.com/news/politics-and-nation/steady-rise-in-literacy-rate-among-delhis-sc-population/articleshow/47802791.cms

Diagrams and Images:

"Elementary Education in India: Where Do We Stand?" *National University of Educational Planning and Administration*, 2015-2016. Accessed July 6, 2017. http://udise.in/Downloads/Elementary-STRC-2015-16/07.pdf

"Secondary Education: State Report Cards." *National University of Educational Planning and Administration*, 2015-2016. Accessed July 6, 2017. http://udise.in/Downloads/SEMIS-STRC-2015-16/07.pdf

Public Facilities - Culture   78

Text:

Garg, Ruchika. "Delhi's Own Festival that Promotes Communal Harmony." *Hindustan Times*, October 19, 2016. Accessed June 22, 2017. http://www.hindustantimes.com/art-and-culture/delhi-s-own-festival-that-promotes-communal-harmony/story-8SggWs1eSW8c5m5rWeLvOJ.html

Singh Sawhney, Isha. "Forget the Bling-Fest, Delhi is Still the Cultural Melting Pot of India." *The Sunday Guardian*. Accessed June 22, 2017. http://www.sunday-guardian.com/young-restless/forget-the-bling-fest-delhi-is-still-the-cultural-melting-pot-of-india

"Central Government Holidays." Indya Tours General Information. 2017. Accessed August 6, 2017. http://www.indyatour.com/india/festivals/list-of-public-holidays-and-festivals-in-india-2017

Public Facilities - Security   79

Text:

"2016 Emerges as Worst Year in Delhi's Crime Graph." *Daily News and Analysis, India*. Feb. 11, 2017. Accessed August 6, 2017. http://www.dnaindia.com/delhi/report-2016-drops-a-blot-on-delhi-s-crime-graph-2319434Images

Public Facilities - Healthcare   80-81

Text:

"Air Pollution Cuts Life of Indians by Average 3.4 years." *Financial Express*, June 8, 2016. Accessed June 22, 2017. http://www.financialexpress.com/india-news/air-pollution-cuts-life-of-indians-by-average-3-4-years-study/276780/

Dutt, Anonna. "Seven Things to Know about Delhi's Mohalla Clinics Praised by World Leaders." *Hindustan Times*, February 7, 2017. Accessed June22, 2017. http://www.hindustantimes.com/delhi-news/7-reasons-why-world-leaders-are-talking-about-delhi-s-mohalla-clinics/story-sw4IUjQQ2rj2ZA6ISCUbtM.html

Diagrams and Images:

Ministry of Statistics and Programme Implementation. "Health in India." *Government of India*, 2014. http://mospi.nic.in/sites/default/files/publication_reports/nss_rep574.pdf

Energy   82-83

Text:

"Discoms Owe RS 4,911.07 Crore to Delhi Government's Power Companies," The *New Indian Express*, March 11, 2017. Accessed June 22, 2017. http://www.newindianexpress.com/nation/2017/mar/11/discoms-owe-rs-491107-crore-to-delhi-governments-power-companies-cag-1580205.html

Malhotra, Aditi. "Who Really Holds Power in Delhi." *The Wall Street Journal*, February 25, 2015. Accessed June 22. 2017. https://blogs.wsj.com/indiarealtime/2015/02/25/who-really-holds-power-in-delhi/

Rao, Kavitha. "Delhi Created Its Own Energy Crisis." The Guardian, June 7, 2013. Accessed June 22, 2017. https://www.theguardian.com/environment/terra-india/2013/jun/07/delhi-created-own-energy-crisis

Diagrams and Images:

Elliot Hannon, "India's Blackout: In the Dark about Being in the Dark," *National Public Radio*, August 1, 2012, http://greencleanguide.com/electricity-scenario-of-national-capital-territory-of-delhi/, (June 16, 2017).

"Power Rates in Delhi to Rise by 2.5% to 25% for Various Levels of Consumption," *Economic Times*, July 18, 2014, http://economictimes.indiatimes.com/industry/energy/power/power-rates-in-delhi-to-rise-by-2-5-to-25-for-various-levels-of-consumption/articleshow/38579924.cms, (June 16, 2017).

Rao, Kavitha. "Delhi Created Its Own Energy Crisis." *The Guardian*, June 7, 2013. Accessed June 22, 2017. https://www.theguardian.com/environment/terra-india/2013/jun/07/delhi-created-own-energy-crisis

Rashmi Kadian, R.P. Dahiya, and H.P. Garg, "Energy-Related Emissions and Mitigation Opportunities from the Household Sector in Delhi," in *Energy Policy*, Volume 35, Issue 12, December 2007.

Shailesh, "Electricity Scenario of National Capital Territory of Delhi," *Green Clean Guide*, August 1, 2013, http://greencleanguide.com/electricity-scenario-of-national-capital-territory-of-delhi/, (June 16, 2017).

Waste   86 87

Text:

Iqbal, Naveed. "At Half the Height of Qutub Minar, Meet Delhi's Garbage High-Rises." *Indian Express*, May 30, 2016. Accessed June 23, 2017. http://indianexpress.com/article/cities/delhi/delhi-the-high-rise-garbage-landfills-2825046/

Lalchandani, Neha. "A Disaster Waiting to Happen in Waste Capital." *Times of India*, April 22, 2010. Accessed June 24, 2017. http://epaper.timesofindia.com/Repository/getFiles.asp?Style=OliveXLib:LowLevelEntityToPrint_TOINEW&Type=text/html&Locale=english-skin-custom&Path=CAP/2010/04/22&ID=Ar00400

Research Unit, Rajya Sabha Secretariat, "E-Waste in Delhi." June 2011. Accessed June 24, 2017. http://www.rajyasabha.nic.in/rsnew/publication_electronic/E-Waste_in_india.pdf

Singh, Shivani. "Metro Matters: Delhi Can't Let This Chance to Sort Its Trash Go Waste." *Hindustan Times*, June 12, 2017. Accessed June 24, 2017. http://www.hindustantimes.com/columns/metro-matters-delhi-can-t-let-this-chance-to-sort-its-trash-go-waste/story-VYiqWJnnnZ6001nWp8z2EO.html

Diagrams and Images:

"Delhi Urban Environment and Urban Improvement Project 2021". Section III - Environmental Infrastructure, Solid Waste Management, 49-54. Accessed October 03, 2017 http://delhiplanning.nic.in/Reports/Delhi21/Chapter_10.pdf

Waste Process   88-89

Diagrams and Images:

Talyan, Vikash and Dahiya, R.P. "State of Municipal Solid Waste Management in Delhi, the Capital of India." *Waste Management*, Vol 28,7. 2008. Accessed December 03, 2017. https://doi.org/10.1016/j.wasman.2007.05.017

Air Quality   92-93

Text:

Feltman, Rachel. "Air Pollution in New Delhi is Literally Off the Charts." *Popular Science*, November 8, 2016. Accessed June 23, 2017. http://www.popsci.com/air-pollution-new-delhi

Joshi, Mallica. "Delhi Air Pollution: Why Graded Action is a Good Idea, But Tough to Implement." *The Indian Express*, January 18, 2017. Accessed June 23, 2017. http://indianexpress.com/article/explained/delhi-air-pollution-control-graded-response-action-plan-government-4479203/

"What Causes Pollution in Delhi?" *Delhi Air*. Accessed June 23, 2017. https://delhiair.org/india-and-delhi/what-causes-pollution-in-delhi/

"Delhi - What's Polluting the Air?" *Urban Emissions*. Accessed August 6, 2017. http://www.urbanemissions.info/delhi-india/whats-polluting-delhis-air/

Rohatgi, Meenakshi. "Life Expectancy Drops 6 Years in Delhi" *The Times of India*, June 9, 2016. Accessed August 6, 2017. http://timesofindia.indiatimes.com/life-style/health-fitness/health-news/Life-expectancy-drops-6-years-in-Delhi/articleshow/52631220.cms

Diagrams and Images:

"A GIS Based Emissions Inventory at 1 km x 1 km Spatial Resolution for Air Pollution Analysis in Delhi, India," *Atmospheric Environment*, March 2013, accessed 15 Sept 2014.

"Six Years of Beijing Air Pollution Summed Up in One Survey Chart" *Quartz*, 10 Apr 2014, accessed 14 Sept 2014.

"PM10 Levels by Region, for the Last Available Year in the Period 2008-2015." Last Updated 2016. *World Health Organization*. Accessed July 6, 2017. http://www.who.int/phe/health_topics/outdoorair/databases/cities/en/

Green Space   96-97

Text:

Gandhi, Nidhi. "Trends in Growth of Open Space in Delhi." 2013. Accessed June 25, 2017. http://shodhganga.inflibnet.ac.in/bitstream/10603/27659/8/08_chapter%203.pdf

Government of National Capital Territory of Delhi. "Extent of Forest and Tree Cover." 2015. Accessed June 25, 2017. http://delhi.gov.in/wps/wcm/connect/doit_forest/Forest/Home/Forests+of+Delhi/

Nath, Damini. "The Grim Reality of Delhi's Green Spaces." *The Hindu*, December 14, 2014. Accessed June 25, 2017. http://www.thehindu.com/news/cities/Delhi/the-grim-reality-of-delhis-green-spaces/article6690615.ece

Yadavi, Pankhuri. "Park Safe Haven for Criminals at Night." *The Times of India*, February 20, 2017. Accessed June 25, 2017. http://timesofindia.indiatimes.com/city/delhi/parks-safe-haven-for-criminals-at-night/articleshow/57239080.cms

Road Network   100

Text:

"Review of Road Network and Transport System." *City Development Plan*. Delhi, 2006. Accessed June 26, 2017. http://ccs.in/sites/default/files/files/Ch11_Review%20 of%20Road%20Network%20and%20Transport%20System.pdf

Ranjan, Rakesh. "Highway to Hell: Research Body Says Delhi's Roads Are Deathtraps After 1,500 People Die in 2016." *Daily Mail India*, April 9, 2017. June 26, 2017. http://www.dailymail.co.uk/indiahome/indianews/article-4395944/Research-body-says-Delhi-s-roads-deathtraps.html

Lakshmi, Rama. "Toll Roads Indian Style." *Independent*, December 22, 2012. June 26, 2017. http://www.independent.co.uk/news/world/asia/toll-roads-india-style-8429794.html

Public Transportation Network   101

Text:
"Introduction." *Delhi Metro Rail Corporation*. Accessed June 26, 2017. http://www.delhimetrorail.com/about_us.aspx#Introduction

Mallapur, Chaitanya. "Delhi's Declining Bus Use Points to Mass Transit Failures." *India Spend*, December 19, 2015. June 26, 2017. http://www.indiaspend.com/cover-story/delhis-declining-bus-use-points-to-mass-transit-failures-39486

Diagrams and Images:
"Delhi Metro." Wikipedia. Accessed July 6, 2016. https://en.wikipedia.org/wiki/Delhi_Metro

Mobility Systems   102-105

Text:
Delhi Ministry of Urban Development. "Report on How to Decongest Delhi." 2014. Accessed June 26, 2017. http://www.indiaenvironmentportal.org.in/files/file/Report%20on%20How%20to%20Decongest%20Delhi.pdf.

Safetipin. "Enhancing Last Mile Connectivit." Accessed June 26, 2017. http://safetipin.com/resources/files/Last%20Mile%20Connectivity.pdf.

Singh, Apula. "Delhi's Urban Transportation System—Challenges Galore." *Innovation Governance of Large Urban Systems*, October 19, 2016. Accessed June 26, 2017. http://iglus.org/delhis-urban-transportation-system-challenges-galore/

Mobility Overlaps   116-117

Diagrams and Images:
Government of National Capital Territory of Delhi. "Statistical Abstract of Delhi 2012." Accessed June 30, 2017. http://delhi.gov.in/DoIT/DES/Publication/abstract/SA2012.pdf

Daily Commute   108-109

Text:
"Home Again, Home Again." *The Economist*, February 6, 2009. Accessed June 27, 2017. http://www.economist.com/node/13047681

S., Rukmini. "India Walks to Work: Census." *The Hindu*, November 15, 2015. Accessed June 27, 2017. http://www.thehindu.com/data/india-walks-to-work-census/article7874521.ece

Diagrams and Images:
Missionary, Willa. "Delhi Metro Blue Line Bombardier." *Wikimedia Commons*. January 2014. Accessed July 6, 2017. https://commons.wikimedia.org/wiki/File:DelhiMetroBlueLineBombardier.jpg

Wikipedia. "Delhi Underground Metro Station." June 13, 2012. Accessed July 6, 2017. https://en.wikipedia.org/wiki/Delhi_Metro#/media/File:Delhi_underground_metro_station.jpg

Delhi's Governance and Efforts to Revitalize its Yamuna   114-119

Text:
Bhattacharjee, Puja. "River Rejuvenation: And Unquiet Flows the Yamuna," *Governance Now*, May 16, 2016.

Bandyopadhya, Simanti. "Local government finance: challenges in revenue raising at the Municipal Corporation of Delhi," *Commonwealth Journal of Local Governance* 16. May 2015. 60-84.

Halder, Ritam. "Two New Committees to Oversee Yamuna Cleaning," *Hindustan Times*, August 6, 2016; *Times of India*, August 5, 2016.

Mahapatra, Dhananjay. "Half of Delhi's Population Lives in Slums," *Times of India*, October 4, 2012.

Mathur, Om Prakash. "New Delhi, India," in Enid Slack and Rupak Chattopadhyay (eds.) *Finance and Governance of Capital Cities in Federal Systems*. Montreal: Queens University Press, 2009. 156.

Mathur, Om Prakash. Interview with Institute of Social Sciences, New Delhi, July 20, 2016.

Nath, Damini. "Yet another Yamuna action plan," *The Hindu*, May 8, 2016.

Nandi, Jayashre, "Review 1994 water pact to revive Yamuna: Experts," *The Times of India*, March 24, 2015.

Nandi, Jayashre, "New Yamuna agency must clear sewage mess," *The Times of India*, August 15, 2015.

Report of the Fourth Delhi Finance Commission, March 2013. 50-54; 56; 186; 214-15. Accessed on August 8, 2016. http://delhi.gov.in/DoIT/DOIT/fdfc/DFC_Final_Report_2013.pdf

"Restoration and Conservation of River Yamuna: Final Report," submitted to the National Green Tribunal, 2013. 63. Accessed on August 8, 2016. http://delhi.gov.in/wps/wcm/connect/55a9380047b2199a9155d5bdc775c0fb/Final_Report_NGT-Yamuna_Restoration%2B%2811-4-2014%29.pdf?MOD=AJPERES&lmod=-287594179

Diagrams and Images:
Delhi Governance Structure. *LSE Cities*. Accessed July 20, 2017. https://lsecities.net/media/objects/articles/governance-structures/en-gb/

03 DELHI AND ITS WATER BODIES

The Dead River   122-123

Text:
Soni, Vikram, Shashank Shekhar, and Diwan Singh. "Environmental Flow for Monsoon Rivers in India: The Yamuna River as a Case Study." Accessed June 5, 2017. https://arxiv.org/pdf/1306.2709.pdf

Floodplain Encroachment   126-127

Text:
Misra, Manoj. "Dreaming of a Blue Yamuna." In Finding Delhi: Loss and Renewal in the Megacity, edited by Bharati Chaturvedi. New Delhi: Penguin Books India, 2010.

Nath, Damini. "Yamuna Floodplains Yet to Recover a Year after Culture Fest." *The Hindu*, April 17, 2017. Accessed June 29, 2017. http://www.thehindu.com/news/cities/Delhi/yamuna-floodplains-yet-to-recover-a-year-after-cultural-fest/article18073355.ece

Vikram, Kumar. "Embankments allong the Yamuna Guard Delhi." *India Today*, June 24, 2013. Accessed October 17, 2017. http://indiatoday.intoday.in/story/embankments-along-yamuna-helped-in-preventing-floods-from-wreaking-havoc-delhi-india-today/1/284963.html

Diagrams and Images:
Agarwal, Ravi and Krause, Till. "Yamuna Manifesto." *Toxics Link*, November 12, 2013. 78. Accessed October 4, 2017. http://toxicslink.org/docs/Final_Yamuna_Book.pdf

Flooding Danger   128-129

Text:
Vikram, Kumar. "Embankments allong the Yamuna Guard Delhi." *India Today*, June 24, 2013. Accessed October 17, 2017. http://indiatoday.intoday.in/story/embankments-along-yamuna-helped-in-preventing-floods-from-wreaking-havoc-delhi-india-today/1/284963.htmlmes.com/city/delhi/Ghats-will-get-better-not-Yamuna/articleshow/38159494.cms

Inaccessible Yamuna   132-134

Text:
Kant, Vishal and Vishnu Sukumaran. "Fatal Leap of Faith into Yamuna." *Deccan Herald*, September 28, 2013. Accessed June 27, 2017. http://www.deccanherald.com/content/360032/fatal-leap-faith-yamuna.html

So Delhi. "Yamuna Riverfront." Accessed June 27, 2017. http://www.sodelhi.com/parks-gardens/yamuna-riverfront

"Ghats Will Get Better, Not Yamuna." *The Times of India*, July 11, 2014. Accessed June 27, 2017. http://timesofindia.indiatimes.com/city/delhi/Ghats-will-get-better-not-Yamuna/articleshow/38159494.cms

The Drain System   136-137

Text:
Singh, Darpan "Stormwater Drains Missing in Delhi." India Today, June 29, 2015. Accessed June 27, 2017. http://indiatoday.intoday.in/story/stormwater-drains-delhi-yamuna-river-monsoons/1/447664.html

Centre for Science and Environment. "Indo-Gangetic Plains: Delhi." in Excreta Matters, 2. Accessed May 30, 2017. cseindia.org/userfiles/delhi_20130314.pdf

Delhi's Drains   138-139

Text:
Kalia, Pallavi. "Natural Urban Drainage: Realisation of an Unrecognised Potential." Accessed June 28, 2017. http://www.devalt.org/newsletter/sep98/of_7.htm

JNNURM, City Development Plan Delhi. "Storm Water Drainage." Accessed June 28, 2017 http://ccs.in/sites/default/files/files/Ch10_Storm%20Water%20Drainage.pdf

Najafgarh and Its Subdrains   140-141

Text:
"Sahibi River." India Mapped. Accessed June 27, 2017. http://www.indiamapped.com/rivers-in-india/sahibi-river/.

YAMUNA RIVER PROJECT

The University of Virginia

Authors
Iñaki Alday Sanz, Pankaj Vir Gupta

Editor
Joseph Brookover Jr

Copy Editor
Wendy Baucom

Publication Design
Graphic Design: Joseph Brookover Jr
Layout: Ramon Prat, Marga Gibert
Cover: Ramon Prat

Publication Research Team
Ben DiNapoli
Scott Getz
Ben Glor
Gabrielle Rashleigh
Marissa Sayers

With Contributions from
Rana Dasgupta, *Novelist*
Peter DeBaere, *Associate Professor, Darden School of Business*
John Echeverri-Gent, *Associate Professor, Politics*
Daniel Ehnbom, *Associate Professor, Art History*
Wu-Seng Lung, *Professor, Department of Civil and Environmental Engineering*
Matt Reidenbach, *Associate Professor, Department of Environmental Sciences*

Photo Essays
Phil Chang; *A Walk to the Yamuna* (120, 230, 234, 242, 256, 282, 296, 312, 336, 348)
Randhir Singh; *Delhi's Nullahs* (84, 98, 110, 136, 168, 174, 184, 192, 193, 198, 206, 216, 326)

Select Projects
Josh Aronson, *MArch 17*
Sally Aul, *BsArch 17*
Eric Barr, *MArch 15*
Aaron Bridgers, *MArch 15*
Joseph Brookover Jr, *MArch 17*
Anna Cai, *BsArch 16*
Phil Chang, *MArch 17*
Ben DiNapoli, *BsArch 17*
Elizabeth Dorton, *BsArch 18*
Yushan Du, *MArch 16*
Brittany Duguay, *BsArch 17*
Sosa Ehearbor, *BsArch 17*
Laurence Holland, *MArch 17*
Meng Huang, *MArch 18*
Audrey Hughes, *BsArch 17*
Joey Laughlin, *MArch 15*
Sam Manock, *BsArch 16*
Lemara Miftakhova, *MArch 18*
Andrew Morrell, *MArch 18*
Lauren Nelson, *MArch 15*
July Qui, *MLA 17*
Gabrielle Rashleigh, *BsArch 17*
Shannon Ruhl, *MArch 17*
Donna Ryu, *MArch 16*
Katie Salata, *BsArch 18*
Abigail Sandberg, *MUEP 16*
Andrew Shea, *MArch 17*
Xiaonian Shen, *MLA 18*
Zhilan Song, *MLA 17*
Michelle Stein, *MArch 15*
Sean Sullivan, *MArch 17*
Chloe Voltaire, *BsArch 16*
Xiang Zhao, *MLA 17*
Fuhou Zhang, *MArch 17*

Select Photographs
Josh Aronson (146); Aaron Bridgers (79); Phil Chang (91, 99, 109, 113); Pankaj Vir Gupta (44, 45); Monisha Nasa (43, 49, 59, 85); Lauren Nelson (77, 125); Xander Shambaugh (47, 48); Andrew Shea (08, 109); Sean Sullivan (98); Missy Velez (46); Xiang Zhao (64)

Yamuna River Project Directors
Iñaki Alday, *Quesada Professor of Architecture*
Pankaj Vir Gupta, *Professor of Architecture*

Yamuna River Project Advisory Council
Ian Baucom, *Former Buckner W. Clay Dean, College of Arts and Sciences*
Ila Berman, *Dean, School of Architecture, Edward E. Elson Professor of Architecture*
John Echeverri-Gent, *Associate Professor, Politics*
Debjani Ganguly, *Director, Institute of Humanities and Global Cultures, Professor of English*
Thomas Katsouleas, *Executive Vice President and Provost*
Karen McGlathery, *Lead Principal Investigator at Virginia Coast Reserve LTER, Professor, Environmental Sciences*
Brian Owensby, *Center for Global Inquiry and Innovation, Professor, History*

Yamuna River Project Research Faculty
Michael Allen, *Assistant Professor, Department of Religious Studies*
Daniel Ehnbom, *Associate Professor, Art History*
Eric Field, *Director of Information Technology; Lecturer, School of Architecture*
Gouping Huang, *Assistant Professor, Urban and Environmental Planning*
Wu-Seng Lung, *Professor, Civil and Environmental Engineering*
Andrew Mondschein, *Assistant Professor, Urban and Environmental Planning*
Bala Mulloth, *Assistant Professor, Public Policy, Batten School of Leadership*
Spencer Phillips, *Lecturer, Economics, Environmental Consultant*
Mahesh Rao, *Research Scientist, Batten School of Leadership*
Matt Reidenbach, *Associate Professor, Environmental Sciences*

Yamuna River Project Research Coordinators
Joseph Brookover Jr (2017-18)
Eric Barr (2015-16)
Megan Suau (2014-15)
Matthew Pinyan (2013-14)

Multidisciplinary Research Teams

2017-2018
Marnissa Claflin, *MUEP '19*
Boning Dong, *MUEP '19*
Rahul Gupta, *BsArch 18*
Jaqueline Hammaker, *BPP '19*
Catherine Harrison, *MEng '19*
Charlie Higginson, *MLA 19*
Erica Mutschler, *MLA 18*
Monisha Nasa, *MArch 19*
Mahesh Patel, *PhD Post-Doctoral Fellow Env Sciences*
Danielle Price, *BsArch 18*
Matthew Reger, *MArch 19*
Alexander Sambaugh, *BsArch 18*
Xiaonian Shen, *MLA 19*
Zhilan Song, *MLA 17*
Hana Thurman, *BS '19*
Siddharth Velamakanni, *MArch 18*
Missy Velez, *MLA 19*
Abe Wilson, *MArch 18*
Timothy D Winchester, *MUEP '19*
Xiang Zhao, *MLA 17*

2016-17
Josh Aronson, *MArch 17*

Sally Aul, *BsArch 17*
Fiorella Barreto, *BsArch 17*
Haritha Bhairavabhatia, *MPlan 18*
Katie Carter, *BaEvsc 16*
Aleksander De Mott, *BsArch 17*
Elizabeth Dorton, *BsArch 18*
Sosa Erhabor, *BsArch 17*
Maggie Grady, *BsCe 16*
Ana He Gu, *BsArch 17*
Laurence Holland, *MArch 17*
Meng Huang, *MArch 18*
Audrey Hughes, *BsArch 17*
Julia Johnson, *BsCe 16*
Sophie Mattinson, *BsArch 17*
Tyler Mauri, *MArch 18*
Emily McDuff, *BsCe 16*
Tianning Miao, *MArch 18*
Lemara Miftakhova, *MArch 18*
Katy Miller, *BsGds 17*
Andrew Morrell, *MArch 18*
Ana Mota, *BsArch 17*
Cristina Preciado, *BsArch 18*
Danielle Price, *BsArch 17*
Justin Safaric, *BS Env 17*
Katie Salata, *BsArch 18*

Vivi Tran, *BsCe 16*
Siddarth Velamakanni, *MArch 18*
July Qiu, *MLA 17*
Tony Zhang, *BsCe 16*

2015-16
Aaron Bridgers, *MArch 15*
Joseph Brookover, *MArch 17*
Cristina Castillo, *BsArch 16*
Philip Chang, *MArch 17*
Ben DiNapoli, *BsArch 17*
Yushan Du, *MArch 16*
Brittany Duguay, *BsArch 17*
Stephen Hobbs, *MLA 16*
Samantha Manock, *BsArch 16*
Gabrielle Rashleigh, *BsArch 17*
Shannon Ruhl, *MArch 17*
Marissa Sayers, *BsArch 17*
Andrew Shea, *MArch 17*
Sean Sullivan, *MArch 17*
Chloe Voltaire, *BsArch 16*
Fuhou Zhang, *MArch 17*

2014-15
Isabel Argoti, *BsArch 15*

Jessica Baralt, *BsArch 15*
Eric Barr, *MArch 15*
Anna Cai, *BsArch 16*
Anna Freidrich, *BsArch 16*
William Keel, *BsArch 16*
Joseph Laughlin, *MArch 15*
Lauren Nelson, *MArch 15*
Donna Ryu, *MArch 16*
Seth Salcedo, *MArch 16*
Abigail Sandberg, *MUEP 16*
Michelle Stein, *MArch 15*
Chris Wallace, *BsArch 15*

2013-14
Henry Brazer, *BsArch 15*
Luke Escobar, *BsArch 15*
Kate Fowler, *BsArch 14*
Rachel Himes, *BsArch 15*
Alexandra Iaccarino, *BsArch 15*
Courtney Keehan, *BsArch 15*
Jaline Mcpherson, *BsArch 15*
Madeline Partridge, *BsArch 15*

Related Researchers
Peter DeBaere, *Associate Professor, Darden School of Business*
Rebecca Dillingham, *Director, Center for Global Health,*
     Associate Professor of Medicine, Division of Infectious Diseases and International Health
Christian McMillen, *Associate Chair, Professor, History*
Luis Pancorbo, *Assistant Professor, Architecture*
Elizabeth Rogawski, *Postdoctoral Fellow, Public Health*
Sreerekha Sathiamma, *Assistant Professor, Global Studies*

With Special Thanks to
Aga Khan Trust for Culture
Embassy of Spain in India
Embassy of Switzerland in India
Katz Family Foundation
Yamuna Biodiversity Park

YES Institute, India
R.M. Bhardwaj
Rana Dasgupta
Jeffrey Legro
Brian Owensby

Bimal Patel
Pradip Saha
Mohammad Shaheer
Dr. Amarjit Singh
Mr. and Mrs. Navjeet Sobti

And for the generosity, wisdom, and support of the Delhi Jal Board team lead by Keshav Chandra, S R Tyagi, and Mriganka Saxena

Published by
Actar Publishers, New York, Barcelona
www.actar.com

All rights reserved
© edition: Actar Publishers
© texts: their respective authors
© design, drawings, illustrations, and photographs: their respective authors

Distribution
Actar D, Inc. New York, Barcelona.

New York
440 Park Avenue South, 17th Floor
New York, NY 10016
T +1 2129662207
E salesnewyork@actar-d.com

Barcelona
Roca i Batlle 2-4
08023 Barcelona, SP
T +34 933 282 183
E eurosales@actar-d.com

Indexing
English ISBN: 978-1-945150-67-8
PCN: 2017952724
A CIP catalogue record for this book is available from Library of Congress,
Washington, D.C., USA

Printed in China